T0311647

Strategies, Markets and Governance

Strategies, Markets and Governance addresses governance concerns at firm, industry, country and international levels. How do regulatory authorities deal with new business models, organizational structures and blurring market relations? What limits regulatory control and what are the implications of corporate self-regulation? What drives the spread of new regulation and what limits its effectiveness? How does 'the organized public' shape political and corporate interests and what is its legitimacy and impact on business? How do corporate strategies turn tighter regulation into profit opportunities, deliver public benefits in the face of predatory states and when is exit the only option left?

The contributing authors are leading researchers on governance and public policy, and present assessments of these questions in a variety of institutional and international contexts. The book is ideally suited to advanced students of business, public policy and business regulation, as well as practitioners and policy makers.

Ralf Boscheck is the Lundin Family Professor of Economics and Business Policy at IMD (International Institute for Management Development) in Lausanne, Switzerland.

Christine Batruch is Vice President, Corporate Responsibility, Lundin Petroleum.

Stewart Hamilton is Professor of Accounting and Finance at IMD.

Jean-Pierre Lehmann is Professor of International Political Economy at IMD.

Caryl Pfeiffer is Director, Corporate Fuels and By-Products, e.on US.

Ulrich Steger holds the Alcan Chair of Environmental Management at IMD and is Director of IMD's research project on Corporate Sustainability Management, CSM.

Michael Yaziji is Professor of Strategy and Organization at IMD.

STRATEGIES, MARKETS AND GOVERNANCE

Exploring Commercial and Regulatory Agendas

Ralf Boscheck

with

Christine Batruch

Stewart Hamilton

Jean-Pierre Lehmann

Caryl Pfeiffer

Ulrich Steger

Michael Yaziji

CAMBRIDGE UNIVERSITY PRESS

CAMBRIDGE
UNIVERSITY PRESS

University Printing House, Cambridge CB2 8BS, United Kingdom

One Liberty Plaza, 20th Floor, New York, NY 10006, USA

477 Williamstown Road, Port Melbourne, VIC 3207, Australia

314-321, 3rd Floor, Plot 3, Splendor Forum, Jasola District Centre, New Delhi - 110025, India

79 Anson Road, #06-04/06, Singapore 079906

Cambridge University Press is part of the University of Cambridge.

It furthers the University's mission by disseminating knowledge in the pursuit of education, learning and research at the highest international levels of excellence.

www.cambridge.org
Information on this title: www.cambridge.org/9780521688451

First published 2008

A catalogue record for this publication is available from the British Library

Library of Congress Cataloging in Publication data
Strategies, markets & governance / Ralf J. Boscheck . . . [et al.].
p.   cm.
Includes bibliographical references.
ISBN 978-0-521-86845-7
1. Industrial policy. 2. Trade regulation. 3. Corporate governance. I. Boscheck, Ralf, 1959–
II. Title: Strategies, markets and governance.
HD3611.S774   2008
658.4′012–dc22
2007052172

ISBN 978-0-521-86845-7 Hardback
ISBN 978-0-521-68845-1 Paperback

Contents

List of Figures, Boxes and Tables

Acknowledgments

The following content, previously published or updating and modifying previously published material, is included with permission of the original copyright holder.

Chapter 2: Competitive advantage and the regulation of dominant firms, is forthcoming under the same title in *World Competition*.

Chapter 3: Delegating Regulation – supply-chain management, partnering and competition policy reforms updates Boscheck, R. (2000) EU Policy reform on vertical restraints, *World Competition*, 23(4), 3–49 in view of the Council Regulation (EC) No. 1/2003, 12 June, 2002.

Chapter 8: Oil and conflict: Lundin Petroleum's experience in Sudan by Christine Batruch originally appeared in Bailes, A.J.K. and Frommelt, I. (eds.) Stockholm International Peace Research Institute (SIPRI), Business and Security; *Public-private sector relationships in a new security environment*, Oxford University Press, pp. 148–60.

Chapter 9: How the clean air interstate rule will affect investment and management decisions in the US electricity sector, by Caryl Pfeiffer, was published in Boscheck, R. (ed.) (2007) *Energy futures*, Palgrave Macmillan, pp. 243–58.

Chapter 10: EU Water infrastructure management: National regulations, EU framework directives but no model to follow is in part based on and updates Boscheck (2002) European water infrastructures, *Intereconomics*, May/June, 138–49 in view of the EU Framework Directives and initiatives of the 2006 Fourth World Water Forum.

Chapter 11: Market-testing healthcare: Managed care, market evolution and the search for regulatory principles, was published in *Intereconomics*, November/December 2006, 328–36.

Chapter 15: EU Constitutional governance: Failure as opportunity!?, was published under the same title in *Intereconomics*, February 2006, pp. 1–12.

Chapter 16: One competition standard to regulate global trade and protection? updates Boscheck, (2001) The governance of global market relations – The case of substituting antitrust for antidumping, *World Competition*, 24(2), 1–18, in view of the failure of the 2004 Doha Work Program.

Preface

Strategies, Markets and Governance addresses governance concerns at firm, industry, country and international levels. How do regulatory authorities deal with new business models, organizational structures and blurring market relations? What limits regulatory control and what are the implications of corporate self-regulation? What legitimizes private and public uses of market incentives to monitor executives, manage demand or shift economic risks and what are the responses to latent moral ambiguities? What drives the spread of new regulation and what limits its effectiveness? How can one separate symptoms from root causes of regulatory concerns to determine the direction and viability of necessary change? How does "the organized public" shape political and corporate interests and what is its legitimacy and impact on business? How do local, national and supra-national agendas align or conflict in governing the use of national or common resources, applying shared regulatory standards, or constituting global trade relations? How do corporate strategies turn tighter regulation into profit opportunities, deliver public benefits in the face of predatory states and when is exit the only option left?

The book is organized in five parts. Part I discusses the concepts of strategy, market and governance and offers an analytical framework for assessing their impact on company operations, managerial and regulatory control, agency and political supervision as well as local, national and international policy coordination. Parts II to IV apply this framework to sixteen contributions discussing governance concerns at the level of the firm, the industry, and international policy. The issues covered range from problems with identifying fraud, organizing board supervision, enforcing competition law, changing investment and market strategies in line with regulation or NGO campaigns, to finding institutional responses to international trade policy distortions, dissecting national economic imperatives governing global energy markets, and assessing political and cultural obstacles to policy reforms in systems as diverse as China and the EU. These contributions exhibit the richness of current governance discussions but also the need to review some of their underlying assumptions. They differ in style and reflect the professional background of their authors. Part V, therefore, traces rising governance concerns to the so-called "paradox of the market", i.e. the apparent need to rely on, yet limit the pursuit of self-interest. The paradox is based on a narrow but popular conceptualization of economic behavior, which takes economic man to be driven by some loutish motivation that proves unsustainable in reality and confuses the means of competitive market selection with the goal of productive cooperation. To tackle this, research and teaching in commerce, economics, and law needs to return to the roots of classical political economy and rehabilitate moral reasoning to deal with unavoidable discretion.

Strategies, Markets and Governance is a group effort. Five contributors are members of the IMD faculty with particular research interests in economic regulation, corporate governance, international political economy, NGO activities and accounting and audit frauds. Two authors offer direct industry perspectives on regulatory and political risk and link technology and commercial aspects with concerns for legal and corporate social responsibilities. My assistant Virginie Boillat-Carrard worked hand-in-hand with Paula Parish at Cambridge University Press to see the manuscript through to completion. I would like to thank all of them. I am above all grateful to my wife Charo for her support and to Jupp for helpful conversations.

Ralf Boscheck
Larr abastera, Vizcaya
2007

Notes on Contributors

Ralf Boscheck is the editor and lead author of this book. He is the Lundin Family Professor of Economics and Business Policy at IMD Lausanne, Switzerland. He undertakes market and competition analyses to define and assess strategies and public policy at the company, industry and country levels. His research has appeared in a range of books, academic journals and the business press. He is on the editorial board of *World Competition – Law and Economics Review*, as well as the *International Journal of Energy Sector Management*.

Christine Batruch is Vice President of Corporate Responsibility, Lundin Petroleum. Hon. BA, BCL, LL.B., barrister and solicitor (University of Toronto, McGill University, Law Society of Upper Canada). Based in Geneva, Christine has worked in the non-profit, academic and business sectors. From 1992 to 1995 she participated in the establishment of a number of non-profit institutions in Ukraine as part of the Soros network of foundations. From 1995 to 1999 she worked at the International Academy of the Environment as executive assistant to the director and later assistant professor. She joined Lundin Oil in 1999 and became Vice President Corporate Responsibility at Lundin Petroleum in 2002.

Stewart Hamilton is Professor of Accounting and Finance at IMD. Prior to joining IMD, he combined a twenty-year career in public accounting practice with teaching at the Universities of British Columbia, Calgary and Windsor in Canada and for more than ten years, in the Law Faculty at the University of Edinburgh. He appears regularly as an expert witness in a wide range of civil litigation cases, including share valuation disputes, professional negligence claims, and loss of profit disputes. Professor Hamilton has served on many professional committees and working parties on Company Law reform, conduct of serious fraud trials and financial services regulation. He has co-authored books on Company Law and taxation and written many articles for the professional and financial press. His current research interests are in corporate failure, risk management and investor protection.

Jean-Pierre Lehmann has been Professor of International Political Economy at IMD International Institute for Management Development since January 1997. His main areas of expertise are the socioeconomic and business dynamics of East Asia, the impact of globalization on developing countries and the government–business interface, especially in respect to the global trade and investment policy process. In

1994 he launched the Evian Group, which consists of high-ranking officials, business executives, independent experts and opinion leaders from Europe, Asia and the Americas. The focus of the Evian Group is on the international economic order in the global era, specifically the reciprocal impact and influence of international business and the WTO agenda.

Caryl Pfeiffer is Director, Corporate Fuels and By-Products e.on US. BA (cum laude) Biology/Business Administration, Wittenberg University, USA; Graduate Fellowship Award, Department of Landscape Architecture, University of Illinois, USA; Graduate work, School of Natural Resources (emphasis on economics and energy development), Ohio State University, USA. As director of corporate fuels and by-products, Caryl is responsible for developing and implementing strategies for the use of solid fuels within the integrated energy business. Prior to that, she was director of Louisville Gas and Electricity's environmental affairs from 1998 to 2003. Before joining LG&E in 1998, she held a series of positions in environmental affairs with the Kentucky Utilities Company and the Columbus and Southern Ohio Electric Company. She has over 26 years' experience in energy and environmental affairs and sits on various state and federal level environmental and energy committees, including the American Gas Association's Environmental Regulatory Action Committee, the Edison Electric Institute Environment and Energy Committee and the US Environmental Protection Agency's FACA Subcommittee on Ozone, Particulate Matter and Regional Haze.

Ulrich Steger holds the Alcan Chair of Environmental Management at IMD and is Director of IMD's research project on Corporate Sustainability Management, CSM. He was a member of the Managing Board of Volkswagen, in charge of environment and traffic matters and, in particular, the implementation of an environmental strategy within the VW group worldwide. Before becoming involved in management education, he was active in German politics. He was Minister of Economics and Technology in the State of Hesse with particular responsibility for transport, traffic and energy. Before that, he was a member of the German Bundestag, specializing in energy, technology, industry and foreign trade issues.

Michael Yaziji is Professor of Strategy and Organizations at IMD. His primary interests are in the areas of non-market strategy, strategy formulation and implementation, and change management. His current research focuses particularly on relationships between corporations and nongovernmental organizations (NGOs, e.g. Greenpeace, Friends of the Earth, PETA, WWF). The range of relationships he studies includes both antagonistic campaigns by NGOs against corporations and partnerships with them. His most recent publication was on partnering with NGOs for competitive advantage *Harvard Business Review* (2004). He has consulted for leading corporations and industry groups and has worked in both the private and civil society sectors.

Part I

Introduction and overview

1 Strategies, markets and governance

Ralf Boscheck

Every day, the news reminds us that the terms making up the title of this book are sadly at odds. We had just sent the manuscript to the publisher, when the European Commission released the findings of its energy sector competition inquiry, concluding that industrial customers and consumers were losing out due to inefficient gas and electricity markets.[1] The report pointed to high levels of market concentration; anti-competitive integration of generation, networks and supply; unequal access to, and insufficient investment in infrastructure, and, possibly, market sharing cartels between operators. Going forward, the Commission intended to prosecute individual cases under EU competition rules and to further liberalize the sector, if necessary against the will of national governments.

At the end of 2006, the average annual salary of a programmer in Hungary ranged from $4,000 to $7,000, in India from $5,900 to $11,000, and in the USA from $60,000 to $80,000. The annual cost of a chip designer in Suzhou (China) was $24,000, i.e. $4,000 less than in Shanghai, $6,000 less than in Bangalore, $276,000 less than in Boston.[2] Business reacts by outsourcing, off-shoring, and relocating production. For recipients, outsourcing provides employment, substitutes for imports and generates export earnings; for outsourcers and importers, like WalMart, contributing nearly one-fifth of China's total export volume, it sustains "every day low prices" to consumers. Still the ILO, WTO, EU, and NAFTA push for internationalizing employment standards and their enforcement through product labeling, trade sanctions and consumer boycotts. Harmonizing labor rights blocks regulatory competition and social degradation; but it also limits development options, protects inefficient practices and raises costs to consumers.

Ongoing healthcare reforms in the US, Germany and the UK are market-driven.[3] Economic motives affect treatment options, patients' choice and payers' financial commitment; they may also result in unwarranted exclusions from vital cures and generally the supply of sub-optimal healthcare.

---

[1] EU Press Release, IP/07/26, Brussels, January 10, 2007. [2] www.cio.de, last visited January 12, 2007.
[3] Boscheck, R., (2004) Healthcare reforms and patient rights, *Intereconomics*, 39(6), 310–13.

Responding to evident risks, countries rely on a mix of market and judicial reviews, regulatory oversight and corporate self-regulation. But procedural and substantive standards are generally unclear and private rules are seen to require public supervision. How can patients, care suppliers and authorities determine whether a given service is fairly offered in competitive markets, requires stronger incentive contracts, or demands direct regulatory control? How should courts pass judgment? What ultimately legitimizes healthcare markets?

Concerns about strategies, markets and governance and how they interact are hardly new. Every day, the news scrutinizes markets and regulatory outcomes and holds private and public actors accountable based on some norm of solidarity, efficiency, equity or fairness. What may be new is that a much larger number of individuals, organizations and nation states on an ever-expanding range of issues reach around the world faster and deeper than ever before. The result is increased complexity in dealing with stakeholders, uncertain motifs, cross-cutting agendas and legitimacy concerns. This chapter offers a perspective: It explores the notions of strategy, market and governance, links them to a framework for assessing a hierarchy of inter-related coordination decisions and structures the contributions to the book.

1. By way of introduction – concepts and cases

Strategies, markets and governance are such familiar concepts today – so why make an effort to explain them at all? After all, one expects private or public actors to use strategies to drive policies and regulations, create markets or shape their structure, conduct and performance. Markets are understood to induce economic activity, allocate resources and rewards and contain or balance the impact of private and public ventures. Governance mechanisms are known to enable and substitute for market and non-market coordination. And yet, while these concepts appear to be well established and to constitute each other, they often actually relate to quite different views on man, his primary motifs and need for authority. In fact, the dominance of any given implied motivation could easily give rise to distinct conceptualizations of institutional, economic and social structures, from the libertarian society to the command economy, whose coexistence alone requires coordination. As strategies, markets and regulations spread, would one such model win out or diversity persist and some common ground be recognized? This section explores the terms and connotations.

Strategies

Almost since its foundation in 1908, the Harvard Business School, possibly *the* reference for modern business strategy thinking, required aspiring managers to enroll in a course on "business policy." Classes and case teaching methods called on participants to shed functional preoccupations and instead develop an integrative and deliberate response to market opportunities and threats. Emulated around the world, the course's curriculum has since been adjusted in line with commercial and industrial developments and advances in analytics. Most importantly, academics and consultants added copious tools for assessing markets, gauging corporate resources and dealing with external and internal stakeholders. In the process, sectors became "clusters," competition "the value-web," and fresh thinking the source of "reengineering." Notably, everything became "strategic." But what made it strategic?

In 2005, Jonathan Oppenheimer privately held and ran DeBeers Société Anonyme, selling an estimated 70% of the world's total rough diamonds with a value of $7.9bn and a reported net profit of $554 m.[4] His great-grandfather, Ernest Oppenheimer, had taken over the company in 1929 and in so doing achieved a nearly complete integration of South Africa's diamond trade. At the heart of DeBeers business was the London-based Central Selling Organization (CSO), which distributed purchased stones to handpicked sightholders, thus controlling quantities, qualities and prices. On the demand side, the DeBeers slogan "a diamond is forever" made stones an invaluable token of love not to be resold; on the supply side, the company's stocks allowed it to flood the market whenever associated mines tried to sell direct. More recently, the diamond trade faced the end of apartheid, the fall of communism, the emergence of major Canadian competitors and NGO campaigns attacking so-called "blood" diamonds. DeBeers reacted by transferring the lion's share of its financial assets into the Swiss-based DeBeers Centenary AG, delisting DeBeers Consolidated Mines from the Johannesburg stock exchange and selling all of its shares to three entities under significant family control. It also acquired and renewed mining contracts in Canada, Botswana, Namibia and Russia. In 2000, DeBeers began to brand its gems and a year later agreed to transfer all its retail-related rights to LVMH Moet Hennessy Louis Vuitton. Since 2002, DeBeers and its distributors have been at the core of the Kimberley Process, an intricate certification system intended to

---

[4] See EU (2007) *Investigation into the rough diamonds market*, reported January 31, 2007; Datamonitor (2006) *DeBeers* – Company Profile; and Spar, D. L., (2006) Continuity and change in the international diamond market, *Journal of Economic Perspectives*, 20(3), Summer 2006, 195–208.

eliminate "conflict diamonds" by tracing all stones from mines to retail. The process solidified supply and enhanced the quality of the brand.

This brief sketch of DeBeers integrates decisions and actions, after the facts, to present a coherent and deliberate business policy. But does it spell out the company's strategy? Were all outcomes intended and consequences foreseen? More importantly, would the Oppenheimers have done so well, if implied rationales had been widely apparent at the time decisions were taken? Could they have sustained their success? While the conventional strategy literature[5] refers back to the Greek *strategos* for "leader" and "military planner," could it be that the modern connotation of the word, emphasizing uncertainty and disguise, is more instructive here? Webster's defines "strategy" as "a plan, scheme, or trick for surprising or deceiving an enemy; ... the skillful use of a stratagem ... any artifice, ruse, trick devised or used to attain a goal or to gain an advantage over an adversary." It is synonymous with "intrigue, maneuver, and contrivance."[6] In fact, reviewing numerous biographies, from Jakob Fugger's to J. P. Morgan's, from Oppenheimer's to Gates's,[7] it seems that it is the combination of shrewdness and guile that separates the strategist from the mere rational planner and spells success in managing expectations, utilizing relations and creating and exploiting market failures. But there is a discomfort in that combination, which raises governance concerns and divides the admirers of the "go-getters" from the prosecutors of the "robber-barons." While the former marvel at superior ability in the face of decentralized market checks, the latter insist on centrally restraining dubious behavior through rules. But in the end both controls may be lacking.

Markets

Throughout history, competitive markets have been deemed to provide non-authoritarian social control merely based on financial sanctions. For Christian and Talmudic thinkers, competitive markets identified just prices; for French and British economic liberals, they established an individual's freedom within and *vis-à-vis* the state. Today, the attractiveness of free markets seems to be based less on the implied working of some natural law than on the lack of regret in the face of change. Markets are seen as

---

[5] See for example Ghemawat, P., (1997) *Competition and business strategy in historical perspective*, HBS-798-010.

[6] Webster's Encyclopedic Unabridged Dictionary of the English Language, Revised 1996 edn, p. 1404.

[7] See Heuser, U. *et al.* (eds) (2004) *Schöpfer & Zerstörer*, Rowohlt; Heller, R., (2004) *Movers and shakers*, London: Bloomsbury.

impersonal, objective promoters of efficiency and progress. Yet this confidence needs qualification.

Since the beginning of the twentieth century, perfectly competitive markets have been assumed to balance individual and common interests, stimulate an efficient allocation and use of resources, and provide a reference to detect market distortions and remedies to them.[8] But this concept has proved to be of limited use in formulating rules for real-life commercial behavior, assessing welfare trade-offs due to scale and technology advantages, or evaluating equity concerns and market failures.[9] Many questions still have no easy answers: Does competitive contracting necessarily lead to efficient contracts? When do sustainable profits reflect monopolizing behavior? Can competition spur optimal technological advances and when does it obstruct the efficiency of a naturally monopolistic supply? More recently, however, market-driven policies have been criticized for their execution rather than their conceptual base and the focus has shifted towards detecting government failures.

In 2003, EU member states converted Kyoto CO_2-reduction targets into renewable obligations for their electricity suppliers; adjustments were to be market-based and facilitated by trading emissions certificates. National governments distributed EU-approved CO_2 allocations as allowances to companies and trading began on January 1, 2005. As planned, companies with low emissions were to profit from selling their quota while emissions above the allotted level engendered penalties; in addition, excess polluters had to surrender allowances in the second year to compensate for overshooting in the first. And yet, although prices for CO_2 allowances rose from an initial \$8 per ton to around \$30 per ton after six months of trading, they did so in part only because the EU Commission rejected plans by some member states to run over their allocations. Also, while early 2006 prices created incentives for using existing fuel mixes in cleaner and more efficient ways, they were too low to avoid subsidizing the switch towards renewables such as onshore or offshore wind or photovoltaic energy. Considering both remarks, observers doubted whether political authorities, at national or EU level, could in fact be relied upon, or even expected, to properly frame the market and capture the true benefits of avoided CO_2 pollution.[10]

Hence, while in a "perfect" market, actual or potential competition would effectively annul any lasting benefit of strategic behavior, so-called

---

[8] See Knight, F. N., (1921) *Risk, uncertainty and profit?* Boston: Houghton Mifflin pp. 51–6.
[9] See Scraffa, P., (1926) The laws of return under competitive conditions, *Economic Journal*, 36, 535–50.
[10] See Bockamp, S., Kruhl, J., (2007) Emissions trading – challenge for utilities. In R. Boscheck (ed.) (2007) *Energy futures*, New York: Palgrave Macmillan, pp. 273–86.

non-economic objectives, ill-determined property rights, distortions in entry or other conditions may call for regulatory intervention to replace market coordination or create "as if competition" outcomes. But real-life policy makers and regulators, far from acting as benevolent guardians, may also be driven by self-interest and the desire to avoid market and non-market controls.[11] Thus, the question is how to regulate the regulator and govern the government?

Governance

"Governance" defines the rules and institutions for coordinating collective activity and the process for deriving these. As such it reaches beyond mere market-based and governmental controls and involves a host of public and private actors in setting agendas, creating rules and monitoring and enforcing compliance. Given that at each level, strategies and alternative approaches affect the process and outcome of coordination, any form of governance inherently poses legitimacy and efficiency concerns.

In democracies, for instance, public rules are seen to reflect either the will of citizens directly, or its interpretation through legislators and courts. Yet, outside of an ideal "committee democracy", relying on the direct initiation of debate and direct votes on single issues, the question is who may instigate the process of setting or developing norms, who is involved in pre-screening rules and in making the final selection and how does one know? Also, if rules need to fit a variety of circumstances and yet be simply and certainly enforced, moving norm-setting, monitoring and enforcement authority closest to the issue at stake may improve the adequacy and efficiency of regulation but at the price of heightened legitimacy concerns. In the extreme, "private order-ing" based on privately set and enforced norms, even if perfectly acceptable to contract parties, may appear to be incompatible with given public rules and unrelated to any abstract citizen-will.

And yet, real-life economic, political and social governance by necessity relies on the interaction of public and private rules and enforcement: for example, by the time that simplified competition laws, set to maintain uniformity, centralized control and legal certainty, are seen to distort commercial behavior, multiple standards and interpretations (re)-emerge, coexist and compete, until, at some stage increased complexity triggers the return to harmonized rules and centralized enforcement. In the process, private parties

---

[11] For an early discussion see Downs, A., (1957) *An economic theory of democracy*, New York: Harper & Row.

change from meeting regulatory defaults to self-regulation and back. Next, economic regulation usually involves regulatory commissions addressing other regulators, industry associations, public-interest groups, firms, particular members of management teams and other parties. *Also*, non-governmental organizations (NGOs) may be granted information and negotiation status to expose regulatory inadequacies or to assume regulatory powers and directly punish corporate non-compliance.

These interactions are not only constantly in flux, but, far from clear cut, are often suspected to be driven by strategic interests. As blunt, central norms are replaced by decentralized forms of self-regulation, whose interest is ultimately being served? How does one, from the outside, know that a regulator's moderation to induce private cooperation in fact is not a symptom of corruption? How can one ensure that an NGO does not side with the political authority whose work it is charged to supervise? When are proposals to co-regulate earnest and when are they merely self-serving? When and how is one to argue for a complete regulatory overhaul?

While in the US and EU, centralized drug authorization has been reformed to speed products to market, decentralized cost containment practices continue to delay patients' access to vital cures; proposals by the pharmaceutical industry to be involved in co-regulation, however have met with suspicion. In brief, US federal law does not regulate drug prices but requires pharmaceutical companies to quote the "best terms" offered to any health plan to the federal Medicare and Medicaid programs. Hence, to sell to the public market, pharmaceutical suppliers need to be listed in the formularies of several private health plans. The European situation is similar and yet more complicated. Approval procedures are harmonized at EMEA level but decentrally applied; reimbursement processes differ from country to country, re-imports provide a market check. Reimbursement decisions in France, for example, emerge from a highly complex interplay between the French Ministry of Health and Social Insurance, the High Authority of Health, the Transparency Commission, and the Pricing Committee. Complexities are such that drug producers increasingly shy away from selecting European countries as first launch markets – put differently Europeans typically have to wait for lifesaving medicines already available in the US.[12]

---

[12] While in the 1990s, 46% of first launches took place in the US, none was attempted in France; 2½ years after their first launch, 85% of all drugs were available in the USA; compared with 55% in France. See Danzon, P. *et al.* (2005) The impact of price regulation on the launch delay of new drugs – evidence from twenty-five major markets in the 1990s, *Health Economics*, 4(3), 147–51.

Addressing these concerns, representatives of the pharmaceutical industry recently suggested joining forces with health authorities in a "Global Health Union." Its purpose was to create transparency on reimbursement standards and levels of healthcare provision; establish directives for committing fixed shares of GNP for healthcare purposes; formalize the structure of global drug development and market introduction, and regulate the speed of generic competition by disease area.[13]

Yet critics, wondering why society would want to hand a blank check to any industry, were concerned that substituting negotiation for market-testing healthcare costs effectively played into the hands of drug suppliers. They pointed out that the pharmaceutical industry, focusing on institutional access, next to quality, safety and efficacy, as the "fourth hurdle" to commercial success, maintains a sophisticated practice of public affairs advocacy. Its purpose is to influence governing bodies directly or by way of key opinion leaders such as healthcare professionals, patient advocacy groups, the media and the courts. Since 2001, no other US industry is estimated to have spent more money to sway state and federal public policy.[14] Politicians, who are understood to react to high-profile issues such as drug pricing and availability, are being targeted in states with large numbers of networked patients and in those areas of disease most feared by the general public. The media are provided with information that arouses emotions such as national pride, sympathy for minorities and anger about disability discrimination or perceived injustice. In 2006, a media storm covered the case of two UK breast cancer patients, unsuccessfully taking their local care providers to the European Court of Human Rights, to reverse an NHS refusal to pay for a specific drug.[15] Whilst critics were unable to directly "charge" the drug company in question with acting against the public interest, they pointed out that NHS funds which are spent in one area are not available to others. They also suggested that drug suppliers may react to cost containment strategies by lowering prices and gaining market share at the expense of high-price substitutes, i.e. by accepting legitimate market and regulatory controls instead of utilizing political agendas to "illicitly" further corporate interests.

But what makes the implied motifs illicit? Does public affairs advocacy inappropriately expand the "role of business?" Do suppliers require scrutiny when key buyers are market makers? Is it regulatory burden or corporate strategy that limits access to vital cure? Is it the seller's price or the buyer's

[13] See SIMI MBS, MCA 2.   [14] See www.publicintegrity.org.
[15] See http://news.bbc.co.uk/1/hi/england/kent/4751471.stm.

unwillingness to pay that should be reviewed? Which criteria should be used and with whose benefit in mind? Beset by the complex interactions between markets, strategies and regulatory concerns, observers typically respond to uncertainties about governance by requiring additional checks and balances. It must be a fundamental trait of guardianship to address distrust with more and more layers of control. But the question is how are the layers to be structured and interact? And is this the best one can do?

In sum

This section provided a first and fairly sketchy assessment of the notions of strategy, market and governance. Perfectly competitive markets eliminate the need for any managerial intervention and the likelihood of any strategic move. Failing market coordination, however, calls for intervention to optimize allocation and production decisions, suppress illicit acts, or attain non-market objectives. Yet by substituting or complementing the "invisible hand" of the market by the "visible hand" of some private or public actor, the pursuit of self-interest becomes cunning, rational market participants transform into strategists and Aristotle's benevolent political man, interested in coordinating life with others, turns Machiavellian in shrewd pursuit of power. Under these conditions, the inability to fully control strategic drives of any party unavoidably generates deep-rooted distrust and layers of control. This is the subject of institutional economics which is discussed next to derive a general framework of analysis.

2. The economics of distrust – market failures and institutional responses

Institutional economists reject the notion that the model of perfect competition is able to reduce the complexities of societal regulation to issues of mere market allocation. Instead their research provides rich but largely disconnected perspectives on the formation, structure, and economic impact of various real-life institutions of governance. Integrating some of their findings,[16] this section outlines an abstract reference for discussing coordination issues that range from intra- and inter-company contracting to the regulation

---

[16] For a detailed discussion see Boscheck, R., (2002) *Market drive and governance*, London: Routledge, Chapter 1, pp. 6–25.

of the global commons; it links individual decisions to collective choice, private with public spheres, and society's economic base to its political institutions. The structure helps to organize the contributions of this book. Parts II to IV briefly address three cross-cutting themes: market-driven governance; regulatory competition and conversion; and the civil economy. The entire framework will be refined in Part V, reviewing the complexity of coordination under distrust that is discussed next.

Strategic behavior, abuse and contracting[17]

Economic, political or social activities differ in terms of complexity, longevity, frequency of occurrence, value and the ease with which they can be assessed on the spot. They may also require specific commitments, i.e. investments that are re-deployable in alternative uses only at loss. The latter creates vested interests on behalf of the investing party and gives his less exposed, opportunistic partner an option on appropriation. To safeguard against abuse, parties invest in information to assess the availability and value of alternative uses of their resources and specify performance expectations. Based on this, an agreement can be struck, its compliance monitored, and, in case of reneging, enforced. Differences in specific information, specification, monitoring and enforcement requirements dictate the choice of contractual formats and institutional provisions.

Depending on the quality of information and the foreseeable complexity of an undertaking, agreements may be specified as comprehensive, complete and explicit contracts, or may require the inclusion of adjustment rules and relational agreements to closely link parties through multiple obligations. Subject to the kind of contract put in place, monitoring may be based on external audits, internal reviews, or incentive-based self-regulation; similarly, enforcement would call for litigation, arbitration or transaction-specific bonds, reputation or ownership guarantees. Put differently, subject to the level of appropriation risk, centralized and decentralized forms of governance are employed. Figure 1.1 sketches coordination options at the level of operational control, company management, regulatory control, agency supervision, political direction, and global governance.

---

[17] For early references see Alchian, A., Demsetz, H., (1972) Production, information costs and economic organization, *American Economic Review*, 62(5), 777–795; and Williamson, O. E., (1986) *Economic organization: Firms, markets and policy control*, New York: New York University Press.

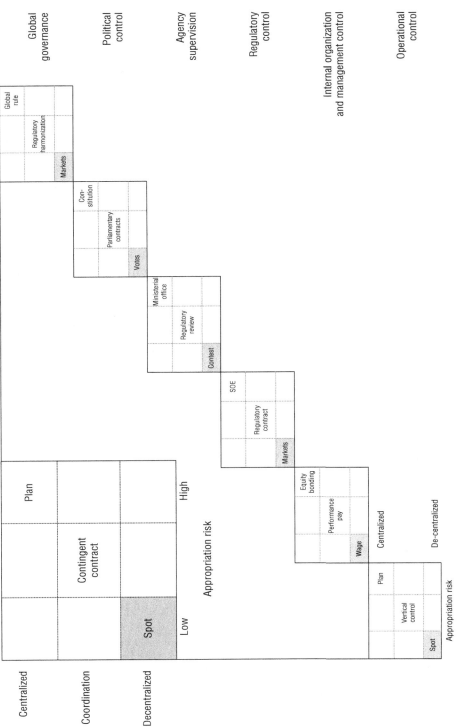

Figure 1.1: Coordination options and levels of governance

Levels of governance – operational control

The ideal spot market is presented at the bottom-left corner of the graphic and provides a starting reference. It is superseded by supply arrangements, relational contracts and vertical integration subject to budget control. Yet, to the extent that internalization reduces shirking of outside parties and economizes on "market-using" costs, it comes at the price of reduced flexibility, bureaucratic degradation and the need of controlling internal organization and management.[18]

Internal organization and managerial control

Observational limits, specific skill and investment requirements are the three main reasons to switch from spot-market labor contracts to offering and asking for long-term employment and careers. However, firm-specific human capital reduces access to the outside market and offers the employer and the employee an option on appropriation. To safeguard against it, employees require employment guarantees, premium wages, or an ensured structure of promotion prior to developing firm-specific skills. Similarly, firms use promotional tournaments, incentive contracts, or obligatory equity participation either to reveal the worker's true contribution or to delegate the task of performance-monitoring to the employee himself. Hence, as managerial control complements external market rates with implicit labor contracts or executive self-monitoring related to the company's performance, analyzing firm-level contracts requires an understanding of the next levels of governance.[19]

Regulatory control over company performance attained in competitive input and output markets may be replaced by regulatory contracts, or, at the extreme, public budget control and asset ownership. The choice among these is apt to reflect the perceived informational advantages of decentralized vs. centralized decision-making, as well as the status of regulatory capacity and supervisory control. While indirect, price-based regulation largely retains management authority, its effectiveness rests on actual or derived market pressures or transparent decision-processes. In the absence of the latter, budgetary

---

[18] For overviews see Cheung, S. N., (1983) The contractual nature of the firm, *Journal of Law and Economics*, 26(1), 1–21; Jensen, M. C., and Meckling, W. M., (1976) Theory of the firm: Managerial behavior, agency costs and ownership structure, *Journal of Financial Economics*, 3(4), 305–360.

[19] For broader perspectives see Hart, O., (1983) Optimal labor contracts under asymmetric information: An introduction, *Review of Economic Studies*, 50(1), 3–35; Lambert, R. A., Larcker, D. F. and Weigelt, K., (1989) *Tournaments and the structure of organizational incentives*, The Wharton School, University of Pennsylvania.

restrictions may be preferred and grow in number and specificity as public agencies, in need of reliable data, are drawn to micro-manage, plan and effectively operate the regulated undertaking.[20] Who then regulates the regulator?

Agency supervision may result from contests among offices and stakeholders, consultative reviews, or direct ministerial oversight. Where regulatory complexity does not allow agency performance to be clearly specified, benchmarked, and contested, adherence to formal procedures may be invoked and parliamentary committees and supervisory boards installed. Ultimately, larger shares of the task may be brought back under direct ministerial supervision. Put differently, for different levels of perceived appropriation risk, more or less centralized patterns of agency supervision and political control emerge.[21] But what are the incentives for re-election minded politicians to provide straight bureaucratic guidance, *ex ante*, or involve themselves in broad-based supervision, *ex post*?

Political direction

The reality of the political market place is that the general citizen cannot stay informed about all issues of interest to him. As a result, one may expect vote-maximizing politicians to target the median voter for general endorsement, and, rather than engaging in broad-based bureaucratic oversight, to respond to specific constituency demands by salient *ad hoc* "fire-alarm" controls. In the same vein, clear agency mandates may be avoided to benefit from "optimal delegation," i.e. claiming credits for agency programs but no responsibility for their costs and unresolved issues. Also, to protect constituency interest against the vagaries of political tenure, incumbent representatives may invoke procedures and time schedules that limit the bureaucratic and legislative discretion – in the extreme by promoting regulation to the level of constitutional law.[22] Still, irrespective of whether political direction

---

[20] See Boscheck, R., (2002) The nature of regulatory contracts, *World Competition*, 25(3), 303–348.

[21] Early analysis of cognitive limits underlying "administrative behavior" gave way to a full-blown theory of discretionary decision-making that is applicable to both private and public offices. See March, J. G. and Simon, H. A., (1957) *Organizations*, New York: John Wiley & Sons; Williamson, O. E. (1964) *The economics of discretionary behavior*, Englewood Cliffs, NJ: Prentice-Hall; Tullock, G., (1965) *The politics of bureaucracy*, Washington, DC: Public Affairs Press; Downs, A., (1967) *Inside bureaucracy*, Boston: Little, Brown; Niskanen, W. A., (1971) *Bureaucracy and representative government*, Chicago: Aldine-Atherton.

[22] For an overview of the public choice literature, see Mueller, D. C. (ed.) *Perspectives of public choice*, Cambridge: Cambridge University Press; see also McCubbins, M. D. and Schwartz, T., (1984) Congressional oversight overlooked: Police patrols vs. fire alarms, *American Journal of Political Science*, 28(1), 165–179; Banks, J. S. and Weingast, B. R., (1992) The political control of bureaux under asymmetric information, *American Journal of Political Science*, 36(2), 509–24.

may rest on direct electoral outcomes, inter-or intra-party agreements, or constitutional rule, it may still face a global market check.

Global governance builds on competition in factor and commodity markets, contingent rules, or central issue-based accords and institutions of varied scope. Free trade, factor mobility and regulatory competition reduce a nation's political autonomy over issues of market regulation; their impact may be constrained by limited market access or harmonizing regulatory standards. With regard to the latter, principles of national treatment, mutual recognition and subsidiarity may be deemed sufficient to promote harmonization; i.e. it is believed that there is no or only limited need for centralized enforcement, uniform rules and dispute settlement. Still, increasingly complex trade-related competition issues and powerful states able to escape discipline require strengthened procedures and institutions of international coordination. Either way, the benefits of uniform rules, reduced transaction costs and competitive distortions or an avoided regulatory "race to the bottom," come with the side-effects of centralization: the risk of regulatory capture, limited legal innovation, and the potential exclusion of those not present at the time when agreements are struck.[23]

In sum

Introducing the language of institutional economics, this section more or less arbitrarily focused on six interrelated levels of governance, each relying on competition, contract-based monitoring and internal control, depending on context. *At each level of governance*, markets are preferred as the most efficient process for handling dispersed information and decentrally coordinating activities. But decentralized market coordination presupposes comprehensive and explicit contract – based on clearly defined supplies, skill-levels, product features, standards of agency performance, single-issue ballots, and undistorted global market conditions. As complexities and risks increase, and non-efficiency considerations matter, necessarily incomplete agreements are complemented by more centralized forms of monitoring and control. Fiat replaces market contest. However, as the emergence of "visible hands" triggers concerns over strategic behavior, rent-seeking, accountability, and fairness, related levels of governance are required to offer market-test and regulatory controls. Hence, while firms are monitored by input and output markets or

---

[23] Trachtman, J. P., (1993) International regulatory competition, *Harvard International Law Journal*, 34(1), 47–104; Siebert, H., *et al.* (1993) Institutional competition vs. centralization: *Oxford Review of Economic Policy*, 9(1), 15–30.

regulatory relations, the regulator faces several mechanisms charged with agency supervision, etc.

Governance across levels of coordination also involves a hierarchy of rules, monitoring and enforcement mechanisms. It may be based on some fundamental principle, which, to the extent that it is broadly shared across various levels of governance, allows decisions to be delegated, standards to be adjusted to circumstance and matters to be kept predictable throughout. Or it may require clearly specified duties to be strictly monitored and sanctioned – level by level. Put differently, unavoidable discretion is either managed by relying on trust in the system or, given limits to regulatory fine-tuning, blunt governance measures at the risk of regulatory breakdown. Whereas the latter outcome is clearly unattractive, the former does not seem to fit with the implied primary motivation of a strategist: Why trust discretion, if one believes that rational market participants and political actors pursue solely their short-term self-interests – with guile? Section 3, taking up three broader governance themes, comes back to this.

3. The process of governance – some observations

Figure 1.1 provides an abstract, economic reference for discussing market and non-market coordination; but it does not indicate what, in actual fact, motivates, produces or limits changes at and across different levels of governance. To shed some light on these issues, this section: (1) presents two brief perspectives on the potential and limits of market-driven coordination; (2) discusses regulatory competition and convergence at the micro and macro levels related to corporate governance and social policy; and (3) examines the assumption of short-term self-interest and the notion of a "civil economy."

Market-driven coordination – Limits and potential

A strong market-drive is causing corporations to focus production and outsource, governments to privatize and deregulate, and economies to liberalize their trade and investment rules. They all answer calls for efficiency and competitiveness by shedding the cost of red tape and internal organization. But in some cases, motivating statistics and enticing rationales are flawed, and market-driven governance proofs incompatible with the underlying activity. In others, market-based solutions cannot simply be imposed by a single authority but, in fact, are required to create enforcement conditions on which future collective action can rest.

Market-driven public policy reforms in OECD countries are often motivated by the need to cut regulatory burden. Regulation is considered a tax that drains economic resources to an estimated tune of 10 per cent of GDP.[24] But the data to back up this claim, drawn from various studies of transition economies, evidence gathered during industrial privatization programs, or macroeconomic models intended to capture the costs of administering business regulation, is far from conclusive. It also typically does not specify the type of regulation or government failure that could be eliminated.[25] Moreover, while it is imperative to continuously challenge regulatory claims in view of viable market alternatives and productivity standards, one should not forget that some regulations target objectives other than efficiency or are explicitly designed to constitute or supersede the market (i.e., they may not meet the market test or, as seen in the next example, only at substantial hidden costs).

In 2001, US President George W. Bush, announcing far-reaching reforms in the area of human capital, sourcing, finance and budgeting,[26] embraced New Public Management as an approach to "reinvent government through decentralization, de-bureaucratization, and privatization."[27] The Department of Defense saw the potential to save up to $18bn chiefly by replacing key personnel, promoting managerial ability ahead of service allegiance, devolving authority and accountability and tendering all non-core activities. Outsourcing was to plough back vital resources to better leverage troops in combat zones. Hence, while during the second Gulf War the contractor-to-troop ratio had still been 1:6, and 1:10 during the Balkan Crisis, going forward, it was expected to exceed the 1:2 relation estimated in the Kosovo conflict.[28] However, by 2004, US Congress had grown critical about the high costs of negotiating with dominant defense contractors and their recorded unwillingness to self-govern.[29] More importantly, however, in the face of the Abu Ghraib scandal, Congress recognized that private military contractors were

---

[24] See UK Better Regulation Task Force (2005) *Less is more*, Report to the Prime Minister.

[25] For a critical review of several calculations see Helm, D., (2006) Regulatory reform, capture and regulatory burden, *Oxford Review of Economic Policy*, 22(2), 169–185.

[26] For the underlying Government Business Reference Model see www.feapmo.gov.

[27] See OECD (1997) *A new paradigm for public management*, Paris; also Kearney, R. C and Hays, S. W. (1998) *Reinventing government: the new public management and civil service systems in international perspective*, Review of Public Personnel Administration 618(4), 38–54; Pollit, C., and Bouckaert, G. (2000) *Public management reform – A comparative analysis*, Oxford: Oxford University Press.

[28] Singer, P. W. (2003) *Corporate warriors*, Ithaca and London: Cornell University Press.

[29] See US General Accounting Office (2004) *Testimony before the permanent subcommittee on investigations, committee on government affairs*, US Senate – February 12, 2004: Financial Management.

not subject to US military law, and therefore could not be held fully accountable for their actions. Under a new law, written into the 2007 military spending bill, private military contractors working in Iraq now fall under the jurisdiction of courts-martial. To some, this reestablishes the government's effective monopoly over the use of force – the *raison d'être* and source of any public authority; to others it has proved sufficient to challenge the constitutionality of the resulting changes in existing employment/agency contracts and, in effect, ask the Supreme Court to review the viability of market-testing national security.

While market-testing national security may be contentious, market-based coordination is generally considered to be the only way to deal with problems of the global commons, as in the case of managing global ecosystems.[30] Yet for markets to work, they need to be constituted by political accords that allocate and enforce property rights and establish regulatory authority for necessary adjustments. But some pattern of ownership may work against good management of ecosystems, as when property rights are concentrated in the hands of those favoring extensive development or unsustainable harvest levels. Also, coordination may break down if some countries free-ride on the efforts of the rest. There is also the fundamental problem of enforcing compliance. Coercion within the multinational environmental arena is virtually non-existent, and most environmental regimes either do not permit compulsory jurisdiction for dispute settlement or exclude arbitration by making third-party involvement subject to common agreement.[31] Here other market-driven mechanisms may take over to induce cooperation.

At its simplest, parties may pay others for reduced environmental destruction – as in the case of the Global Environmental Facility pursuant to Agenda 21 of the Rio Summit, or the EU's Cohesion Fund targeting sustainability investments in backward regions, or the "debt-for-environment" swaps of the Paris Club financing similar investments through debt relief. Next, countries may protect their own regulatory standards by imposing countervailing duties on imports from countries that simply refuse to make polluters pay. Such action appears WTO-legal if, in a second step, tariff revenues are channeled back to exporters for use in the upgrading of their own environmental regime.[32] Finally, there are a host of mechanisms that could compensate

---

[30] For a review see Helm, D., (2005) Economic Instruments and Environmental Policy, *The Economic and Social Review*, 36(3), Winter, 205–228.

[31] See Braithwaite, J. and Drahos, P., (2000) *Global business regulation*, Cambridge: Cambridge University Press.

[32] See Daly, H and Goodland, R., (1994) An ecological-economic assessment of deregulation of international commerce under GATT, *Ecological Economics*, Vol. 9, 73–92.

for the lack of global enforcement by building up pressures in domestic political and commercial markets. These range from the promotion of eco labels, brands and emissions certificates to the high-profile endorsement of models of corporate self-regulation and legislative benchmark rules, to the upgrading of NGOs' participation in contesting regulatory outcomes and the linking and broadening of issues in parliamentary vote trading.[33]

Hence, while there are limits to market-testing, certain governance structures, particularly those designed to constitute or supersede the markets, in other cases, may even substitute for the lack of central enforcement. The following examples also look at the option of tightening regulation versus improving market processes but they do so not only for addressing a particular governance concern but also for dealing with alternative systems of governance.

Regulatory competition, convergence and collusion

There are good arguments for avoiding harmonizing standards and for devolving regulatory powers to lower-level governments. Decentralized regulation is apt to better reflect local conditions and citizen preference, broaden regulatory experience, and limit the impact of failure or corruption. In the extreme, decentralized regulation could be sanctioned by issue-based voting and lead to market-driven law-making, reduced regulatory capture and increased legal innovation. From this perspective, harmonizing rules or centralizing regulation means colluding in markets for regulatory and political control. But for regulatory competition to work, factors must be mobile, markets open and rules predictable. Put differently, regulatory harmonization is often a precondition for regulatory competition. But in real-life coordination, other considerations may come into play.

Recent corporate governance scandals have led to a global tightening of rules concerning the remuneration of directors, the composition and functioning of corporate boards, and the role of auditors, institutional investors, analysts and shareholders. At the same time, initiatives to improve the disclosure of information, market access and rules governing takeovers were to enhance the regulatory function of markets. And yet, given that capital markets differ in shareholding structures and type of agency concerns,

---

[33] See Keohane, R. *et al.* (1993) The effectiveness of international environmental institutions. In Peter Haas *et al.* (eds.) *Institutions for the earth: Sources of effective international environmental protection*, Cambridge, MA.: MIT Press.

in which areas would the convergence of standards enhance the quality of regulation and where would it reduce the level of regulatory competition?

Executive pay is typically higher in capital markets with dispersed rather than concentrated shareholdings, e.g. higher in the US than in Continental Europe. This means that the former relies on high-efficiency wages to induce managerial self-monitoring and performance and/or that the latter provides stronger incentives to concentrated shareholdings to engage in active governance. Recent increases in the perks of US executive perks, unrelated to performance and control and out of line with conditions in executive labor markets,[34] have consequently given rise to drastic board reforms and calls for harmonizing take-over codes. But should these changes be emulated in Europe?

Corporate board reforms, centerpieces of SEC or OECD governance initiatives, typically focus on constraining board discretion largely to the benefit of shareholders and auditors, increasing directors' reputation and liability risk, or reinforcing board independence.[35] But measures designed for large, widely held US corporations, in need of constraining senior executives, are unlikely to be fit to protect minority investors under threat in Europe's blockholder-dominated corporations. Looking for one standard to fit all may improve administrative efficiency but at the cost of taking wrong decisions; it is not an efficient rule. Instead, observers have proposed to work on simple, principle-based rules and to broaden the regulatory community to monitor and enforce them.[36] In this context, the *de facto* harmonization of takeover rules that can be observed in Europe[37] is not an anachronism that masks the continued diversity of corporate governance systems in Europe, it rather facilitates market control over it. Yet, the same logic – devolving rule writing while enhancing widest market control – that seems efficient in promoting

---

[34] During the period 2001–3, the compensation of the top five executives of US corporations totaled around \$92bn, i.e. in excess of 10% of aggregate corporate earnings. During the decade up to 2003, compensation of the top five executives increased by 76%, the CEOs' pay by 96%; the cash component in each case grew by 56% and 45% respectively. See Bebchuk, L. and Grinstein, Y., (2005) The growth of executive pay, *Oxford Review of Economic Policy*, 21, 283–303.

[35] See Hertig, G., (2005) Ongoing board reforms: One-size-fits-all and regulatory capture, *Oxford Review of Economic Policy*, 21, 269–282.

[36] *Ibid.*

[37] Goergen *et al.* assess takeover regulation in twenty-nine Continental European countries and show that standards converged *de jure* with takeover regulation in the UK and the US. They measure convergence in nine dimensions: adoption of a mandatory-bid rule; the equal treatment principle; transparency of ownership and control; squeeze-out rules; sell-out rules; one-share-one-vote; implementation of a breakthrough rule; imposition of board neutrality; and bans on *ex post* defenses. Goergen, M. *et al.* (2005) Corporate governance convergence: Evidence from takeover regulation reforms in Europe, *Oxford Review of Economic Policy*, 21(2), 243–68.

European corporate governance, in the case of European social policy could prove deleterious to regulatory standards and politically unsustainable.

Since its beginning in 1957, European integration efforts have focused on economic not social objectives; attempts to create standards of social policy, such as the European Social Charter (1989) or those embedded in the European Constitutions, either did not gain unanimous support or were rejected. Currently, the EU's Open Method of Coordination (OMC) with respect to social policy does not set minimum standards for all members through directives, but instead encourages a process of learning from best practices of other member states. However, models are diverse and adjustment costs high.

Traditional European social models, labeled as social-democratic, conservative and liberal,[38] have been blurred by market-driven changes in fiscal, regulatory and labor market policies. Aggregate perspectives block the view on vital differences. Europe is but a label. At the beginning of 2006, it covered nations with GDP growth rates ranging from 8.6% to −1.2%, export expansions varying from 38.4% to −15.9%, and national unemployment rates stretching from 3.1% to 18.1%. Europe houses economies in which industry/ agriculture share more than 65% of GDP, others in which economic activity is more than 80% service-related. In terms of labor productivity, in 2004, a European employee generated as much as US$56.44 or as little as US$9.11 worth of output per hour; hourly manufacturing wages ranged from $35.37 to $0.53. In addition, while disparities among European nations are pronounced, regional differences within them are becoming economically and politically even more important.[39] Among the Union's 25 regions, GDP per capita was almost three times higher in the ten wealthiest locations than in the ten at the bottom of the scale.[40] Differences in skills and infrastructures explain patterns of economic activity and rising income polarization – the coexistence of regional growth magnets and poverty traps. Enlargement adds to this. In Denmark, Austria, the Netherlands, Germany and France, expenditure on social protection is three to four times higher than in Hungary or Slovakia.

The EU, as an alliance, is only viable to the extent that it creates and maintains procedural and substantive consensus and deference to it. Alliances tend to expand to the point of saturation and then disintegrate once membership

---

[38] In the *social democratic model*, the state provides universal and homogenous social insurance benefits; the *conservative model* looks at the family as the nucleus of the welfare state and differentiates contributions and pay-outs. The *liberal model* emphasizes market models and private as opposed to public responsibility for retirement and health insurance plans. Based on Esping Andersen, G., (1990) *The three worlds of welfare capitalism*, Princeton: Princeton University Press.

[39] Maza, A., Villaverde, J., (2004) Regional disparities in the EU, *Applied Economic Letters*, 11(8), 517–523.

[40] Second Report on Economic and Social Cohesion, EC Commission, Brussels.

grows further in numbers and diversity. Its leadership is closed to participation or does not deliver benefits, and necessary reforms are delayed or not pursued by all.[41] Does the combination of the OMC and market pressure drive regulatory competition to the bottom? Would collusion on a minimum social policy standard eliminate or enable viable market competition? Or is there at times a need to relax the market-based allocation logic and embrace the concept of a "civil economy"?

Towards a 'civil economy'?

Figure 1.1 provides an audit trail for assessing the relative efficiency and possible fairness of a given pattern of economic or commercial coordination. There is clearly very limited scope for any *a priori* judgment; rather, an integrative view on the interaction of multiple levels of governance is required when assessing the specifics of the case at hand. But is this enough? Figure 1.1 presents a two-dimensional conceptualization that limits the discussion to issues of decentralized market-based coordination or centralized non-market rules. Classical (institutional) economists were also concerned with decentralized non-market coordination based on principles overriding short-term self-interest. In fact, one may argue that without understanding individual and societal norms, analyses of market and non-market coordination remain incomplete and efficient responses to governance concerns are unexplored.

Recent work on the so-called "civil economy,"[42] at first sight, appear to address this concern. Sharing a broad, sociological conceptualization of economic and commercial activity, contributors in this area advocate substituting and complementing governmental and market coordination by notions of community orientation, civil association and self-regulation – at local, national and global level. Yet a closer look reveals why the theme has so far not resulted in any systematic and testable account. In proposing methods of mutual governance, social accountability and communal responsibility, which should substitute profit with non-profit organizations, industrial enterprises with employee cooperatives, and the public sector with civil privatization, contributors, possibly unwittingly, substitute self-interest with universal altruisms, and positive analysis with normative reasoning. Their arguments often emanate from the urge to confront the "paradox of

---

[41] For a review see Dougherty, R. and Pfalzgraph, J., (1984) *Theories of international relations*, New York: Harcourt Brace.

[42] For an overview see Bruyn, S., (2000) *A civil economy – Transforming the market in the 21st century*, Ann Arbor MI: The University of Michigan Press.

the market," that is, the apparent need to rely on and yet limit the pursuit of short-term self-interest. Yet, as will be argued in Chapter 15, that paradox is based on a flawed but popular conceptualization of economic behaviour. It assumes that economic man is driven by some loutish motivation, which proves unsustainable in reality and confuses the means of competitive market selection with the goal of productive cooperation. In particular, Chapter 15 examines the link between self-interest, self-restraint and essential market functions and evaluates the function of conventions and norms in supplementing incomplete market and regulatory governance. For markets to work there is a need to rehabilitate moral reasoning to deal with issues of trust and unavoidable discretion.

4. Strategies, markets and governance – structure and overview

Strategies, markets and governance is a group effort. Five contributors are members of the IMD faculty with particular research interests in economic regulation, corporate governance, international political economy, NGO activities and accounting and audit frauds. Two offer direct industry perspectives on regulatory and political risk and link technology and commercial aspects with concerns for legal and corporate social responsibilities. Their work is organized to highlight governance concerns at the level of the firm, the industry and international policy.

Parts I to III focus on firm-level governance, in particular the tension between competitive strategy and competition policy standards, theories about harmonizing corporate governance and its failure in practice, fraud and moral ambiguity, the legitimacy, nature and impact of NGO campaigns and the challenges of stakeholder management in hostile national environments.

Chapter 2 addresses issues related to Competitive advantage and the regulation of dominant firms. More than 110 years after passing the US Sherman Act and nearly half a century following the enactment of EU competition rules, antitrust authorities on both sides of the Atlantic continue to search for general principles to assess the abuse of market power by dominant firms. But just as recent, high-profile cases, involving corporations such as American Airlines, 3M, Michelin, Deutsche Telekom, IMS Health and Microsoft, left the law unsettled, ongoing policy reviews, organized by the European Commission, the US Department of Justice and the Federal Trade Commission, have yet to clarify standards for dominance abuse as well as viable efficiency defenses. Business needs guidance on permissible practices, but drafting acceptable rules is far from simple. The EU's ongoing review of the application of Article

82 to exclusionary conduct intends to provide an effect-based, economic approach to dominant firm regulation.[43] It will have a major impact on the range of price and non-price strategies as well as the protection of intellectual property rights. But is the Commission's initiative likely to address vital policy and strategy concerns? Or will it merely continue its approach of delegating regulation and shifting the burden of proof to the dominant, successful players in the market?

Chapter 3, Delegating regulation: Supply-chain management, partnering and competition policy reforms, discusses regulatory reforms when dealing with increasingly complex inter-firm contracts. Accompanying the enlargement of the European Union (EU) on May 1, 2004, the Commission ushered in a complete overhaul of the procedural rules applicable to Articles 81 and 82 of the EC Treaty.[44] As a result, the EU's competition law regime shifted from a highly centralized notification and authorization process to a decentralized system that broadly relies on national competition authorities (NCAs), courts *and* the undertakings themselves for case assessment and law enforcement. By delegating regulatory tasks, the Commission hopes to free resources for the proactive appraisal of key cases and new policy areas, and to ensure the uniform application of EU competition law through economic, "effect-based" substantive rules, procedural guidance and outcome controls. But while the lack of economic references makes stipulating substantive and procedural standards far from trivial, specifying these still does not guarantee effective regulatory delegation at Member State and corporate level. In fact, the Commission falls short of structuring a proper approach to assess vertical agreements. This raises concerns about how to assess any over- or under-regulation and how to ensure the uniformity of law and the effectiveness of regulatory devolution and corporate self-regulation. These are concerns that are generally applicable to the broader EU competition law reform.

Chapters 4 and 5 shift the perspective towards corporate governance and offer an historical perspective on the diffusion of regulation and a "hard-nosed" reality check. Chapter 4, Diffusion of corporate governance regulation: France, Germany, the UK and the USA presents, following a timeline, the reasons why corporate governance regulations, such as the liability and independence of boards, the creation and use of audit committees with non-executive, independent directors or remuneration rules, did or did not spread through different countries. Drivers of diffusion include high-profile corporate

---

[43] For background information see http://ec.europa.eu/comm/competition/antitrust/art82/index.html.
[44] Council Regulation (EC) No. 1/2003, 12.6.2002, O.J. Ll/1.

crises, growing capital market orientation, the widespread use of the internet and modern communication media, as well as privatization and regulatory harmonization in line with common market measures. Diffusion was typically blocked due to unequal legal, institutional and regulatory bases, particularly ownership structures, differences in remuneration and legal systems.

Chapter 5, Corporate governance after Enron *et al.*, is less academic and decidedly more opinionated. Enron, World Com, Metallgesellschaft, Rolls-Royce, Guinness and Barings Bank, Tyco, Marconi, Ahold, Swissair, Parmalat are used to illustrate six fundamental conditions of governance failure, the combination of which turned out to be lethal: (a) ineffective boards that lacked distance, financial and resource independence and the technical competence to perform the monitoring tasks required; (b) strategic failures, due to lack of preparation, due diligence – and ultimately – arrogance; (c) the dominant CEO – dominant leaders driving group thinking at executive and board level and, not facing any serious inside or outside control, ultimately believing their own PR; (d) hubris and greed – executive pay levels linked to asset value and perceived performance – a race that exploded CEO pay fivefold during the 1990s and promoted a "take what you can" mentality; (e) ill-judged acquisition and over-expansion to justify claims; (f) control failure – due to growing organizational complexities, the lack of internal audit processes and CFOs with fundamental professional weaknesses. Two solutions are being proposed: the separation of operations from monitoring and the need to align executive pay with long-term viable strategies. But even then, no legislation or corporate structure will ultimately offer sufficient safeguards. If one cannot legislate for a direct, rigorous monitoring attitude or financial moderation, how can this become the reliable norm as the ultimate reference for effective corporate governance?

Chapter 6, Tackling healthcare fraud!?, deals with norms and moral hazards. Aiming to contain vast and fast rising expenditure levels, estimated to amount to 8.2% of GDP across OECD countries in 2003, national healthcare reforms cannot avoid rationing – withholding beneficial interventions from needy individuals. Yet, a substantial part of a nation's healthcare spending is typically diverted in illicit ways – rendering otherwise feasible care unattainable and undermining the legitimacy of private and public services. In the United States, healthcare fraud and abuse reportedly accounts for around 10% of total outlay – about $120bn per year.[45] In the UK, prescription crime in 2003 was

---

[45] See Hyman, D. A., (2001) Health care fraud and abuse: Market change, social norms, and the trust "reposed in the workmen", *Journal of Legal Studies*, Volume 30(2), 531–68.

estimated to amount to £115 m. In Lower Saxony, one of Germany's 16 Länder, insurance fraud alone accounted for €40 m in 2003. But cases are not always clear-cut and not always easily dealt with. There is often substantial ambiguity in defining what is actually improper conduct, identifying such behavior among the vast numbers of cases that are handled annually, separating errors from deliberate criminal intent, and choosing adequate regulatory responses. Three cases – involving the "upcoding of fertility treatment," the "importation of low cost dentures" and the "confessions of a Managed Care Medical Director" are presented but not discussed. Rather the chapter ends with a brief note on moral standards to help structure a debate.

A firm's stakeholders may challenge its regulatory and moral legitimacy. Chapter 7, Watchdog and proxy war campaigns against firms, deals with NGOs confronting firms over a broad range of issues – from the environment to labor, and human and animal rights. Corporate managers often fail to appreciate the deeper dynamics behind these campaigns and, as a result, respond to them in ineffective or even counterproductive ways. The chapter distinguishes between two very different types of NGO campaigns: watchdog campaigns and proxy war campaigns, which need to be understood and responded to in very different ways. How it is that small "David" NGOs can beat "Goliath" corporations? How can managers avoid and effectively respond to these campaigns?

Chapter 8, Oil and conflict: Lundin Petroleum's experience in Sudan, details stakeholder management in practice. Lundin Petroleum obtained the rights to explore for, and produce oil and gas in concession Block 5 A, Unity State, Sudan, in February 1997; it sold these rights in June 2003. During the period in which the company was active in Sudan, it operated in the belief that oil could benefit the economic development of the area and the country as a whole, and that this would have a catalyzing effect on the peace process. The problems which it encountered in the area, however, led the company to constantly reassess its activities, role and responsibilities there. This chapter examines the reasons why Lundin decided to operate in Sudan, the challenges it faced in the course of its activities, the steps it adopted to satisfy both its commercial objectives and ethical concerns, and its efforts to promote a peaceful resolution of the conflict.

Focusing on drivers of industry regulation and market evolution rather than their direct firm-specific impact, contributors to Part III discuss mechanics, options and alternatives for market-driven policies in the area of energy, water, healthcare and the environment. Chapter 9 presents a perspective on How the clean air interstate rule will affect investment and management decisions in the US electricity sector. Following an introduction to the US Acid Rain Cap and Trade Program, its regulatory drivers and political subtleties, the chapter discusses compliance options including investing in air pollution control technologies, lowering emitting generation sources, switching fuel or relying on the emissions trading market. The way in which tightened air emission standards impact any individual utility depends on each company's generation mix and regulatory status. The chapter concludes with a discussion of the business case of LG&E Energy's own compliance program and its fit with the company's overall strategy.

Chapters 10 and 11 focus on the political process shaping and diluting regulatory outcomes and the need to reconsider fundamental options. Chapter 10 evaluates whether EU water infrastructure management offers a role model that is worth emulating around the world. It is projected that by 2025 at least 3.5bn people or 48% of the world population will live in "water-stressed" conditions, that is, experience severe water scarcity and gravely strained aquatic ecosystems.[46] To arrest this development, current efforts to identify transferable solutions also focus on European resource management, particularly on national approaches to operating and charging for water and infrastructure investments as well as the EU's Water Framework Directive (WFD). But Europe does not offer simple answers either. There is no common European performance standard to benchmark given supply schemes or to suggest a model to be followed. Next, the EU's WFD, drafted under the impact of a protracted power struggle among EU institutions, Member States and stakeholder groups, has resulted in vague objectives and unclear monitoring criteria that threaten to dilute pre-existing regulatory norms. The chapter offers a set of recommendations.

Chapter 11 discusses US and UK experiences with Market-testing healthcare. With 30% of the OECD's GDP projected to be spent on healthcare by 2030, numerous Member States attempt to market-test healthcare. The 2003/4 Bush Administration's Medicare bill offered $500bn prescription drug benefits to motivate pensioners to join for-profit health maintenance plans that manage costs by substituting closed budgets for fee-for-service arrangements. Similarly, reforms of the UK National Health Service (NHS), intended to improve the system's overall capacity to respond to patient needs, employed fixed-price performance contracts to stimulate competition in primary and hospital care. In each case, determining cost-effective therapies as a condition for coverage amounts to "managing care" and continues to raise concerns about the legitimacy and constestability of results and

---

[46] See UNESCO World Water Assessment, at www.uesembassy, i/file200303/alia/a3030516.htm.

standards. Governance concerns relate to treatment guidelines, patient rights and the legal status of various stakeholders. This chapter deals with market reactions to regulatory changes and vice-versa. It initially focuses on recent developments in the UK NHS and the transformation of US managed care towards what President Bush in his 2006 State of Union address, called consumer-driven healthcare. It then discusses US antitrust rationales for curbing specialty hospitals and upholding apparently anti-competitive settlements between generic and branded drug producers. While observers may be pessimistic about market-testing healthcare, there is a need to recall the characteristics of its principal alternatives.

While the previous two contributions discuss options for complete policy reversal, Chapter 12, On governing natural resources, urges for a necessary turnaround. Environmental degradation, defined by the UN as one, and possibly *the* main, threat facing mankind, meets with little effective response. This is partly due to the way issues are presented. Discussions about environmental sustainability are often heated and seldom rational. Analysis mixes with cynicism, denial with defeatism. Issues are intricate, forces interacting and findings hopelessly conditional. Any attempt to express a vital concern in its entirety and complexity is necessarily abstract, indirect and therefore often deemed irrelevant by the intended audience; however, more catchy phrases, simplified assumptions and statistics are quickly discredited by skeptics. Yet even if hype were to be avoided and concerns were concisely presented, acting on crucial issues often requires agreement on policy instruments, institutional contexts and enforcement mechanisms that may not be forthcoming if adjustment costs are prohibitive or freely shifted onto others. Continued inaction in the face of critical concerns is often justified based on some overarching principle that ultimately blocks any progress. Chapter 12 offers a perspective on some of these issues: it sketches the plight of global marine fishery as a case-study of non-adjustment and identifies the key issues underlying that case as constituting the main challenges in managing natural resources. The chapter discusses issues of globalizing environmental standards and challenges the need for economic growth. Is mankind able to change the chip? Are policy makers and business executives able to see opportunities and lead the way?

Contributions to Part IV link national market contexts to issues and challenges of international policy coordination. They review national economic imperatives governing global energy markets, political and cultural obstacles for policy reforms in systems as diverse as China and the EU and the need to find institutional responses to international trade policy distortions.

Chapter 13, Governing oil supply, initially wonders why current oil price speculations – broadly concerned with fuel substitution or technological supply constraints – hardly ever seem to account for the role of national oil companies (NOCs). Is it because NOCs, habitually secretive and subject to political discretion, typically do not render information in any timely, market-relevant way? Or does it reflect the perception that NOCs simply operate outside the realm of conventional market, corporate and regulatory controls? But it is the NOCs that control roughly 90% of the global hydrocarbon reserves and whose operating and investment decisions affect prices, demand adjustments, but also their own country's policy options. Recent endeavors to substitute analysis for prevailing economic and political clichés, clarify important but largely unconnected questions. The chapter charts an integrative approach. It ties current oil price discussions to conceivable supply adjustments and the importance of NOCs. It proceeds to rationalize NOCs – conceptually, historically and in current market contexts – and to discuss NOC governance in general and on the basis of the experience in Norway, Saudi Arabia and Nigeria. It links NOC governance to the challenges of steering resource-based economic development. Understanding that linkage is vital to be able to predict the ability of resource owners to adjust, and thereby assess, market outcomes.

While also focusing on the capacity of national adjustment to changing market conditions, the approach taken in Chapter 14, China – External imperatives and internal reforms, is quite different. China – in a dramatic turnaround – opened its closed economy and, in numerous ways, redefined the basis of global competition and trade. While China's relations with the West – the intimate link between "two actors sharing one bubble" – are the focus of frequent policy discussions, this chapter takes the reader inside the country to appreciate the dynamics of domestic policy reform. China's insulation is legendary. While the West focuses on the fact that from the mid – nineteenth century to the second half of the twentieth century, China's contribution to global GDP fell from roughly 30% to 5%, a broadly shared national perspective holds that until the 1970s, China appeared "entirely self-sufficient" whether in terms of products or ideas. And there are at least three strands of strong internal opposition to the reform process: the old and the new left, nationalists, and the cultural center of the world, perspective. Will liberal China succeed in improving the accountability and transparency of the government? What are the prospects for party–industry relations and the options for establishing sound social security and pension systems? How will all of this impact on China's role in the global economy?

The EU's future role in the global economy will largely depend on the consistency of political and economic decision-making within it. Chapter 15, assessing EU constitutional governance, evaluates the process and prospect of political reform within the EU. Fifty years since the signing of the Treaty of Rome, the EU is trying to restart its drive for a constitution that was rejected just two years ago. Why did it fail? On June 17, 2005, the European Union summit broke up in a bitter dispute over the EU's budget and the future of its constitution. The popular rejection of the proposed EU constitution by France and the Netherlands, two major advocates of European unity, just prior to the meeting had raised deep questions about the union's legitimacy and purpose. Hopes by some that successful ratifications in the remaining EU countries would change the French and Dutch stance were soon dispelled. To some, the union had been thrown off course and into "one of the deepest crises in its history;"[47] to others, Europe had just been given a unique opportunity for political, economic and institutional renewal. The chapter briefly sketches some elements of the EU's current economic status, its institutional aspirations and *Realpolitik*, and the range of challenges that a European constitution was envisioned to meet. It then outlines key considerations for assessing the origin and performance of constitutional governance and the political economy of federalism. Based on this, the reader is invited to speculate about alternative strategies for "re-engineering" EU governance in line with European regional economic activity and a growing interest in the devolution of political control.

The lack of policy coordination is also the focal point of Chapter 16. This chapter asks whether there could be One competition standard to regulate global trade and protection?, and tackles the issue of antidumping distortions of global trade relations. Today, 103 years after the first antidumping law was passed in Canada, and with ninety-eight countries enacting such rules to potentially cover more than 90% of worldwide imports,[48] antidumping proceedings only rarely live up to domestic competition standards or general economic principles. Rather, with tariffs, voluntary export restraints or safeguards drastically reduced, banned, or enjoining compensation, WTO-condoned antidumping action has turned into a powerful trade weapon. Its threatened use alone can cause international competitors to raise prices and

---

[47] Jean-Claude Juncker, Prime Minister of Luxembourg, chairman of the Brussels summit. Quoted in *The Economist*, Europe's identity crisis deepens, June 18, 2005.

[48] Zanardi, M., (2006) Does antidumping use contribute to trade liberalization? University of Tilburg Working Paper.

effectively agree to collude at consumers' expense. Mounting welfare losses are only topped by the cost of corrupted global trade.

Reform initiatives abound – ranging from the promotion of unilateralism to diverse models of multilateral coordination, often involving the use of common, centrally or decentrally applied competition standards. Yet, while the drawbacks of the former are sufficiently clear, the latter usually presuppose that broadly diverse regulatory criteria can be harmonized and objective enforcement, review and arbitration institutionally ensured. But multilateralists typically don't answer why national authorities, in reality, would limit their discretion over the domestic allocation of trade protection and which preconditions would be required for this outcome to be achieved. This chapter aims to do just that.

In **Part V**, Chapter 17, Addressing the market paradox, offers an observation to close out the book. Dealing with governance concerns at the firm, industry and international level, the chapters included in this volume shed light on the benefits and limits of market-based coordination. Structural conditions permitting, markets are recognized to be efficient in allocating resources and stimulating their adept and innovative use as long as market participants pursue their self-interest. At the same time, for markets to work, strategic behavior, in its modern, Websterian definition, may be problematic as the pursuit of interest should not extend to forms of opportunistic behavior, misrepresentation and guile. In other words, market coordination requires the vigorous pursuit and clear limitation of self-interest. Dealing constructively with this apparent *market paradox*, successful, capitalist economies rely on habits and behavioral norms to buttress more formal institutions in sustaining system trusts and dependable, decentralized coordination. Conversely, institutional deficiencies cause market failures, legitimacy concerns and the loss of faith in economic and even political liberties; they are ultimately linked to economic backwardness. While, none of this is new, its importance is often not recognized by both proponents and critics of market-driven life. Along with an appreciation of the regulatory value of conventions, there is a need to rehabilitate moral reasoning.

Part II

Firm-level

Competitive advantage and the regulation of dominant firms

Ralf Boscheck

More than 110 years after passing the US Sherman Act and nearly half a century after the enactment of EU competition rules, antitrust authorities on both sides of the Atlantic continue to search for general principles to assess the abuse of market power by dominant firms. But just as recent, high-profile cases, involving corporations such as American Airlines, 3M, Michelin, Deutsche Telekom, IMS Health or Microsoft, left the law unsettled, ongoing policy reviews, organized by the European Commission, the US Department of Justice and the Federal Trade Commission, have yet to clarify standards for dominance abuse as well as viable efficiency defenses.[1] Business needs guidance on permissible practices, but drafting acceptable rules is far from simple. This chapter contrasts business and regulatory views on competitive advantage and offers a non-technical sketch of US and EU approaches to assessing market power and its potential abuse. Do current EU reform initiatives address vital policy concerns?

1. Competitive advantage – business and regulation

The tasks of devising a competitive strategy and assessing its economic impact focus on the same question: *How can a company attain and sustain above-industry-average profitability?* Answers provided by business and antitrust authorities frequently differ, which is surprising, given that both sides are often guided by the same economic references.

Regulatory authorities apply concepts from industrial and institutional economics in assessing and, for the purpose of rule writing, pre-judging the viability and welfare effects of diverse market structures and types of firm behavior.[2] Quoted out of this original context, the same tools have since been

---

[1] See www.abanet.org; http://ec.europa.eu/comm/competition/antitrust/art82/index.html for the latest perspectives.

[2] For a review see Whinston, M., (2006) *Lectures on antitrust economics*, Boston: MIT Press.

borrowed by the field of competitive strategy to systematize earlier business policy discussions and replace the "art of strategy" with a set of "scientific techniques" for analyzing markets and shaping competition. The resulting industry analysis framework, initially outlined by Porter, provides an understanding of a sector's attractiveness and helps companies to determine specific operational and organizational decisions to effectively offset the forces of competition.[3] More recent discussions of resource-based strategies expand the analysis by identifying those skill-sets which companies must nurture, leverage and protect to sustain and extend their position across a variety of commercial arrangements. In the process, the conventional view of firms competing in clearly defined arenas has been replaced by a more realistic notion of networks of vertically and horizontally related activities whose coordination involves a mix of competition and cooperation both inside and outside traditional market relations. A competitive advantage, that is, above-average profitability, results from controlling those decisions that make it impossible, or at least difficult, for other stages of production to substitute for what a given company has to offer. This may be based on a superior offer or the preclosure of alternative supplies, or both; in some cases it may also be the prerequisite for any valuable economic activity to take place at all. Yet, for regulators the question is how to distinguish the creation of a superior offer from the build-up and abuse of a monopoly position, and how to stipulate general, predictable rules.

Consider three landmark cases. In 1990, three years after its patent in Canada had expired, *NutraSweet* continued to hold a 95% share in the Canadian market for aspartame. The Director of Competition Policy reviewed NutraSweet's supply, promotion, and pricing policies and concluded that the company had engaged in exclusionary and predatory practices.[4] Authorities considered that NutraSweet's US patent, which had been extended up to 1992, enabled the company to afford price-cuts in the Canadian market that made any serious competitive market entry non-viable. The patent had also created sufficient leverage to tie Pepsi and Coke into exclusive supply contracts outside the US, thus foreclosing a substantial proportion of the Canadian market. Next, NutraSweet was charged with interfering in the market for dietary and low-calorie foods by offering Canadian industrial buyers rebates for US imports containing NutraSweet aspartame. Furthermore, the company's policy of

---

[3] For a review see Porter, M. E., (1980) *Competitive strategy*, New York: Free Press; and Ghemawat, P., (1997) *Competition and business strategy in historical perspective*, HBS 9-798-010.

[4] See *Canada (Director of Investigation & Research) v. NutraSweet Co.*, (1990), 32 C. P. R. 3rd 1 Competition Tribunal.

advertising directly to consumers by inducing food producers to display the NutraSweet logo and brand name on their own product, was argued to increase food producers' switching costs and was only in NutraSweet's interest. Nevertheless, the company paid a volume-based trademark display allowance of up to 40% of the gross price of aspartame. As a result of this so-called "branded ingredient strategy," the net-allowance price of branded NutraSweet aspartame was frequently below the price of the commodity product. Any new competitor not only had to sustain below-commodity prices, but also had to overcome massive scale-based entry barriers in production as well as the barrier in distribution created by NutraSweet's branding, pricing and rebate scheme. Finally, NutraSweet's supply conditions included "meet or release clauses," which committed the company to meet any competitive price quotation and, through "most-favored-nation agreements" (MFN), to pass these prices on to any one of its customers. In evaluating the Director's piece-by-piece assessment, "[t]he Tribunal [saw] little purpose in ... determining whether each clause constitutes an anticompetitive act; rather it was persuaded that the agreements had an exclusionary *purpose*."[5]

In its decision on *TetraPak* in July 1991, the EC Commission argued that the Swedish packaging supplier held a 90% market share in its core business of aseptic milk cartons, which it was said to have leveraged to tie the sales of its various products and services, lock its customers into exclusive long-term arrangements, and exclude its competitors, even in other markets.[6] The attestation of market dominance relied on the inferred unwillingness of final consumers to switch between UHT milk (requiring aseptic packaging) and fresh milk, as differences in taste and convenience made both products incomplete substitutes and the consumer-price impact of packaging material prices charged to dairies was too insignificant to effect such substitution. Against the background of a 90% market share in aseptic milk cartons, TetraPak's differential pricing decisions, its policy towards extensive patenting and technology acquisition, its exclusive and conditional supply of machine, material, and services, and its aggressive and coordinated targeting of reference accounts appeared to further an abuse of dominance and to completely prevent inter-brand and intra-brand competition. Yet, given a broader market definition, would TetraPak's conduct have been considered questionable at all?

---

[5] Ibid, p. 42, italics added.
[6] See TetraPak II, *Official Journal of the European Communities*, No 18/3 (1992): No L 72/1–68.

Following a US Supreme Court decision against *Eastman Kodak* in November 1992,[7] a 1987 antitrust lawsuit against the photographic equipment giant was reinstated and heard by a jury in the fall of 1993. Eighteen independent service companies, represented by the California State Electronic Association (CSEA), had sued the company for refusing to sell independent service groups parts to fix its copiers, which in their view not only amounted to an illegal tying of services to product sales, but was intended to drive independent service companies out of business. They furthermore argued that an independent, cost-efficient service sector was required to check on the performance of a few original equipment manufacturers, otherwise likely to dominate the service provision in the US. For Kodak, reclaiming services as an integral part of the business generated by their product seemed natural; alternative suppliers, requiring independent service support, maintained the viability of an independent service sector; and the legal action of independent service companies interfered with its product, pricing, and distribution policies. Revoking its one-product defense, for Kodak, meant destroying the key lever of any company's strategy – the freedom to define its business.

The three cases illustrate the difficulties in determining the scope of a company's market, as well as the sources, effects, and legitimacy of its ability to control decisions within it. One may argue that because NutraSweet was the first to adopt a large-scale process, its production, marketing, and distribution strategies were aimed at maintaining its cost advantage at prices that deterred entry into its market. The intention to exclude is deduced from attempts to contract large volume long-term, escape commoditization through brand-differentiation, and pass on scale advantages through cost-based pricing, with or without display allowance. Furthermore, the use of "meet or release" and MFN-clauses, rather than foreclosing competition, may be deemed to enhance market transparency and foster the intensity of market contests. Does market power turn pro-competitive behavior anti-competitive?

Similarly, in the case of TetraPak, a narrow and static view of the relevant market might have overstated the company's position and qualified its behavior as "abusing and leveraging dominance" rather than supporting a systems solution that called for coordinating decisions across related markets. In fact, by emphasizing the final consumer, authorities not only might have misjudged the relevant buyers – the filler and indirectly the trade – as well as the range of the packaging and distribution options available to them. They also apparently failed to grasp the essence of TetraPak's business idea to offer

---

[7] *Eastman Kodak Co.* v. *Image Technical Services, Inc.*, 504 U.S. 451, 112 S. Ct. 2072 (1992).

liquid packaging and distribution solutions. In the context of this broader and very different competitive environment, TetraPak's overall position had been much closer to the self-assessed 14% share of the liquid packaging market – hardly characterizing dominance.[8] Within this broader context, the very same data – previously interpreted to manifest abusive behavior – appears to support a legitimate interest in leveraging control over otherwise loosely related parties so as to build and protect the company's vital key assets and skills.

Likewise, the discussion of Eastman Kodak demonstrates the need for clarity in defining permissible means of controlling and defining one's business, lest regulatory stipulations on "abuse of dominance" turn into viable tools for manipulating unwelcome decisions taken by suppliers, buyers, or competitors. In each case, the defendant argued that judicial market definitions neglected actual or potential substitutes and for that reason overstated its relative power in affecting market choices. Where contracts and tacit agreements indeed constrained such choices or even forestalled competition altogether, they were held to be vital for creating what markets perceived to be superior offers. Hence, rather than reducing economic choice, they ultimately improved upon it.

More than a decade has passed since these decisions gave rise to calls for competition law reforms and the need to clarify limits to aggressive competitive conduct. Have regulatory systems adjusted? Have standards for assessing price and non-price strategies been spelled out? Section 2 contrasts the current US and EU philosophies towards dominant firm regulation in general and in the areas of pricing and rebates, bundling and refusal to deal.

2. Abuse of dominance under Section 2 of the US Sherman Act and Article 82 of the EC Treaty

"The successful competitor having been urged to compete must not be turned upon when he wins." *US* v. *Alcoa*, 148 F2d 416 (2d Cir. 1945) at 430

"Dominant undertakings have a special responsibility not to impair competition on the market concerned." ECJ on 28.9.2006 rejecting appeal of CFI's judgment Case T-65/98 *Van den Bergh Foods* v. *Commission* [2003] ECR II-4653.

Differences in US and EU approaches to regulating dominant firms have been characterized as "protecting competition" vs. "protecting competitors."[9]

---

[8] See Boscheck, R., (1993) Competitive success and the law: TetraPak, *European Management Journal*, 11(2) 190–99.

[9] The characterization stems from Charles James, quoted in Antitrust chief reacts to EU decision to prohibit GE/Honeywell deal, *Antitrust and Trade* (BNA) 15, July 6, 2001.

But this dichotomy is conceptually questionable and does not give an adequate description of current case law and regulatory challenges. There is rather an attitudinal difference that manifests itself in the relative emphasis that, at any given point in time, is put on the concern for "consumer welfare" vs. "economic liberty" and the different sources of harm that relate to these.[10] Focusing on consumer welfare, the currently predominant US approach is performance oriented and aims to avoid price increases, output reductions, and allocative, productive and technological inefficiencies rather than controlling dominance and questionable conduct *per se*. Less optimistic with regard to the ability of markets to adjust, today's mainstream continental European position concentrates on maintaining the freedom to compete and competition as an institution. Accordingly, there is a stronger focus on market structure, a concern for even likely distortions and an implied responsibility of a dominant firm not to harm. Since World War II, both mindsets have played an important role in the antitrust discourse on either side of the Atlantic.[11] Today, while concerns about "consumer welfare" vs. "economic liberty" capture the general difference in US and EU regulatory outlook, recent court decisions and reform initiatives paint a less consistent and less predictable picture.

To prove a monopolization offence under section 2 of the Sherman Act, courts require plaintiffs to establish that the defendant willfully acquired and maintained market power and engaged in predatory or anti-competitive behavior with the specific intention and high likelihood of monopolization. A firm that due to superior products, business insights or chance, legally acquired a monopoly position does not violate section 2 merely by exploiting the situation and charging a monopoly price. US courts typically have held conduct to be anti-competitive, in the sense of predatory and exclusionary, if it would be economically irrational except for the goal of monopolization or otherwise exclusionary without any legitimate business justification. A business justification relates to the direct or indirect advancement of consumer welfare due to increases in quality and efficiency. Hence, in essence, market dominance is seen to reward business skills and to create an incentive for others to follow and to compete for profits; authorities must ensure that markets remain contestable, but must also protect dominant players against unfounded allegations from their less efficient competitors that stifle, rather than promote, competition.

---

[10] For a discussion see Bundeskartellamt A (2006), BKartA/competition forum debate on reform of Article 82: A "dialectic" on competing approaches, *European Competition Journal*, 2(0), 211–227, and also Fox, E. (2003) We protect competition, you protect competitors, *World Competition*, 26(2), 149–65.

[11] See, for example, Langenfeld, J., Scheffman, D. T., (1986) Evolution or revolution – What is the future of antitrust? *Antitrust Bulletin*, 31(2), 287–300.

Article 82 of the EC Treaty prohibits any abuse by dominant undertakings within the Common Market or a substantial part of it, provided that trade between Member States is affected. Abuse is defined as both exclusionary conduct, that is, exclusive dealing, predatory pricing or refusal to supply, and exploitative practices, including unfair prices and trading conditions. The latter also includes applying dissimilar conditions on equivalent transactions (discrimination and non-discrimination offences) as well as extracting concessions from contract parties unrelated to the subject of the contract. Although Article 82, in its present form, does not provide for an efficiency defense, the European Court of Justice (ECJ) has held that dominant undertakings cannot be disentitled from protecting their own commercial interests if they are attacked. A dominant firm therefore has the possibility to justify business conduct that does not strengthen its position and is not abusive on economic grounds. Nevertheless, the ECJ has imposed on dominant undertakings a "special responsibility not to impair competition." Put differently, "market dominance entails particular duties not incumbent on other market players."[12] Seen this way, in the EU, market success has lately been on the defensive. Yet relative to these stark differences in outlook, US and EU variations in evaluating potentially objectionable exclusionary and pricing behavior are much more nuanced.

Exclusionary conduct

In general, in the US, a firm may unilaterally restrict output or product development for the purpose of maximizing its profits without violating section 2 of the Sherman Act; there is also no obligation for a monopolist to deal with another firm. In the EU, a refusal to deal may constitute an abuse under Article 82 where a dominant undertaking is seen to act arbitrarily, disproportionately or in the pursuit of anti-competitive aims. The termination of an existing supply relationship is subject to stricter standards than the refusal to establish a new one. However, recent case law on both sides of the Atlantic – particularly in view of essential facilities and intellectual property rights – blurs this clear-cut distinction.

In *Trinko*,[13] a case involving the refusal by a telecommunication operator to share its local network with its rival, the US Supreme Court reaffirmed its position in *US* v. *Colgate & Co*, that "(i)n the absence of any purpose to create

---

[12] Wesseley, T. W. *et al.* (2005) Seeking rules for "the only game in town", *Global Competition Review: Dominance*, 3.

[13] *Verizon Communications Inc.* v. *Law Offices of Curtis Trinko LLP*, (02 – 682) 540 US 398 (2004), 304 F.3d 89, reversed and remanded.

or maintain a monopoly, the Sherman Act does not restrict the long-recognized right of a trader or manufacturer, engaged in an entirely private business, to freely to exercise his own independent discretion as to parties with whom he will deal."[14] In the process, the Court cast doubt on the general validity of the essential facility doctrine invoked in lower courts decisions to oblige monopolists to supply rivals that were otherwise unable to compete.[15] Still, the Court also suggested that a refusal to deal motivated entirely by the desire to eliminate competition might constitute illegal monopolization. This resembles the EU Commission's view on *Clearstream*,[16] a major provider of clearing and settlement services in the EU, which was found to have abused its dominant position by refusing to supply such services to its competitor Euroclear. It also ties with similar US and EU positions on evaluating exclusionary conduct in the presence of intellectual property rights, even though remedies differ.

In March 2004, following five years of investigation, the European Commission handed down its decision against *Microsoft*, resulting in the highest ever fine levied against a single firm under EU competition law (€497m).[17] The Commission found that the software supplier had abused its dominant position by refusing to supply information required to ensure interoperability between Windows and competing operating systems and by bundling its Media Player with the Windows software. Three years earlier, US antitrust authorities had found Microsoft's strategies in the browser market to warrant condemnation under section 2 of the Sherman Act, especially as Microsoft failed to provide an adequate justification for it. Yet, while the EU ordered Microsoft to offer an unbundled version of Windows to PC makers, that remedy had been explicitly rejected by US regulators, as stifling innovation and competition to benefit Microsoft's competitors.

Addressing these concerns, the ECJ's judgment on *IMS Healthcare*[18] stipulated that a firm may be required to license its intellectual property rights, if such property rights were indispensable for carrying on a particular business, competitors were not merely intending to duplicate existing products,

---

[14] *United States* v. *Colgate & Co.*, 250 U.S. 300 (1919).

[15] The essential facilities doctrine establishes liability if a plaintiff shows: (i) control of the essential facility by a monopolist; (ii) the competitor's inability practically or reasonably to duplicate the essential facility; (iii) the denial of use of the facility to a competitor; and (iv) the feasibility of providing the facility.

[16] For background on Clearstream see IP/04/705, 02/06/2004; see also Case C-7/97, *Oscar Bronner GmbH & Co KG* v. *Mediaprint Zeitungs- und Zeitschriftenverlag GmbH & Co KG*, (1998) ECR I-07791.

[17] EU Commission, IP/04/382, 24/03/2004; http://ec.europa.eu/comm/competition/antitrust/cases/microsoft/index.html.

[18] Case C-418/01, *IMS Health GmbH & Co. OHG* v. *NDC Health GmbH & Co. KG* (2004) (Judgment of the Court (Fifth Chamber) of April 29, 2004), available at www.curia.eu.int/en/content/juris/index.htm (April 29, 2004).

and if market demand was sufficient. But the court did not address the degree of novelty or difference that the newcomer would have to offer, nor any pricing considerations for access to intellectual property. To the extent that IMS Healthcare is interpreted to contribute to a relaxing of IPR protection, US courts appear to be moving in the opposite direction. While in 1992, Kodak saw courts rejecting its unilateral refusal to sell and license patented parts to independent service organization, in 2000 Xerox's identical refusal was granted absolute immunity from antitrust liability.[19]

Pricing

Widespread pricing practices may nevertheless constitute a violation of antitrust law when carried out by a dominant firm; US and EU positions differ in legal focus and regulatory practice.

Whilst exploitative prices by a legally acquired monopoly do not violate section 2 of the Sherman Act and price discrimination is only caught if it is predatory by intent, Article 82(2) explicitly refers to price discrimination and nondiscrimination, unfair prices, and trading conditions as forms of abuse. Yet, besides offering rather general pointers for benchmarking charges and costs, neither the ECJ nor the Commission has offered any well-founded explanation for how to establish the reasonableness of prices. In addition, US regulators define predatory prices as below-cost pricing by dominant firms – the ability to recoup profits when competition has exited the market.[20] Given this high burden of proof, only a few successful predatory pricing cases are brought under section 2 of the Sherman Act. So far, the EU has not established whether recoupment is a necessary part of its predation test. Up to now, neither the ECJ nor the Commission have accepted a "meeting competition" defense, that is, the ability of a dominant firm to charge prices posted by (smaller) competitors.

Exclusionary pricing involving, among others rebate schemes, loyalty programs and pricing aligned with growth targets, has been at the core of recent antitrust attention in both the EU and the US. In *Michelin II* and *British Airways*,[21] the European Court of First Instance (CFI) established that

---

[19] See *In re: Independent Service Organizations Antitrust Litigation* (*CSU et al.* v. *Xerox Corporation*), 203 F.3d 1322. Compare with *Eastman Kodak Co.* v. *Image Technical Services.*

[20] In *Brooke Group* v. *Brown & Williamson Tobacco Corp.* (92–466), 509 U.S. 209 (1993), the US Supreme Court held that two elements must be proved to establish predatory pricing under section 2 of the Sherman Act: (a) below-cost pricing by the monopolist; and (b) a dangerous probability of recoupment by the monopolist once the rival has been driven from the relevant market. *Corp.* [(92–466), 509 U.S. 209 (1993)].

[21] Case T–203/01 *Michelin* v. *Commission*, judgment of September 30, 2003; Case T-219/99 *British Airways* v. *Commission*, judgment of December 17, 2003.

rebate schemes involving standardized quantity discounts, payments for services provided by customers or purchasing targets may only be accepted if undertakings can demonstrate that any potential market foreclosure is overcompensated by substantial efficiencies, and that conduct is not *likely* to have any negative effect on the market. Similarly, a recent US court decision created uncertainty about the legality of rebate schemes of dominant firms. The Third Circuit Court of Appeals, in its decision on *LePage's vs. 3M*,[22] held that a bundled pricing program that extended deep discounts to customers for purchasing across a number of product lines violated section 2 of the Sherman Act – even if final prices covered costs. The business community is awaiting a Supreme Court review.

These and other high-profile cases have sparked a renewed debate on the limits of dominant firm conduct, the role of antitrust and the validity of US and EU regulatory outlooks. Responding to analytical uncertainties and calls for clearer regulatory guidance, competition authorities are undertaking policy reviews. In Europe, Article 82 has been reassessed in the light of economic thinking to deliver a less formalistic and more evidence- and effect-based standard that could facilitate legal certainty and consistency as well as a reliable delegation of enforcement action to national authorities. A discussion paper, entirely focused on exclusionary conduct, was published by the Director General of Competition in December 2005 and was subject to public review. Section 3 evaluates its contribution.

3. EU discussion paper on the application of Article 82 to exclusionary abuse[23]

Paragraph one of the discussion paper states that it is meant to set out "possible principles for the Commission's application of Article 82 of the Treaty to exclusionary abuses. By exclusionary abuses are meant behaviors by dominant firms which are likely to have a foreclosure effect on the market, i.e. which are likely to completely or partially deny profitable expansion in, or access to, a market to actual or potential competitors and which ultimately harm consumers. Foreclosure may discourage entry or expansion of rivals or encourage their exit."[24] The paper describes the relationship between Article

---

[22] *LePage's* inc. v. *3M Corp.*, 324 F. 3d 141 (3d Cir.2003), cert. denied U.S. (2004).

[23] For the paper, comments and a public hearing see http://ec.europa.eu/comm/competition/antitrust/art82/index.html.

[24] See DG Competition (2005), p. 4.

82 of the Treaty with other provisions (paragraphs 8–10); market definition issues (paragraphs 11–19); the principles used for finding a dominant position (paragraphs 20–50); the general framework for the analysis of exclusionary abuses (paragraphs 51–92); the application of this general framework to a number of exclusionary abuses (paragraphs 93–242); and the analysis of aftermarkets (paragraphs 243–265). The following paragraphs offer a number of specific comments with regard to the proposal's compatibility with prior regulation, and the standards for assessing dominance and exclusionary conduct.

Relationship of Article 82 with other provisions

There are at least three alignment issues with regard to other provisions and policies that need to be addressed. Firstly, while Article 82 dealing with abuse is typically understood not to provide for any balancing of pro- and anti-competitive effects, paragraph 8 holds that "if the conduct of a dominant company generates efficiencies and provided that all the other conditions of Article 81(3) are satisfied, such conduct should not be classified as an abuse under Article 82 of the EC Treaty." Paragraph 58 details three steps for establishing whether or not a firm is infringing Article 82: (a) is the conduct capable of foreclosure? If so, (b) is the conduct likely to foreclose? If so, (c) are there any countervailing pro-competitive effects'? Yet, given that companies typically aim to retain existing customers and win new ones, dominant players nearly by definition foreclose markets and hence require an efficiency defense. However, the fact that the DP, most clearly in paragraph 78, puts the onus on the dominant firm to establish efficiencies contradicts Regulation 1/2003 which requires that abuse be substantiated and proven by competition authorities or, in a private action, by the plaintiff.[25] Secondly, national regulatory structures may affect industry performance in ways not adequately incorporated in the DP's elaboration on market definition and dominance. In the pharmaceutical industry, for example, differences in healthcare finance affect the weighting of drug-specific efficacy and side-effect scores and thereby prices and substitution patterns. Thirdly, to the extent that an effect-based approach to regulating dominant firm behavior may be oriented towards assessing its impact on competition, competitors, consumer welfare and possibly the broader public interest, it may be important to clarify the regulation's relation with other EU initiatives, such as the EU's Lisbon

---

[25] Council Regulation No. 1/2003, 16.12. 2002 on the implementation of Art. 81 and 82 of the Treaty [2003] J OJ L 1/1.

strategy, particularly with respect to the link between intellectual property rights and investments in research and development R&D, (see below).[26]

Market definition and dominance

Referencing concentration, share and contestability of the market as key indicators for establishing dominance, paragraph 13 insists that "(i)t is necessary to rely on a variety of methods for checking the robustness of possible alternative market definitions;"[27] paragraph 31 suggests that firms with above 50% of the market share are presumably dominant, while those with below 25% of the market share operate in a safe harbor; paragraphs 34–40 present a list of barriers to entry and expansion. The Commission's presumption of dominance, although itself inconsistent with an effect-based approach, is not based on market share alone. But the conceptualization of barriers to entry and expansion is questionable. Paragraph 40 cautions that "(w)hen identifying possible barriers to expansion and entry it is important to focus on whether rivals can reasonably be able to *replicate* circumstances that give advantages to the allegedly dominant undertaking." Hence, a viable competitive check is seen to require an "as efficient" competitor (see below) offering more or less a carbon copy of what is already available in the market. There is no appreciation of the difference between market and business definition, differences in business models, cost structures and return requirements, or other non-efficiency related characteristics that may make unequal rivals offer a viable check on the potential abuse of market power by dominant firms. Seen this way, a market leader's brand, reputation and financial resources easily appear as barriers to entry rather than as signs of superior efficiency and business acumen. Can innovation not circumvent these obstacles? Also, the Commission apparently thinks that inefficiencies in capital markets should drive the design of competition policy rather than being dealt with by financial sector reforms. Clearly, to avoid over-enforcement, the Bainian list of entry barriers needs to be brought forward into post-Chicago times.[28]

---

[26] The 2004 Report "*Facing the challenge – The Lisbon strategy for growth and employment*," the High Level Group chaired by Wim Kok, effected a change in the Commission's strategy towards promoting R&D and innovation.

[27] The paper lists the SSNIP test, the need to reconstruct competitive prices to assess true substitution patterns, market power leverage in related markets, product differentiation making demand inelastic, inter-regional price comparisons etc. As a first cut, EU Commission and US enforcement agencies and courts typically determine market power by assessing whether a "small but significant and non-transitory increase in price" (SSNIP), normally 5% above the competitive market price, would induce buyers to switch to other products and suppliers.

[28] See Boscheck, R., (2002) Contract logic and efficiency concerns, *World Competition*, 25(4), 435–63.

Framework for analysis of exclusionary abuses

In general, considering only conduct which would exclude a hypothetical "as efficient" competitor as potentially abusive, the DP outlines four types of behaviors to illustrate refutable presumptions of lawfulness or illegality. There is a sliding scale that relates higher degrees of dominance to an increased capacity to foreclose and heightened regulatory concern. Paragraph 58 holds that "(f)oreclosure may discourage entry or expansion of rivals or encourage their exit. Foreclosure thus can be found even if the foreclosed rivals are not forced to exit the market: *it is sufficient that the rivals are disadvantaged and consequently led to compete less aggressively*." Paragraph 60 states that "(w)here a certain exclusionary conduct is clearly not competition on the merits, in particular conduct which clearly creates no efficiencies and which only raises obstacles to residual competition, such conduct is presumed to be an abuse." Conduct may nevertheless be defended based on efficiencies, objective necessity or to meet competition, with the latter not being applicable to nonprice abuses. The DP relates back to courts which imposed an obligation of "proportionality" on dominant companies in response to challenges from smaller competitors. Also paragraph 67 point 4 suggests that not-yet-efficient competitors may be protected "sometimes". Three comments need to be made:

By suggesting an "as efficient" competitor test[29] the Commission asks whether the dominant company itself would survive its own exclusionary conduct if targeted. But the impact of a strategy is not only a function of the efficiency of competitors, but also of timing and circumstance. Acting on a market opportunity first may foreclose the market to an equally efficient player who is just late. In addition, as pointed out above, the standard equates market and business definition and only allows a business to compete in one way. Hence, even without considering the analytical problems in identifying or modeling "apparently efficient competitors," the use of an "as efficient" competitor benchmark would need to be reviewed to avoid over-enforcement. Paragraph 60 is likely to lead to an open-ended discussion of what may be meant by "competing on the merits." While plaintiffs would want to limit "merits" to conventional price, quality and other product dimensions, defendants have an interest in broadening the scope of legitimate competition to include ancillary and necessarily exclusionary contracts. Finally, while the

---

[29] For a background discussion see Elhauge, E., (2003) Defining better monopolization standards, *Stanford Law Review*, 56(2), 253–86.

compatibility of the efficiency defense with Regulation 1/2003 needs to be clarified, the standard that it imposes on dominant firms is very high. The requirement to prove that a particular arrangement is "indispensable" (para 84, point 4), would numb even the most vigorous player in any market and stifle, rather than promote competition.

Predatory pricing

Paragraphs 93–133 tackle the question "When can a dominant company's pricing strategy be presumed not to be intended to compete but to eliminate or discipline its rivals or to prevent entry of potential competitors?" The paper discusses pricing above and below average total cost as well as, and for the first time, average avoidable costs. The latter toughens the predation test, as it focuses on costs that could have been avoided by not producing the output in question. But the standard not only creates legal uncertainty because it is new, but also because some conceptual and analytical issues are far from clear. While the discussion paper recognizes the need to recoup losses as an important element of predation, it does not require proof of it in finding abuse. To substantiate profit sacrifice, price-cost comparisons often need to be made across ill-defined or non-standardized cost-accounting principles and methods for allocating costs across companies of different sizes and product mixes. Any attempt to avoid this by modeling "apparently as efficient competitors" is apt to open up a debate on modeling approaches and principles. Business needs more guidance here.

Single branding and rebates

Suppliers may have superior offers or use rebate schemes and exclusivity contracts (single branding in Commission language), to attract and sustain customers. Recognizing welfare trade-offs involved in accepting single branding obligations and conditional and unconditional rebates, the paper sets out the criteria for evaluating the risk of foreclosing equally efficient competitors. For instance, to assess rebate systems, the Commission outlines an entry-limiting pricing model to identify five conditions to determine abuse: (i) rebates apply to all purchases provided customers exceed minimum purchasing threshold; (ii) the threshold set by a dominant supplier is so high that switching to other suppliers is not easy and (iii) exceeds the commercially viable amount per customer; (iv) the rebate system covers a "good part" of the dominant company's customers, thus having a market impact; (v) foreclosure is appreciable. The Commission's focus on likely effects is clearly superior to relying on formal distinctions between loyalty, target and volume rebates. Still, it seems doubtful that a complex concept such as "commercially viable amount" or "required share" will be useful in guiding courts or structuring an efficiency defense. Simplified tests are needed.

Refusal to supply

The discussion paper recognizes that undertakings, including dominant companies, are generally entitled to determine whom they will or will not supply. A dominant company's refusal to supply, or the threat of it, may be anticompetitive if it is used as an instrument to punish buyers for dealing with competitors, force them to accept exclusive or tying arrangements, or exclude them from participating in a given economic activity. Also, the Commission distinguishes between terminating existing supply relations and refusing to start supplying an input and considers the hurdle to finding abuse lower in the former. Next, while the paper recognizes that an obligation to license intellectual property rights would effectively annul the right, refusing to license may, under exceptional circumstances, be considered an abuse. This also pertains to information that may be indispensable to ensure interoperability in and across markets, even if it is considered a trade secret. Some comments are required.

First, as the freedom to contract may be (ab-)used to restrain the right to compete, competition law needs to set standards of permissible behavior. Applying more severe standards for assessing refusals to continue vs. to embark on new relations, however, may create a disincentive to offer supplies to begin with – exit barriers are entry barriers. Second, trade secrets must remain secret to receive legal protection; a forced disclosure would devalue the property right. Third, US and EU case law recognize the general right to refuse access to intellectual property. *Trinko* confirms that in the US, it is not unlawful for a firm to exploit its market power, that it has the right to refuse to deal and that exceptions to that rule will be very rare. The court stated that "compelling that firms share the resources that give them a competitive advantage is in tension with the underlying purposes of the antitrust laws." A duty to share lessens incentives for a firm, and its rivals, to invest in developing those resources. Forced sharing also requires the courts to determine when resources are competitively advantageous and indispensable and at what price they should be made available, a set of decisions better left to the market. Compelling cooperation between competitors may facilitate collusion, "the supreme evil of antitrust."[30] Also, as pointed out in section 2, in ECJ case law a refusal to license by a dominant firm would only be considered abusive if exceptional harm to competition could be shown. The discussion paper does not clarify the nature of exceptional circumstance that would result in an abuse. Particularly, the language of paras 239 and 240 introduces concepts such as "follow-on innovation" or "identifiable new goods" that are highly imprecise and lower rather than increase legal certainty. The Commission may want to review the need to reconsider the clear and narrow concept of "exceptional circumstances" as outlined in the IMS Health decisions.

4. In sum

Although US and EU competition law offer a well-established framework for regulating commercial conduct, its quintessential focus – the behavior of dominant companies – is still unsettled. Asked to distinguish, and for the purpose of rule making, prejudge which conduct is apt to lead or has led to superior offers and which front for the mere build up and abuse of market power, legislators and regulators often mix assessing forms of conduct with their faith in the intrinsic ability of markets to adjust.

The EU's review of the application of Article 82 to exclusionary conduct intends to move beyond form and belief. Intended to provide an effect-based, economic approach to dominant firm regulation, the Commission's discussion paper largely replaces formal typecasting of business conduct with principles and methods for assessing its ability to foreclose markets to equally efficient competitors. In the process, the Commission avoids pre-judging actual behavior and, by allowing for an efficiency defense, in actual fact shifts the burden of proof to the dominant firm. Yet, even if this could be made compatible with prior regulation, to make the approach useful in regulatory practice and judicial review standards for assessing dominance and exclusionary conduct would need to be clarified and data requirements reduced.

Most importantly market share limits, the conceptualization of entry and expansion conditions and the notion of an "as efficient competitor" need to be reviewed to avoid overlooking viable checks on dominant undertakings. The predation test should be strengthened by insisting on proving the recoupment of losses and by further operationalizing the assessment of

---

[30] See above at 13, paragraph 408.

average avoidable costs. Similarly, clarifying the limit-pricing framework underlying the assessment of rebate systems may ensure its application in court. Issues around refusals to license or disclose interoperability information are bound to be addressed in the course of the continuing Microsoft discussion.

While some of the assessment principles outlined in the discussion paper are more convincing than the standards currently offered by EU competition law, it remains to be seen whether its implied regulatory model is ultimately more efficient. Efficient regulatory systems minimize the total cost of law enforcement and the cost of taking wrong decisions. Enforcement costs depend on the process of case initiation, fact finding, and review and the means and location of enforcement; wrong decisions may come as type I "false positive" errors, which arise when rigid policies lead to over-enforcement and effectively chill pro-competitive and innovative conduct; conversely, type II "false negative" errors arise when lax policies lead to under-enforcement that result in inefficiencies and lasting damage to markets and competition. It could be argued that effectively shifting the burden of proof to dominant firms may economize on overall enforcement costs and trigger self-regulation – but the latter may also stifle the level of pro-competitive activity. Similarly, whether the increased use of economic reasoning will enhance legal predictability and legal certainty remains to be seen.

Irrespective of this, the Commission should be applauded for trying to break new ground in attempting to outline a consistent dominant firm regulation in line with economic reference. At the same time one needs to be aware of the limits to this undertaking. When reading the discussion paper one is often reminded of the sobering perspective offered in the introduction to Areeda and Turner's Antitrust Law:

Economics does not lay down a blueprint for antitrust law. Economic theory is inadequate in some areas and in conflict in others. Moreover, the relevant empirical data may be unavailable or unobtainable within the time and resources that can reasonably be devoted to the determination of individual cases. A concern that the law be reasonably administratable, predictable, and consistently enforced may, in many instances, dictate relatively simple rules and presumptions that limit the scope of case by case economic inquiry.[31]

Clearly, there will always be a gap between the theoretically conceivable and the practically feasible – both in markets and in court.

---

[31] Areeda, P., Turner, D., (1978) *Antitrust law*, Boston: Little Brown, Vol. I, pp. 13–14.

3 Delegating regulation: Supply-chain management, partnering and competition policy reforms

Ralf Boscheck

Accompanying the enlargement of the European Union (EU) on May 1, 2004, the Commission ushered in a complete overhaul of the procedural rules applicable to Articles 81 and 82 of the EC Treaty.[1] As a result, the EU's competition law regime shifted from a highly centralized notification and authorization process to a decentralized system that is to rely more broadly on national competition authorities (NCAs), courts *and* undertakings themselves for case assessment and law enforcement. By delegating regulatory tasks, the Commission hopes to free resources for the proactive appraisal of key cases and new policy areas and to ensure the uniform application of EU Competition Law through economic, "effect-based" substantive rules, procedural guidance and outcome controls. But while the lack of economic references makes stipulating substantive and procedural standards far from trivial, specifying these still does not guarantee effective regulatory delegation at Member State and corporate level.

This chapter addresses four aspects of the modernization of EU competition policy: Section 1 sketches the challenges of devising welfare economic default rules for assessing and prejudging company behavior; Section 2 illustrates these with reference to currently the most demanding area of antitrust – vertical restraints; Section 3 appraises the "EU block exemption regulation for vertical restraints" in the context of broader EU competition policy reform. Section 4 discusses preconditions that allow delegated regulation to be effective and reliable.

1. Contracts, laws and economics

"Partnering" or "supply-chain management" label the recurrent trend towards corporate disintegration and the substitution of rules for ownership

---

[1] Council Regulation (EC) No 1/2003, 6.12.2002, OJ Ll/1.

in shaping the actions of formally independent parties. Restricting purchasing, pricing, service, or location decisions of independent but vertically related parties can improve efficiency and profits, but may also lower consumer welfare and total surplus. The freedom to contract may be (ab-)used to restrain the right to compete. The principal concern here is what constitutes legitimate control that any party may wield over decisions taken by related stages. In determining which contracts the law will enforce, or otherwise recognize as creating legal rights, regulatory authorities require evidentiary standards to appraise, and for the purpose of policy formulation, prejudge arrangements. The standards differ in adequacy and ease of use.

For instance, section 1 of the US Sherman Act, holding restraints to trade legally unenforceable and unlawful *per se*, soon enjoined broad judicial discretion to uphold ancillary restraints based on the *rule of reason*.[2] Over time, attempts to marry administrative efficiency with the complexity of the required assessment tasks have resulted in "a crude dichotomy between a formalistic but administratively simple rule of *per se* illegality and an administratively hopeless, but generally exculpating, *rule of reason* defense."[3]

In Europe, institutional features of EU competition policy make the situation worse. Article 81(1) broadly forbids as incompatible with the treaty agreements that affect trade between Member States and have the object or effect of restricting competition within the Common Market. Such agreements are rendered void by Article 81(2) but can be exempted under Article 81(3). The bifurcation of Article 81(1) and (3), together with a severely under-staffed Commission, guarding its monopoly for granting exemption subject to notification, led Brussels to develop a practice of sending "comfort letters" and devising group exemptions for entire categories of contractual agreements. But the Commission's limited capacity, delayed reviews and comfort letters neither constituted exemptions nor provided validity to contracts. At the same time, the Commission's unwillingness to formally clear agreements with ancillary restraints undermined national enforcement and the contract laws of Member States. Group exemptions enhanced the efficiency of law enforcement, but asked parties to distort transactions to fall within the straitjacket of what one critic called "legal formalism void of

---

[2] *Chicago Board of Trade* v. *United States* 246 US 231 (1918). The first formulation of the doctrine of ancillary restraints in modern antitrust law dates back to *United States* v. *Addyston Pipe & Steel Co.*, 85 Fed. 271 6th Cir. (1898).

[3] Gellhorn, E., Kovacic, W. E., (1994) *Antitrust law and economics*, 4th edn., St. Paul, MN: West Publishing, pp. 177–78.

economic logic."[4] Clearly, on both sides of the Atlantic there was an urgent need for more efficient rules. But what are "efficient rules"?

An efficient administration of competition rules minimizes the sum of two types of interrelated costs: (1) enforcement costs incurred in notifying, analyzing, and litigating a case including the uncertainty and time involved and its effect on behavior, and (2) the costs of permitting (prohibiting) efficiency-reducing (-increasing) clauses. The former are apt to vary subject to the structure of the enforcement processes, that is, case initiation, fact-finding, review, and the required level of data access and means of enforcement. The latter differ in line with the quality of foregone contract alternatives and the extent of welfare distortion until removed. Both costs are related to the quality of policy input. Clearly, the closer a rule matches the specifics of a case at hand, the higher the enforcement costs, and the lower the costs of a wrong decision. Conversely, simplifying rules by aggregating business relationships based on some shared characteristics is efficient to the extent that reductions in enforcement costs more than compensate for the likely increases in the costs of wrong decisions. The resulting "rules of thumb" enhance administrative efficiency and legal certainty but may overly limit contract choice and, to the extent that new arrangements receive less certain treatment, discourage organizational innovation.

The inherent "dilemma of regulation" – devising efficient standards that fit a variety of situations and yet can be easily applied – may be solved through a hierarchy of rules and levels of enforcement. Regulatory delegation avoids the pitfalls of ordering complexities centrally. But it requires fewer and simpler meta-rules to be able to guide lower-level decisions, adjust principles to circumstance and keep matters predictable. Hence, next to the mechanisms to motivate, monitor and contest lower-level regulatory outcomes, delegation in the area of competition policy is limited by the adequacy of the economic reference that it employs. Economic theory offers a wide yet insufficient menu of advice.

The two mainstream market models – commonly labeled as the Harvard vs. Chicago schools of antitrust analysis – are unable to directly assess the reasonableness of a given contract, but deduce conceivable welfare effects in line with conflicting views on output market pressures. While the price-theoretic reference of a "competitive market" may be useful in issuing general policy directions, it cannot guide the analysis of contracts that, by definition,

---

[4] Korah, V., (1994) *EC competition law and practice*, 5th edn., London: Sweet & Maxwell, p. 213.

block market review.[5] Transaction cost economics discusses the reasons and conditions for contracting prior to its effects, and thereby offers an audit trail to assess whether a given restraint is, in fact, proportional, reasonable or necessary for a transaction to occur. But evidentiary standards are such that the approach may be out of reach for authorities aiming to devise simple, higher-level default standards. (Yet, transferred as an assessment tool to lower-level regulation, it may provide for regulatory delegation and the stipulation of truly efficient rules.)[6] Judging vertical control presents the case in point.

2. Strategy, economics and law of vertical control

Firms engaged at different levels of the production and distribution process, realizing the effect of each other's decisions on final market outcomes, may restrict their commercial freedom to mimic integrated supply. Most distribution contracts, for example, include provisions other than a uniform wholesale price to directly or indirectly control decisions and activities that may be prone to free riding.

Figure 3.1 focuses on three *types* of coordination issues that can be dealt with by such vertical restraints: (1) successive pricing decisions, (2) sales effort and service, (3) and manufacturer free riding. Common *types* of restraints that may be used include two-part tariffs, royalties or commissions, required or recommended resale prices (maintaining price ceilings or price floors), fixed sales quantities, minimum levels of sales revenue, territorial and customer provisions, exclusive dealing, full-line forcing, tie-ins and requirement contracts. From the standpoint of profitability, various combinations of these clauses may be interchangeable in dealing with a given situation, yet their welfare effects, that is, their effect on total surplus, may differ substantially *per se* or in line with market conditions. Provisions may be interchangeable in dealing with some circumstances but lead to quite different results in others. Whether a given provision or contractual format enhances or reduces welfare depends on upstream and downstream market conditions – actual as well as potential – and on its comparative efficiency in addressing a given coordination task. Prejudging the former involves the screening of

---

[5] Boscheck, R., (1988) Cooperative R&D as institutional choice: Implications for antitrust analysis, *Aussenwirtschaft*, 43, 97–139; Kirchner, C., (1996) Symbiotic arrangements as a challenge to antitrust, *Journal of Institutional and Theoretical Economics*, 152, 226–42.

[6] Boscheck, R., (2002) Contract logic and efficiency concerns, *World Competition*, 25(4), 435–63.

Cause	Means	Effect CS = Consumer surplus PS = Producer surplus
Successive price determination Upstream and downstream market power	Max. RPM Quantity forcing Two-part pricing	Σ(CS, PS) ▲ Σ(CS, PS) ▲ Σ(CS, PS) ▲ Ambiguous in case of downstream risk aversion
Sales effort and service level Upstream and downstream market power	Contract Two-part pricing Third party Contract	Σ(CS, PS) ▼▲ Σ(CS, PS) ▼▲ Σ(CS, PS) ▼▲ Σ(CS, PS) ▼▲
Upstream market power, downstream competitive	Two-part pricing Third party Exclusive distribution Customer allocation	Σ(CS, PS) ▼▲ Σ(CS, PS) ▼▲ Σ(CS, PS) ▼▲ Σ(CS, PS) ▼▲ infra-marginal consumer, inter-brand competition, risk of cartelization
Manufacturer free riding	Exclusive dealing	Σ(CS, PS) ▼▲

Figure 3.1: Vertical coordination – issues, means and presumed welfare effects

"common-sense" results in line with one's accepted market model; assessing the latter has to step beyond that. To quote Tirole (1988):

Theoretically, the only defensible position on vertical restraints seems to be the rule of reason. Most vertical restraints can increase or decrease welfare, depending on the environment. Legality or illegality *per se* thus seems unwarranted. *At the same time, this conclusion puts far too heavy a burden on the antitrust authorities.* It seems important for economic theorists to develop a careful classification and operative criteria to determine in which environments certain vertical restraints are likely to lower social welfare.[7]

As pointed out above, simple economic market models may be useful in limiting the number of cases to be reviewed, but are inadequate for assessing a provision's comparative efficiency in handling a given coordination task. They rather deduce the appropriateness of a given arrangement from the conditions of the market to which it caters. More recent advances in economics could provide a direct and complete assessment of the case at hand, but would drastically add to evidentiary requirements. For many years, the legal treatment of vertical restraints in both the US and Europe – bifurcated as "per se vs. rule of reason" or "Article 81(1) vs. 81(3)"– reflected this.

---

[7] Tirole, J., (1988) *Theory of industrial organization*, Cambridge, MA: MIT Press, p. 188, emphasis added.

Reviews of US case law on vertical restraints show that both price and non-price restraints, definitions of market power, redeeming virtues, or reasonableness are far from clear.[8] A legal system that creates an "apparent dichotomy between *per se* illegality (the plaintiff always wins) and the rule of reason (the defendant generally wins) magnifies characterization and evidentiary issues."[9] Yet, whilst members of the US antitrust community continue to view vertical restraints as either latently anti-competitive or generally justified by some compensating efficiencies,[10] enforcement agencies appeared to have moved on in search of "useful rules (...) to decide whether to challenge a *particular* practice or not."[11] The Federal Trade Commission and the Department of Justice appear to have pushed aside Chicago's pro-competitiveness presumptions but need to balance the cost and time of case- analysis against the clarity of simple rules and the certainty of their application. Whether "post-Chicago" economics will effect a retreat from Chicago-style policy depends on its ability to be persuasive in courts, provide "efficient rules" and sell these throughout a highly decentralized system of antitrust enforcement. Unfortunately, the most recent thinking presented by the Federal Trade Commission[12] falls substantially short of offering a structured rule of reason but merely identifies options for screening vertical contracts and leaves it up to "the court or decision-maker to resolve" the most important issues of inference. The relevant EU reforms may have an edge here.

Traditionally, the Commission's overriding concern for "market integration", and "freedom of action" explained its strongly negative presumption against any restraints of trade and its own ability to delegate their assessment. It also created the need to harness the resulting over-regulation by administratively simple rules: European competition law captured vertical restraints in distribution along six types of arrangements in descending order of integration and presumably increasing competition policy concern: distribution by affiliate (full integration), agency contracts, franchise

---

[8] For a review of the evolution of legal standards in US case law, EU block exemptions and Court decisions, see Boscheck, R., (2000) EU policy reform on vertical restraints, *World Competition*, 23(4), 3–49.

[9] Gellhorn, E., Kovacic, W. E., (1994) *Antitrust Law and Economics*, 4th edn., St. Paul, MN: West Publishing, pp. 318–19.

[10] For a recent restatement of the Harvard vs. Chicago positions see Scherer, F. M. (2004) Vertical relations in antitrust: some intellectual history, *The Antitrust Bulletin*, 49(4) Winter 2004, 841–58, and Posner, R. (2005) Vertical restrictions and "fragile" monopoly, *The Antitrust Bulletin*, 50(3), Fall 2005, 499–509.

[11] See Cooper, J. C. *et al.* (2005) Vertical antitrust policy as a problem of inference, *International Journal of Industrial Organization*, 23, 639–64.

[12] See Cooper, J. C. *et al.* (2005).

agreements, exclusive purchasing agreements, selective distribution agreements, and agreements between an enterprise and an independent distributor. To be sure, block exemptions cleared types of not-notified agreements irrespective of market share or combined turnover simply based on their fit with pre-drawn lists of contract clauses. Problems of over-and under-inclusion were inherent as were the administrative and legal costs resulting from a system that aimed to centrally control highly complex market relations. EU Regulation No 2790/1999 changed this and created a new block exemption model to spur EU competition policy reform.

3. The White Paper, Commission Regulation No 2790/1999 and guidelines[13]

In its White Paper *Modernizing the rules for implementing Articles 81 and 82,* the Commission argued that centralized authority, vital for establishing coherent EU competition standards, is no longer adequate to guarantee regulatory supervision, legal certainty and the freedom to contract. The resources available do not match the complexities of an ever-expanding market. Efforts to cut notification requirements and assessment tasks, by either screening minor cases and block exempting others, or by shelving authorizations and delegating complaints,[14] had proved insufficient to allow the Commission to more actively pursue critical policy areas. Options to relax resource constraints by, for instance, waiving prior notification requirements, generally applying non-opposition procedures to all restrictive practices, or permitting national competition authorities to adopt constitutive exemptions, were considered unlikely to reduce the level of notification, but to risk the predictability and uniformity of Community law. Deeming the current system beyond repair, the Commission envisioned future regulation to rest on four pillars: clear legal standards, corporate self-assessment, a "network of authorities" and a system of *ex-post* controls.

Ending the notification process, a new generation of block exemptions was to apply economic reasoning to clear broad categories of agreements subject only to a list of prohibited or conditional restrictions and market-share

---

[13] First published as Commission Regulation (EC) No 2790/1999, OJ L 336, December, 29 1999, pp. 21–25. Commission Notice: Guidelines on Vertical Restraints, at http://europa.eu.int/comm/competition/antitrust/legislation/vertical_restraints/guidelines_en.pdf.

[14] Decentralized processing of complaints is outlined in the Notice on Cooperation between the National Competition Authorities and the Commission OJ C 313, 25.10.1997, p. 3.

thresholds. Based on these, and, where necessary, with the aid of notices and guidelines, effective corporate self-assessment had to be the source of legal certainty, monitored by *ex-post* controls and a network of authority. Presiding over that network, the Commission was to retain its sole right to propose legislative texts and take on individual cases to guide policy. National competition authorities were to be empowered to withdraw block exemptions and investigate cases of application of Community law based on complaints or own initiative. National courts, already employing Article 81 in proceedings on contractual and non-contractual liabilities and injunctions, were also able to apply Article 81(3). Corrective measures were needed to ensure the uniform application of law by national authorities. As part of this, an amended Regulation 17 required national authorities to promptly inform the Commission of any case in which Articles 81 and 82 were applied. At any rate, the Commission retained the right to take a case out of national jurisdiction or intervene in court proceedings. Finally, this system was to be reinforced by measures of enhanced *ex-post* control, granting the Commission broader powers of inquiry, encouraging and increasing the importance of complaints, and significantly raising the level of penalties as well as procedural and periodic fines. The 1999 EU Block Exemption on Vertical Restraints (BerV) was the first application of this kind of reasoning.

Following numerous rounds of consultation and revisions, the BerV set a 30% market share threshold, below which, in the absence of severely anti-competitive restraints, it is presumed that efficiency-enhancing effects of vertical restraints will outweigh any anti-competitive effects. Articles 4 and 5 provide a blacklist of restraints precluding exemption. Hardcore restraints are: (1) minimum and fixed resale price maintenance; (2) territorial and customer restrictions except in specified cases counteracting free riding in selective distribution and after-market competition; (Article 4(b) and (c)); (3) direct and indirect non-compete obligations for more than five years unless in specific cases related to the buyer's occupancy of supplier's land or premises, (Article 5(a) or (b)) or to protect know-how transferred by the supplier to the buyer for not more than one year, unless the know-how has not entered the public domain, (Article 5(b)). Article 5(c) bans any direct or indirect obligation causing the members of a selective distribution system not to sell the brands of particular competing suppliers.

The Guideline accompanying the Regulation aims "to help companies to make their own assessment of vertical agreements under the EC competition rules" and cautions that "each case must be evaluated in the light of its own facts" and hence apply the Guidelines "reasonably and flexibly."[15] It reiterates that due to the extension of Article 4(2) of Regulation 17/62, no precautionary notification needs to be made, and in the absence of litigation in national courts or complaints, notifications as such will not be given any priority in the Commission's enforcement policy. Agreements that have not been notified, because parties assumed in good faith that the market share threshold was not exceeded, will not be fined.[16] The remainder of the Guideline is concerned with issues of market definition and market share calculation and details the EU's "philosophy" *vis-à-vis* vertical restraints. Paragraphs 103–118 present the Commission's view on the economics of verticals, that is, its negative and potentially offsetting positive effects. Paragraphs 119–137 present a step-by-step approach for analyzing vertical restraints, which is then illustrated by assessments of most common arrangements and combinations that are covered by the block exemption, but may still have to be reviewed due to combinations and market share.

Both parameters used in the Regulation to screen contracts with potential efficiency risks are not unproblematic. The use of *market share* data requires an agreement on, and an understanding of, the methods for defining markets and the criteria for assessment. Articles 9 and 10 of the Regulation and paras 78–90 of the Guidelines reflect the Commission's respective approach as presented in its Notice on Defining the Relevant Market.[17] Still, market share is but a proxy of a proxy to establish an undertaking's position relative to actual, and not even total, competition. It provides an input to calculating market concentration that controls for factors such as the minimum efficient scale of production, market growth, average level of non-amortized sunk-cost investments etc., and may indicate some level and share of market power. But "(n)o consensus exists on the critical levels of concentration in predicting the conduciveness of particular markets to adverse competitive effects."[18]

---

[15] EU Guidelines on Vertical Restraints, as approved on May 23, 2000, p. 2, para 3.

[16] EU Guidelines on Vertical Restraints, p. 14, paras 62–65.

[17] The Commission's Notice on Defining the Relevant Market, OJ C 372/5, September, 12 1997. An attempt is made to employ economic criteria of demand and supply substitutability, the former being emphasized due to investment inflexibilities on the supply side. In considering the extent of demand substitutability, the Commission relies on a mix of the following criteria and evidence. Functional interchangeability, product characteristics, "shock analysis" (new product entry), quantitative tests (e.g., elasticity of prices), marketing studies, regulatory/economic barriers preventing substitution, different categories of customers (in case of price discrimination) and finally patterns of purchases/trade flows.

[18] Azcuenaga, M. L., (1993) The evolution of international competition policy. In Hawk, B. (ed.) *International antitrust law and policy*, 1992 Annual Proceedings, Fordham Corporate Law Institute, pp. 1–15.

In addition, the theory of contestable markets points to the need to focus on conditions for market access rather than concentration and market share.[19]

The Commission maintains that its market share threshold provides mere screens to identify potentially risky undertakings. But its level and use remains arbitrary. The switch from two to a single 30% threshold between May 1998 and December 1999 legitimizes previously objectionable contracts (e.g., quantity forcing and tying) and creates a risk of under-enforcement. To minimize the danger of over-enforcement, undertakings are encouraged to substantiate any efficiency advantages of contracts caught by the Regulation. But the Guidelines, particularly paragraphs 116–118, are limited to providing only crude pointers related to general contracting efficiencies. The Regulation prescreens based on *types of restraints*, which cuts the link between contract cause and effect and judges restraints solely based on the type of conceivable market effects. The EU outlined this logic in a paper entitled the "Economics of Verticals".[20]

Following this view, hard-core restraints are those clauses or combinations of clauses that are seen to effectively eliminate substitution potential or provide total territorial or market protection. This is the case of non-compete and tying arrangements that eliminate intra-brand and (in-store) inter-brand competition or may result from combined selective systems. It also covers exclusive distribution that only permits passive sales. The final Regulation restates, with minor changes, the blacklist restraints, but, given its single market-share limit, treats non-compete obligation s.t. time-limits and implied efficiency reasoning. Yet, whereas Articles 4 and 5 are at the same time more precise and in total less restrictive than their predecessors, it is affirmed that agreements using "not indispensable restrictions", restrictions that "eliminate competition", or restrictions with alternatives having generally less anti-competitive effects will be caught. Although the Commission maintains that it operates from a presumption of legality, "individual exemption of vertical agreements containing such hard-core restrictions is ... unlikely."[21]

---

[19] Paras 126–129 of the EU Guidelines on Vertical Restraints. barely deal with the analysis of entry barriers, informing that "actual competition is in general more effective and will weigh more in the assessment of a case than potential competition."

[20] Peeperkorn, L., (1998) The economics of verticals, 2nd edn., *Competition Policy Newsletter*, EU Commission.

[21] EU Guidelines on Vertical Restraints, para 46, p. 10.

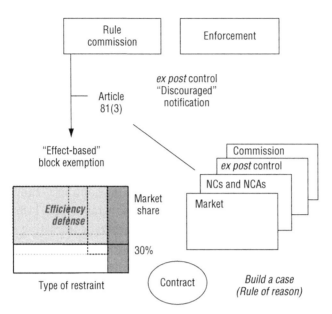

Figure 3.2:   "Effect-based" block exemption within system of strengthened *ex post* control

In fact, *every single entry into the Commission's classification could be either substantiated or challenged.* To take the most contrary perspective, a stylized Chicago position would certainly point to the general neglect of entry conditions, not in product markets, but in markets for contractors catering to them. Or, it would debate the extreme narrowness of relevant markets, which, as in the case of single-branding restraints, seems to go to the level of a single shelf-space that, once it is occupied by one brand, by definition excludes intra-brand and inter-brand competition in stores. But, with the exception of blacklisted restraints, none of these concerns really matter as, in the case of individual review, the Commission has the burden of proof but undertakings are required to substantiate any efficiency claims. Accepting the need for detailed case assessment and its efficient organization, the Commission effectively out-sources that task and merely provides two filters – market share and a blacklist. But the implications are broader than this.

Figure 3.2 captures the procedural and substantive changes brought about by the new block exemption regulation and the reforms outlined in the Commission's White Paper on competition policy reform. Under the "old regime", undertakings either opted for legal certainty by contracting around form-based regulatory defaults, or notified with the questionable benefit of comfort letters. The new approach involves more private initiatives. Undertakings with below 30% market share, no blacklist clause, no non-compete arrangement outside efficiency-defense or time-limit, no cumulative effects, and no *"nevertheless"* have no problem. The rest are asked to self-assess: this means to build a case based on economic analysis, assess competitive situations and scenarios, evaulate impacts on market choice, outline and substantiate an efficiency defense, monitor evolution over time, and, to ensure legal certainty, keep records as evidence and enforce the internal standard against oneself. It means self-assessment becomes rule writing as the basis of self-regulation subject to the risk of detection and punishment.

The process induced by present EU reforms could be a step towards creating a "regulatory win-win". Companies are apt to prefer "self-regulation" as a way to write simpler yet more specific, adaptable rules that reduce compliance costs. Their contract assessments could provide the basis for regulatory reviews, structure in-house compliance programs, and together be considered as mitigating factors in case of prosecution and penalty. For public authorities, assessing specific rules, linking economic causes and effects to changing circumstance, presents both better prosecutorial evidence and an opportunity for learning. Hence, self-regulation offers an attractive vehicle to maintain contractual options and freedom and avoid the return to inefficient straitjackets. That is, provided efficient regulatory monitoring and *ex-post* control is guaranteed. With regard to the former, the EU's elimination of notification requirements cuts the need for resources used in authorizing private case assessment standards and, by that, any concerns for regulatory co-optation and capture. It still offers the Commission the opportunity to ask for contract reports to be filed without review. With the resulting emphasis on *ex-post* controls (penalties and complaint procedures), these need to be structured to ensure that privately written rules have the public interest in mind and in-house compliance processes are indeed independent. Given the informational advantages of those directly involved, the focus here has to be on the incidence of inquiry, the height of the penalty and the contractual status and professional position of the in-house legal council. Clearly, the new regulatory process also relies on a mix of private and public rule writing, monitoring and enforcement. But by stressing self-assessment, and implying self-ruling and self-enforcement, it makes use of decentralized, informationally more efficient means.

Rather than structuring a rule of reason for assessing vertical control, the EU block exemption responds to the lack of substantive policy guidance, symptomatic for legal treatment of vertical restraints in both the US and the

EU, by more broadly involving national authorities and delegating the assessment task and the choice of tools to contractors themselves. But how can concerns for the uniformity of law be reconciled with the "risk of forum shopping" viz. the "interest in regulatory competition"? Can firms at the bottom of the enforcement pyramid, and clearly closest to the contract and requisite information, be relied upon to enforce competition rules themselves?

4. Reliable regulatory delegation

The EU's ability to maintain general control over its competition policies and efficiently delegate enforcement is based on the reliability of national agencies and private actors. But should national authorities merely be executing and can private actors effectively self-regulate?

Regulatory cooperation vs. competition

Following the pre-Maastricht period and its focus on removing internal barriers and designing common policies with regard to agriculture, trade, and competition, the Commission moved towards the large-scale harmonization of national rules. But with harmonization requiring consensus on detailed legislative standards and their translation into national technical norms, the program soon gave way to the principle of "mutual recognition" which forced competing regulators to identify the floor of common rules. Regulatory competition, in turn, increased the diversity and complexity of rules and led to the reemergence of interest in centralizing policy making within functional directorates or external agencies with rule-making and direct enforcement powers. The present debate pitches the proponents of more unified European policy-making against those who are concerned about the representation of national interests or the control of potentially unwieldy federal bureaucracies. There are strong arguments in favor of regulatory competition and delegation.

Public choice theorists argue for the devolution of regulatory powers to junior levels of government.[22] Decentralized regulation is seen to better reflect local conditions and citizen preference, create a bundle of regulatory experience, and limit the negative impact of failure or corruption. In the

---

[22] For a review see Mueller, D. C., (1997) (ed.) *Perspectives on public choice*, Cambridge: Cambridge University Press.

extreme, decentralized regulation could be sanctioned by issue-based voting and lead to market-driven law making, reduced regulatory capture and increased legal innovation. From this perspective, harmonizing rules or centralizing regulation means colluding in markets for regulatory and political control. But for regulatory competition to work, markets must be open, factors mobile and rules predictable. Put differently, regulatory harmonization, especially in the area of competition policy, is often a precondition for regulatory competition.

The need for harmonized competition standards, however, should not preclude the use of regulatory competition in the drafting of new uniform rules, nor its decentralized application. Yet, given that the Commission, as the guardian and guarantor of the Treaty, maintains the sole right to propose legislative texts, how can EU law-making be effectively contested without politically stalemating it? Is it possible for institutions, such as the Advisory Committee on Restrictive Practices and Dominant Position, to play a broad role in balancing the allocation of cases or identifying new areas of law? Conversely, given the Commission's increased reliance on decentralized enforcement, and the broad discretion provided by Article 81(3), how can the monitoring of a national authority's performance be reduced so as to avoid wasting the resources that current reforms are trying to save? Addressing a range of similar inter-agency concerns stemming from observational limits, and incomplete regulatory and competitive controls, the debate around the Commission's White Paper invoked the spirits of a *Common Competition Culture.*[23] These principles should guide agencies in using self-restraint to avoid short-term free riding on incompletely enforceable regulatory relations for the long-term benefits of their economies. Yet, it is not self-evident that any rational authority, national or otherwise, would submit its self-interest to self-regulation based on some broader, reasonable principle. But if one cannot expect "rational" regulatory authorities to submit to self-restraint, would it reasonable to expect companies to do so?

Self-regulation

Relative to previous, form-based block exemptions, leading undertakings to contract around regulatory defaults, the 1999 EU block exemption on vertical restraints appealed to "corporate self-responsibility" and offered more discretion in self-regulating restraints subject to the ability to substantiate the

---

[23] See Lowe, P., (2005) Introduction, European antitrust review 2005, p. 3.

efficiency benefits of arrangements. Having gone that far, why not take a step further and discuss broader options of company and industry self-regulation – also, or especially – in the area of antitrust?

In the broadest sense, self-regulation pertains to firm- or industry-level initiatives that establish standards of behavior or assist in complying with, or exceeding, existing statutory requirements. The advantages are obvious. Standards, tailored to fit the circumstances of a given firm or industry, present simple and adaptable alternatives to overly strict or overly lax regulatory defaults; decentralized enforcement can reduce private compliance costs and efficiently extend an agency's range of regulatory mechanisms. But self-regulation may also present unsought risks and complexities.[24]

First, free riding, inherent in firm-level self-regulation, may be avoided by industry-wide mandatory standards, but such norms typically require governmental safeguards against anti-competitive abuse. Second, private rules, that affect or replace statutory requirements, demand regulatory approval and a level of ensured enforcement that may not be guaranteed by private compliance initiatives. Clearly, private and public regulations at firm-level are complementary not substitutable. Their interaction channels economic activities, reinforces distinct commercial values and patterns of acceptable inter-company behavior, and thus creates the institutional bases of unique sectoral and national economic cultures.[25]

There is a tendency for regulatory authorities *and* analysts to abstract from the specifics of these institutional fabrics, as this facilitates the broad-brush categorization and modeling of commercial practice, the harmonization of

---

[24] Garvin (1983) outlines a regulatory spectrum ranging from pure self-regulation, to self-regulation plus governmental information, policing of deception, and rule-making authority. See Garvin, D. A., (1983) Can industry self-regulation work? *California Management Review*, 25(4), 37–52. For a broader perspective see Boscheck, R., (2002) *Market drive and governance*, London: Routledge Chapter 5: The constitution of economic coordination.

[25] Differences in inter-company contracting reflect differences in institutional conditions as much as in values. The German "Allgemeine Geschäftsbedingungen," for example, offers a concept of legally binding general conditions of business that allows standard contract terms to be detailed and partly sanctioned by industry associations in line with the overarching requirements of "good faith". The latter is often held to imply a view of contracting as supporting long-term, non-adversarial dealings, and of regulation as guidance. By comparison, as Deakin *et al.* (1997) point out, "English contract law is above all influenced by notions of individual liberalism and autonomous contracting, to the point that notions of good faith in commercial dealings have only achieved limited recognition." Legal regulations of standard norms are less extensive, contractual mechanisms are seen to retain their flexibility in meeting conditions in largely adversarial commercial and regulatory relations. See Lane, C., and Bachmann, R., (1997) Cooperation in inter-firm relations in Britain and Germany, *British Journal of Sociology*, 48(2), 226–54; Deakin, S., Lane, C. and Wilkinson, F., (1997) Contract law, trust relations and incentives for co-operation. In Deakin, S., Michie, J. (eds.) (1997) *Contracts, Cooperation and Competition*, Oxford: Oxford University Press, pp. 105–39.

regulatory structures and enforcement methods, and, in the process, presumably strengthens the rule of law. But it commits to one set of implied behavioral motifs, commercial objectives and regulatory conduct, and requires an insistence on the letter, not the spirit, of any agreement. It weakens the appreciation for and the reliability of self-regulation. Given failing markets and incomplete regulatory control, the ability to trust in some broader standard, taking precedence over short-term self-interest, reduces the uncertainty and complexity of trading relations, allows for more discretion among parties, and therefore improves economic efficiency. This concern applies across all levels of governance – from political control to inter-agency relations to company contracting.

Economies differ in terms of the availability and legal standing of the requisite "institutions of good faith", including industry contracts, compliance programs or mechanisms of corporate and bureaucratic self-regulation. They also differ in terms of the effectiveness of these institutions in creating "systems trust" and legitimately exercising extra-legal, non-market governance. However, proposing to complement market and regulatory control with some broader reliance on "self-restraint" not only requires a better understanding of the specific case at hand but also of the principal interactions among these three sources of governance in constituting economic coordination. It calls for a return to the broader concerns of classical political economy and its focus on the interplay between economics, law and ethics.

5. In sum

In an effort to streamline and harmonize the application of EU competition law across an enlarged EU, Regulation 1/2003, effective as of 1 May 2004 ushered in a modernization of the procedural rules applicable to Articles 81 and 82 of the EC. As a result, the EU's competition law regime shifted from a highly centralized notification and authorization process to a decentralized system that is to more broadly rely on national competition authorities (NCAs), courts *and* undertakings themselves for case assessment and law enforcement. By delegating regulatory tasks, the Commission hopes to free resources for the proactive appraisal of key cases and new policy areas and to ensure the uniform application of EU Competition Law through procedural guidance, outcome controls and economic, "effect-based" substantive rules. But with economic references forever at odds, achieving the latter is far from trivial. It is generally most complex for vertical agreements.

The EU Commission's new block exemption for vertical restraints employs two parameters – market share and type of agreement – to blacklist illicit obligations, clear large numbers of previously notified cases, and provide public and private parties with a set of contingent standards for assessing the rest. The reform reflects the Commission's interest in delegated and consistent regulation but falls short of structuring a rule of reason approach for assessing vertical agreements. It also raises concerns for how to assess any over- or under-regulation, and how to ensure the uniformity of law, and the effectiveness of regulatory devolution and corporate self-regulation. These are concerns that are generally applicable to the broader EU competition law reform.

4 Diffusion of corporate governance regulation: France, Germany, the UK and the USA

Ulrich Steger

1. Introduction

Numerous developed nations have introduced legislation and codes to regulate corporate governance over the last years. Efforts to harmonize corporate governance regulations can be noticed, especially in the European Union (EU), but also on a more international level through the OECD. Moreover the discussion in the media about corporate governance is picking up pace.

But what has caused this recent "excitement"? At the beginning of the twenty-first century, investors' trust was severely shaken, not only through the always cited – and I am not trying to be the exception – collapse of Enron in 2001, but also through other corporate disasters like Vivendi in France in 2002.[1] Authorities felt the need to react and to create and amend regulations concerning corporate governance. Certainly the most prominent example of corporate governance regulation is the Sarbanes-Oxley Act (SOX or Sarbox) in the United States, which became effective on July 30, 2002 and is still being updated.[2]

The Sarbanes-Oxley Act has been the first real change in US corporate governance regulations since the Investment Advisor Act of 1940[3] and according to Wiesen,[4] it is the most important change after the Securities Exchange Act of 1934. Like the Sarbanes-Oxley Act, "the 34 Act" was preceded by a crisis

---

[1] See Almond, P., Edwards, T., Clark, I., (2003) Multinationals and changing national business systems in Europe: Towards the 'shareholder value' Model, *Industrial Relations Journal*, 34(5), 430–45.; Steger, U., Aguirre, I. P. (2004) *The French corporate governance system* (Lausanne: IMD Global Corporate Governance Research Initiative).

[2] See US Securities and Exchange Commission (SEC) (2005) *The investor's advocate: How the SEC protects investors, maintains market integrity, and facilitates capital formation*, available at www.sec.gov/about/whatwedo.shtml, accessed on February, 15 2006.

[3] See ibid.   [4] See Wiesen, J., (2003).

and the second worst loss of investors' confidence in the stock market[5] – the world economic crisis of 1929.

It would seem that any change must be precipated by a crisis or as Tricker[6] writes: "Changes in corporate governance are often a response to corporate crisis"[7].

As you read through this chapter, you will recognize that crises are not the only cause for changes in corporate governance regulation. This chapter describes the history of corporate governance, analyzes the timing and the direction of the changes as well as the drivers and barriers for changes of corporate governance regulations with a focus on the diffusion of corporate governance regulation in the US, the UK, Germany and France over the last 40 years. Those focal nations are developed countries and have been chosen because the corporate governance systems of the US and the UK are considered as prime examples of the Anglo-Saxon model and follow the shareholder approach or the outsider model (dispersed ownership system) of corporate governance. The corporate governance models of Germany and France are characterized as the insider model (concentrated ownership-structure) or the stakeholder approach to corporate governance.[8]

In order to get an historical overview of corporate governance and its diffusion, this chapter is written chronologically, starting at the original problem of the principal-agent theory. It continues through the last 40 years to discuss today's issues of corporate governance. The changes are identified and summarized and an analysis of the general movements in corporate governance regulation is undertaken. Finally, the results are summed up and the outlook for the future of corporate governance is discussed.

2. The history of corporate governance regulation

The early development of corporate governance

Although the expression "corporate governance" was first used in the 1980s,[9] the *issue* of corporate governance is as old as the division of capital/ownership

---

[5] See Sykes, A., (2002) Overcoming poor value executive remuneration: Resolving the manifest conflicts of interest, *Corporate Governance*, 10(4), 256–60.

[6] See Tricker, B., (2005) Corporate governance – a subject whose time has come, *Corporate Ownership and Control*, 2(2), 11–19.

[7] See Hönsch, H., Behncke, N., Wulfetange, J., (2005) *Corporate governance in Deutschland: Entwicklungen und Trends vor internationalem Hintergrund* (Frankfurt a.M., Berlin: PriceWaterhouseCoopers AG (PWC) Bundesverband der Deutschen Industrie (BDI)).

[8] See Almond, P., Edwards, T., Clark, I., (2003); Coffee, J. C. J., (2005) A theory of corporate scandals: Why the USA and Europe differ, *Oxford Review of Economic Policy*, 21(2), 198–211.

[9] See Huizenga, C. J., (ed.) (1983) *Proceedings of Corporate Governance: A Definitive Exploration of the Issues* CA, UCLA.

and management (principal-agent theory), where the investor (principal) gives a manager (an agent) responsibility to administer the capital he has invested – an arrangement that may result in a conflict of interest.[10]

The possibilities to separate ownership and control were unprecedented, as it become possible to establish limited liability companies, first in Britain in the 1850s, followed by its colonies of Australia, New Zealand, South Africa and India.[11] This was then followed by the US as well as Germany and France (although the latter two countries were more regulated). Corporate governance issues, although – as mentioned above – this term was not used, were imminent.

In 1932, interestingly, shortly after the World Economic Crisis of 1929, the "first seminal work of corporate governance"[12] was published by Berle and Means, who noted that corporations were becoming ever more powerful – even more powerful than the political powers.[13] This, they argued, was threatening democracy and needed to be controlled.[14] Shortly after Berle and Means's book was published and – according to Tricker[15] – because of its influence, the Securities and Exchange Control was established to control publicly traded companies in the US.

Development of corporate governance in the 1970s

At the beginning of the 1970s, Mace challenged the ability of a company's board of directors to fulfill its governing duties of:
- establishing basic objectives, corporate strategy and board policies;
- asking discerning questions; and
- selecting the president.

He maintained that these functions "were not borne out in practice" in the US.[16] To re-establish the board's control of supervising functions, investors as well as the SEC started to call for independent outside directors and for more checks and balances at board level.[17] During the 1970s, the SEC even

---

[10] See Colley, J. L. J., Doyle, J. L., Logan, G. W. Stettinius, W., (2003) *Corporate governance*, New York: McGraw-Hill.

[11] See Tricker, B., (1994) *International Corporate Governance – Text, Readings and Cases*, New York: Prentice Hall.

[12] See Tricker, B., (2005).

[13] See ibid.; Berle, A. A., Means, G. C., ([1932] (1968)) *The modern corporation and private property*, New York: Harcourt, Brace and World.

[14] See Mizruchi, M. S., (2004) *Berle and Means revisited: The governance and power of large U.S. Corporations*, available at www-personal.umich.edu/~mizruchi/tsweb.pdf, accessed on February 21, 2006.

[15] See Tricker, B., (2005).

[16] See Mace, M. L., (1971) *Directors: Myth and Reality*, Boston, MA: Harvard University Press; See also Tricker, B. (1994); op. cit.; Tricker, B. (2005).

[17] See Tricker, B., (2005).

called for standing audit committees to be composed of independent outside directors.[18] This movement was followed in the UK, where a Green Paper requiring audit committees was created,[19] based on Sir Brandon Rhys-Williams's call for the employment of non-executive directors and the use of audit committees.[20] However, this failed in Parliament in 1977.

On a European level, the European Economic Commission's fifth draft directive tried to replace the unitary boards system with the two-board system, practiced, for example, in Germany. This proposal was criticized by the UK because of its requirement that there were employee representatives on the board. UK directors thought the one-tier board was viable and therefore saw no need for change.[21] Following the implementation of this directive, the Bullock report was published in the UK, suggesting the continuation of the unitary board but with worker representation. Again, this did not go down well with UK directors, as it suggested worker representation.[22]

The 1970s saw "a questioning of the role of the large corporation in society,"[23] especially in the US and the UK (e.g. Watkinson Report, PEP report by Fogarty[24]). The argument was that companies had a broader responsibility to society as a whole, rather than just what was written in the law.

The drivers for theses demands and suggestions for changes in corporate governance behavior and corporate governance regulation (although the expression "corporate governance" was still not used at that time) were shareholders in the US, who became more litigious[25] and started to sue companies and their auditors for financial gain. It was thought that improvements in the governance could protect against these lawsuits. In Europe, the main drive for new corporate governance regulation was aimed at creating a harmonized European market.[26]

Development of corporate governance in the 1980s

The 1980s saw more focus on the shareholder and shareholder-value, due to the politics of Margaret Thatcher in the UK and Ronald Reagan in the US.[27]

---

[18] See Securities and Exchange Commission (1972), *Standing Audit Committees composed of Outside Directors.*
[19] See HMSO (1977), *The conduct of company directors; White Paper,* UK Cmnd. 7037.
[20] See Rhys-Williams, S. B., (1976), *The case for audit committees,* London: Accountancy Age.
[21] See Maclean, M., (1999) Corporate governance in France and the UK: Long-term perspectives on contemporary institutional arrangements, *Business History,* 41(1), 88–116; Tricker, B., (ed.) (2000) *Corporate governance,* London: Ashcroft Publishing; See Tricker, B., (2005).
[22] See Tricker, B., (ed.) (2000).   [23] See Tricker, B., (2005).
[24] See Tricker, B., (ed.) (2000).   [25] See ibid.; cf. Coffee, J. C. J., (2005).
[26] See Cernat, L., (2004) The emerging European corporate governance model: Anglo-Saxon, continental, or still the century of diversity? *Journal of European Public Policy,* 11(1), 147–166.
[27] See ibid.; Tricker, B., (2005).

In the UK in the 1980s, to increase the profit orientation of the state-owned companies and obviously to fill the treasury coffers, the telecommunication, mining, and electricity industries were beginning to be privatized,[28] creating revenues of US$96.7bn for the UK treasury from 1985–1995.[29] Germany and France followed this approach about ten years later.[30]

This time lag was partly due to a different perception of the market for corporate control as, especially in the UK, the constant threat of hostile takeovers was seen as an "incentive for strong board level performance."[31] In Germany and France this market did not exist to this extent due to a less diffused stock-ownership structure and a stronger role of the banks[32] and because the market for corporate control was rather seen as a threat for the strategy of the companies.

In the US, the American Law Institute was starting to discuss a more differentiated role of the executive and the supervising members of the board (monitoring model),[33] resembling the the two-tier board practiced in Germany.

It was in the 1980s that the term "corporate governance" first appeared and spread through the literature,[34] indicating the growing awareness of issues of corporate governance. As described above, this attention was partially due to a number of high-profile IPOs in conjunction with the privatization of state-owned companies.[35] Formerly state-run companies, previously responsible to a variety of stakeholders due to political reasons, were now facing profit-oriented stakeholders and therefore had to adopt new governance structures. Furthermore, a number of corporate failures and scandals such as insider trading in the US through Ivan Boesky, Michael Levine and Michael Milken or the Guinness case, where an attempt was made to influence the stock

---

[28] See Tricker, B., (2005); Huffschmid, J., (1996) Privatisierung in Westeuropa – Tafelsilber für die Währungsunion, *Blätter für deutsche und internationale Politik*, (8), 1013.

[29] See *Privatisierungserlöse zwischen 1985 und 1995*, (1996) *Financial Times*, June 14.

[30] See Nelson, M. M., (1994) Privatization. *The Wall Street Journal Europe*, October 10. Germany and France started their major wave of privatization around ten years later than the UK (Germany, for example, privatized its telecoms industry in 1995, whereas the UK privatized in 1985).

[31] See Tricker, B., (2005); See also Keasey, K., Thompson, S., Wright, M. (eds.) (2005) *Corporate governance – accountability, enterprises and international comparisons*, Chichester: John Wiley & Sons Ltd.

[32] See Almond, P., Edwards, T., Clark, I., (2003).

[33] See Theisen, M. R., (2002) *Corporate Governance als Gegenstand der Internationalisierung*, Wiesbanden: Gabler.

[34] See Huizenga, C. J., (ed.) (1983); Mintzberg, H., (1984) Who should control the corporation? *California Management Review*, 27, 90–115; Baysinger, B. D., Butler, H. N., (1985) Corporate governance and the board of directors: Performance effects of changes in board composition, *Journal of Law, Economics and Organization*, 1, 101–124.; See also Tricker, B. (2005).

[35] See Maclean, M., (1999).

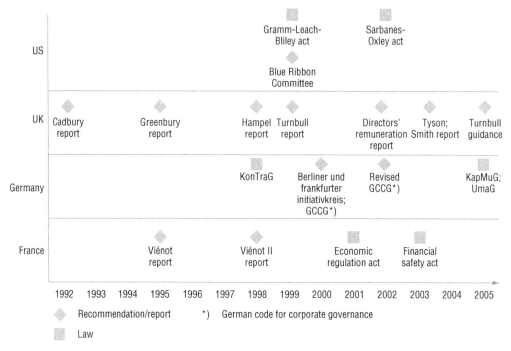

Figure 4.1:   Major laws and reports for corporate governance 1992–2005

market to increase the value of Guinness stocks in the UK, had an influence on corporate governance perception and regulation.[36] A growing number of people were depending on the stock market either directly through personal investment or through pension funds – (the equity market value in the UK grew from £36bn in 1971 to £514bn in 1989[37] and in the US, the number of shareholders grew from around 31m in 1970 to around 51m in 1990).[38]

Development of corporate governance in the 1990s

The late 1990s saw a further rise in awareness for corporate governance all over the focal countries. An array of reports, guidelines and best practice codes were

---

[36] See Tricker, B., (ed.) (2000).
[37] See London Stock Exchange (2004) *Historic Statistics*, available at www.londonstockexchange.com/NR/rdonlyres/D02B7655-EBC0-4445-8C5B-97DDDF86198D/0/Historic2004.pdf, accessed on March 20, 2006.
[38] See NYSE (1990) *Highlights of NYSE shareowner census reports (1952–1990)*, available at www.nysedata.com/nysedata/Default.aspx?tabid= 115, accessed on June 20, 2006.

issued in various nations[39] as well as the OECD guidelines on corporate governance in 1998. All these reports and laws were calling for more transparency, checks and balances, conformance and compliance at board level.[40]

In 1992, a "landmark in thinking on corporate governance", the Cadbury Report, was published in the UK, dealing with "directors' service contracts, interim reporting, the effectiveness and perceived objectivity of the audit and the role of institutional investors".[41] In 1993, this report became obligatory for companies listed in the UK and any divergence from it had to be explained in annual reports published from June 30, 1993.

In France a "number of embarrassing business scandals"[42] led to the creation of the Rapport Viénot in 1995 ("The Board of Directors of Listed Companies in France"[43]), which is said to have been spurred by the Cadbury Report.[44] The Viénot report suggested the removal of cross-shareholdings and cross-directorships and the establishment of nomination and remuneration committees, all on a voluntary, not a statutory, basis. In 1995, the Greenbury Report on directors' remuneration was published in the UK,[45] recommending the full disclosure of management remuneration.

1998 saw the publication of the Hampel report ("Combined Code: Principles of Good Governance and Code for Best Practice"[46]) in the UK and the second Viénot Report in France. The Hampel report combined the Cadbury and Greenbury codes and concluded that corporate governance regulations generally shouldn't be mandatory but rather unsolicited. Furthermore it suggested that the board should only be accountable to the company's shareholders as there is no need to redefine managers' responsibility to other stakeholders[47] – a clear statement for the shareholder approach to corporate governance commonly accepted in UK. Nevertheless, the Hampel report also suggested the separation of the role of CEO and chairman of the board, giving more emphasis to the supervisory role of the board.

---

[39] See Cadbury, S. A., (1992) *The financial aspects of corporate governance – A report of the Committee of Corporate Governance*, London: Gee and Co.; CNPF, A.-. (1995) *The boards of directors of listed companies in France – Viénot Report*, available at www.ecgi.org/codes/country_documents/france/vienot1_en.pdf, accessed on February 15, 2006; Greenbury, S. R., (1995) *Directors' remuneration: The report of a study group*, London: Gee and Co..

[40] See von Rosen, R., (2001) Corporate governance: Eine Bilanz, *Die Bank*, 4/2001.; See Tricker, B., (2005).

[41] See Maclean, M., (1999).   [42] See ibid.

[43] See Corporate governance advisor (1999) will Viénot II spur change in French capitalism? 7(5), 17–26.

[44] See Maclean, M., (1999); Corporate Governance Advisor (1999).

[45] See Maclean, M., (1999); See Tricker, B. (2005).

[46] See Hampel, R., (1998) *Committee on corporate governance – final report*, available at www.ecgi.org/codes/country_documents/uk/hampel_index.htm, accessed on February 15, 2006.

[47] See Tricker, B., (2005); (1998) Summary of the major recommendations of various committees and institutions concerning corporate governance, *OECD Economic Surveys: United Kingdom*, 1998(13), 163–171.

The second Viénot report from 1998 aimed to change the formerly secondary goal of achieving shareholder value in French companies with a call for greater transparency in response to investors' demands. This report also called for performance-related pay for top managers as well as the disclosure of the directors' remuneration policy (not so the disclosure of individual director compensation), to spur managers to increase shareholder value. The second Viénot report was said to "embrace the Anglo-Saxon practices of good corporate governance".[48]

In Germany, movement on the corporate governance agenda was visible with two laws concerning the transparency and control of corporations (KonTraG) and the access to capital (Kapitalaufnahmeerleichterungsgesetz – KapAEG) being passed. The KonTraG was the first major company law reform since 1965[49] and had to satisfy the countervailing demands for "securities market modernization and more stringent, shareholder-protective regulation, as well as normative commitment to effective employee representation on supervisory boards under codetermination law"[50]. The law dealt with cross-shareholding, the use of "golden shares", which allowed for disproportionate voting rights, and with transparency and shareholder democracy. It was passed after a number of corporate scandals like Daimler-Benz AG which disclosed losses of over $1 bn when publishing its annual report with GAAP calculations, having reported a profit under German accounting rules.[51] These differences in reporting unsettled international investors.

In 1999, the US saw changes to corporate governance regulations through the Gramm-Leach-Bliley Act and the recommendations of the "Blue Ribbon Committee". The latter contained ten suggestions about issues like transparency, accountability of external auditors and independence of external directors for audit committee and was aiming to improve the effectiveness of corporate audit committees. The recommendations were made compulsory by the NYSE, NASDAQ and AMEX in 1999.[52]

The creation of these reports and laws for the improvement of corporate governance as well as the growing awareness of corporate governance issues was driven by a changed worldwide economy as well as individual events or crises in the nations (See Daimler-Benz AG above). Major drivers for diffusion in corporate governance regulation of the 1990s include:

---

[48] See Corporate Governance Advisor (1999).
[49] See Cioffi, J. W., (2002) Restructuring "Germany Inc.": The politics of company and takeover law reform in Germany and the European Union, *Law & Policy*, 24(4), 355–403.
[50] See *ibid.*   [51] See *ibid.*   [52] See Hönsch, H., Behncke, N., Wulfetange, J., (2005).

- *Globalization and the spread of the internet*:[53] during the 1990s, the internet made communication and information sourcing easier, faster and cheaper. Boundaries of information and boundaries for international investment quickly vanished. This led to easier cross-national investments and a more internationalized capital market that demanded more transparency.
- *A stronger focus on shareholder value*:[54] this can be seen, for example, in Germany where banks, which were formerly more interested in the long-term success of the companies and held a high proportion of seats on the supervisory board, became increasingly interested in short-term benefits, believing "that more money could be made in underwriting and the lucrative market for company buying and selling".[55] The share of chairmanship of German banks therefore fell from 44% in 1992 to 23% in 1999 in the 40 largest German companies.[56] This changed the governance situation for German companies significantly[57] as it "reduced the willingness and capacity [of the banks] for insider monitoring".[58]

Development of corporate governance since 2000

In January 2000, having been exposed to a lot of criticism from international investors because of its opaque corporate governance regulations,[59] the Frankfurt Commission for Principles on Corporate Governance and the Berlin Initiative Group started to document the German system of corporate governance to create a code of best practice in corporate governance for German companies.[60] In June 2000, the "German Code of Corporate Governance" was introduced, which deals with the responsibilities of the Vorstand – the executive part of the German two-tier board. The German Code of Corporate Governance gives recommendations on issues like performance-linked remuneration, the use of the internet for reporting and annual meetings, the use of international accounting standards, the creation of audit committees and the use of a sufficient number of independent directors. The compliance with the Code in its revised form was made compulsory for German companies in

---

[53] See Maclean, M., (1999).

[54] See Engelen, E., (2002) Corporate governance, property and democracy: A conceptual critique of shareholder ideology, *Economy and Society*, 3(3), 391–413.

[55] See Lane, C., (2003) Changes in corporate governance of German corporations: Convergence to the Anglo-American model, *Competition and Change*, 7(2–3), 79–100.

[56] See Hoepner, M., (2001), *Corporate governance in transition: Ten empirical findings on shareholder value and industrial relations*, Discussion Paper 01/5 (Cologne: Max-Planck-Institut für Gesellschaftsordnung).

[57] See Cernat, L., (2004).   [58] See Lane, C., (2003).   [59] See von Rosen, R., (2001).   [60] See *ibid*.

2002 and any divergence from it had to be explained.[61] The creation of this code was driven by international shareholder pressure but also – again – by corporate failures such as Flowtex AG, Cargolifter and Philipp Holzmann AG.[62]

In 2001 the French passed the Economic Regulation Act, giving shareholders the right to sue members of the board in cases of bankruptcy for management fault and conflict of interest.[63] In 2002, the US passed the Sarbanes-Oxley Act, the "most far reaching reforms of American business practices since the time of Franklin Delano Roosevelt" [US president from 1933 to 1945].[64] This act had a serious impact on corporate governance of US companies as well as foreign companies listed on American stock exchanges. Major regulatory changes amending prior regulations through the Sarbox include:[65]

- the CEO and CFO have to certify the accuracy of corporate financial reports;
- companies are required to publish information related to material changes in their financial situation in a timely manner;
- companies must prepare reports assessing and describing the effectiveness of their internal control structures and financial reporting procedures.

The Act's drivers were certainly a number of major corporate scandals in 2001 of which Enron was probably the most (in-)famous in the US.[66] The Enron failure was shortly followed by the scandals of WorldCom and Tyco International in 2002, both involving major accounting frauds. Accounting problems and frauds, visible, for example, in financial restatement announcements, were increasing significantly in the US up to an estimated 250 in 2002 from only 92 in 1997.[67] In order to enhance corporate responsibility, financial disclosures and combat corporate and accounting fraud and certainly to re-establish investor's trust, the US legislation felt the need to pass an Act as comprehensive as Sarbanes-Oxley.

---

[61] See PriceWaterhouseCoopers (2006) *Themenpool: Corporate Governance*, available at www.pwc.com/de/ger/ins-sol/online-sol/themenpools/tpool_corp-governance.htm, accessed on February 16, 2006.

[62] See Dörner, D., Müller, H., Orth, C., (2002), *Entwicklungstendenzen der deutschen Corporate Governance* Ernst &Young; At Philipp Holzmann AG losses of DM 2.4 bn surfaced in November 1999; FlowTex had to file for insolvency with DM 3 bn of debt after dramatically exaggerating its sales figures over the years; see Aalund, D. (1999) *Holzmann braces for shareholders' flak - meeting to convene today on bailout plan*, The *Wall Street Journal Europe*, published December 30, 1999.

[63] See Steger, U., Aguirre, I. P., (2004).   [64] See US Securities and Exchange Commission (SEC) (2005).

[65] See Bednarz, A., (2005) *Thinking ouside the Sarbox*, NetworkWorld, published February 7, 2005.

[66] See Almond, P., Edwards, T., Clark, I., (2003); von Rosen, R. (2003) *US corporate governance kein Vorbild mehr*, Börsen-Zeitung, published November 28, 2003; Wiesen, J., (2003).

[67] See Coffee, J. C. J., (2005) for a closer study.

On the other side of the ocean, the EU made a number of directives and recommendations to push the harmonization process of the European market in 2005. The directives include the disclosure of management remuneration, the personal liability of management internally to the company (the external liability is subject to state regulation), the publication of half- and full-year reports as well as interim reports when necessary as well as the use of international accounting standards. Some of these directives (e.g. the Publication Directive) are similar to the Sarbanes-Oxley Act. The recommendations include the use of remuneration, audit and nomination committees as well as the liberty to choose between the one-tier and the two-tier board system. According to the Winter Report, the EU is solely interested in harmonizing national regulations through directives and recommendations. It does not try to establish a European Codex for Corporate Governance.[68]

A number of the EU recommendations and directives came into force in Germany in 2005, for example, the personal liability of the management to the shareholders. Filing lawsuits for small investors has become easier, increasing the power of minor shareholders. Furthermore, the German government now requires the publication of managers' remuneration, a highly controversial decision in Germany.[69]

French legislation introduced a law requiring publicly traded companies to disclose directors' and general managers' remuneration as well as retirement bonuses in 2005. Furthermore, *sociétés anonymes* (limited liability companies) have to publish information on board organization as well as the company's internal control procedures, again, similar to the Sarbanes-Oxley Act. Unlike the other focal nations, France does not yet have a corporate governance code. Corporate governance practices in France are said to be less initiated through regulations but rather through main employer organizations (MEDEF and AFEP) and the French market regulator (AMF).[70] The reports by Viénot and by Bouton – both instigated by the employer organizations – have led to the New Economic Regulations Act of 2001 as well as the Financial Safety Act of 2003, defining the competences and responsibilities of main actors within the company in detail and "leaving little room for self-governance".[71]

---

[68] See Hönsch, H., Behncke, N., Wulfetange, J., (2005); EurActiv.com (2005) *Corporate Governance*, available at www.euractiv.com/Article?_lang=EN&tcmuri=tcm:29-137147-16&type=LinksDossier, accessed on February 23, 2006.

[69] See Hönsch, H., Behncke, N., Wulfetange, J., (2005).

[70] See Grimonet, A., (2005) France, *International financial law review*, (corporate governance), pp. 43–45; Hebert, S. (2004) Corporate governance 'French style', *Journal of Business Law*, Nov 2004, 656–71.

[71] See Hebert, S., (2004).

3. Analysis of corporate governance regulation diffusion

Converging corporate governance and its drivers

Figure 4.2 shows how selected issues on corporate governance have diffused over the last ten years, many stemming from the Anglo-Saxon model. Especially evident are the issues concerning board remuneration as well as issues concerning audit committees. Also visible in this chart is the evolving nature of corporate governance and the diffusion of corporate governance in general. Many issues, like the personal liability of the board for the accuracy of the company's statements experienced awareness only over the last five to ten years.

The diffusion of corporate governance regulation is not converging in one direction only, i.e. that regulation diffuses from the Anglo-Saxon model to the continental-European model. A more differentiated view has to be taken, as in some instances corporate governance approaches and rules are diffusing from the Anglo-Saxon model, for example, remuneration disclosure, regulation for transparency and the use of audit committees. Other issues diffuse from continental Europe – the distinction between the executive and the supervising members of the board as well as the separation of the chairman of the board and the CEO.[72] While the share of split roles in the US was at only 8% in 1998, it rose to 29% in 2005 for S&P 500 companies.[73]

This diffusion of corporate governance regulation is caused by a variety of drivers, as described above. The main drivers identified include:

- scandals and corporate crises;
- internationalized capital markets;
- harmonization of capital markets through political powers;
- growing importance of investment for a broader part of the population;
- privatization.

A further driver for the diffusion of corporate governance, although not on a regulatory (*de jure*) level, is the export of corporate governance models to subsidiaries, as companies building subsidiaries in foreign countries often export the company's culture including corporate governance into this subsidiary. In this *de facto* diffusion, the continental model to corporate governance is – according to Engelen as well as to Boyer – more influential: "In

---

[72] See Tieman, R., (2003) *German two-tier structure seen as role model*, in *Financial Times*, published February 24, 2008.
[73] See (2006) *Separation of CEO and chairman role increases*, in *Business Wire*, published February 1, 2006.

CG Issue	Country	1994	1995	1996	1997	1998	1999	2000	2001	2002	2003	2004	2005
Remuneration pay by performance	Germany							R	R	R	R	R	R
	France						R	R	R	R	R	R	R
	UK	S	S	S	S	S	S	S	S	S	S	S	S
	USA	S	S	S	S	S	S	S	S	S	S	S	S
Remuneration disclosure	Germany							R	R	R	R	R	S
	France							R	R	R	R	R	S
	UK		R	R	R	R	R	R	R	R	S	S	S
	USA	S	S	S	S	S	S	S	S	S	S	S	S
Audit committee creation	Germany							R	R	R	R	R	R
	France		R	R	R	R	R	R	R	R	R	R	R
	UK	S	S	S	S	S	S	S	S	S	S	S	S
	USA						S	S	S	S	S	S	S
Audit committee independence	Germany							R	R	R	R	R	R
	France										R	R	R
	UK	R	R	R	R	R	R	R	R	S	S	S	S
	USA	R	R	R	R	R	R	R	R	S	S	S	S
Board independence	Germany							*	R	R	R	R	R
	France	R	**	R	R	***	R	R	R	R	R	R	R
	UK	R	R	R	R	R	R	R	R	R	R	R	R
	USA									S	S	S	S
Removal of cross-shareholding	Germany							R	R	R	R	R	R
	France							R	R	R	R	R	R
	UK	S	S	S	S	S	S	S	S	S	S	S	S
	USA	S	S	S	S	S	S	S	S	S	S	S	S
Liability of board	Germany												S
	France								R	R	R	R	R
	UK												
	USA									S	S	S	S
Comply or explain	Germany									R	R	R	R
	France										R	R	R
	UK					S	S	S	S	S	S	S	S
	USA									****	R	R	R
Separation of Chairman/CEO	Germany	S	S	S	S	S	S	S	S	S	S	S	S
	France							R	R	R	R	R	R
	UK					R	R	R	R	R	R	R	R
	USA												

▨ Recommended
▪ Statutory/common practice

*	"Sufficiently independent"
**	2 independent directors
***	1/3 independent directors
****	Law-driven

Figure 4.2: Diffusion of selected corporate governance issues 1994–2005

Germany, US transplants have adopted German practices, whereas German transplants in the US have created German-like environments within the 'host' country."[74]

Persistent corporate governance and the barriers for diffusion

In many issues of corporate governance differences prevail, like in the approach to corporate governance regulation, where the US "prefers the hammer of Sarbanes-Oxley, while the Europeans lean towards a voluntary approach".[75] This does not connote that the other focal countries, for example Germany, do not also have statutory regulations concerning corporate governance systems, but rather that the US corporate governance system is currently the most regulated with almost all issues being statutory, whereas in Germany and the UK some issues are still regulated with a "comply or explain" rule.

Persistence concerning issues of corporate governance also exists in the size of individual shareholders (concentrated versus well dispersed). In Germany, for example, cross-shareholding has just seen a new rise, as Porsche AG bought 18.5% of the stock of the VW AG for €3.5 bn in 2005[76] and will soon have a blocking minority with more than 25% of the stock after a share buy-back from VW;[77] however, in the UK and the US shares are very well dispersed under a variety of shareholders.[78] Furthermore, the difference in the board structure (one-tier vs. two-tier) currently prevails, as for German companies the two-tier system of the board including the co-determination with employees will be the only legal form for companies, as long as companies don't change their legal form of organization to SE (Societas Europeae). French companies are still able to choose between both practices, while UK and US companies will continue governing their enterprises with a one-tier board, although with a high percentage of independent directors.

[74] See Engelen, E., (2002); Boyer, R., Drache, D. (eds.) (1996) *States against markets: The limits of globalization*, London: Routledge.

[75] See Melnitzer, J., (2003) US presses Europeans to implement governance reforms, *Corporate Legal Times*, 13(137), 36–7; cf. also Albert-Roulhac, C., Breen, P., (2005) Corporate governance in Europe: Current status and future trends, *Journal of Business Strategy*, 26(6), 19–29.

[76] See Moore, M., (2006) *VW's Piech to step down in 2007; Porsche CEO to join board*, Associated Press, published January 20, 2006.

[77] See Hofmann, J., (2006) *VW verhilft Porsche zur Sperrminorität, Handelsblatt*, published February 14, 2006.

[78] See Almond, P., Edwards, T., Clark, I., (2003); Cernat, L. (2004); Coffee, J. C. J. (2005); Maclean, M. (1999).

The barriers for total assimilation of corporate governance laws and the persistence of manifold differences in the regulations have been mentioned in this chapter. The main barriers can be summarized as:

- differences in the capital/financial structure;
- differences in remuneration policies;
- differences in the system of law; and
- differences in the economic systems and economic environment.

As mentioned above, the capital/financial culture in the Anglo-Saxon system is characterized by a highly dispersed ownership structure where stocks are held by a variety of shareholders and no big shareholders exert power over the strategy of a company. The relationship between owners and managers is described as "arm's-length."[79] On the other hand, the continental system as still seen in France and Germany is characterized by long-term commitment with block- and cross-shareholding and a high involvement of the state (France) and banks (Germany). Those block-shareholders are not interested in the day-to-day share prices but rather in longer-term profit and exert power directly through seats on boards.[80] Achieving control of an economic entity through the market or through the influence of major shareholders is different and the need for regulation comes with it.

Remuneration policies differ significantly between the countries. US and to a lesser extent UK managers still receive a much higher proportion (in 2001 it was 66% for US CEOs) of their compensation in equity than their German or French counterparts. Furthermore, senior management income as a multiple of average employee compensation in the US and the UK is essentially higher (531:1 in the US in 2004, 25:1 in the UK in 2004) than in France (16:1) or Germany (11:1).[81] Managers who are reimbursed through equity feel the need to push the stock price, even by artificial or illegal financial statement inflation,[82] to sell their options/stock as part of their salary. Therefore, a different approach to corporate governance might be necessary since "governance protections that work in one system may fail in the other".[83]

Another barrier for a unitary diffusion of corporate governance is found in the difference between the law systems in the UK/US and the one practiced in Germany and France. The UK and the US both have a common law body, where mostly precedent decisions and their analogies determine the law. As long as there are no incidents or scandals, laws will not be created in the common law system. In the UK, for instance, the corporate governance system

---

[79] See Almond, P., Edwards, T., Clark, I., (2003); See Hall, P., Soskice, D. (2001).
[80] See Coffee, J. C. J., (2005).   [81] See *ibid*.   [82] See *ibid*.   [83] See *ibid*.

generally relies on guidelines, whereas in the US, corporate scandals have triggered the creation of the SOX. Germany and France have a civil law body with codified laws. In Germany, for example, many of the issues addressed in the German Code of Corporate Governance are a summary of already existing laws, which provide guidelines about corporate governance[84] and which were amended with recommendations for best practice to be used on a voluntary basis.[85] A unitary diffusion of corporate governance regulation from this point of view is unlikely, since the approaches to regulation are already different in the systems.

The last barrier to be discussed here is concerned with cultural differences in the economic system. The perception of the market versus the individual differs between the focal nations. The Anglo-Saxon corporate culture is emphasizing self-responsibility, so the individual is able to take action possibly without state restrictions. The US and the UK are consequently classified as "liberal market economies". The most important stakeholder for the economic entity in this system is the shareholder – who also gets the necessary protection; other stakeholders are secondary (therefore "shareholder approach"). Germany and France are considered as "coordinated market economies", where the state tries to integrate a variety of stakeholders in its legislative actions, so a broader range of stakeholders has to be taken care of when operating an economic entity in these two countries (therefore "stakeholder approach").[86] This again makes the need for differing corporate governance regulations apparent.

A general assessment of the value of corporate governance regulation diffusion

So far, this chapter has analyzed how corporate governance regulation has spread or not spread through different countries and the reasons encouraging or encumbering it. Some of the advantages and disadvantages of diffused corporate governance regulation are now discussed.

For years, international investors have demanded a more common approach to corporate governance, especially in terms of transparency and accountability, obviously to be able to better compare investment options on an international playing field. Therefore adoption of those corporate governance standards known to major investors might be beneficial for countries

---

[84] See von Rosen, R., (2001).
[85] See von Rosen, R., (2005) *Die Selbstregulierung muss das Grundprinzip bleiben, Börsen-Zeitung*, published June 3, 2005.
[86] See Almond, P., Edwards, T., Clark, I., (2003).

with great need of international investment. Also multinational companies can profit from a more international approach to corporate governance, especially companies that are listed on different stock exchanges, as they currently face different issues of corporate governance in the different countries, and therefore have to bear high costs to be able to comply with more than one corporate governance system. These are just two examples of stakeholders of corporate governance regulation, and they see great advantages in a more converged regulatory environment.

There are also disadvantages to a unitary approach of corporate governance regulation. Due to differences in the social and economic environment in a country, a "one size fits all" approach would not match the demands of a certain country setting and would not bring full economic benefit available. Countries, due to their different location factors, also try to attract different industries. Not all industries are interested in the same governance regulations, rather they demand different laws. This spurs competition for governance regulations between nations to attract those industries in which they are interested. Countries which just follow others in their regulatory approach could lose competitive advantages; moreover, a diverse approach to corporate governance regulation can create industry clusters, raising the attractiveness of the location even more.

4. Conclusion and outlook

This chapter summarized the changes in corporate governance regulation over the last fifty years. It has been discovered that although corporate governance is a fairly established issue, as it arises as soon as ownership and management are separated, it was only in the 1980s that the term "corporate governance" was developed. Since then, changes in corporate governance regulation have been numerous, concerning issues such as liability of the board against shareholders, independence of the board, creation of audit committees with non-executive and independent directors, directors' remuneration and its disclosure etc.

The diffusion of corporate governance regulation has been driven by a number of causes. Firstly, corporate crises have triggered regulatory changes as can be seen by the creation of the Sarbanes-Oxley Act in 2002 after the fall of Enron and WorldCom in the US. Secondly, an internationalization of the capital market and (especially important in Germany) a growing orientation of the long-term banks towards a more short-term view, has changed the necessity of shareholder perception. Also, technological advances like the emergence of the internet and with it the possibility of quick information sourcing and evaluation gave the financial markets the possibility to act faster, making investment capital more fluid. The EU with its effort to create a single European market passed a number of directives and recommendations towards a harmonized approach to corporate governance and therefore made changes for corporate governance regulations on a national level necessary. Last but not least, the wave for privatization and deregulation in the 1980s and 1990s has led to a changed economy in the focal countries (especially France, Germany and the UK), as formerly state-owned companies started to face shareholder demands and had to put greater efforts into the creation of shareholder value.

Nevertheless, numerous differences in corporate governance regulations prevail. Corporate governance regulation in the US is now very law-based, whereas the UK, France and Germany "enforce" a number of corporate governance issues with codes or in the case of Germany and the UK with a "comply or explain" regulation. France does not yet have a code of best practice and consequently has no "comply or explain" regulation. Also regulations concerning codetermination of the board and the employees as well as the one-tier vs. the two-tier board structure seem to stay different across the nations (Germany enforcing the two-tier board system; France offering the possibility to choose; the UK and the US opponents of the two-tier board structure). These differences are due to a number of barriers, which encumber convergence towards a unitary approach to corporate governance. These barriers can be found in the capital culture (UK and US dispersed ownership system; Germany and France concentrated ownership system with block- and cross-shareholding as well as state participation), differences in management remuneration, differences in the law systems (common law in the UK and the US vs. civil law in France and Germany) and differences in the economic systems ("liberal market economy" in the UK and the US vs. "coordinated market economies" in Germany and France).

The way to good corporate governance regulation is neither straightforward nor obvious. It is no surprise that some of the issues concerning corporate governance regulation are being generally accepted by the different national regulators as well as by the players on the markets, such as more independence of the board or the creation of audit committees. Other issues of corporate governance legislation, such as rules concerning disclosure or accountability, are viewed rather more skeptically by some of the market participants and sometimes the regulators have to row back. In August

2006 for instance, US Treasury secretary Hank Paulson announced that the Sarbanes-Oxley Act could have been an overreaction,[87] raising the hopes of those critics claiming that the costs especially through section 404 don't justify the benefits of this piece of corporate governance regulation.

Academic research has often tried to discover trends of convergence towards a more insider-oriented model or a more outsider-oriented model of corporate governance over the last years, with very different outcomes. It has also tried to evaluate good corporate governance, although mainly from a shareholder's perspective.[88] It seems at this stage of corporate governance research though that the way to a common approach of "good" corporate governance regulation is difficult if not impossible. This has also been recognized by international organizations such as the EU and the OECD which have kept their demands and suggestions for good corporate governance general, embracing issues such accountability and transparency very broad.[89]

Overall, diffusion in corporate governance regulation can be observed in a lot of issues, but a global convergence towards one corporate governance model – whatever it may be – is neither likely nor sensible in the near future. In the end, corporate governance depends not only on the regulatory environment, but also on the relevant capital markets, on the business model and strategy and, last but not least, on the personalities responsible for the companies and the authorities.[90]

---

[87] See Freeland, C., Grant, J., (2006) *Brokering change: How Cox is building a consensus as regulation goes global, Financial Times*, published August 4, 2006.

[88] See Chang, K., Noorbakhsh, A., (2006) Corporate cash holdings, foreign direct investment, and corporate governance, *Global Finance Journal*, 16(3), 302–16; Stulz, R. M., (2005a) Corporate governance and financial globalization, *NBER Reporter*, Fall 2005, 13–15.; Stulz, R. M., (2005b) The limits of financial globalization, *The Journal of Finance*, 55(4), 1595–638; La Porta, R., Lopez-de-Silanes, F., Shleifer, A. Vishny, R. W., (1998) Law and finance, *Journal of Political Economy*, 106(6), 1113–155.

[89] See Witherell, B., (2004) Corporate governance, *OECD Observer*, May 2004 (243), 41–3.

[90] See Steger, U., (ed.) (2004) *Mastering global corporate governance*, Chichester: John Wiley & Sons Ltd.

5   Corporate governance after Enron *et al.*

Stewart Hamilton

1. The millennium meltdown

When Enron, the seventh largest (by recorded revenues) corporation in the US, collapsed in December 2001, it caused a shock across the globe. But once the shockwaves had died away, the collapse was largely dismissed as an unfortunate aberration in the system, "the one bad apple." Europeans, and others, looked on with a measure of *Schadenfreude*. This was to be short-lived. Then when WorldCom went down a few months later in the biggest corporate bankruptcy the world had ever seen, and reports emerged of other – if smaller-scale – disasters, from the UK, Switzerland, the Netherlands, Australia and elsewhere, it became clear that this was a global phenomenon.

As tales of trouble at ImClone, Adelphi, Tyco and Global Crossing, among others, continued apace in the US, these were paralleled elsewhere in the world. In the UK, TXU Europe collapsed, major problems at Marconi were revealed and, later, Equitable Life only just managed to come back from the brink; in Switzerland the failure of the national carrier, Swissair, rocked the country; in Holland, serious accounting fraud at Ahold was uncovered; and in Australia the scandal of HIH came to light. Perhaps most spectacular of all was the implosion of the Italian food giant, Parmalat, in Europe's biggest ever corporate failure, which removed any residual belief that these were solely American problems.

Worldwide, there was something rotten at the core of corporate life. Politicians and financial commentators alike pronounced themselves to be aghast at the losses to misled shareholders, as the tales of excess, corporate wrongdoing, shoddy accounting and supine boards unfolded.

Many commentators – politicians, the media and some academics[1] – have chosen to describe events in terms of "accounting scandals," exhibiting an

---

[1] See for example, Dembinski, P. H., Lager, C., Cornford, A., Bonvin, J.-M., (eds.) (2006) *Enron and world finance: A case study in ethics*, Houndsmill: Palgrave Macmillan/Geneva: Observatoire de la Finance.

inability to understand the root causes of the disasters. Few, if any, of the failures were the direct result of accounting irregularities. To be sure, so-called aggressive accounting policies and earnings management[2] were part of the stories. Often embarked upon to meet analysts' expectations, these primarily served to conceal, for far longer than should have been possible, much more significant problems, namely flawed or failed business strategies or decisions. The problems were, of course, exacerbated by the abject failure of public auditing firms to do their job properly.

Similarly, it is too simplistic to ascribe events to the raging bull market of the 1990s. What is true, however, is that in long bull markets there is a tendency for even the most rational individuals to get caught up in the excitement of the times and act less prudently than they might otherwise do. Similarly, companies face ever-increasing pressure to perform, quarter after quarter, in terms of reported earnings growth and to maintain or increase their share price. Growth must be pursued at almost any price, often through aggressive acquisitions that increase leverage levels, thus putting further pressure on management. At the same time, if a company's share price continues to rise, board members find it harder to question and challenge senior management even if they have misgivings about the strategy being pursued.

This chapter is not about stock market "bubbles" or the "irrational exuberance" that characterized the last decade of the twentieth century.[3] Nor is it about accounting scandals and craven auditors. Nor does it seek to identify in detail why companies fail.[4] Nevertheless, some understanding of what has happened in the recent past is a necessary context for the governance changes that are being forced upon, or voluntarily adopted by, companies worldwide.

The intention of this chapter, rather, is to focus on the main causes of failure, which are rarely captured in the financial media and less often seriously analyzed. Much of the academic research on corporate failure[5] has been obsessed with trying to develop predictive empirical tools that would

---

[2] A problem highlighted by SEC chairman, Arthur Levitt in a speech at New York University in September 1998, *The Numbers Game.*

[3] For a comprehensive coverage of these events see Stiglitz, J., (2003) *The roaring nineties*, New York: W. W. Norton.

[4] See Hamilton, S., Micklethwait, A., (2006) *Greed and corporate failure: The lessons from recent disasters*, Houndsmill: Palgrave Macmillan.

[5] For a review of the literature, see Morris, R., (1997) *Early warning indicators of corporate failure: A critical review of previous research*, London: Ashgate.

enable investors to avoid companies at risk. Of these, Altman's Z-score[6] is probably the best known. Little in the literature has addressed the behavioral issues of directors, although some references exist.[7]

History suggests that the "rational investor" from time to time loses his critical faculties. Rational judgment is suspended, despite overwhelming evidence that market levels are unsustainable, as is well illustrated by the dramatic events of 1929.

2. The great crash – history repeats itself

On September 3, 1929 the Dow Jones reached 381, up from 257 a year earlier, prompting a distinguished academic to observe: "Stock prices have reached what looks like a permanently high plateau."[8] Many were convinced that a new order had arrived: is it not entirely possible that conditions at present are so different from conditions in the past that the old standards of comparison are worthless?

This euphoria had been fed by the proliferation of "tip sheets"[9] and the widespread use of brokers' loans and margin trading, which in turn led to a strong public appetite for new issues of stock. When the crash came it was, as everyone knows, dramatic in scale and impact. On Black Tuesday – October 29, 1929 – the Dow dropped 13%, and by the end of the month it had plunged 40% since the beginning of September. The Great Depression had begun. By June 8, 1932, the Dow had sunk by 89% from its 1929 high, to 41, barely above the level on its first day of existence in May 1896. In the aftermath, 9,800 banks failed, unemployment rose to over 25% and gross national product (GNP) fell to 50% of its 1929 peak. In the 1920s the US securities market had seen some $50 billion of new securities issued, with fully half, or $25 billion, proving to be worthless.[10]

---

[6] Altman, E. I. (1971) *Corporate bankruptcy in America*, Lexington MA: Heath Lexington Books. The Z score was a multiple discriminant analysis which he believed was a good predictor of failure, where $Z = 0.012X_1 + 0.014X_2 + 0.033X_3 + 0.006X_4 + 0.010X_5$ when X_1 is working capital/total assets, X_2 is retained earnings/total assets, X_3 is EBIT/total assets, X_4 is market value of book equity/book value of total debt and X_5 is sales/total assets. A score less than 1.8 was regarded as a danger sign and greater than 3.0 an indicator that the company was unlikely to fail.

[7] See, for example, John Argenti, J., (1976) *Corporate collapse: The causes and symptoms*, London: McGraw-Hill.

[8] Irvine Fischer, Professor of Economics, Yale, September 1929.

[9] A tip sheet was an unregulated document circulated by stockbrokers and others, encouraging investment in particular shares.

[10] US House of Representatives report, 1993, quoted by Commissioner Isaac C Hunt, Lisbon, May 2001.

Sixty years later, in the 1990s, stock markets around the world were enjoying the greatest bull run since that golden age of the twenties. The NASDAQ which had closed at 357 on January 9, 1991, reached a peak of 5049 on March 10, 2000.

All indicators showed that prices were at an unsustainable level. Price/earnings ratios were at an all-time high, as was Tobin's "Q."[11] In the dot-com arena, companies that had never earned a penny were being valued at many times the worth of their more traditional counterparts. One of the most extreme examples was that of e.Toys, an online retailer competing with Toys "Я" Us. At the height of the dot-com boom, e.Toys, with sales of $117m, 300 employees and losses of $126m, had a market capitalization of $5.6bn compared with that of its "bricks and mortar" competitor, which was valued at $3.9bn and generated profits of $12m on sales of $11.9bn and had 70,000 employees worldwide.

The cheerleaders this time around had been the investment banks and their conflicted analysts; the tip sheets of the past had been replaced by CNBC and Bloomberg and the unlikely valuations of these "new economy" companies were justified by the consultants McKinsey,[12] among others. We saw the emergence of "day traders" whose activities were enabled by the technological revolution in which they were investing. We also witnessed the phenomenon of "momentum" investment strategies born out of a fear of missing out and the suspension of rational thought by those who should have known better.

There were some voices of caution. In his prescient book, *Irrational Exuberance*, published in 2000, before the crash, Robert Shiller, professor of economics at Yale, expressed his concerns "that the present stock market displays the classic features of a *speculative bubble*: a situation in which temporarily high prices are sustained largely by investors' enthusiasm rather than by consistent estimation of real value."[13] Most chose to ignore or dismiss such concerns.

Despite the fact that politicians and others claimed that this time things were different, that there had been a "paradigm shift" and that boom and bust were a thing of the past, the stock market crash of 2000 proved the opposite, with the dot-com and telecom companies replacing the banks of the 1920s. Failures occurred across continents and industries, among small and large companies alike.

---

[11] Tobin's "Q" is the ratio of the stock market value of a firm's assets (as measured by the market value of its outstanding shares and debt) to the replacement cost of the firm's assets.

[12] Driek Desmet *et al.*, (2000) Valuing dot.coms. *McKinsey Quarterly*, Iss.1, p. 148.

[13] Shiller, R. J., (2000) *Irrational exuberance*, Princeton: Princeton University Press, p. 5.

3. The Enron saga

Amidst all this came the almighty collapse of Enron in November 2001, which sent legislators in the US scurrying to find ways to prevent a repeat.

Enron, in the space of little more than a decade, had grown from a traditional gas pipeline company to become a major player in that market but had also become the world's largest energy trader. Enron had pursued dual strategies of continuing to invest in traditional energy generation and pipelines, and of developing a huge energy trading operation, both of which required a great deal of cash, always in short supply. The traditional energy business came unstuck when Enron expanded into areas its management did not really understand. Its most notorious failure was the Dabhol power project in India, which even the World Bank would not support, and which eventually cost Enron $3bn. Other international ventures had lost some $7bn in value by 2000 but, extraordinarily, the necessary write-downs were postponed with Arthur Andersen's consent.

The trading side was initially profitable, but as more and more competitors joined in, margins decreased and Enron turned to increasingly exotic products, such as weather derivatives and oil tanker freight rates, in its search for profits. To compound matters, Enron then moved into broadband, in which there was already burgeoning capacity, laying fiber optic cables and trading bandwidth. Although the business never made any profit, this did not stop Enron CEO, Kenneth Lay, and others from hailing broadband as a major part of Enron's future.

Reluctant to issue new shares to fund such activities, Enron was heavily reliant on borrowing, the extent of which potentially jeopardized its investment grade credit ratings, a must to support its trading operations. This pressure led to many schemes to disguise the scale of Enron's borrowings and to artificially inflate reported earnings. Ultimately it was determined that the hidden debt amounted to some $25 billion.[14]

Enron's ethos added to the problems. Remuneration linked to quarterly profits and the "rank or yank" performance assessment system, whereby the bottom 10% of employees were shown the door on a regular basis, fueled the drive to do deals and book ever-increasing profits regardless of whether

---

[14] US Bankruptcy Court, Southern District of New York, Second Interim Report of Neil Batson, Court Appointed Examiner in re: Enron Corp, *et al.*, January 21, 2003.

the underlying contracts generated cash. These deals, while not necessarily illegal, certainly painted an optimistic picture of Enron's performance.

In another company, effective risk management and a strong internal audit team would have prevented the worst excesses, but these controls were absent at Enron. A complacent and supine board failed to call a halt to Enron's reckless expansion or to monitor its internal controls. Finally, inadequate external auditing permitted the highly dubious financial engineering and reporting that enabled Enron to hide its problems for much longer than should have been possible and kept the company afloat long after it had become insolvent.

While the scale and combination of problems at Enron were unprecedented, the problems themselves were not.

4. Underlying causes of corporate failure

Reacting to the media outcry and the worries expressed by the many who had lost jobs, pensions and savings, the US Congress was quick to pass an ill-considered and hasty piece of legislation, the Sarbanes-Oxley Act (SOX) in early 2002. The Act established a range of new standards particularly with a view on public accounting firms, covering such issues as auditor independence, management oversight and enhanced financial disclosure. It sought to prevent future "Enrons," an objective in which it will fail as it does not and cannot address the underlying problems. But the fundamental causes of corporate failure are more complex. Accounting or, more accurately, the misuse of accounting, was not the main problem. Rather the uncontrolled pursuit of flawed strategies coupled with greed on the part of many was the real reason for the downfall of several household names and previous stock market favorites.

From our research into recent corporate failures, and into earlier examples like Metalgesellschaft, Rolls-Royce, Guinness and Barings Bank, we have identified what we believe are the six main causal factors.[15] Only when these are clearly understood can we identify what needs to be done to reduce the likelihood of future repetitions.

The recurring, and interrelated, themes are poor strategic decisions; over-expansion, especially through (ill-judged) acquisitions; the dominant CEO,

---

[15] Failure is defined to include shareholder value destruction in companies that do survive in a legal sense, e.g. Marconi, Tyco, Ahold, Parmalat.

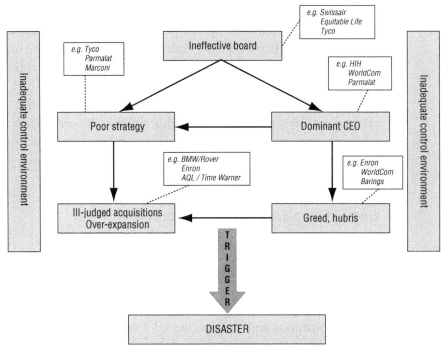

Figure 5.1:   The downward spiral

or "one man band"; the greed, hubris and power lust of CEOs and other "star" performers; poor risk management and weak internal controls, particularly with regard to cash; and, most importantly, ineffective boards and their audit committees. While any one of these on its own would not necessarily be sufficient to cause the collapse of a company, the combination of two or more is likely to be lethal. Figure 5.1 shows the linkages between the various factors.

In examining the linkages between the six main causal factors behind corporate failure, the starting point must be the board itself. A company board has a number of clear responsibilities and duties, and with a weak and ineffective board these responsibilities are not met.

Link 1: Ineffective boards

Recent events have underlined the lack of genuinely independent directors. A board is supposed to provide a non-partisan judgment of the senior management's actions and strategic proposals and to look after the interests of shareholders. Board members may not do this effectively if they are financially beholden to the company (although they need to be paid properly for the job), as their judgment might well be clouded. Many so-called independent directors may not have been so independent after all. At WorldCom, many of the directors came from companies it had acquired and who owed much of their wealth to Bernie Ebbers. At Tyco, some of the "independent" directors either depended indirectly on Tyco for the bulk of their income or had benefited from the use of company assets at the discretion of the CEO, Dennis Kozlowski.

Most importantly, boards, blinded by ever increasing share prices and the apparent success of the company, fail to critically scrutinize corporate strategy or demand sufficiently rigorous analysis and due diligence of the project under discussion. Sometimes they are simply inadequately prepared for the job.

Many audit committee members have too little financial expertise, making it difficult for them to understand complex accounting matters. Instead, they have tended to go through the motions of reviewing controls rather than undertaking a much more detailed study which would involve posing challenging questions. Enron's audit committee, despite being chaired by a distinguished academic accountant,[16] clearly failed in this regard. In this respect at least, SOX may make a difference.

Link 2: Strategic failures

One of the primary consequences of an ineffective board is the likelihood of poor strategic thinking and decision making. Strategic decisions should be based on proper research, analysis and considered debate to ensure the proposals on the table are robust. Without any of this there is a real risk that the company's strategy and decisions will suffer, with potentially dire consequences.

In particular, companies often fail to understand the relevant business drivers when they expand into new products or geographical markets, leading to poor decisions. For example, Marconi quite simply did not clearly understand where rapid technological change was driving the market and therefore persistently made incorrect strategic choices. Similarly, Tyco, in trying to emulate GE's success with GE Capital, had not fully understood how that business worked. Both Enron and WorldCom did not appreciate how a growing market overcapacity in fiber cables would impact their investments

---

[16] Dr Jaedicke, R. K., former Dean of Stanford Business School and author (with Robert T. Sprouse) of *Accounting flows: Income, funds and cash*, Englewood Cliffs, N. J.: Prentice-Hall, 1965.

in that field. The board of Barings, rooted in the traditional banking business, did not realize the risks associated with the relatively new derivatives markets. From a geographical and cultural perspective, neither Ahold nor Parmalat (in South America), nor Enron (in India) really understood the country and political risks that they faced. When Swissair made a large minority investment in Sabena (Belgium), it failed to judge the difficulties associated with achieving necessary change in a government-controlled company.

Often a lack of adequate due diligence, whether building a new plant or making an acquisition, exacerbates the problems. Tyco did not research the cable market adequately and moved into it when there was already over-capacity; Ahold failed to uncover fraud before buying USF; WorldCom, in its acquisition of Intermedia, blindly accepted its advisors' overvaluation of the company's local network assets.

Link 3: The dominant CEO

A further consequence of a weak board can be the emergence of a dominant CEO. These individuals often appear after a period of successful (or apparently successful) management. The company becomes packed with like-minded executives who (usually) owe their position to him and are reluctant to challenge his judgment. A complacent board, lulled by past achievements, stops scrutinizing detailed performance indicators and falls into the habit of rubber-stamping the CEO's decisions. His drive, commitment, (often) charisma and streak of ruthlessness have contributed to the previous success. But later, the dominant CEO becomes a major contributor to the company's downfall. With no challengers or critics within the company, he may begin, perhaps unconsciously, to behave as though it is his own creation and – as Dennis Kozlowski did at Tyco, Bernie Ebbers at WorldCom and Calisto Tanzi at Parmalat – use it as his own piggy bank. Shareholders and the board become irrelevant. Seduced by the prospects of yet more power and wealth and with a strong belief in his own infallibility, he goes all out for growth. Think of Jean-Marie Messier's obsession with turning Vivendi into a media company. The rationale behind such a campaign is difficult to fathom in the cold light of day.

Of course, there are some who argue that very successful dominant CEOs can and do exist. Indeed, Jack Welch is one who would spring immediately to mind. But there is a fine line between the CEO as hero and as villain. The danger is that, with the passage of time, powerful CEOs begin to believe in their own PR and start to have difficulty in distinguishing between their own personal interests and those of the company. Boards, needed to provide a reality check, often fail to question senior management decisions and competence and merely rubber-stamp decision and compensation packages. This is what happened at WorldCom, Enron, Marconi, Ahold, Parmalat, Swissair and Tyco.

Link 4: Greed and hubris

Along with the expanding power base of the CEO invariably comes a level of greed and hubris which is barely contained. High achievers, such as top executives, are particularly ambitious and eager for more power and wealth. Certainly towards the late 1990s and beyond, executive compensation and share options, in particular, were moving exponentially upwards – in the US more than anywhere else. As of 1990, the median CEO compensation of S&P 500 Industrial Companies was $1.25m, with 94% of that amount paid in cash and 6% equity; by 2001, the median CEO of an S&P industrial company was earning above $6m, of which 66% was in equity.[17] There is a clear and direct link between the size of a company and the level of executive compensation, which naturally drives a CEO to grow his company by the fastest route possible.

Link 5: Over-expansion and ill-judged acquisitions

The quickest way to grow a company is often by acquisition. The greedy CEOs of WorldCom, Tyco, Ahold, Parmalat and others, often frustrated by their inability to grow organically sufficiently quickly, needed little encouragement to embark on a spending spree. Despite the conventional wisdom holding that less than half of all acquisitions deliver the sought-after or promised returns, AOL and Time Warner being a prime example, this acquisition trend shows little sign of abating, even today.[18] Very often, the desired synergies are ephemeral, and the integration costs far exceed the anticipated benefits. Furthermore, cultural differences and lack of management capacity often add to the obvious problems.

---

[17] See Hall, B. J., (2003) Six challenges in designing equity-based pay, *Accenture Journal of Applied Corporate Finance*, 15(3), 21.

[18] Indeed the statistical reference is a bit more complicated than this. Moeller *et al.* (2005) show that for the period of 1998–2001, the largest transactions (87 out of 4,136 deals) destroyed value = $ 379bn; the remaining 4,049 deals created value = $157 bn). Put differently, value creation of smaller acquisitions was unable to over-compensate for the value destruction of the very big deals. See Moeller, S. *et al.* (2005) Wealth destruction on a massive scale? A study of acquiring-firm returns in the recent merger wave, *Journal of Finance* 60, 757–82.

The examples are countless but to name a few of the better-known transactions, consider the DaimlerChrysler mega-merger in 1998 which by 2006 resulted in a combined company worth less than half of the sum of its former individual parts. The major accounting firms did not escape the trend. The majority of former Price Waterhouse and Coopers & Lybrand clients were firmly opposed to the merger between the two firms, and it is no small wonder it made it through the prevailing competition law. Too often, a tendency to pay too high a price to secure the deal – perhaps as a result of hubris – adds to these difficulties. This is what happened with Enron and Wessex Water, and with WorldCom and Intermedia, for example, and in an earlier era, Robert Maxwell and Macmillan US.

Link 6: Control failures

Underlying all this are weak internal control environments. The basic concept of risk management is elusive to many companies, too focused on ensuring that the petty cash float adds up to consider the risks which might threaten the very core of the business. It is thirteen years since traces of benzene were allegedly discovered in Perrier bottled mineral water. In 2005, the volume of Perrier (since bought by Nestlé) sales was at 80% of the pre-benzene level. Put this in the context of the massive growth of the mineral water market over the last 13 years, and the scale of loss of value becomes clear. There are too many companies where the controls are not in place to ensure that the effects of an oil spill, or of a rating agency downgrading stock, does not translate into disaster.

Blurred internal reporting lines within an organization also leave holes in control systems, nowhere more obvious than in the case of Barings, where no one believed that they had overriding responsibility for the activities of rogue trader Nick Leeson, who had been sent to work in the bank's various locations. Dispersed departments can add to the problem: it is more difficult to pool knowledge of goings on when departments do not work closely together. In WorldCom, where the finance and legal functions were scattered over several states, communications were poor and employees lacked the support to question the actions of the CFO, Scott Sullivan.

Changing the organizational structure can often leave gaps in information flow and responsibilities until the new one matures. Vital data can be overlooked. At Marconi, for example, when responsibility was delegated to division heads and the system of ratios and trend lines put in place by former CEO Arnold Weinstock was abandoned, the result was that the deterioration in the working capital position was not addressed early enough.

Remote operations, far from head office, are often difficult to manage since head office is heavily reliant on local management and cannot always judge whether correct and sufficient information has been transmitted. This is a particular problem with new, or unfamiliar, operations such as in the cases of Barings and Ahold and, earlier, at Daiwa Bank and Showa Shell.[19]

A fundamental contributor to control failure is a weak, or ineffective, internal audit function. Often this is regarded as an expensive and unnecessary overhead. As a result, in many companies, such as Barings and WorldCom, the function is understaffed and has chosen, or been forced, to perform mostly operational audits with the objective of uncovering potential cost savings rather than financial audits with the objective of safeguarding company assets. A recurring feature is poor cash control: At Marconi the spiraling level of working capital was not detected and dealt with early enough; at WorldCom, revenue was more important than collecting debts; at Enron, profit over the life of a contract was more important than the fact that it made losses and consumed cash in its early years.

A CFO without a professional accounting qualification (Andrew Fastow at Enron; Michiel Meurs at Ahold) is a significant additional risk factor. Bankers, or for that matter MBAs (even with a finance specialization), do not have the broad range of skills to oversee the finances of a large company and certainly not ones as complex as Enron and Ahold.

In many cases, inappropriate financial structures have played a part. Tanzi's desire for Parmalat to remain a family-controlled company precluded the issue of new shares to fund acquisitions, and instead it relied upon bond issues. In the Enron case, it was a desire not to dilute earnings per share (EPS) – and thus the share price and value of executive options – which gave rise to the same tactic. Thereafter, both companies suffered under heavy debt burdens and manipulated their accounts to disguise the effects of these tactics.

5. Making such failures less likely

There is a massive literature on improving corporate governance from the point of view of policy and strategy – ranging from improving third party,

---

[19] In 1995, Daiwa Bank (Japanese) revealed accumulated losses of US$1.1bn, run up by a trader in US treasury bonds over an eleven-year period. Similarly, Showa Shell, a Japanese associate company of Royal Dutch/Shell saw losses of US $1.5bn accumulate between 1989 and 1993 as a result of unauthorized trading in foreign exchange futures.

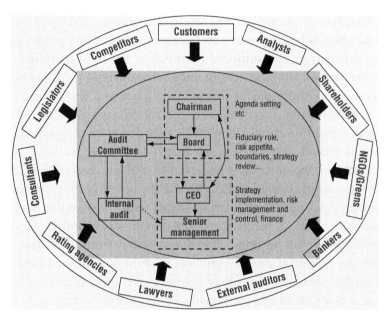

Figure 5.2: Forces affecting the financial health of companies

multilateral audit mechanisms, processes for enhancing shareholder activism to policies for increasing the efficiency in markets for corporate controls.[20] Figure 5.2 lists multiple factors that affect the financial health of the corporation. This chapter focused on the interplay between the board, the CEO and senior executives – three groups that have clear and separate roles to play. In each of the examples cited, the board has failed in its responsibilities to the shareholders and other stakeholders. Too often cronyism has been evident; the directors have not had the necessary knowledge or specific industry experience required to make an effective contribution; and in most cases have allowed themselves to be dominated by the CEO. Two general and rather practical sets of recommendations emerge from these accounts:

Back to basics – Separating operations from monitoring

The chairman should set the agenda for board meetings, in consultation with the CEO, and appropriate papers should be sent out to directors in good time

[20] See among others Hertig, G. (2006) On-going board reforms, *Oxford Review of Economic Policy*, 21(2), 269–82; Jensen, M., Murphy, K. (2004) *Remuneration*, ECGI Financial Working Paper No. 44/2004 available at www.ecgi.org/wp; Kraakmann, R. (2004) Disclosure and corporate governance. In G. Ferrarini *et al.* (eds.) *Reforming company and take-over law in Europe*, Oxford: Oxford University Press; Romano, R. (2005) The Sarbanes-Oxley Act and the making of quack corporate governance, *Yale Law Journal*, 114(7), 1521–611.

so that they can properly prepare for the meeting. An effective board which reviews strategy plans and questions management thoroughly should act, at the very least, as a brake on poor decision making, and at best be a positive force, using its wider vision and experience to direct the company onto the most profitable path.

The roles of chairman and CEO should not be combined. One key task of the chairman should be to assess the CEO's performance in running the company. This is impossible if he is the CEO himself. Furthermore, a retiring CEO should not step up to the chairman's position, as this risks emasculating or at least overshadowing the new incumbent, or, conversely, limits the independence of monitoring.

A competent audit committee is essential to ensure that the appropriate internal controls are in place and working adequately; to ensure that company financial statements give a true and fair view of the company's affairs; and to appoint, oversee and, if necessary, remove, external auditors.

Aligning executive pay

Executive compensation packages should be designed to encourage long-term thinking with a focus on long-term achievement plus some penalty for poor performance. The granting of share options, which are just a one-way bet, should be avoided. If share options are used, they should be expensed immediately. A better incentive scheme would involve restrictive shares, whose value can go down as well as up. Awards based, partially at least, on relative performance – say, on how the share price moves relative to an index of its peers – would avoid the problem of excessive, or negligible, rewards because of general improving, or deteriorating, market conditions and these should be conditional on their being held for a minimum of a year after the beneficiary (CEO or other senior executive) has left the company (apart from any sale necessary to pay tax on the award) or, if still with the company, until a suitable period, perhaps three years, has elapsed. Guaranteed bonuses, which are simply salary by another name, should be eliminated, and all executives should be on no more than an annual rolling contract, except in very special circumstances such as inducing individuals to assist a company to emerge from Chapter 11. Company perks such as private use of airplanes should be disclosed in annual reports at their pre-tax value.

While it is impossible, and indeed not desirable, to entirely remove greed and the desire for power from CEOs' ambitions, compensation packages that focus on long-term performance should reduce their incentive to increase short-term earnings at the expense of the long-term health of the company.

This might act as a curb on making reckless acquisitions, since they would need to deliver the promised performance before the CEO could benefit. In 2002, in response to a public outcry, the US Congress passed the Sarbanes-Oxley Act (SOX) in the biggest shake-up of corporate regulation since the 1930s. Once again, scandal had forced the regulators to act, a pattern dating back to the early nineteenth century.[21] The act has four main thrusts: the implementation or improvement of internal controls (the, by now, infamous section 404); the independence of non-executive directors; and the requirement that directors explicitly recognize their responsibility for the company's financial statements. There is also a requirement to provide support for "whistle-blowing" for concerned (or, as feared, disgruntled) employees. In addition, SOX prohibits auditing firms from providing many other services to their audit clients to prevent conflicts of interest.

Of course, SOX is in addition to the existing listing requirements and regulations of the exchanges and the SEC. Furthermore, SOX is in part enabling legislation with many of the detailed rules delegated to the Public Company Accounting Standards Oversight Board (PCAOB).[22]

In the UK and some other countries, a less prescriptive route has been chosen with the emphasis on voluntary compliance with a code of good practice[23] and the requirement of those companies not following it in any specific regard to explain why not. The proponents of this "comply or explain" approach claim that it is less rigid and easier to adapt to changing circumstances.

Predictably, these various codes and requirements, especially SOX, have received widespread criticism. Many companies are finding compliance to be expensive and onerous and doubt the effectiveness of it all.

While some requirements amount to little more than "box ticking," or ensuring that procedures are adequately documented, the general thrust of these codes, by encouraging greater director independence and better all-round controls, has validity.

Regrettably, the passing of legislation like the Sarbanes-Oxley Act will do little to prevent future corporate failures, as it cannot address the underlying causes. Conversely, in the process, by focusing on accounting controls, SOX has undeservedly enriched the very accounting firms who were, in part, culpable in the recent disasters. None of this will prevent companies pursuing

---

[21] Banner, S., (1997) *What causes new securities regulation? 300 years of evidence*, 75 Wash ULQ 849.
[22] See PCAOB (2004) *Auditing standard No. 2: An audit of internal control over financial reporting performed in conjunction with an audit of financial statements.*
[23] E.g. Financial Reporting Council (London, June 2006) *The combined code on corporate governance.*

flawed strategies or making poor acquisitions. Nor will it rein in the overly ambitious and greedy CEO unless there is a strong, knowledgeable and challenging board.

In any case, no legislation or corporate structure will ultimately offer sufficient safeguards. One simply cannot define and legislate for the independence of non-executive directors – in the way that most of the new codes require. More than financial autonomy, independence is a state of mind, the willingness to ask the tough questions, walk away if not satisfied and force companies to explain the sudden departure of board members. Similarly, it is not possible to impose external limits to "excessive" greed. But if one cannot legislate for a direct, rigorous monitoring attitude or financial moderation, how can they become reliable norms as the ultimate reference of effective corporate governance?

6 Tackling healthcare fraud!?

Ralf Boscheck

Aiming to contain vast and fast rising expenditure levels, estimated to amount to 8.2% of GDP across OECD countries in 2003, national healthcare reforms cannot avoid rationing, that is withholding beneficial interventions from needy individuals.[1] Yet, a substantial part of a nation's healthcare spending is typically diverted in illicit ways – rendering otherwise feasible care unattainable and undermining the legitimacy of private and public services. In the US, healthcare fraud and abuse reportedly accounts for around 10% of total outlay, i.e. $120bn per year.[2] In the UK, prescription crime in 2003 was estimated to amount to £115 m. In Lower Saxony, one of Germany's 16 Länder, insurance fraud alone accounted for €40 m in 2003. But cases are not always clear cut and are not always easily dealt with. There is often substantial ambiguity in defining actually improper conduct, identifying such behaviour among vast numbers of cases that are handled annually, telling errors apart from criminal intent, and choosing adequate regulatory responses.

Four classes of corruption in healthcare are typically distinguished:[3] *bribes* may be paid to get access to better service (demand-side) or service contracts (supply-side). Some of these, such as kickbacks and fee-splitting for referrals, may be induced by receivers who are deliberately not delivering services or decisions; others may be given to enable otherwise impossible service provision; others again may involve a gratitude payment to ensure better treatment in the future. *Theft* ranges from pilfering supplies, to so-called "creeping privatisation," that is the use of public equipment, supplies and

---

[1] For most recent data see www.kff.org/insurance/snapshot/chcm010307oth.cfm, last visited February 20, 2007.

[2] See Hyman, D. A., (2001) Health care fraud and abuse: Market change, social norms, and the trust "reposed in the workmen", *Journal of Legal Studies*, Volume 30 (2), 531–68.

[3] See, for example, Ensor, T., Duran-Moreno, A., (2002) Corruption as a challenge to effective regulation in the health sector. In Saltman, R. B. *et al.* (2002) (eds.) *Regulating entrepreneurial behavior in health care*, Buckingham: Open University Press, pp. 106–124; World Bank (1997) *Helping countries combat corruption*, Washington, D.C.: World Bank.

> ## Box 6.1: The Webster's Encyclopedic Unabridged Dictionary of the English Language defines:
>
> **Corruption:** n. the act or state of corrupting or of being corrupt. 2. moral perversion and depravity. 3. pervasion of integrity. 4. corrupt or dishonest proceedings. 5. bribery. 6. debasement or alteration as of language or a text. 7. a debased form of a word. 8. putrefactive decay; rottenness. 9. any corrupting influence or agency. – Synonym: abandon, dissolution, immorality, baseness, dishonesty, rot, putrefaction, putrescence, foulness, pollution, contamination, Antonym : purity, honesty.
>
> **Fraud:** n. 1. deceit, trickery, sharp practice, or breach of confidence used to gain some unfair or dishonest advantage. 2. a particular instance of such deceit or trickery: mail fraud, election frauds. 3. any deceit, trickery or humbug: That book is a fraud and waste of time. 4. a person who makes deceitful pretences; impostor.
>
> **Cunningness:** n. shrewdness, artfulness, wiliness, trickery, finesse, intrigue, slyness, deception.
>
> **Legitimacy:** n. the state or quality of being legitimate. Legitimate: 1. according to law. 2. in accordance with established rules, principles or standards.

time to offer private service, to large-scale misappropriation of public money. *Bureaucratic and political corruption* describes cases of abuse of office to maintain political posts and/or channel funds into private businesses. *Misinformation for private gain* may involve activities resulting in patients consuming more or less than the optimal amount of care, or in reclassifying patients into more attractive reimbursement categories. It may also entail the collusion of practitioners with patients or pharmacists against payer organisations, or patients making false claims on insurance premium forms.

Given its economic impact, healthcare fraud attracts a lot of political attention. The National Healthcare Anti-fraud Association in Washington, DC estimates that with $100 m spent on anti-healthcare fraud campaigns in the US in 2001, the government recovered $1.2bn of ill-gotten gains. In Britain, the National Health Service (NHS) maintains a 200-strong anti-fraud team. The German government operates a specialized police force investigating healthcare fraud and its 2003/4 healthcare reform obliged the country's 350 sickness funds to set up similarly specialized investigative units. Yet, there is also growing concern about the dangers of over-regulation. Law-abiding and professional healthcare providers may react cynically to growing levels of public interference in what they may perceive to be a traditionally trust-based system of private self-regulation. As a result, they may shun any type of discretion and decide to follow the letter, rather than the spirit of agreements. What would be the components of a viable system of healthcare governance and how would one assess its performance? How would that ideal system deal with the following cases?

Case 1: *Up-coding* fertility?[4]

On January 9, 2001, Niels H. Lauersen, 64, a well-known Manhattan obstetrician was convicted of defrauding insurance companies. He had billed them for gynaecological procedures that were covered by policies while in fact performing fertility treatments which were not covered. The trial's outcome was expected to set a precedent regarding costly procedures that are rarely covered by payers – something women had challenged in other courts. In New York, insurance companies must cover all gynaecological problems deemed medically correctable, but they are not obliged to cover procedures that are intended strictly to induce pregnancy. The lawyers for Dr Lauersen and his anaesthesiologist, Dr Magda Binion, who was tried with him and convicted on similar charges, said they would appeal and that the verdict had "disturbing social implications."

Dr Lauersen had a thriving Park Avenue practice and a celebrity clientele. But as malpractice lawsuits mounted against him, he was forced to resign from one New York City hospital. In 1999 he had been indicted on healthcare fraud and conspiracy but the charges ended in a mistrial. In this case, prosecutors said the doctor not only billed for services he had not delivered but had also urged some patients to lie about their care. In two cases it was claimed that he had urged patients to lie to a federal grand jury. In his defence, Dr Lauersen's lawyer argued that he often had done dual procedures, correcting ailments that impeded fertility, as well as carrying out fertility treatment. Also, he stated that Dr Lauersen often had swallowed the loss when insurances would not pay for the treatments, and that it was immoral of the companies not to pay. The doctor denied tampering with witnesses. Prosecutors argued that the doctor made at least $2.5m from 1987 to 1997 from "phantom procedures," and, regarding the defence of charity, "his cause may have been noble but that's not the point."

Prosecution relied heavily on a former anaesthesiologist for Dr Lauersen who testified about his role in the billing in exchange for a lesser punishment.

---

[4] Based on Steinhauer, J., Day, S., (2001) Doctor convicted of insurance fraud in fertility procedures, *The New York Times*, January 10, 2001, p. 1, col. 3.

That doctor had admitted a lengthy history of drug abuse, as well as other attempts to defraud the government, such as draft dodging.

Different from Dr Lauersen's first trial, jurors, five men and seven women, seemed to get along well. Former patients of Dr Lauersen's made regular appearances at his first trial, many with babies in tow, and one even approached a juror and was harshly admonished. In this trial, patients showed up for closing arguments and the verdict. As the foreman was preparing to read the verdict, a row of people whom Dr Lauersen described as friends, relatives and patients were sitting close together, clutching one another's hands. Some of them began to cry quietly, while one young woman sobbed.

Dr Lauersen and Dr Binion each faced maximum possible sentences of five years in prison on a conspiracy charge, ten years on a healthcare fraud charge, and five years each on mail fraud charges. Dr Lauersen also faced a maximum sentence of five years on false statement charges, and ten years for each count of witness tampering.

Case 2: Kick-backs *or* arbitrage – Globudent?[5]

In June 2003, prosecutors in Wuppertal, Germany were investigating 450 dentists and 22 staff of Globudent, a medical supplier that allegedly paid illegal kickbacks worth at least €8.9 m to dentists who used dentures, which the company had imported cheaply from China. Globudent was assumed to have reaped profits of up to €700 for each set of dentures that were charged to health funds at high German prices. Company executives then supposedly gave 20–30% of this to the dentists involved – often in envelopes stuffed with cash. About 95,000 dentists' bills were being examined.

Although this was considered to be the biggest scandal in recent years, investigators were looking into more than sixty similar cases involving dentists and dental laboratories importing dentures from Bangkok, Thailand, Morocco, Jordan, Hungary, and China at prices up to 80% below the German level.

In a bid to avoid further scandals, the national dentists' association and health funds signed an agreement in February 2003 under which dentists could claim only "for costs that they actually incur". Meanwhile, the founders of Globudent, while still on bail, re-established their business operations under a new name, again offering cheap dentures from China.

---

[5] Based on Williamson, H., (2003) Corruption is "plaguing" German health industry; *Financial Times*, June 12, 2003.

In Germany, fraud commonly arises from secret deals between doctors and medical suppliers, who conspire to inflate their medical bills. In addition, relationships between doctors, hospitals, medical suppliers, drug companies and chemists tend to be loosely defined, with few independently monitored control mechanisms.

Jörg Engelhard, head of Medicus, a special Berlin-based police team investigating health fraud, added: "The doctors' payment system is based on trust: doctors have to control themselves, because other control mechanisms hardly exist. The increase in fraud represents a breakdown of this trust." Manfred Richter-Reichhelm, chairman of the doctors' main lobby group – the 100,000 strong, self-governing KBV – admitted that the way doctors charge for their work is "not exactly opaque but is certainly problematic – it leaves lots of room for maneuver. We are trying to deal with this gray zone."

Case 3: Confessions of a managed care medical director

On May 30, 1996, Dr Linda Peeno delivered the following statement along with a written testimony to a hearing of the US Congress Commerce Subcommittee on Health and the Environment on "Contracting Issues and Quality Standards for Managed Care."[6]

"My name is Linda Peeno, and although the witness list does not reflect this, I am a physician. I am a former medical director and medical reviewer. I did the job that was referred to repeatedly in the first panel as a physician manager for three health care organizations. I currently, though, primarily work in medical and health care ethics.

I am here primarily today to make a public confession. In the spring of 1987, as a physician, I denied a man a necessary operation that would have saved his life and thus caused his death. No person and no group has held me accountable for this because, in fact, what I did was I saved the company a half a million dollars for this. And furthermore, this particular act secured my reputation as a good medical director, and it ensured my advancement in the health care industry; in little more than a year, I went from making a few hundred dollars per week to an annual six-figure income.

---

[6] US House of Representatives' Committee on Commerce, Subcommittee on Health and Environment, chaired by Michael Bilirakis. Her entire testimony can be found at the National Coalition of Mental Health Professionals and Consumers (www.nomanagedcare.org/DrPeenotestimony.html), last visited November 21, 2006.

In all my work, I had one primary duty and that was to use my medical expertise for the financial benefit of the organization for which I worked and according to the managed care industry... [In the managed care industry] it is not an ethical issue to sacrifice a human being for a savings, no matter how those savings occur. And I was repeatedly told that I was not denying care. I was simply denying payment.

I am not an ethicist whose primary background has come from the books. For me, the ethical issues were born in the trenches and pit of the pain that I have come to realize that I cause. And if I am an expert here today, it is because I know how managed care maims and kills patients. So I am here to tell you about the dirty work of managed care and this is the kind of straight talk that I wish Ms Ignagni [President and CEO of the American Association of Health Plans] could hear now.

Now, let me explain to you the ways that I was a good medical director. I was regularly consulted by marketing on ways to change expensive benefits or change the language to give me loopholes to make denials when requests came. For example in one plan, we were able to structure our investigational language exclusion so that I was often able to use it to deny almost anything that was expensive, and particularly out-of-network requests.

I turned preexisting exclusions into a game as I tried to connect almost any prior medical complaint or visit as a reason to deny payment. There are many more things that I could tell you about, but, ultimately I was only as 'good' – and I put that in quotation marks – as the doctors in my network, for it was their numbers that I needed to prove that I was doing my job.

That meant that I did whatever it took to control them: intimidation, hassling, humiliation, I have done it all. I have used inadequate and inaccurate data to create reports to get doctors to make their numbers better, in other words, decrease their usage. I have used 'economic credentialling' to select the best inexpensive physicians and rarely correlated these with quality factors.

I have helped design contract provisions to ensure our payment and monitoring schemes got the results we wanted at the plan, and I have threatened de-selection to numerous physicians who were especially difficult or costly.

However, there is one last activity that I think deserves a special place in this list. This is what I call the 'smart bomb' of cost containment and that is medical necessity denials. Let me take you to the heart of managed care.

Even if a plan denies using all the other things that I could list, it is impossible for them to deny their use of this practice because it is vital to managed care; that is making medical decisions about access, availability, and use. And even when medical criteria are used, it is rarely developed in any kind of standard traditional clinical processes. It is rarely standardized across the field. The criteria are rarely available for prior review by physicians or the members of the plan. So, even if a plan has a clear benefit package and has all the perks, like free eye exams or free screening tests for cancer, and other marketing ploys, the member's physician will never be the final authority on what his or her patient will get.

This might go unnoticed for simple needs, like a regular office visit or a bout of the 'flu, but I can tell you that when something unexpected or expensive happens, it is like a bucolic pasture turned battlefield. The land mines will start exploding everywhere.

And somewhere in every coverage booklet for every managed care plan is a claim that establishes the plan as the final authority for medical necessity. What that means is that there is some physician at some plan doing what I did. That person rarely is continuing a clinical practice. They are sitting behind a desk making decisions about a patient they will never see or touch, completely removed from the consequences of their decisions. They are getting paid by someone to make decisions for the benefit of the plan and not for the benefit of the members.

I would like to conclude by saying, what kind of system have we created when a physician can receive a lucrative income for adding to the suffering of patients? I became a physician to care for, not bring harm to, my patients, and I am haunted by the thousands of pieces of paper on which I have written that deadly word, 'denial' Thank you."

On its website, the US Citizen Council on Healthcare[7] adds the concluding statement of Dr. Peeno's prepared written testimony.

"I contend that managed care, as it has become, can exist only through serious ethical transgressions against individuals and society. Furthermore, I contend that a health plan's resistance to ethical correctives is proportionate to its reliance on ethical transgressions for its 'success.' Disclosure and exposure would present serious disadvantages in competition for cost-cutting and profit making. In summary, it is a fair assessment to claim that managed care's 'success' depends upon the following:

- use of non-medical agendas to drive medical policies and practice;
- collapsing of the rights of individuals for purported greater collectivist goals;

---

[7] www.cchc-mn.org.

- super-session of the care of the individual by the care of the collective;
- creation of poor relationships between professional ambitions and the absence of moral inhibitions;
- reliance upon righteous ideologies about reform and societal benefits coupled with cost-cutting policies;
- disparagement of the 'weaker' (i.e. costly) groups within society;
- linkage of economic imperatives and professional self-interest;
- direction of medical professionals by parameters set by health care and financial administrators;
- establishment of quotas and internal processes for control with little regard for the physical and psychological cost of their effects;
- selection of professionals who are ideological converts and 'good' practitioners of its goals;
- enticement of physicians as agents of an organization, so that organizational goals are supplied with medical validation;
- facilitation of unethical professional practice by financial rewards and bonuses, as well as job security and advancement;
- generation of moral void by use of propaganda;
- degradation of moral expressions of compassion and sympathy for persons who have been designated costly or needy;
- induction of guilt into those who are made to feel a drain on resources or a threat to the collectivist goals.

The list could go on, however, there is enough here to suggest a drastic need for change. Of course, each of these points would be vehemently contested by the managed care industry. If they are inaccurate, then it seems that the industry should have no reservations about supporting transparent and publicly accountable activities.

We know, though, they do object to this. Why? Because control of patients and doctors depends upon unethical practices. To this, at least, we should object. Manipulation and exploitation for any reason, even beneficence, is unethical and destructive of social good.

We have enough evidence from history to demonstrate the consequences of secretive, unregulated systems which go awry. The list above is not new. In fact, it comes from a book detailing the characteristics of a dire period of recent history.[8]

---

[8] Burleigh, M., (1994) *Death and deliverance: "Euthanasia" in Germany 1900–1945*, Cambridge: Cambridge University Press.

The last time this combination of forces worked in concert, over 200,000 individuals lost their lives in Nazi Germany (even before the Final Solution). Most of these persons were German citizens sacrificed for medical reasons set by economic and social agendas. I find the parallels chilling. One can only wonder: how much pain, suffering and death will we have before we have the courage to change our course?

Personally, I have decided even one death is too much for me".

A brief note on moral standards

Debating these or similar cases calls for separating disagreements over facts (how many abortions were administered?), concepts (is a fetus a human person?) and moral judgment (is abortion right or wrong?). Also legality does not imply morality, just as illegality does not imply immorality. But are there moral standards for what is good and right? And if so, how are they to be applied in practice?

Morality should not be confused with norms shared by a group of people. It is a neutral standard of behaviour that is rationally justified, and consciously and consistently applied across a variety of circumstances. Two main types of moral justification, based on teleological vs. deontological reasoning, relate to the benefits that stem from a given act vs. the respect for persons regardless of consequence.

Ethical relativists believe that moral principles are valid relative to culture or class, (conventional or cultural relativism) or individual choice (subjective relativism), i.e. that there is no universal moral truth. Also, even if absolute standards were to exist, teleological moral skeptics would hold that one may never know what they are, so why live pretending to be guided by them? Conversely, moral absolutism claims that, even if individuals and societies deal differently with a given concern, this does not necessarily mean that there are no absolute moral standards (as claimed by ontological moral skeptics). One simply may not have discovered them yet. Or one may simply avoid facing up to moral dilemmas and the need to identify some overarching principle by claiming that morals are relative.

So, while for a deontologist like Kant, insisting on "rules that have no exceptions", lying to save the life of an innocent is still wrong, a utilitarian consequentialist is apt to justify it as a lesser evil, and an ethical egoist would favor the behavior that would suit him best. It is the underlying ethical theory that, like any meta-rule, shapes the application of absolute ethical standards in line with circumstance. Moral behavior requires conscious, rational and consistent choice – not the agreement of others. Again, some may argue that absolute moral standards need to be absolutely applied.

A utilitarian analysis of a moral question involves identifying who will be affected by it, establishing the effects of alternative action on the same audience, and finally deciding which decision would lead to the greatest overall utility. There is an evident concern that utilitarianism may cause injustice to certain individuals and that those who lose out ought to be compensated. It could be argued that this is partly anticipated in deontological reasoning which applies principles of universality and reciprocity to ensure respect for individuals.[9] But, superimposing one's own standard of judgment onto a group may result in overly permissive or restrictive outcomes for its average member. Therefore one may disaggregate issues and standards and may even think of individuals as possessing a hierarchy of rights, from the most elementary and vital to those related to the total fulfillment of one's overall potential. Insisting that an individual's rights may only be overridden to protect another individual's more basic right (rather than to increase some abstract level of utility),[10] a rights-based assessment of alternative actions would then compare the seriousness of the actual or potential rights infringement that may be involved.

In this context, it is important to note that there are no inalienable patient rights. Although the World Health Organization (WHO) identifies a range of conceptualizations of patient rights and implied differences in provider-patient relations,[11] the question is to what extent patients have the legal standing to enforce their patient rights – and patient rights to what?[12]

Patient rights may be formulated in three ways: as "legal rights" they pertain to well-defined areas and have no limitations related to resources. If violation occurs, patients can appeal to judicial authorities for compensation and sanctions. "Quasi-rights" are performance targets or framework conditions obliging healthcare providers subject to available resources at a given

---

[9] In its simplest from this is expressed in the "Golden Rule": "Do unto others as you would have them do unto you."

[10] See most importantly, Gewirth, A., (1999) *Self-fulfilment*, Princeton: Princeton University Press.

[11] In its "paternalistic model", for example, "the best interest of the patient, as judged by the clinical experts, is valued above the provision of comprehensive medical information and decision-making power to the patient." By contrast, the "informative model", "sees patients as consumers who are best to judge what is in their own interest, and thus view the doctors chiefly as provider of information." See www.who.int/genomics/public/patientrights/en/print.html.

[12] See Boscheck, R., (2004) Healthcare rationing and patient rights, *Intereconomics*, Nov./Dec. 2004, 310–313;

point in time. Non-legal policy documents, such as patient charters, formulate mere "moral commitments". Comparing national standards, patient rights in cases of malpractice and injury are generally more widely recognized than any right to treatment. Legal redress in case of malpractice can hardly ever be directed against professionals, only against provider organizations. Here, judicial proceedings are not geared towards establishing guilt but instead aim to compensate the injured patient and to accumulate knowledge to preempt injuries in the future. The "legal right" to treatment is even more limited and is largely restricted to particularly vulnerable groups, such as the disabled. For anyone else, real economic limits abolish any pretense of inalienable rights to treatment.[13]

In Europe, the conflict between ambitions and resources is clear. Not even Nordic countries, at the forefront of care guarantees, offer any legal right to treatment. Although patient rights are enshrined in some Eastern European constitutions, their application and enforcement is limited to rare cases of "ministerial regulation." The UK Patient's Charter mentions a limited number of patient rights related to access, quality assurance, and complaint management. But the Charter does not confer legally enforceable patient rights and does not provide for any external monitoring and enforcement.[14] In Germany, patient rights have no explicit legal standing. Civil law has established individual rights in some of these cases, but they may be restricted by the social security system.

The US model of decentralized healthcare governance would require patients to be given proper legal standing. Recognizing this, the Clinton Administration's Consumer Bill of Rights and Responsibilities, issued in March 1998, was to strengthen the patient's role in the healthcare system. Since then, its underlying principles have spawned a plethora of divergent Patients' Bills of Rights offered by states, providers, health plans, and patient groups. But operational standards and enforcement mechanisms are often ill-defined and not every state that endorses a Patients' Bill of Rights also adopts the necessary complementary legislation and administrative guidance. The debate surrounding the US Patient Protection Act and the Supreme Court's intention to open up the patient-doctor relationship for review is unlikely to establish any right to treatment.

---

[13] Silver, M., (1997) Patients' rights in England and the United States, *Journal of Medical Ethics*, 23(4), 213–21. Fong, T., Tieman, J., (2004) Politics front and center, *Modern Healthcare*, 34(2), 26–9.
[14] See Halford, J., (2001) Patient's rights, public law and the Human Rights Act, *Consumer Policy Review*, 4, 118–25.

Watchdog and proxy war campaigns against firms

Michael Yaziji

Firms are increasingly facing campaigns by nongovernmental organizations (NGOs) over a broad range of issues such as the environment, labor, human rights, consumer rights and animal rights. The number of international NGOs has increased by 400% in the last decade and the number of mentions of NGOs in the *Wall Street Journal* has increased twenty-fold during this period. Corporate managers often fail to appreciate the deeper dynamics behind these campaigns and, as a result, respond to them in ineffective or even counterproductive ways. These managers are also often surprised at how effective small – and often ideologically radical – NGOs can be in tackling much larger firms. In this chapter I will (1) differentiate between two very different types of campaigns – watchdog campaigns and proxy war campaigns, which need to be understood and responded to in very different ways; (2) explain how it is that these small "David" NGOs can beat "Goliath" corporations; and (3) provide some guidance for managers on how to avoid and respond to these campaigns. The discussion presented here draws on three years of qualitative research including interviews, case studies and a large-scale global survey of NGOs that have campaigned against firms.[1]

1. Differentiating watchdog campaigns from proxy war campaigns

Early neo-institutional theory focused on how organizations, in order to gain and maintain the legitimacy necessary to survive, must conform to institutional demands in the form of norms and rules.[2,3] While institutions are

---

[1] For more detailed information on the research results and research methods, see Yaziji, M., (2004) *Institutional change and social risk: A study of campaigns by social movement organizations against firms*, Fontainebleau: INSEAD.

[2] DiMaggio, P. J., Powell, W. W., (1983) The iron cage revisited: Institutional isomorphism and collective rationality in organizational fields, *American Sociological Review*, 48(2), 147–60; Meyer, J. W., Rowan, B., (1977) Institutionalized organizations: Formal structure as myth and ceremony, *American Journal of Sociology*, 83(2), 340–63.

[3] For more of an introduction on institutions, please see Chapter 17 in this book.

broad and often diffuse, institutional pressure must ultimately be brought to bear on organizations by other organizations that give expression to institutional norms. These "institutionally expressive" organizations might be governmental bodies, professional associations or nongovernmental watchdog or advocacy groups. In its most elementary structural form, a single institutionally expressive organization puts "institutional" pressure on a single organization. An example of this is a regulatory body fining a firm for failing to meet federal environmental guidelines. In some cases, this pressure is applied blindly or "impersonally," i.e. without regard to differences in institutionally neutral attributes of the organization. For example, only hospitals that meet a certain explicit set of requirements will be granted accreditation by a given accrediting agency.

In other cases, however, the institutional pressure is applied strategically. This is the case in NGO campaigns against corporations. The NGO behind the institutional pressure will apply pressure strategically, carefully choosing the target and tactics that it will employ depending on the goals it is trying to achieve.

The advocacy campaigning organizations that carry out these campaigns are institutionally proactive in that they either hold firms accountable to dominant institutional norms, or they pursue institutional change through their campaigns against firms. Critically, these two categories of campaigns – holding firms accountable to dominant institutional norms and pursuing institutional change – are fundamentally different. These two different types of campaigns – "watchdog" and "proxy war" campaigns – have different goals, often select their targets differently, use different kinds of rhetoric with different audiences, and use different kinds of tactics. In the sections that follow I will highlight the differences between these two types of campaigns along these dimensions.[4]

Watchdog campaigns

A watchdog campaign is one in which the goal is to pressure the targeted firm to *comply* with dominant institution standards. These standards may or may not be formalized in regulation. Watchdog campaigns are often run by local organizations that are responding to a perceived threat or harm to their local

---

[4] These two sorts of campaigns are "ideal types" and in reality there is a continuum between the two. Nonetheless, as we shall see, there are some important qualitative differences between the two that need to be appreciated for practical as well as theoretical reasons.

interests. An example of such campaigns would be a local NGO campaigning against a firm for its local impact, such as polluting a local river in violation of existing normative and/or regulative standards. These campaigns fit within the category of "isomorphic pressure" described by early neo-institutional scholars.[5]

Watchdog target selection

NGOs engaged in watchdog campaigns select their target firms most commonly because (1) the NGO perceives the firm to be infringing upon local *interests* through its specific actions; and (2) there is a plausible story to be told about how these activities are in violation of accepted regulatory and/or social standards.

Watchdog rhetoric and audience

NGOs running watchdog campaigns accept, and draw on, the dominant institutions, in terms of both the content of the rhetoric and the key audiences. In these campaigns the NGOs do not want to change the institutional standards, but merely to better enforce them; the message is institutionally conservative. The campaigning NGO has the potential to appeal to a wide audience (since it is drawing on broadly accepted norms) including judicial, legislative, and regulatory bodies.

In the case of isomorphic pressure campaigns, the *rhetoric* and framing of the complaint against the targeted organization is often in terms of specific violations of existing standards by the targeted organization. Whether the institutional standards are formalized as regulations or not, these standards will be invoked as the appropriate measure by which the activity of the firm can be judged. In cases where formal regulatory standards exist, the existing standards are assumed to be the appropriate bases of evaluation. The campaigning NGO will make claims to the effect that the targeted firm is in violation of these regulations.

Where there are no specific regulatory standards related to the activity of the firm, terms like "accepted community standards" will be invoked. An example of this would be a campaign against a firm for its perceived "tasteless advertising." In such a case, the campaigning organization may recognize that regulation is either impossible or is not needed. The rhetoric will focus on

---

[5] See DiMaggio, P. J., Powell, W. W., (1983).

demands for the firm to change its advertising practices, and claims will be made to the effect that the advertising is in violation of what is considered decent by the community.

With respect to targeted *audiences* in isomorphic campaigns, we would expect – in cases where there are formal enforcement systems – that regulators and other enforcement agencies and professional associations would be key audiences for the campaign. In the "purest" watchdog campaigns, courts would be used in cases where the issue is a "question of fact" rather than a "question of law." A campaigning organization may use the courts to enforce particular regulatory requirements, e.g. to get a court injunction for a particular type of behavior or to fine the targeted organization. They would not need to argue that the laws need further refinement, only that the facts of the case fall under the purview of a given law.

In cases where there are informal enforcement mechanisms, we would expect the campaigning organization to target its rhetoric to both members of the firm – to tap into their sense of shame – and broader society and other stakeholders that can apply pressure on the firm through social opprobrium and/or withholding of resources. For instance, in the "tasteless advertising" example above, the company may be shamed into complying with demands and third-party stakeholders, such as banks, may be more hesitant to do business with the offending firm.

Watchdog tactics

Tactics can be described by the degree to which they use existing political, legal and regulatory institutions to attain the ends sought, and by how broadly accepted they are within the community at large. We can thereby identify three different categories of tactics. First, lawsuits, lobbying of regulators and lobbying of politicians are tactics which can be described as "highly institutional"; second, press conferences, rallies and marches might be considered "institutionally neutral" in that they rely less on political, legal and regulatory institutions, but do not contravene these institutions; finally, civil disobedience, direct action to disrupt businesses and streets, destruction of property and violence are all tactics which, generally being illegal, can be labeled as "contra-institutional."

The tactics employed in watchdog campaigns tend to be "highly institutional" and/or "institutionally neutral." The tactics often draw on established sources of institutional power, which are, after all, institutionally aligned with the goals of the campaign and may include for example, appeals to courts and regulatory bodies. Mainstream and moderate advocacy organizations will tend to have more access to, and reliance upon, the resources housed within the dominant institutional bodies. Furthermore, more radical tactics will be more likely to alienate the institutionally conservative audiences that are being targeted, thus the NGO will be loath to use legitimacy-threatening radical tactics.

Proxy war campaigns

Proxy war – also called "social movement" – campaigns are designed to challenge and change the institutional framework, whether in terms of the formal regulatory and legal systems or accepted social norms and values. As carriers of a challenging ideology, the social movement organizations (SMOs, a subcategory of NGOs) behind a campaign often engage in *institutional proxy campaigns* in which opposing institutions generate a proxy conflict between organizations which strategically interact to promote, sustain or represent the opposing institutions.[6] In proxy war campaigns the goals of the targeting organization are: (1) to extend the application of the campaigning organization's own "home" institutions (whether values or regulations) to a new context; (2) to delegitimize the competing institution; and/or (3) to establish a meta-institutional rule that holds that the home institution dominates or takes precedence over the competing institution in cases where the two institutions are in apparent conflict. All proxy wars concern the truth, appropriateness, applicability and importance of the beliefs, norms and values in conflict.

While the campaign appears to the casual observer to be a conflict between two organizations, it is, at a deeper level, actually an expression of a broader conflict over norms, values and regulatory environments, in short, institutions. This is represented in the figure below.

This framing is highly generalizable. A timely example concerns what Samuel Huntington calls a "clash of civilizations" which is reified through proxy wars between organizations such as al-Qaeda and the US intelligence and defense departments. Other examples include campaigns over free trade and globalization, and civil rights campaigns in the 1950s–70s.[7]

---

[6] NGO is a term of art and can include anything from church groups to chess clubs to watchdog groups to radical social movement organizations bent on the destruction of the status quo. Social movement organizations pursue institutional change, from moderate to radical.

[7] Huntington, S. P., (1996) *The clash of civilizations and the remaking of world order*, New York: Simon & Schuster.

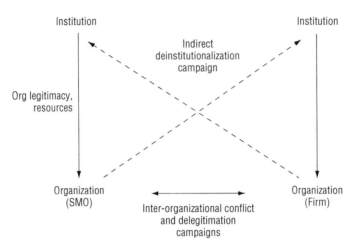

Figure 7.1: Institutional proxy wars

SMO campaigns against corporations are increasingly common. In these campaigns, the campaigning organization targets a given firm, but the goal is not simply to delegitimize the focal firm, but rather to use it as an example of a dominant institution and to thereby show that the institution is problematic. Examples include campaigns against McDonald's as a representative organization of a larger institution, e.g. US multinational corporations; People for the Ethical Treatment of Animals (PETA) campaigns against firms when the goal is actually a change of social norms and laws rather than just the change of a single firm's practices; and Oxfam's campaign against GlaxoSmithKline apparently concerns AIDS drugs in South Africa, but is more fundamentally about the World Trade Organization's TRIPS accord, concerning intellectual property protection, and the WTO itself. Other examples include campaigns against Nike's suppliers' labor practices in Southeast Asia, the catch methods of Starkist Tuna's suppliers and Monsanto's use of genetically modified organisms.

Proxy war target selection

In choosing which firm to target, SMOs take multiple factors into account, including prior public beliefs about the firm; how egregious the firm's behavior can be portrayed to be; the firm's willingness and ability to resist the campaign; and how well it can be presented as exemplary or expressive of the institution that the SMO is attempting to undermine. This last basis of target selection merits further clarification.

First, firms are often targeted and face greater institutional pressure not because they fail to conform to dominant institutional standards (as classically portrayed in most neo-institutional theory) but precisely because they *do* conform. In watchdog campaigns, the campaign is a form of institutional pressure to conform; in proxy wars, the campaign is a response to the firm's conforming to the "problematic" institution.

Second, they are targeted because they are exemplary representatives of an institution that is itself under challenge. For example, some anti-globalization protestors have protested against McDonald's. They readily aver that their main reason for choosing McDonald's as a target is because they take it to represent globalization and multinational corporations in general. One advocacy group, the McInformation Network, writes on its website, "Yes, we appreciate that McDonald's only sell hamburgers, and loads of other corporations are just as bad. But that's not the point. They have been used as a symbol of all multinationals and big business relentlessly pursuing their profits at the expense of anything that stands in their way."[8]

Proxy war rhetoric and audience

In proxy wars, the campaigning organization must put forward two different narratives – one which shows how egregious the focal firm is, and the other which highlights how this egregiousness is a natural outgrowth, expression or instantiation of a problematic institution.[9]

The tone and content of the rhetoric is often more ideologically radical than that of watchdog campaigns. The more fundamental the level of institutional change, the more radical the rhetoric tends to be. A more moderate campaign might call, for example, for a new system of carbon trading or a carbon tax, while a more radical campaign might call for nothing less than an immediate and complete end to the use of fossil fuels.

The degree of radicalism also affects which audience is targeted. In more moderate campaigns, key audiences will often be courts, regulators and /or legislators, since in this context these generally sympathetic groups often hold the power to quickly reshape regulatory institutions. Minor modifications in laws, their interpretation or their enforcement may be feasible through direct appeal to the various branches of government.

---

[8] www.mcspotlight.org/help.html, November 2, 2003.
[9] The rhetoric of proxy war campaigns would operate at the "Levels of Generality" 1–2 and perhaps 3; watchdog campaigns would operate at Level 4. Much of the detail of the nature of this rhetoric is discussed there.

Where more radical change is desired, these audiences are less likely to be sympathetic, since they tend to reflect or be dependent upon the ideological status quo. As a consequence, more radical campaigns often first attempt to appeal to the hearts and minds of the public at large or some more politically active segment of the population.

Proxy war tactics

Proxy war campaigns tend to rely on "institutionally neutral" and "contra-institutional" tactics. Contra-institutional tactics have a number of attributes that make them more attractive as an option for ideologically radical organizations than for more mainstream or moderate organizations. First, these tactics tend to be less resource-demanding. An individual or group of people, with little or no training or capital or networks, can engage in civil disobedience, direct action and violence. By contrast, political and regulative lobbying, for example, tends to require established networks among institutional players such as politicians and regulators and a large resource base. Radical organizations, at odds with the dominant institutions, are less likely to have these resources and networks than mainstream or moderate organizations.

Second, positive feedback systems will tend to enforce this dynamic, as the use of radical tactics may tend to isolate the radical organization from more mainstream sources of capital as well as from key players in the dominant institutions. The mainstream holders of capital and individuals ensconced in institution networks have their own resource-dependencies – most likely on the dominant institutions – and will thus tend to avoid jeopardizing their own legitimacy within their field by providing support to radical organizations.

Third, radical organizations, being less reliant on dominant-institution resources, will be free to pursue these radical tactics. Likewise, by using contra-institutional tactics, radical organizations have already put themselves out of contention for access to resources tied to more ideologically mainstream resource providers. As a result, further use of radical tactics will not threaten the resources of the radical campaigning organization. (This is a form of tactical "lock-in" which I will describe in more detail in the section below.)

Finally, radical ideologies may justify and even demand radical tactics more easily than more moderate ideologies. For example, many of the members of PETA take seriously ethical theories that may *demand* radical tactics. Some are ethical utilitarians who believe that we must maximize the welfare of all *sentient beings* and that an animal's suffering is as morally significant as a human's welfare. Others are rights theorists who believe that if severely mentally handicapped humans have whatever attributes give them rights, then higher animals that share those capacities also have similar rights. Thus, from this perspective, animal "holocausts" are ongoing and whatever means necessary should be employed to stop them. Similarly, internally consistent reasoning may lead some pro-life groups to sanction, if not publicly, violence against abortion practitioners.

2. How radical "David" social movement organizations beat mainstream "Goliath" firms

The efficacy of small and radical SMOs can seem puzzling to both managers and scholars. SMOs are, by definition, working against the mainstream – either in terms of values and beliefs or in terms of regulatory systems – of their societies. It is often a mystery to corporate managers just how they manage to be so effective in affecting firms.

A parallel paradox also faces neo-institutional scholars attempting to understand institutional change. Institutions are highly resilient social structures consisting of logics – beliefs, norms and values that guide practical action – and governance structures through which power and authority are exercised.[10] How can institutional change take place when dominant institutional logics, governance systems and resources are all stacked to favor the status quo? And more puzzling still: how can small, resource-poor and ideologically unconventional SMOs successfully challenge dominant institutions?[11]

The key to answering these practical and theoretical mysteries is in terms of institutionally circumscribed resource pools. Because of their dedication to institutional change, the SMOs tend to have a relatively small institutionally circumscribed resource pool from which to draw. (We can think of pools of resources as being attached to particular institutions, such that these resources are preferentially available to those organizations that conform to

[10] Scott, W. R., (2001) *Institutions and organizations.* In D. Whetten (ed.) *Foundations for organizational science*, Newbury Park CA: Sage.

[11] Snow, D., (2002) Social movements as challenges to authority: Resistance to an emerging conceptual hegemony, Working Paper, University of California; Zald, M. N., Roberta Ash, R., (1966) Social movement organizations: Growth, decay and change, *Social Forces*, 44(3) 327–41.

the given institution's demands.) Most of the potentially available resources are likely to be withheld from SMOs, since most of the individuals and organizations that control these resources will be loath, all things being equal, to provide resources to organizations with which they are at ideological loggerheads. The resources that are potentially available to SMOs are restricted to those small niches that are controlled by individuals or organizations that share their ideology and support the institutional change being pursued by the SMO.

Yet, the fact that the SMO is dedicated to undermining a dominant institution, although limiting the pool of available resources, simultaneously ensures that the SMO has a relatively institutionally homogenous set of individuals and organizations upon which it is resource dependent. Given the wide ideological range of possible organizations to which they could contribute, the suppliers of capital and labor to a particular SMO will tend to be relatively homogenous in their support of the ideological goals of the SMO. If their views diverge from that of the SMO, they can easily direct their resources elsewhere. (Clearly, as the SMO grows in size and takes on multiple and divergent campaigns, it will tend to draw resources from more – and more heterogenous – constituencies. Nonetheless, given their generally small size and their dedication to narrowly defined forms of institutional change, a given SMO will generally tend to have a small but relatively institutionally homogenous set of resources and resource-dependencies.)

In contrast, the corporations that SMOs target are usually gigantic organizations, fulfilling multiple functions in multiple countries for a multitude of stakeholders. The mere size of the throughput, in terms of labor, capital and resources, ensures a vast set of resource dependencies. The fact that the corporation is driven primarily by practical rather than political ends also allows for greater institutional heterogeneity in the resources upon which it is dependent. Employees, customers and suppliers, for example, could believe in very different ideologies, but deal with the corporation for practical reasons.

Thus, the truism in organizational theory that most organizations exist in a context of institutional complexity, applies more to large corporations than to small SMOs. Thus, the conflicting demands placed on organizations operating in institutionally complex fields are more severe for corporations than for the SMOs that campaign against them.

How does this insight fit with current research? In their fascinating paper, Padgett and Ansell put forward the proposition that multivocality – having single actions interpreted coherently from multiple perspectives simultaneously – can provide an advantage through the use of robust actions, actions which are interpreted differently by multiple, separated audiences.[12] But the current context suggests that multivocality can be a cost or a constraint. The actions of the SMO are univocal; the SMO speaks to a relatively narrow range of constituencies and has a relatively narrow ideological range of resource-dependence. Being deeply embedded in a single institutional context, the SMO faces fewer conflicting institutional demands. In contrast, the firm has a wider range of stakeholders that abide by multiple, conflicting institutions. Thus, the firm's actions are multivocal and subject to multiple conflicting evaluative criteria and demands. So, an action that satisfies some stakeholders (e.g. analysts and shareholders) may well appear illegitimate to another set of stakeholders who uphold a different set of rules, values and beliefs (e.g. consumers, employees and citizens). Thus, while occupying a "structural hole" in the network provides informational advantages from an institutional perspective, it can come at a cost of multivocality and generate multiple and conflicting demands.[13]

Let's consider an example of how SMOs are able to leverage their small but homogeneous resource niche to attack with univocality the corporation whose response is constrained by the multivocality forced upon it by its institutionally heterogenous resource dependencies. For example, SMOs campaigned against pharmaceutical companies for their pricing and patent enforcement efforts in South Africa. Some of the SMOs were created in response to this very issue. The SMOs did not have to worry about losing support from their capital and labor providers over the goals of the campaign. The individuals and organizations upon which the SMOs were dependent were virtually unanimous in their ideological stance on the issue.

In contrast, the pharmaceutical corporations under attack were in a *multi-vocal* position, speaking simultaneously to multiple, separate constituencies including: the South African government; developed world consumers; South African, American and British SMOs; intergovernmental organizations responsible for international patent agreements; and financial analysts. These audiences had a wide range of worldviews and values – as well as interests – and the pharmaceutical companies had great difficulty in addressing or sidestepping the conflicting demands. The institutional ideologies of patents and shareholder capitalism came into direct conflict with ideologies of the pre-eminence of public health concerns. The corporations – burdened

---

[12] Padgett, J. F., Ansell, C. K., (1993) Robust actions and the rise of the Medici, 1400–1434, *American Journal of Sociology*, 98(6), 1259–1319.

[13] Burt, R. S., (1992) *Structural holes: The social structure of competition*, Cambridge MA: Harvard University Press.

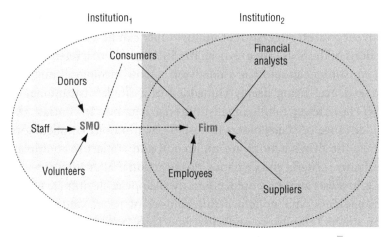

Figure 7.2:   Institutional homogeneity and heterogeneity of resource providers

with multivocality and aggressive SMOs that were demanding explicit action –
vacillated ineffectively in their response. For example, the corporations filed a
lawsuit against the South African government to enforce their patent (explicitly out of concern for the institution of patents, rather than immediate
concern about profits), only to drop the suit six weeks later when further
pressure was exerted by the SMOs. The greater institutional complexity of
firms (relative to that of SMOs) underlies the need for multivocality and
thereby limits the options for both responding to conflicting institutional
pressures and being institutionally entrepreneurial. This is represented in
Figure 7.2.

3. Understanding and managing watchdog and proxy war campaigns

In addition to being of theoretical interest, SMO campaigns are of significant
managerial relevance. The phenomenon of SMO campaigns against corporations has received very little attention from strategy or organizational theory
scholars, although it is of increasing importance and is likely only to grow in
significance because of communications technologies, the increasingly trans-
national operations of corporations, and the ongoing spread of liberal and
democratic regimes. These campaigns represent a new form of risk for firms –
which I call "social risk" – which is unique and needs to be studied as such.
These campaigns are also an increasingly important process through which
institutions are challenged and changed.

There are a number of other managerial implications from this research that reflect the unique aspects of social risk. They include the issues over which campaigns begin, the dynamics of the campaigns, the source of strength of SMOs in these attacks, and firm-specific risk factors. I will now briefly discuss these before turning to specific managerial recommendations for avoiding and managing these campaigns.

Issues of campaigns

Corporate managers are generally focused on key variables of competition such as product characteristics and price. However, the issues that concern SMOs are often different, and thus managers tend to be less cognizant of them. Campaigns are often over production processes (such as labor practices); the worthiness of the product itself (e.g. protesters are not complaining about furs not being soft enough or cigarettes not being tasty enough); and negative input and output externalities such as the opportunity costs of the clear-cutting of forests or the costs incurred by third parties as a result of pollution. Recognizing the broader range of potential issues is the first step towards dealing with social risk.

Campaign dynamics

The dynamics of campaigns are also fundamentally different from the dynamics of market competition, and managers must recognize and deal with these differences. First, having a big brand is often a source of social risk for a firm as it is more likely to be readily identifiable by third-party audiences of SMO campaigns and it is also more easily construed as a symbol of an institution or industry in a proxy-war type campaign. Additionally, the larger the company the easier it is to portray the battle to third parties as a David-and-Goliath type contest, thereby drawing out the audience's sympathies for the SMO.

Second, in market competition, it is usually "every firm for itself" in a contest for market share and profits. By contrast, SMOs, being relatively resource-poor and often sharing similar social, political and economic goals, tend to join in coalitions or "swarms" to attack a particular targeted firm through myriad tactics. In my research I found coalitions of 200 or more SMOs in a single campaign to be common.

Third, the impact of market competition is generally on market share or margin, but in the case of SMO campaigns, the effects – while ultimately including these – are broader. For example, Sir Mark Moody-Stuart, the former chairman of Shell, said in an interview that the gravest impact of SMO campaigns against the oil giant were not on direct loss of sales or margin but on employee morale and the ability to attract and retain high-quality employees. SMO campaigns, particularly those pursuing more fundamental social change, can also lead to changes in the regulative rules of the game in which firms compete; SMO campaigns can lead to changes in regulative oversight and legislation and taxation and subsidies.

Why SMOs are effective

In speaking with firm managers and studying campaigns, I have been struck by the way firms are normally caught off guard by the impact of SMO campaigns. There are a number of attributes of SMOs that support their effectiveness: first, as highlighted in the section above, the advantage of univocality and institutionally homogenous resource pools puts a wider choice of tactics at the disposal of SMOs embarking on a proxy war campaign. Second, SMOs have, as an "industry," much greater legitimacy than firms. As indicated in Figures 7.3–7.5 below, which draw from Edelman surveys,[14] SMOs are trusted more than firms – and often even governments. Third, in addition to their greater legitimacy, they are also regularly seen as underdogs which can bring audience sympathy. Fourth, NGOs, as mentioned above, tend to cooperate more with one another than firms do, so when an SMO "industry" goes up against a market industry, it has a competitive advantage. Fifth, SMOs are designed around and focused on their causes, whereas firms are primarily focused on and designed to optimize their market performance. Thus, while firms are, at root, economic agents, SMOs are social and political agents. As a result, SMOs tend to be good at social and political maneuvering, whereas firms are often more maladroit. Also, as dedicated political/social players, SMOs do not need to balance their goals or campaign resources against some other organizational imperative such as maximizing economic performance to the same extent as firms do. Although targeted firms often have tremendous resources, most of them are dedicated to goals of market competition, not responding to SMO campaigns. Finally, another source of effectiveness of SMOs in their campaigns is that they are the initiators and on the offense. This means that they get to choose their targets, tactics, and timing, and can frame issues to optimize their impact.

---

[14] See Edelman Trust Barometer at www.Edelman.com (2003).

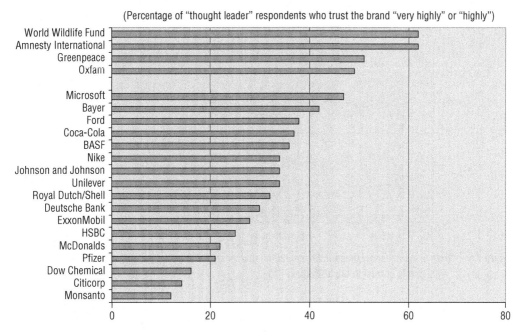

Figure 7.3: European trust in brands (Edelman, 2003) (percentage of "thought leader" respondents who trust the brand "very highly" or "highly")

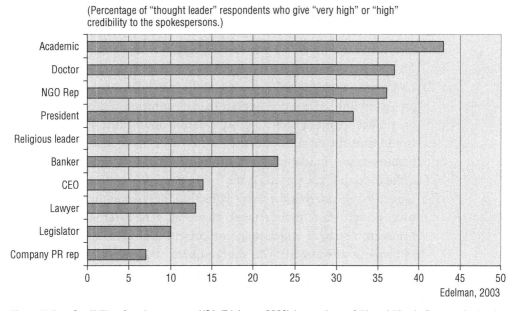

Figure 7.4: Credibility of spokespersons, USA (Edelman, 2003) (percentage of "thought leader" respondents who give "very high" or "high" credibility to the spokespersons)

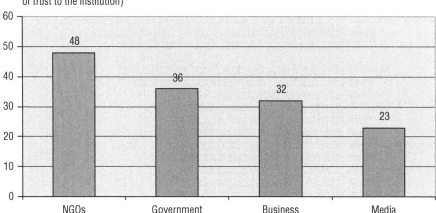

(Percentage of thought leaders who give "very high" or "high" levels of trust to the institution)

Figure 7.5:   Trust in institutions, Europe (Edelman, 2003) (percentage of thought leaders who give "very high" or "high" levels of trust to the institution)

Firm-specific risk factors

Through my research, a number of firm-specific risk factors have been identified and these have obvious managerial relevance. Firms at the greatest social risk include those which:

(1) *Offer life-saving or life-threatening products* (e.g. pharmaceuticals, health care, arms and tobacco). It is easy for SMOs to cast these situations as "people versus profits."

(2) *Confront changing social mores* (e.g. fashion, media, alcohol, pornography, gambling). Firms that operate in environments of institutional flux or conflict are more likely to get drawn into an institutional proxy war. In addition, the magnitude of the risk, as well as its probability, is higher because more fundamental institutional changes – and thus major changes to the "rules of the game" – are possible.

(3) *Generate large externalities* (e.g. extraction, heavy manufacturing, electrical power, waste management, chemical). The externalities of these firms are felt by a wider range of citizens and consumers and thus campaigns are more likely to gain resources and garner support.

(4) *Have high power in the supply chain or market.* Firms such as Wal-Mart and Microsoft can often extract a high percentage of the surplus value in the supply chain. This will tend to increase the degree to which there is a negative pre-existing attitude toward the firm. As a result, SMO claims

against the firm are more likely to find a positive reception among relevant third-party audiences.

(5) *Have high brand awareness* (e.g. retail, clothing, food and beverage, automotive, media, finance). As mentioned before, these firms make better targets for SMOs because they are already known to potential audiences of a campaign, and are more easily cast as symbols of industries or institutions.

(6) *Use new technologies* (e.g. genetic engineering, stem-cell-based research, personal data collection). New technologies can raise new questions about whether the arising practices are legitimate and appropriate.

(7) *Do business in different regions with differing ethical or social expectations* (e.g. virtually every multinational, particularly those operating in both developed and developing countries). This increases their exposure to institutional complexity.

(8) *Are representative of controversial institutions* (e.g. being a US-based multinational).

Recommendations for managing social risk

Through my qualitative research, some apparent "best practices" for managing social risk and campaigns have become apparent. I will divide the suggestions into two categories: (1) avoiding attacks and (2) responding to attacks.

Avoiding attacks

The first steps are to identify and minimize exposure. Thus, managers should consider what risk factors their firms face (as discussed above). Also, they must remain cognizant of the distinction between what is legal and what is legitimate. SMOs engaged in efforts to change industry-wide practices, laws or institutions often attack firms regardless of whether they are law abiding.

Firms should also try to map out the relevant SMOs. These include radical organizations that could only be considered as potential threats as well as less radical organizations which might be partners rather than attackers. Preemptive engagement with NGOs can reduce the downside of social risk and increase the upside.[15]

Managers should keep in mind the relative lack of trustworthiness or credibility that most firms have. If a more legitimate SMO makes claims

---

[15] See Yaziji, M., (2004).

against a less legitimate firm whose motives in defending itself are immediately suspect, firms begin at a basic disadvantage in the court of public opinion. Building legitimacy and trust as a good corporate citizen should be an ongoing effort.

Responding to attacks

Responses to campaigns invariably include a component of maintaining or regaining legitimacy. Suchman identified generic strategies (compromise, ignore, defend, counter-attack) for doing so. However, two complications are worth discussing.[16]

Suchman assumed that the loss of legitimacy was the result of failing to meet existing dominant institutional standards. But since campaigns are often launched as a form of proxy war, closer adherence to the dominant standards is unlikely to satisfy the campaigning organizations. Firms under attack need to determine the goal of the attack – is it to change the firm's behavior (as in a watchdog campaign), or to change the rules of the game (as in a proxy war campaign)? The optimal response could well depend on the goals of the attacking SMOs.

Additionally, the short-, medium- and long-term consequences must be taken into account. Some firms negotiate and make concessions as soon as they are challenged. This may relieve the immediate pressure, but will invite further attacks. So, seen from the medium term, making concessions might seem like a bad idea. But in the long term, reputations and relationships matter and having a good reputation and having positive ongoing relationships with all the stakeholders that can affect the firm greatly reduces the firm's social risk.

This reasoning only captures a partial truth and actually confuses the medium term with the long term. For very high-profile organizations, it is likely that evaluation and critiques should best be taken as a permanent condition. Given this, close and ongoing cooperation and communication and compromise with relevant SMOs might actually be the optimal long-term approach. Earning a good reputation and the trust of SMOs might be difficult and costly over the medium term, but beneficial over the long term.

---

[16] Suchman, M.C., (1995) Managing legitimacy: Strategic and institutional approaches, *Academy of Management Review* 20(3), 571–60.

4. Conclusion

NGO campaigns against firms are growing in frequency and impact. These campaigns are theoretically useful for understanding institutional change and are practically relevant for managers trying to understand and manage their social risk. In this chapter I attempted to differentiate between two very different types of campaigns – watchdog and proxy war campaigns – which play very different roles in terms of institutional pressure and institutional change and which require very different responses from managers of firms. I have further tried to explain the surprising effectiveness of small social movement organizations and tried to give some guidance to managers facing these formidable, and growing, stakeholders.

8 Oil and conflict: Lundin Petroleum's experience in Sudan[1]

Christine Batruch

1. Introduction

Lundin Petroleum[2] obtained the rights to explore for and produce oil and gas in concession Block 5A, Unity State, Sudan, in February 1997; it sold these rights in June 2003.

During the period in which the company was active in Sudan, it operated in the belief that oil could benefit the economic development of the area and the country as a whole, and that this would have a catalyzing effect on the peace process. The problems which it encountered in the area, however, led the company to constantly reassess its activities, role and responsibilities there.

This chapter examines the reasons why Lundin decided to operate in Sudan, the challenges it faced in the course of its activities, the steps it adopted to satisfy both its commercial objectives and ethical concerns, and its efforts to promote a peaceful resolution of the conflict.

2. Sudan's war

Sudan has been embroiled in a civil war that began shortly after it gained independence from the UK in 1956. It is one of the longest and most tragic

---

[1] This chapter originally appeared in Bailes, A. J. K. and Frommelt, I. (eds), Stockholm International Peace Research Institute (SIPRI), *Business and security: Public–private sector relationships in a new security environment*, Oxford: Oxford University Press, pp. 148–60 and is reproduced here with permission from SIPRI.

[2] On the independent Swedish oil and gas exploration and production company Lundin Petroleum AB – hereafter referred to as Lundin, or the company – see www.lundin-petroleum.com. Lundin was the operator of Block 5A on behalf of the consortium which included OMV (Sudan) Exploration GmbH, Petronas Carigali Overseas Sdn Bhd and Sudapet. For a map showing the location of Block 5A, see www.lundin-petroleum.com/eng/sudan3.shtml.

wars of modern history: fighting has taken place for nearly 50 years, with a single reprieve between 1972 and 1983.[3] The Government of Sudan and the Sudan People's Liberation Movement/Army (SPLM/A), led by rebel leader John Garang, are the main protagonists in the conflict which resumed in 1983, although armed militias in different parts of the country have also been involved at various times. The fighting has taken place chiefly in the southern-most parts of the country although other areas, such as the Nuba Mountains region, Unity State and more recently the Darfur region of western Sudan, have also witnessed periods of intense combat.

It is difficult to ascertain the root causes of the war and the contributing factors over such a long period of time. Nonetheless, certain elements have, at various times, played a role in the conflict. They include: (a) the country's extreme poverty – Sudan is ranked among the poorest nations of the world;[4] (b) the religious/racial divide – northern Sudan is mainly Arab and Muslim, while southern Sudan is African and animist or Christian; (c) the competition for power – political opponents seek a greater participation in power, while regions seek greater autonomy from the central government; and (d) the competition for resources – southern regions contest the government's control over national resources such as water and oil, which originate in the south.

When peace is achieved, it will be easier to determine which of these elements played the decisive role in the conflict and its eventual resolution. What is clear, however, is that the war began years before the presence of oil was even suspected, and it was only after oil was produced that a material basis for a sustainable peace was seen to have been achieved. It was only then that an active, internationally mediated peace process began.[5]

Until that time, Sudan's war had been largely ignored, except from a humanitarian perspective. The conflict was seen as a typical African war:

---

[3] For an account of recent developments in this conflict see Wiharta, S. and Anthony, I., (2003) Major armed conflicts. In *SIPRI yearbook 2003: Armaments, disarmament and international security*, Oxford: Oxford University Press, pp. 101–104. At the time of writing, peace negotiations held under the auspices of the Intergovernmental Authority on Development (IGAD) were in their final phase and a comprehensive agreement was expected to be signed by the end of 2007. On the peace process see "Sudan: peace talks, humanitarian action", www.irinnews.org/webspecials/sudan/default.asp; and Powell, C. L., "An opportunity for peace in Sudan", October 28, 2003, www.sudan.net/news/posted/7274.html.

[4] For a discussion of Sudan's economy and the positive impact of oil in the past few years see the US Department of Energy Internet site at www.eia.doe.gov/emeu/cabs/sudan.html.

[5] The current phase of peace negotiations originated with the activities of Senator John Danforth, who was appointed by President George W. Bush as Special Envoy for Peace in Sudan on September 6, 2001. See Danforth, J. C., "Report to the President of the United States on the outlook for peace in Sudan, April 26, 2002," at www.sudan.net (under "Latest news," "Press releases and commentary," posted on May, 14 2002). The oil issue and the means for resolving the conflict are also discussed there.

over local issues and involving local parties. The situation seemed insoluble because of the many problems to be resolved and the slight foundations for sustainable peace. However, in the course of the 1990s a number of developments brought Sudan to the world's attention.

The early 1990s had seen the rise of Islamic fundamentalism, which figured prominently in the Sudanese government; the harboring of renowned terrorists such as "Carlos the Jackal" and later Osama bin Laden; and the suspicion that Sudan was linked to the 1995 assassination attempt on Egyptian President Hosni Mubarak. At this stage, Sudan was considered a "rogue nation" which had to be isolated from the community of nations.[6] In the latter part of the 1990s, however, the government adopted certain progressive measures, which the international community interpreted as signals of impending reform and of Sudan's interest in shedding its pariah status. The steps taken by Sudan included the handover of "Carlos the Jackal" to French authorities, the expulsion of Osama bin Laden, the purging of key Islamic fundamentalists from the government, allowing the return of political opponents from abroad, the signing of the 1997 Khartoum Peace Agreement with southern opposition groups (see section 3), improved relations with neighboring countries, and the adoption of a new Constitution and Bill of Rights.

Whereas the United States was reluctant to recognize these efforts immediately, the European Union (EU) decided to engage in a constructive dialogue with the Sudanese Government because it believed that this approach was more likely to bring results than keeping Sudan isolated. Thus, when Lundin acquired the rights to explore for and produce oil and gas in Block 5A, world opinion regarding Sudan was beginning to change.

3. Lundin in Sudan

The company's primary concern when considering a new area for activities is geological. If an area presents the required geological profile – that is, if it is assumed to contain oil reserves – Lundin proceeds to study the technical and commercial feasibility of exploiting the oil. In the case of Sudan, the main risk identified in the course of the company's risk analysis was financial. The company decided, however, that the estimated potential oil reserves were

---

[6] Because of Sudan's perceived connection with international terrorism, the UN and the US imposed sanctions against Sudan, the former through a travel ban on Sudanese officials and the latter in the form of a ban on the conduct of business in the country by US companies.

important enough to justify the significant investments required for the venture, in particular investments in infrastructure development. It did not identify any legal risks – there were no international or EU sanctions against Sudan that prohibited a European company from doing business there – or political risks – there were no SPLA forces in the concession area, as the civil war was proceeding further south.

The company therefore engaged in negotiations to obtain a licence to explore for and produce oil and gas in Block 5A. As in most countries, mining rights in Sudan belong to the central state. Negotiations were therefore held with representatives of the Sudanese Ministry of Energy and Mining (MEM). The terms of the agreement were standard for the trade, with an initial period for oil exploration – in exchange for a work commitment and the carrying of costs – followed by a period of oil production, with cost recovery sought after initial production. The only terms that were specific to the exploration and production-sharing agreement (EPSA) concerned the "Sudanization" of the operations. At the request of the MEM, the company committed itself to hire and train Sudanese workers with a view to their constituting 50% of the staff within five years of the commencement of operations and 80% within 10 years. There was also a provision that the company would carry the costs of its Sudanese partner, Sudapet, which had a 5% interest in the venture.

On its first visit to the concession area, Lundin met with key representatives of the local community, who welcomed oil activities as the only way to promote long-term economic development in their area.[7] They also committed themselves to providing a safe environment for the company to operate in. This commitment arose out of the terms of the Khartoum Peace Agreement, which they had signed with the Sudanese Government and which set out the parties' respective rights and responsibilities in the area.[8] Security, however, proved to be elusive. The prevalence of arms, coupled with the division of tribes into various factions, contributed to making the situation

---

[7] The company met with Dr Riek Machar, who, pursuant to the 1997 Khartoum Peace Agreement, was Vice-President of Sudan and President of the South Sudan Co-ordinating Council (the government representative for the south); with Taban Deng Gai, the Governor of Unity State; and with representatives of the local factions.

[8] The text of the Khartoum Peace Agreement, signed in April 1997, is available at www.sudani.co.za/ Documents%20 and%20Issues/Khartoum%20Peace%20Agreement.htm. It was signed between the Government of the Sudan, the South Sudan United Democratic Salvation Front (UDSF) – comprising the South Sudan Independence Movement (SSIM) and the Union of Sudan African Parties (USAP) – the SPLM, the Equatoria Defence Force (EDF), and the South Sudan Independents Group (SSIG).

volatile.[9] Within a few years, instances of fighting started to increase. While the company was not directly affected by the fighting at the time, it was nevertheless worried about the safety of its staff and its operations. It was also concerned about the criticisms that were being directed against an oil consortium situated in a nearby concession. To better understand these developments, Lundin decided to commission a socio-political assessment of the area [in 1999].

The study, conducted both at the Lundin head office in Geneva and in Sudan, was based on an analysis of reports on the political and human rights situation in Sudan, on interviews with company representatives in the head office and in Sudan, and on meetings with members of the Government of Sudan and humanitarian organizations. It also included a visit to the concession area.

The report's conclusion was that, despite the lack of evidence of a direct link between the sporadic fighting that had taken place in the concession area and company activities, there was a potential risk of deterioration if the local communities ceased to perceive the role of oil companies as beneficial. The report also noted that in view of the limited positive benefits of the oil activities at the time – revenues were not expected for a number of years, since activities were at the exploration stage – there was a distinct possibility that the local communities would grow disgruntled.[10] The report's main recommendations were that the company should continue to monitor socio-political developments in the concession area and reinforce its existing relationship with the local community.

Community relations

From the time it started its activities in Block 5A, Lundin adopted a proactive approach to community relations. The company not only met with representatives of the local community but also sought to show goodwill towards the population by hiring local staff and improving the infrastructure in the

---

[9] The main tribe in the area is the Nuer tribe, which has five sub-groups: the Bul, Lek, Jikany, Jagei and Dok Nuer. In turn, these groups are affiliated with local militia.

[10] Oil exploration and production are by nature a long-term activity: it takes a number of years before oil is found, and several more before it is brought into production and sold. It therefore takes years for revenue from oil to accrue to an area, which, in the meantime, has observed construction activity, equipment being brought in, and teams of people going back and forth. In many areas of the world, this poses no particular problem, but in an area like southern Sudan, where the majority of the population live in very precarious conditions, this issue requires special attention.

area.[11] The company believed that if the local population obtained tangible benefits from oil activities they would be even more supportive of these activities. However, given the lack of required skills locally, the number of people who were hired was minimal, so the impact of this effort was limited. Similarly, while infrastructure developments such as bridge and road building increased local mobility, because they had been carried out for operational purposes the company did not consider them as community projects. It therefore sought ways to make a more direct contribution to the local community. It initiated a number of projects, which later became an integral part of the company's Community Development and Humanitarian Assistance Programme (CDHAP). The projects had three main objectives: (a) to promote better health, hygiene, education and general quality of life for the current and future inhabitants of the concession area of Block 5A, Unity State; (b) to contribute to the economic and social development of the area; and (c) to reinforce relationships between the local community and the company.

Through this program, the company also wished to demonstrate to the local and central authorities that it was concerned with the interests and welfare of the population and was prepared to make significant contributions, despite the fact that it would not obtain any revenues from its activities for a number of years.

In order to ensure that its projects were relevant, Lundin had consulted with a number of local actors, in particular non-governmental organizations (NGOs) that were active in the area. With their assistance, it identified areas of need where it felt it could make a contribution, such as the supply of fresh water, health, education and capacity building.

In the three years Lundin ran CDHAP, it spent over $1.7m on its various projects. These ranged from the delivery of fresh water by trucks, to the drilling of water wells and the construction of a water filtration unit. In the field of education, Lundin started by supplying educational materials to existing schools and orphanages, then built schools with local materials, and eventually constructed a permanent building to accommodate several hundred children. Through a team of five Sudanese doctors, assisted by local nurses, Lundin provided medical assistance first in mobile tent clinics, then temporary straw clinics and eventually built a fully equipped permanent clinic. Similarly, it relied on two veterinarians and local para-veterinarians whom it had trained to tend to local cattle in a vet station and in mobile vet clinics. The capacity-building

---

[11] The uniqueness of Lundin's approach did not go unnoticed. Indeed, in a meeting with representative of an international NGO, Dr Riek Machar, who had then defected from the Government of Sudan, stated that Lundin was different in that it had consulted with the local people and tried to involve them in its activities.

projects included the creation of a mobile brick factory, a women's development center and a nursery as well as a program for training local people as midwives, para-veterinarians, nurses, bricklayers, vector control specialists, and computer analysts. In times of emergency brought about by climatic or security conditions, the company provided *ad hoc* humanitarian assistance by supplying people with water containers, soap, blankets, mosquito nets and medical services.[12]

From its inception, CDHAP was a constant element of the company's presence in Unity State. Not only were CDHAP staff members often the first to go to projected areas of activities and the last to be pulled out when the security situation deteriorated, but they stayed there even when operations were suspended. During the company's temporary suspension of activities in 2001 and 2002, services to the community continued to be rendered in the two main towns of the area, Rubkona and Bentiu, and in surrounding villages. Maintaining its presence in the area through CDHAP was the company's way of demonstrating its long-term commitment to the local community and the area.[13]

If CDHAP was the company's most tangible way of showing its concern for the people in the area, it was by no means the only way. Outbreaks of fighting, coupled with allegations that these conflicts were related to oil, led Lundin to reassess its role and responsibilities and to seek ways of exercising a positive influence on the protagonists in the conflict.

Internal review

In the latter part of 1999, civil rights activists started to question the role of the Greater Nile Petroleum Operating Company (GNPOC) oil consortium in the conflict.[14] This consortium, which was operating in a concession area adjacent to Lundin's, had participated in the construction of a pipeline linking the southern oilfields of Unity State to the northern city of Port Sudan and was beginning to produce oil. Activists claimed that human rights violations, such as population displacement, had taken place to pave the way for the consortium's activities. The consortium consistently refuted these claims. The activists also believed that the revenues obtained by the Sudanese

---

[12] For a review of CDHAP activities in 2001–2002 see www.lundin-petroleum.com/eng/comdev.shtml.

[13] This commitment has been passed on to Petronas Carigali Overseas Sdn Bhd, Lundin's successor in the area, which has decided not only to pursue the projects initiated by Lundin, but also to expand the activities under CDHAP.

[14] The GNPOC was at the time a consortium of Chinese, Malaysian, Canadian and Sudanese companies.

Government from GNPOC operations would be used to build up its military arsenal and quash the rebel SPLA.[15]

There was a marked discrepancy between Lundin's first-hand experience in its concession area and reports about what was being alleged to have taken place in the neighbouring GNPOC concession. The report commissioned by Lundin confirmed that many elements distinguished the two operations. First, the GNPOC concession area was sparsely inhabited, which gave credence to the claim that population displacement had taken place prior to the commencement of operations, even though this was disproved by satellite images.[16] Second, the local community there was partly of Dinka origin, the main tribal group behind the SPLA; it was therefore conceivable that there could be clashes between them and government forces. Finally, GNPOC operations had started generating revenue for the government, of which little, if any, appeared to be reinvested by the government in the area.

Despite these differences, Lundin recognized that negative perceptions of the effects of oil operations could also come to be applied to its area and therefore decided to set out, in a Code of Conduct, the conditions under which it was prepared to operate.

The Lundin code of conduct

The process of development of the Code of Conduct was important for Lundin, as it required the company to assess the role of its business from a different perspective. Lundin's management had always seen (and continues to see) itself as making a positive contribution to economic growth by providing a necessary source of energy. It had also witnessed how oil revenues in undeveloped areas acted as a catalyst for economic development, paving the way for other businesses and international loans.[17] Lundin was aware of the potential negative impact of its operations on the environment, and took mitigating measures to address them. The socio-political dimension of its activities, however, was not

---

[15] The consortium contested these allegations. It provided evidence of population growth in the area and divulged the nature of its discussions with the government regarding the use of its facilities for military purposes.

[16] The Canadian company in the consortium hired Kalagate Imagery Bureau, a British company specializing in the analysis of satellite images, to ascertain population patterns in its concession area in the 1980s and 1990s. The conclusions were that there was no evidence of appreciable population migration from the area.

[17] It had felt this way about Sudan, and in many ways it turned out to be right. Over a period of five years Sudan shed its pariah nation status and became an attractive place for the international business community (sanctioned by the International Monetary Fund).

something the company had had particular reason to consider before the Sudan experience. It believed that these were issues beyond its field of competence.

When faced with the possibility that its activities could have a negative impact on the conflict in Sudan, senior management reexamined the company's role from this wider perspective. Lundin established its objective to play a positive role not only directly, in the economic field, but also indirectly, in the socio-political field as well. It stated that the company's "aim is not only to find oil and gas, we are also committed to developing this valuable resource in the best socio-economic manner possible for the benefit of all our partners, including the host country and local communities".[18]

The Code of Conduct was developed after the company had consulted documents in the field of corporate responsibility[19] and after discussions with members of the board of directors as well as senior corporate and country-based management. The Code was adopted as a consensus document which served as a guide for the company's activities worldwide.

The Code set out the company's values, responsibilities and the principles by which it was guided. The company recognized that it had specific responsibilities towards its shareholders, employees, host countries and local communities, as well as to the environment. It committed itself to act in a fair and honest way, to observe both national and international laws, and "to act in accordance with generally accepted principles on the protection of human rights and the environment".[20] After the Code of Conduct had been adopted by the board, Lundin disseminated it to its employees in Geneva and in Sudan, and to the company's affiliates. It became an integral part of the company's contract of employment.

The adoption of the Code was followed by other initiatives, such as the publication of the company's policies on health and safety, the environment and community relations. The company also arranged for an awareness session on human rights and developed a human rights primer, explaining the origins of, and guiding principles for, the protection of human rights and how they relate to business. The company's security liaison personnel in Sudan were provided with information regarding human rights and security,

---

[18] Code of Conduct, "Message from the Chairman". The text of the Lundin Code of Conduct and related documents are available at www.lundin-petroleum.com/Documents/ot_lupe-code_e.pdf.

[19] These include the Caux Principles, the Global Sullivan Principles, the UN Declaration of Human Rights, the International Labor Organization's Tripartite Declaration of Principle concerning Multinational Enterprises and Social Policy, the Organization for Economic Co-operation and Development's Guidelines for Multinational Enterprises, Amnesty International's Human Rights Code for Companies, the Prince of Wales Business Forum on Operating in Conflict Zones, and so on.

[20] Code of Conduct (note 17).

to sensitize them to such issues in conflict situations, and were encouraged to report any violations they witnessed.[21]

The internal dissemination of the Code of Conduct was necessary to ensure that the staff understood what the company stood for and what was expected of each and every one of them. It also became the basis for discussions with stakeholder groups in Sudan.

Stakeholder engagement

In the course of developing its Code of Conduct, the company defined more precisely who its stakeholders were in relation to its activities in Sudan. In the first few years of its operations in Sudan, it had cultivated friendly relations with business partners, government representatives at the central and local levels, and community representatives. It also had informal relations with other oil companies and NGOs active in the area. However, it decided, that in view of the competing claims being made about the impact of oil in the region, it needed not only to widen the scope of these contacts but also to alter the content of its discussions to include socio-political issues.

The company's early consultations with central and local authorities had revealed a shared view that oil represented a momentous opportunity for the development of the country and the area. Even the humanitarian and development organizations it had consulted at the time recognized this potential, but they remained more reserved as to whether the wealth produced would be properly shared among the population.

This general consensus began to erode, however, when representatives of the local communities whom Lundin had met at the outset accused the Sudanese government of reneging on its commitments under the Khartoum Peace Agreement and decided to resign from their governmental posts. Their decision, coupled with the defection of a local tribal faction to the SPLA, represented a turning point both in the conflict and for the company. Interfactional fighting escalated into a conflict which pitted militias against each other that were backed by the two contenders in the civil war – the government of Sudan and the SPLA.

---

[21] The relevant personnel received information about the Voluntary Principles on Security and Human Rights for the Extractive Sector, available at www.amnesty.org.uk/business/newslet/spring01/principles.shtml; Amnesty International's 10 Basic Human Rights Standards for Law Enforcement Officials, www.web. amnesty.org/aidoc/aidoc_pdf.nsf/Index/POL300041998ENGLISH/$File/POL3000498.pdf; the 1990 UN Basic Principles on the Use of Force and Firearms by Law Enforcement Officials, www.unhchr.ch/html/ menu3/b/h_comp43.htm; and the 1979 UN Code of Conduct for Law Enforcement Officials, www.unhchr.ch/html/menu3/b/h_comp42.htm.

Judging the situation as representing an undue risk to the safety of its staff – the SPLA having then indicated that it considered oil operations and staff as legitimate military targets – Lundin decided to temporarily suspend its operations. It made its resumption of activities conditional upon a peaceful environment, noting that this could only be achieved with the support of the local community.

Lundin also decided to enhance its knowledge of the situation by consulting not only those with whom it had formal relations, such as its partners in the consortium and the government, but also those with particular knowledge of, or interest in, the conflict in Sudan. The purpose of these discussions was to share information and opinions about the conflict and to establish what was required for company operations to resume.

The institutions with which the company met included the following:

The Sudanese government (host government) and the government of Unity State (local government)

Discussions with the Sudanese and local governments focused on the means to render the area conducive to oil operations. The company expressed its view that the long-term security required for sustainable oil activities could only be achieved with the support of the local community. Lundin made it clear that, in its view, military action – except for defensive purposes – was not an acceptable option.

The Nuer opposition (local community)

In its discussions with representatives of the Nuer opposition, the company attempted to convey its view that oil presented the best opportunity to achieve sustainable peace and growth in the area and encouraged them to seek a peaceful way to assert their rights to the area.

The Swedish Ministry for Foreign Affairs (home government)

It was important for Lundin, as a Swedish company, to share with the Swedish Ministry for Foreign Affairs (MFA) its views about the situation in Sudan and its approach there. Given the allegations about wrongdoings committed in its area of operations, the company kept the MFA informed of its first-hand experience in the area and the steps taken to address local needs and concerns. As a member of the EU, Sweden had adopted a policy of constructive engagement in Sudan: the activities of the company fell within this approach, in so far as it ensured that its activities were not affecting the conflict negatively.

United Nations relief organizations (the humanitarian community)

UN organizations were present in Sudan mainly to deliver humanitarian assistance under the umbrella organization Operation Lifeline Sudan (OLS).[22] Set up both in Khartoum to service government-controlled areas and in Lokichoggio, Kenya, to service parts of the country under SPLA control, the OLS had witnessed the unbearable toll of the war on civilians. Its main concern was to have full access to all areas of the country to be able to provide humanitarian relief in the case of crises. As the company had itself offered assistance to internally displaced people fleeing from areas of natural or man-made catastrophe, it shared the view of the OLS that unrestricted humanitarian access was required and raised this issue in its meetings with government and Nuer representatives.

The United Nations Commission on Human Rights

The UN Commission on Human Rights (UNCHR) had two representatives for Sudan: an in-country representative, whose role was to promote respect for human rights by the Sudanese government and in government-controlled areas, and a Special Rapporteur on the Situation of Human Rights in Sudan, whose role was to assess and report on the human rights situation throughout the country. In 1999 the Special Rapporteur claimed that oil activities had exacerbated the conflict, although he had not visited the oilfields or even consulted with the oil companies. Lundin therefore contacted him to inform him of its first-hand experience and knowledge of the situation in the area and invited him to visit the oilfields instead of relying on secondary, sometimes biased, sources. The eventual visit of the Special Rapporteur to the area took place at such a time and was of such short duration (a mere three hours) that he could not conduct an in-depth inspection. In the course of discussions with company representatives, however, he admitted that the civil war was the cause of the human rights problems and that oil, if properly channelled, could contribute to a sustainable peace.

Non-governmental organizations

The NGOs with a focus on Sudan may be categorized by two broad groups: (a) those which have a permanent presence in Sudan, and assist the population through local humanitarian or development projects; and (b) those

---

[22] At that time, the OLS was composed of 42 intergovernmental and non-governmental development and humanitarian organizations, among which were the UN Children's Fund (UNICEF), the UN Office for the Coordination of Humanitarian Affairs (OCHA) and the UN Development Programme (UNDP).

which are based outside Sudan, and promote special interests such as human rights, religious rights, development rights, and so on. Lundin was in contact with both groups to exchange views about the situation in Sudan and the means to improve it. Not surprisingly, it found that organizations with a humanitarian focus were generally supportive of the company's efforts to contribute to the local communities in its area of operations. They were prepared to talk to company representatives and even work with them on certain projects. When the stigma surrounding oil activities became significant, most chose not to be publicly associated with the company and therefore only a few cooperative ventures continued, on a confidential basis.

Lundin's experience with special-interest NGOs was more difficult. In many cases, views about the situation in Sudan were so very different that discussions rarely went beyond each side trying to convince the other that its views were correct. This was particularly true with respect to religious-based organizations, which characterized the conflict as an attempt by Muslims to eradicate the Christian population in the south of Sudan in order to gain access to the oil there. Although the company responded to their claims, in discussions and in writing, it felt that not much would be gained from this effort. These NGOs believed that the cessation of oil activities was a means to achieve peace, while the company believed that oil activities would be the basis for peace.[23]

There were two notable exceptions in Lundin's relations with special-interest groups: Amnesty International, particularly the Swedish branch; and the Church of Sweden. Both organizations believed in the benefits of constructive engagement with companies operating in Sudan and met with Lundin on a number of occasions. Lundin invited their representatives to visit its concession area, but because of its suspension of oil activities and later the sale of its assets the visits never materialized. Nonetheless, some of these groups' views and recommendations were taken into consideration and, where appropriate, were integrated into Lundin's business conduct.[24]

Think tanks

The think tanks which had been following and reporting on Sudan for a number of years also considered how oil could act as an incentive for peace in

---

[23] In March 2001 Lundin posted a report on its website "Lundin in Sudan" which described company activities to date and responded to allegations regarding the nature of the conflict in its area of operations.

[24] Amnesty International (AI) had issued recommendations for oil companies operating in Sudan; these were circulated among relevant company staff, as were copies of the ten Basic Human Rights Standards for Law Enforcement Officials (note 20).

Sudan.[25] Above and beyond the obvious positive benefits of oil for the overall economic performance of the country, they were interested in ascertaining whether oil could be used as a peace incentive. Discussions with representatives of think tanks were dedicated to a review of oil exploration, production and revenue distribution schemes. It was generally accepted that a fair distribution of oil resources was a necessary condition for peace, and in this regard the company drew their attention to the equitable sharing scheme laid out in the Khartoum Peace Agreement.

The media (representing public interest)

When allegations of a possible connection between the war and Lundin's operations surfaced in the press, the company decided that the best way to respond was to invite both Swedish and international journalists to visit its concession area. Until that time, journalists who had reported from the field had been able to do so only with the support of rebel forces; therefore their reports presented only one side of the story. The company believed that if they had the opportunity to visit the area without support or interference from either rebel or government forces, they would have a more balanced and realistic view of the situation. A number of journalists took up the company's suggestion and visited the area in 2001 and 2002. They produced articles for the press as well as video recordings that were shown on both Swedish and Swiss television.

Peace negotiators

As a general principle, Lundin refrains from getting involved in the political affairs of a country; it believes that it cannot make a meaningful contribution in this sphere and prefers to restrict itself to its commercial mission. The situation it encountered in Sudan, however, was exceptional, and the company needed to make clear to the protagonists in the conflict that it saw peace as the best means to ensure sustainable oil operations. In this endeavor it relied on the skills and competence of Carl Bildt, a member of Lundin Petroleum's Board of Directors, whose experience as the UN Secretary-General's Special Envoy for the Balkans in 1999–2001 was particularly relevant. In a series of trips to Brussels, Cairo, Khartoum, Nairobi and Washington, Bildt met with high-level representatives of the Sudanese Government, including the President, his peace adviser, the Minister of

---

[25] Two US-based think tanks devoted particular attention to this issue: the Center for Strategic International Studies (CSIS), Washington, DC and the Carter Center Peace Program, Atlanta, Georgia.

Energy and Mining, the Minister of Foreign Affairs, and the main representative of the Nuer community (later the deputy chairman of the SPLA), as well as with representatives of the key nations acting as peace mediators, such as Kenya, Norway, the UK and the US. Bildt delivered the same message to all: oil represented an incentive for peace in so far as oil activities could not be pursued in a war context. He also underlined how oil provided the material basis for a sustainable peace. The company's repeated suspensions of activities were a proof that oil activities could not flourish in a conflict situation, and experience in various other countries demonstrated that a conflict of this nature could not be resolved militarily. In Bildt's view, the parties had to determine for themselves their minimum, not maximum, requirements for the achievement of peace. The mediators' role was to help the parties achieve this compromise by offering them support, in the form of international monitoring and monetary assistance for purposes of reconstruction.

4. Lessons learned

During the seven years in which it acted as operator of Block 5A in southern Sudan, Lundin was faced with a constantly changing environment. The company learned that, despite its desire to restrict itself to a commercial role, it could not ignore either the socio-political developments in its area of operations or the claims – even if unfounded – of a possible connection between its activities and the conflict.

A reaffirmation of its values in a Code of Conduct, a greater involvement in community life, stakeholder engagement and the suspension of activities were the tools adopted by the company in response to the challenges it faced.

In the spring of 2003, the company sold its interest in Block 5A at a profit. The transaction was satisfying not only from a commercial perspective but also from the perspective of corporate responsibility. At the time the company left, active peace negotiations were under way and its community development programme was maintained by its successor. This reinforced Lundin's belief that it is possible for business to pursue commercial objectives while meeting ethical concerns, even in areas of conflict.

Part III

Industry-level

9 How the clean air interstate rule will affect investment and management decisions in the US electricity sector

Caryl Pfeiffer

1. Introduction: Overview of the Clean Air Act Interstate Rule (CAIR)

The Clean Air Act (CAA) of 1970 (amended in 1977 and in 1990) is the US framework for establishing National Ambient Air Quality Standards (NAAQS) to protect public health and welfare and to control harmful emissions from sources of air pollution to achieve those standards. The Clean Air Act is administered by a federal agency, the US Environmental Protection Agency (EPA).

In July 1997, the EPA revised the National Ambient Air Quality Standards for ozone and particulate matter. The new NAAQS for ozone changed the existing standard from one that measures ozone concentrations over a one-hour period to one that measures over an eight-hour period, and tightened the concentration of the pollutant from 120 parts per billion (ppb) to 80 ppb. For particulate matter less than 2.5 microns in diameter ($PM_{2.5}$), the EPA identified NO_x from fossil-fired power plants as a major contributor to ozone pollution, and acid aerosols (nitrogen oxides (NO_x) and sulfur-dioxide (SO_2)) from fossil-fired power plants as fine particulates likely to be subject to additional controls.

The EPA designated eight-hour ozone and $PM_{2.5}$ nonattainment areas (counties) based on ground-level monitoring of pollutant levels. If an area's monitored concentration of a pollutant exceeds the standard, then EPA categorizes that as nonattainment. Each state with a nonattainment area(s) then submits a plan for attainment (a State Implementation Plan or SIP).

The EPA determined that attainment of these new NAAQS in the Eastern United States could only be achieved through a combination of emission reductions from:

(a) sources located in or near nonattainment areas (such as mobile sources); and

(b) sources (such as fossil-fired power plants) located further from the nonattainment areas to deal with interstate transport of air pollution.

To address the regional transport of air pollution and its "significant" contribution to ozone and fine particulate matter nonattainment in downwind areas, the EPA promulgated the Clean Air Interstate Rule (CAIR), finalized on March 10, 2005. This requires significant SO_2 and/or NO_x reductions from fossil-fuel fired power plants in twenty-eight Eastern states and the District of Columbia.

The rules are intended to reduce further ground-level ozone (by requiring further reductions in NO_x during the summer) and to reduce fine particulates or $PM_{2.5}$ (by reducing SO_2 and NO_x on an annual basis).

It requires the following reductions from fossil-fired electric generating units (EGUs) compared to their 2003 levels:

	Applies during:	28 States	Kentucky
Annual NO_x	2009–2014	53%	42%
Annual NO_x	2015 and beyond	61%	58%
Annual SO_2	2010–2014	45%	36%
Annual SO_2	2015 and beyond	57%	49%

and imposes the following caps of emissions:

	SO_2	NO_x
2004	7.9 m tons	2.7 m tons
2011	3.6 m tons	1.5 m tons
2015	2.5 m tons	1.3 m tons

Ozone Season NO_x replaces the current NO_x SIP Call (which caps NO_x emissions during the May–September ozone season) with CAIR NO_x caps, also during May–September. For Kentucky, the new cap is identical to the NO_x SIP Call for 2009–2014 and is reduced by about 15% for 2015 and beyond. Therefore, beginning in 2009, there will be two overlapping restrictions on NO_x emissions, and EGUs must comply with both. They must emit less than a given amount during the ozone season and emit less than another given amount on an annual basis.

The rule requires states to submit a plan to EPA on how they will achieve the reductions, either by participating in a regional "cap-and-trade program" (similar to the Acid Rain and NO_x SIP Call programs) or by an alternative of the states' choosing. The plans were to be submitted by September 2006.

Note on acid rain cap-and-trade program

The Acid Deposition Control Program was established under Title IV of the Clean Air Act Amendments of 1990. Title IV's purpose was to reduce the adverse effects of acid deposition through a permanent 10 million ton reduction in SO_2 emissions and a 2 million ton reduction in NO_x from 1980 levels in the 48 contiguous states. The Acid Deposition Control Program established a cap on annual SO_2 emissions at approximately 8.9 million tons by the year 2000. The legislation obtains these SO_2 emission reductions from electric utility plants through the use of a market-based system of emission allowances. Under the system, "affected units" are allocated allowances in an amount based on their historic fossil fuel consumption and a specified emissions rate. Affected units are required to hold sufficient allowances to cover their annual level of SO_2 emissions, but are given the flexibility to reduce their emissions in the most cost-effective manner. Once allocated, allowances may be used by affected units to cover SO_2 emissions, banked for future use, or sold to others. SO_2 allowances are not unit-specific and can be sold or traded. Utilities have incentives to reduce SO_2 emissions so that they can use allowances to cover growth, to make additional off-system sales, or to sell or trade allowances on the open market, offsetting the cost of compliance. Utilities that reduce the amount of SO_2 emitted below their authorized level may bank their allowances for future use or sell or trade them to other utilities who expect to exceed their authorized emission level, or to other allowance market participants such as emission brokers.

1.2 Note on NO$_x$ SIP call

In September 1998, EPA finalized the NO_x SIP Call rule, requiring 19 Eastern states, including Kentucky and the District of Columbia, to revise their State Implementation Plans. The new SIPs must achieve additional NO_x emissions reductions that the EPA believes are necessary to mitigate the transport of ozone across the Eastern half of the United States. The final rule required fossil-fired power plants in the 19-state area to retrofit their electric generating units with NO_x control devices by May 2004.

It is likely that Kentucky and most of the other affected states will choose the cap-and-trade approach. Under a cap-and-trade program, each combustion unit is awarded a set number of "allowances." Historically, the unit would surrender allowances in an amount equal to its emissions to be in compliance; the new rule modifies the surrender ratio for SO_2, explained later. Each allowance has an associated vintage year and cannot be used for compliance before its vintage.[1] Allowances can be traded between units, plants, companies, and so on.

The allowance programs will be complicated since different states are subject to different combinations of requirements under the Acid Rain Program, the NO_x SIP Call, CAIR ozone-season reductions, and CAIR SO_2/NO_x annual reductions.

The following is a simplified summary based on the EPA's model emissions trading rule:

1.3 Sulfur dioxide

Existing Acid Rain allowances would be used. Allowances with vintage 2009 and earlier would be surrendered on a "one-for-one" basis throughout the CAIR program. Vintages 2010–2014 would be surrendered on a "two-for-one" basis (surrender two allowances for each ton of emissions) and vintages 2015 and beyond would be surrendered on a "2.86-for-one" basis. This acts as an incentive to reduce emissions and bank SO_2 allowances before 2010.[2]

1.4 NO_x

LG&E Energy's allocation will not be known until the state of Kentucky develops an in-state allocation process. A range of estimates has been provided below.

The EPA will allocate predetermined numbers of NO_x allowances to each state and the individual states will determine how to allocate these to individual units, similar to the current process under the NO_x SIP Call. Because Kentucky is required to reduce NO_x for both ozone and $PM_{2.5}$, there will be ozone season allowances and annual allowances.

For ozone-season control, Kentucky's allocation is the same as under the NO_x SIP Call for 2009–2014. For 2015 and beyond, its ozone season cap is about 15% lower (nominally based on 0.125 lb/mmBtu vs. 0.15 lb/mmBtu).

---

[1] Allowances cannot be surrendered to cover emissions earlier than the vintage year. For example, SO_2 allowances have already been awarded for thirty years into the future and have been placed by the federal government in individual accounts for each generating unit/company. When allowances are surrendered for operations in 2005, the company can use allowances dated with a vintage year of 2005 or earlier, but cannot pull allowances forward from a year in the future to cover emissions at the present time. Hence, "No allowance can be used before its time – before its vintage year."

[2] Increases in the exchange rates of allowances over time speed up the reduction of SO_2 emissions. In 2010 the exchange rate will be increased to 2 for 1, so that two allowances must be surrendered for every one ton of emissions into the air and in 2015 that goes to 3 for 1. So utilities are encouraged to reduce emissions because their allowances are worth less and less going into the future.

For $PM_{2.5}$ control, Kentucky's annual NO_x allocation is 83,205 tons during 2009–2014 and 69,337 tons for 2015 and beyond. These figures are about 7% higher than in the proposed regulations, largely because EPA applied a weighting factor that allocates more allowances to coal-fired generation than to oil and gas; thus, Kentucky's allocation increased because of its high percentage of coal-fired generation. A ballpark estimate of LG&E Energy's possible allocation is provided below. However, Kentucky may choose to set some allowances aside for new sources or to withhold some and auction them. For example, under the NO_x SIP Call, Kentucky withheld 5% of the 2004–2006 allocation and auctioned them, with proceeds going to the Kentucky General Fund.

Estimate of Annual NO_x Allowances (assuming no withholding)

	2009–2014	2015 and beyond
KU	16,300	13,400
LG&E (75% TC)	12,600	10,500

The EPA determined that the most "cost effective" way to attain the new ground level NAAQS for ozone and fine particulate matter was with emission reductions from fossil fuel-fired boilers. The EPA also calculated that CAIR costs are "modest in light of benefits expected."

The EPA estimates that CAIR will result in substantial human health and environmental net benefits (up to $100bn per year) while helping urban areas in the East to achieve the new, more stringent NAAQS for ozone and fine particles. Cost is estimated at $3.6bn per year (the investment required by the electric utility industry in the East). Since these costs will fall upon the electricity consumers, EPA estimates that electricity prices will increase 2.0–2.7% within the CAIR Region in the 2010–2015 timeframe. Natural gas production is estimated to increase 1.6%, coal by 25%.

2. Regulatory drivers leading to CAIR

The principal drivers leading to the introduction of CAIR are:
(1) Emission reductions
    In the US, there is an on-going push by public health and environmental advocates, as well as by regulatory agencies, for emission reductions from coal-fired generation. There is 244 GW of installed coal-fired

capacity in the CAIR footprint which represents 80% of the coal-fired capacity in the US. The electric generation power sector represents 69% of the total SO_2 emissions and 22% of the total NO_x emissions in the United States.

(2) Local governments' inability to regulate mobile sources

Even though mobile sources account for the overwhelming majority of emissions resulting in ground-level ozone in urban areas, local elected officials have been unwilling to impose additional restrictions on passenger vehicles because the passengers in those vehicles vote.

(3) Need for local governments to get reclassification of their counties to attainment status

If a nonattainment area is not on an EPA-approved State Implementation Plan to attain the national ambient air quality standards, federal government funding for transportation projects is halted. If local governments adopt (through their SIPs) the EPA regional solution that only affects coal-fired power plants (not mobile sources), then they have an EPA-approved plan without making hard choices about local emission reductions.

(4) Disparity of electric prices in the Eastern United States

East Coast electricity producers have not achieved the lower rates promised through deregulation and are looking for ways to increase their competitive edge. Some East Coast utilities are hoping that rate equalization will occur as environmental compliance costs are pushed onto the heavily coal-dependent (and lower cost) electric generators in the Midwest and South. Currently, East Coast electric providers charge an average retail rate of 12¢ per kWh, as compared to providers in the Midwest and South who come in, on average, at 7.7¢ per kWh.

3. LG&E Energy's current situation

LG&E Energy is a coal-fired electric utility located in Kentucky. It has 9,005 MW of installed capacity of which 8,190 MW is coal-fired. Its 27 coal-fired units, at ten sites throughout Kentucky, burn 21 million tons of coal per year. As shown in Figure 9.1, 98% of the kWh generated and sold comes from coal-fired units.

LG&E Energy's position in the marketplace is based on three main factors:
1. Cost – LG&E Energy has the lowest electric rates in the US, due to:
   - a low embedded cost of generation;

• Emission reductions fall most heavily on coal-fired generators

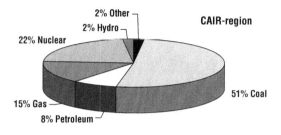

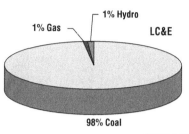

(Database 2003)

LG&E – Current situation:

9,005 MW installed power

8,190 MW from coal power plants

27 coal units at 10 sites

60% equipped with FGD

84% equipped with SCR

CAIR – New requirements for LG&E

For 2,400 MW – 6 new FGD for coal fired power plants

No additional SCR required

SCR – Selective Catalytic Reduction
FGD – Flue Gas Desulfurization

Source: LG & E

Figure 9.1:   Electricity generated by energy sources

- the location of power plants adjacent to low-cost coals (the Illinois Basin, the Appalachian Basin and Pittsburgh 8);
- its historic position as leader in air pollution control – LG&E installed the first flue gas desulfurization system (FGD) in the US (1974), enabling the company to gain experience with this control equipment while burning higher-sulfur, lower-cost coals. The company also invested early in selective catalytic reduction systems and has demonstrated among the highest NO_x removal rates for this technology in the US;
- 60% of the company's installed coal-fired capacity being equipped with FGD for SO_2 control;
- 84% of its installed coal-fired capacity being equipped with SCR for NO_x control;
- good utility management and fair regulatory agency oversight
2. Reliability – LG&E has:
   - adequate reserve margin in generating capacity;
   - a robust transmission system across the service territory, although there are certain constraints in extreme Western Kentucky under peak flow conditions (not caused by LG&E's system, but by those it is interconnected to – TVA and BREC);

• **Clean air machine or electricity generator?**

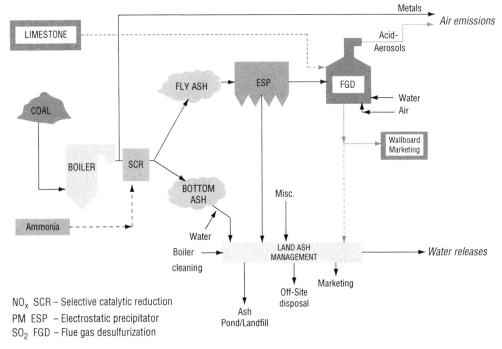

NO$_x$ SCR – Selective catalytic reduction
PM ESP – Electrostatic precipitator
SO$_2$ FGD – Flue gas desulfurization

Source: LG&E

Figure 9.2: Air pollution control technologies for coal-fired units

3. Customer service
   • LG&E Energy has been awarded the JD Powers customer service award (for both residential and commercial customers) for the past six years running;
   • the company has highly qualified and dedicated customer service representatives for each of the customer classes – wholesale, industrial, commercial and residential

4. CAIR compliance options for coal-fired electric generating units

The principal choices facing LG&E are:
• invest in air pollution control technologies or lower emitting generation sources;
• fuel switch;
• rely on the emissions trading market

Note that non-compliance is not an option. There are civil penalties of $27,500 per violation, and criminal penalties, where a utility's designated representative under the CAA is held personally liable, including the potential for jail time.

5. LG&E Energy CAIR compliance strategy

In response to the proposed CAIR rules, LG&E Energy undertook an assessment to determine the most cost-effective means of meeting these environmental requirements (within the emission limitations and deadlines imposed by the rule) and to provide the timeframe for construction and the estimated cost of the projects. This is contained in the 2004 SO_2 compliance strategy study which is a result of the company's continual environmental compliance analysis review process. As identified in its 2002 SO_2 Environmental Compliance Analysis (contained in the company's 2002 Integrated Resource Plan), the company has a rapidly depleting bank of SO_2 allowances that will soon require the addition of new control technologies or the purchase of SO_2 allowances. The company's SO_2 allowance bank reached a peak of 297,000 in 1999 and has diminished substantially since then due to load growth and the resulting increased utilization of the coal-fired generating units. By end of 2004, the bank was projected to have around 160,000 allowances and it was likely to be completely depleted before the end of 2007. The shortfall that was due to begin in 2007 will be further exacerbated by the implementation of the Clean Air Interstate Rule in 2010. The study identified that unless additional SO_2 reductions are achieved, LG & E will be forced to acquire SO_2 allowances from the allowance market, where prices have rapidly escalated from approximately $175 per ton in July 2003 to nearly $700 per ton in November 2004 (and over $900 in October 2005).

The 2004 SO_2 Compliance Strategy study identified that Ghent Units 2–4 and Brown Units 1–3 account for over 55% of the company's future SO_2 emissions and were the most logical and economical choice for installing control technologies to reduce overall SO_2 emissions. The study utilized the PROSYM^{TM} detailed hourly production costing computer model from Henwood, and the Strategist$^{®}$ Capital Expenditure and Recovery (CER) module from New Energy Associates, to analyze twenty-two cases. The analysis included the evaluation of numerous strategies utilizing wet FGD processes, dry FGD processes, and fuel switching for these units, and the purchasing of allowances to determine the most cost-effective means of mitigating the expected SO_2 allowance shortfall. It explored the use of low sulfur coals such as Powder River Basin and Eastern Compliance, but determined that fuel switching at both Ghent and Brown failed to significantly improve the overall SO_2 position. Sensitivities to capital cost and the market price of SO_2 allowances were also considered in the analysis.

The company's least-cost plan results in the construction of wet-limestone, forced oxidation FGD systems on Brown Units 1, 2 and 3 and Ghent Units 2 and 3. The anticipated costs and completion schedule are identified in the table below. It is expected to take 18–24 months to complete each FGD, with some portions of the engineering and design being undertaken simultaneously.

	In-service	Total cost
Location	*Date*	($m)
Brown 1–3 FGD	May '09	$234.19
Ghent 2 FGD	May '08	$149.57
Ghent 3 FGD	May '07	$129.02
Ghent 4 FGD	May '09	$146.15
		$658.93

NOTE: The SO_2 price forecast used in this analysis was a combination of actual market prices and forecast prices. The prices from 2005–2009 reflected the market prices at the end of June 2004 adjusted for inflation. The market prices at the time the forecast was established were the highest in the history of actively traded SO_2 allowances. The anticipated impact of CAIR on the allowance markets was reflected in the 2010 forecast allowance price. In the remaining years the prices were escalated based on the company's assumptions for inflation.

The supply side of the SO_2 allowance market has remained very conservative with the credits available, due to the projected impact of CAIR. These factors have contributed to the current high market prices for SO_2 allowances.

The 2004 SO_2 Compliance Strategy study recommends the construction of wet FGD systems on Ghent Units 2, 3 and 4 and Brown Units 1, 2 and 3, with the simultaneous switching of the units to high sulfur coal and the purchasing of allowances on an as needed basis as the most cost-effective plan for continued environmental compliance. While the addition of the FGD systems does not eliminate the need to purchase SO_2 allowances, the installation of controls significantly reduces the company's exposure to the SO_2 allowance market and further assures continued economical compliance with the environmental requirements of the Clean Air Act. The study also showed that, compared to purchasing SO_2 allowances, the construction of the wet FGD systems and the simultaneous conversion of the units to high-sulfur coal provided the following ratepayer benefits over the twenty-year analysis period:

1. Decreases the cost of SO_2 compliance, with cost savings projected to be more than $110 million (PVRR[3]), and provides the most reasonable least-cost approach for continued environmental compliance.
2. Limits significant exposure to the SO_2 allowance market by reducing the companies' anticipated shortfall.
3. Increases fuel procurement flexibility (lowers fuel costs).
4. Improves position for meeting future regulations regarding mercury.

Note that under Kentucky state law, regulated utilities that retrofit air pollution control equipment in compliance with emission reduction requirements under the Clean Air Act, as amended, can apply for Environmental Cost Recovery (ECR) from the Kentucky Public Service Commission. This mechanism allows for the dynamic recovery of environmental control costs without the need to file a full rate case. Upon a demonstration that the utility's proposed Environmental Compliance Plan represents the least-cost option for meeting the new requirements, the utility can recover the actual costs (plus a rate of return) associated with the capital investment in the air pollution control equipment. These incremental environmental compliance costs are recovered through an ECR bill surcharge.

Since the company's evaluation, there have been significant upward movements in SO_2 market prices. This trend is positively correlated to the value that the company's compliance plan provides its ratepayers. As discussed in the 2004 SO_2 Compliance Strategy, a 10% increase in the SO_2 price forecast increases the value of the project by more than $54 m (from $110 m savings for the companies' ratepayers to $164 m). As recently as October 15, 2005, SO_2 allowances were priced at $950 a ton, more than double the forecast 2005 price of $392 a ton used in this analysis. Therefore, the economics supporting the decision to construct wet scrubbers at Ghent and Brown would be enhanced by the incorporation of today's SO_2 market prices.

6. Impact on LG&E Energy and its competitors

The intention of CAIR is to force SO_2 and NO_x emission reductions from coal-fired generation in the Eastern United States. In order to achieve the SO_2

---

[3] Present value of Annual Revenue Requirements.

emission reductions imposed by the rule, LG&E will install FGD on 2,400 MW of coal-fired generation (six electric generating units) at a capital cost of $678 million. The project will decrease SO_2 compliance costs by $110 million over the twenty-year life of the investment and will result in a net present value of $14.8bn. Furthermore, LG&E FGD retrofits will be installed at an average cost of $275/kW. LG&E is already in compliance with the NO_x emission reductions imposed by the rule, so no additional investment in SCRs will have to be made.

LG&E Energy's investment will result in a 13% rise in revenue requirements for its retail customers or an increase of approximately $7 per month for a typical residential customer using 1,000 kWh per month.

LG&E's major competitors (based on MWh sales and associated revenues) in the states that surround Kentucky are:

- Tennessee – Tennessee Valley Authority
- Missouri – Ameren
- Illinois – Excelon
- Indiana – Cinergy
- Ohio – American Electric Power
- West Virginia – American Electric Power
- Virginia – Dominion

Only TVA in Tennessee and AEP in West Virginia command rates today that could compete with LG&E on "price" after LG&E realizes its rate increase due to compliance with the Clean Air Interstate Rule.

TVA has announced a $1.5bn investment in FGD on 4,350 MW to reduce SO_2 emissions (in addition to a $1.3bn investment in SCR on 9,875 MW to reduce NO_x emissions that it has recently completed) in order to comply with CAIR. The effect of this investment will be to raise their rates by an additional 16%. FGD retrofits will be installed at an average cost of $340/kW.

AEP has announced a $1.2bn investment in FGD on 3,500 MW to reduce SO_2 emissions (in addition to an investment of more than $1bn in SCR to reduce NO_x emissions that it has recently completed). This, too, will raise their rates by an additional 16%. FGD retrofits will be installed at an average cost of $343/kW.

Since LG&E Energy's rates will continue be lower than both TVA's and AEP's, after compliance with CAIR, the company will maintain its position as a cost leader. This is due to LG&E's having not only a lower installed cost for its FGD systems but also fewer coal-fired megawatts that needed to be retrofitted with SO_2 control equipment. LG&E, as a regulated coal-fired generator, benefits from CAIR and will be able to not only recover the costs of compliance through the addition of air pollution control capital expenditures to its regulated rate base, but also have a resultant increase in regulated earnings.

Sources

CAIR information

Clean Air Act of 1970, as amended, 42 USC 7401 *et seq.*, PL 91–604
> Revisions to the National Ambient Air Quality Standards for Fine Particulate Matter and Ozone, 40 CFR Parts 50, 51 and 52, July 1997

Rule to Reduce Interstate Transport of Fine Particulate Matter and Ozone (Clean Air Interstate Rule);

Revisions to Acid Rain Program;

Revisions to NO_x SIP Call, 40 CFR Parts, 51, 72, 73, 74, 77, 78 and 96, March 2005

A New Rule for Clean Air, Electric Perspectives, July/August 2004

Clean Air Interstate Rule at www.epa.gov/cleanairinterstaterule

Clean Air Interstate Rule at www.epa.gov/cair

Electric Utility Trade Association information at www.eei.org/industry_issues/environment/air

Emissions information

State-by-State Utility Emissions and Heat Input Data, Nationwide Utility Emissions and Heat Input Data, Emissions Scoreboard 2003 epa.gov/airmarkets/emissions

Energy supply, consumption and revenue information

Annual Energy Outlook, 100 Largest Electric Company Net Generation 2003, US Average Monthly Bill by Sector and State 2003, Net Generation by Fuel by State 2003, at www.eia.doe/cneaf/electricity
> Utilities: Electricity at www.worldmarketsanalysis.com/servlet

LG&E Energy information

Assessment of Clean Air Interstate Rule Final Rule by Glenn Gibian, Senior Environmental Engineer, LG&E Energy Services, March 18, 2005

Control Technology Cost and Process Description information from Roger Medina, Senior Environmental Engineer, LG&E Energy Services Testimonies of Robert M. Conroy and John P. Malloy in the Matter of: The Application of Kentucky Utilities Company for a Certificate of Public Convenience and Necessity to Construct Flue Gas Desulfurization Systems and Approval of its 2004 Compliance Plan for Recovery by Environmental Surcharge, Case No. 2004–00426 at www.psc.state.ky.us

SO_2 compliance strategy

Integrated resource plan

Rate impacts of least cost compliance plan

Internal investment proposal to construct wet limestone FGD Systems at Brown Units 1–3 and Ghent Units 2–4 and Fuel switch to high sulfur coal, October 2004

Competitor information

Ameren:	www.ameren.com/corporateFacts & www.dynegy.com/Generation/Facilities/MAIN
	17,340 MW: 11,350 coal
	4,040 Oil + NG
	800 hydro
	1,150 nuclear
Excelon:	www.exceloncorp.com/generation/power
	30,000 MW: 10,000 fossil
	1,610 hydro
	18,390 nuclear (20% of US nuclear capacity)
Cinergy:	www.cinergy.com/sustain/environment-improvement.asp
	10,105 MW of coal (35% equipped with FGD/50% equipped with SCR)
AEP:	www.aep.com/environmental/performance/emissionsassessment
	www.aep.com/environmental/emissionscontrol/
	www.aepchio.com/about/serviceTerritroy
	www.indianapower.com/about/serviceTerritory
	www.kenntuckypower.com/about/serviceTerritory
	www.apcocustomer.com/about/serviceTerritory
	23,805 MW: 21,650 fossil (90% coal)
	2,155 nuclear

Dominion: www.dom.com/about/overview
            www.dom.com/about/stations/fossil
            www.dom.com/about/stations/hydro
            www.dom.com/about/stations/nuclear
            23,860 MW: 5,140 coal
                        10,200 Oil + NG
                        2,430 hydro
                        6,090 nuclear
TVA: www.tva.gov/power/powerfacts
            www.tva.com/environment/reports/envreports/aer2003/
            envcompliance
            coal: 61% of TVA's generation
            nuclear: 29% of TVA's generation
            hydro: 9% of TVA's generation
            other: 1% of TVA's generation

10 EU water infrastructure management: National regulations, EU framework directives but no model to follow

Ralf Boscheck

During the twentieth century, global water withdrawal increased by a factor of six, i.e. more than twice the rate of population growth;[1] extrapolating developments during the last five years of that period for the hundred years to come results in an annual extraction twenty-three times the current level. But already the present yearly use of around 5000km^3 represents more than half of the amount readily available to humans; this resource is unequally distributed around the globe and seriously compromised by wastage, pollution, deforestation, land degradation and lowering water tables. If current trends persist, by 2025 at least 3.5bn people or 48% of the world population will live in "water-stressed" conditions, that is, experience severe water scarcity and gravely strained aquatic ecosystems.[2] To arrest this development, UN members, at the Johannesburg Summit in 2002, agreed to employ methods of efficient river-basin management by 2005, and in March 2006, at a meeting of water legislators during the Fourth World Water Forum, declared water to be "a property of the public domain" rather than a commodity, and access to it possibly a human right.[3]

Current efforts to identify transferable solutions also focus on European resource management, particularly on national approaches to operating and charging for water and infrastructure investments as well as the EU's Water Framework Directive (WFD).[4] The latter is said to facilitate integrated, economic river-basin management while considering water a non-commodity. But Europe does not offer simple answers either. For one, Europe's national or regional water systems reflect specific climatic, demographic and

---

[1] Shiklomanov, I., (1999) *World water resources*, St.Petersburg: United Nations; United Nations (1999), *World Freshwater Resources*.

[2] See also UNESCO World Water Assessment, at www.uesembassy,i/file200303/alia/a3030516.htm.

[3] See www.worldwaterforum4.org.mx/files/World_Encounter_of_Water_Legislators.pdf. Fourth World Water Forum 2006 Declaration of Water Legislators; Scanlon, J. *et al.* (2004) *Water as a Human Right?* IUCN Policy Paper No. 51.

[4] Directive 2000/60/EC of the European Parliament and the Council of 23 October 2000 establishing a framework for Community action in the field of water policy, (2000) OJ L327/1 (WFD).

topographic situations and are the product of the particular cultural, political and social fabric of the society they serve. Both sets of factors explain the absence of common performance standards, which makes it difficult to benchmark given supply schemes or suggest a model to be followed. Next, the EU's WFD, drafted under the impact of a protracted power struggle among EU institutions, Member States and stakeholder groups, does not constitute the unifying European reference it was intended to be. Built on vague objectives and unclear monitoring criteria, it is a compromise that risks diluting pre-existing regulatory norms, invokes national discretion to close EU legislative gaps, and, for all practical purposes, may be unenforceable. Finally, and linking both previous issues, lacking a unified reference hampers the EU's ability to assess a Member State's capacity to comply with WFD requirements, identify appropriate remedial actions, and develop central regulations beyond the level of the lowest common denominator.

The argument is presented in three parts. Section 1 characterizes the main challenges facing the European water industry, before sketching the governance methods currently applied in Germany, France and England and Wales. Section 2 traces the evolution of EU institutional bargaining that shaped the EU Water Framework Directive and discusses its impact on national sector regulation and concerns about remaining uncertainty and enforceability. Section 3 sums up governance concerns and offers a conclusion.

1. EU water industry – regulatory structures and challenges[5]

At present, almost 30 bn cubic meters of water are being consumed annually by the EU's industry (56%), households (24%) and agriculture (20%). Regional shares reflect diverse climatic conditions, levels and types of economic activity, population size, consumption habits, and regulations. Industrial users differ widely with respect to the quantity and quality of water they require. Patterns of domestic consumption reveal variations in the use of labor-saving appliances and the adoption of water-efficient technologies. EU water consumption over the last decade of the twentieth century has grown by on average of 2% but the figure hides major increases and decreases in consumption as in Spain, (+17.3%), France (+21.15%), the

---

[5] This section is based on, but updates parts of, Boscheck, R., (2002) European water infrastructures, Intereconomics, May/June, 138–49.

UK (+19.4%), and Denmark (−9.4%) and Germany (−9.1%), respectively.[6] Still, any statistical variance among EU water markets cannot distract from a range of common challenges.

For one, even though nearly 98% of EU households are connected to running water further investments are needed to refurbish aging pipe work, increase system capacity and ensure supply and operating efficiency. Next, in the early 1990s, concern about the quality of ground and drinking water translated into EU purity standards which, more than a decade later, are still unmet by many Member States.[7] Less than 10% of Europe's rivers are considered pristine, and only the upper sections of the fourteen largest rivers retain "good ecological status."[8] In response, the EU Commission set out to prosecute members for infringing environmental rules and to promote the adoption of more stringent WFD norms. The question is how to finance regulatory compliance?

Since the beginning of the 1990s, EU water utilities invested more than €45 bn annually to enhance the efficiency and compliance of their waste- and clean-water infrastructures. Mobilizing the required finance, European utilities improved operational efficiencies, cross-subsidized public budgets or increased revenues from higher water charges and outsourced activities. In this context, privatization became attractive not only to tap financial resources but also to seek market-driven efficiencies and a "covert" opportunity to introduce cost-sufficient pricing policies. Yet, while numerous privatization schemes increased the level of internationalism and corporatism in the EU's national water supplies,[9] only England and Wales have moved towards broadly selling off water assets and centrally regulating private operators of integrated river-basin systems. And even here, recent regulatory reforms and corporate initiatives may end up reversing the pattern of asset ownership and governance. Other economies experimented with more restrained forms of private sector involvement and decentralized methods of regulatory control. Going forward, most EU Member States will need to reconsider the links between asset ownership, regulation and governance. (Box 10.1 sketches some fundamentals of economic regulation.)

---

[6] Data is calculated based on statistics supplied by International Water Association (2000) at www.iwahq.org.uk.

[7] The 1991 Urban Wastewater Directive called on towns exceeding 20,000 inhabitants to have waste-water treatment in place by the year 2000, (2007) and directed industry to pre-treat emissions.

[8] UNESCO, (2003) at www.Unesco.org/water/wwap/facts_figures/protectingecosystems.shtml.

[9] Consider the Vivendi-RWE joint venture in Berliner Wasser Betriebe and Budapest, the Thames Water-EDP joint venture, or the high-profile concessions in Brussels, the Delfland, Poznan, Brdo-Modrice or Santa Maria da Feira.

Box 10.1: Regulatory control

Various consumption, investment and production characteristics are typically seen to require the public organization, or at least a close regulatory control, of water service provision. *First,* while making water consumption exclusive may be seen to be either ethically indefensible or for all practical purposes impossible, the fact that consumption affects the quantity and quality of water available to others requires market and non-market coordination based on some enforceable water rights. In Europe, such claims have traditionally been based on land ownership, rationed use or community membership, or established as common property ultimately under state control.[10] *Second,* investments in pipeline networks offer distant and risky paybacks but immediate and wide-ranging benefits. As societal gains exceed private returns, market-based investments will not reach the social optimum, unless subsidized or at least motivated by publicly enforced, cost-sufficient pricing. *Next,* while sunk investments may make the resulting "natural monopoly" virtually non-contestable and invite abuse by the incumbent, exposing the incumbent to potential competition in part of its market may also prove futile. Even an efficient naturally monopolistic operator cannot defend itself against entrants allowed to cherrypick some unbundled service and undercut the incumbent's average price. Here, continued monopolistic supply is preferable if efficient behavior could somehow be presumed. To deal with these situations, regulatory options range from broadly decentralized control of private undertakings, subject to antitrust and price regulation, to public asset ownership, ministerial guidance and budgetary control. Between these nodes, institutional formats differ in how they allocate ownership, funding obligations and operational and commercial responsibilities among public and private parties, and the type of regulatory, statutory or contractual rules used to hold management accountable.

While there seems to be strong consensus among theorists on the superior performance of private firms over government-owned ones in competitive industries, that presumption is not always empirically tested and evidence in network industries is far less clear cut.[11] Systematic reviews of the water industry are rare but seem to contradict conventional wisdom. Recent studies on comparative public-private efficiency either find private operators to be less efficient or are unable to detect any significant difference with their public counterparts, and this conclusion appears to be robust irrespective of the time period, the sample and the estimation methodology employed. Others show that efficiency differences are largely explained by the regulatory framework – rate of return vs. price-cap regulation – and the degree of transparency that a regulator is able to achieve.[12]

---

[10] These are so-called "riparian", "appropriation" or "community" rights. Private property of surface water is typically limited to small quantities; only France and Spain recognize private property of ground water. However, tradable water rights exist in the UK.

[11] See Megginson, W. L., Netter, J. M., (2001) From state to market: A survey of empirical studies on privatization, *Journal of Economic Literature,* 39(2), 321–89. See Newberry (1999) for a review of the evidence in network industries, Newberry, D., (1999), *Privatization, restructuring, and regulation of network industries.* Cambridge MA: MIT Press.

[12] Conti (2005) concludes that policy makers should focus more on competition and incentive regulation issues rather than on ownership *per se.* Conti, M., (2005) Ownership relative efficiency in the water industry: A survey of the international empirical evidence, *International Economics,* August, 58(3), 273–306.

Box 10.1 (*cont.*)

For much of the twentieth century, regulatory policy towards natural monopoly was dominated by average cost pricing through rate-of-return regulation. It allows firms to freely make input, output and pricing decisions provided that their return on capital remains below some specified level. Firms are insured against cost increases but have little efficiency incentive. While rate-base regulation conceptually duplicates long-term competitive market outcomes, the built-in incentive problems forestall the actual attainment of that goal. Hence, regulators are driven to scrutinize operational decisions and *reveal* the true status of companies. Practical experience with more "incentive-compatible" forms of regulation, in particular with profit-sharing schemes and price-cap formulas, shows that aligning incentives to *delegate* coordination decisions to the firm is not easily achieved. In fact, a range of factors may prompt agencies to retain a larger degree of supervision and forego the advantages of delegation.

Replacing return limits with profit-independent, periodic price-caps provides firms with clear incentives for cost reduction. To ensure that this stimulus is maintained and efficiencies are shared, regular reviews need to reestablish price limits and efficiency targets. In the process, regulators aim to apply informed reductions to presumably inflated company cost and investment forecasts. If underlying assessments are correct, the utility returns its cost of capital. A too lenient or too abrasive cut hurts consumers as it either generates excess profits or threatens the firm's capital stock and long-term viability. Setting targets will be less precarious and *delegation* easier for short-term reviews given readily available and unambiguous references, i.e. stemming from firms or industries with comparable investment profiles and asset bases, as well as stable technology and market environments. Absent such secure benchmarks, regulators can be expected to maintain close supervision. This is even more so as, under these conditions, *companies profit by managing and outperforming regulators' expectations so that corporate success appears as regulatory failure.*

Aubert and Reynaud (2005) review the regulation of water utilities in Wisconsin which is interesting as different firms can be under different regulatory regimes (price cap or rate of return (RoR)) in the same geographical area at the same time.[13] They find that, on average, the most efficient utilities are those operating under a RoR regime in which the regulator gathers extensive information. The least efficient water utilities are those regulated under a hybrid scheme corresponding to a rate of return regulation with much less information, together with an upper bound on water price increases. All other things being equal, the cost of a water utility under a hybrid rate of return regulation is 10.7% higher than the cost of water utilities under a RoR framework with extensive information acquisition. Finally, water utilities operating under an interim price-cap scheme are shown to be quite efficient, although not quite as much as those operating under a RoR procedure.

Figure 10.1 details functional implications for major institutional options. At the end of the 1990s, more than two-thirds of the EU water infrastructure was managed under direct public operational control; the rest relied to a greater degree on private risk-taking in operating public assets. Only one-sixth

---

[13] Aubert, C., and Reynaud, A., (2005) The impact of regulation on cost efficiency: An empirical analysis of Wisconsin Water utilities, *Journal of Productivity Analysis*, 23, 383–409.

Weighted average of European water management systems, based on EURAU Classification

	Government department	Public Enterprise (PE)	PE and corporatized and commercial	PE and service contract	PE and management contract	Leasing contract	Concession contract	Built, operate transfer	Private ownership and operation	Community self-help buyer integration
	63.5%					20.5%			16%	
Asset ownership	Public	Public	Public	Public	Public	Public	Public	Private	Private	Private/Common
Investment planning	Public	Public	Public	Public	Public	Public	Public	Public/Private	Public/Private	Public/Private
Regulation	Parent ministry, Economic, quality, Environment regulators, NGOs	Parent ministry, Economic, quality, Environment regulators, NGOs	Parent ministry, Economic, quality, Environment regulators, NGOs	Parent ministry, Economic, quality, Environment regulators, NGOs	Parent ministry, Economic, quality, Environment regulators, NGOs	Parent ministry, Economic, quality, Environment regulators, NGOs	Parent ministry, Economic, quality, Environment regulators, NGOs	Parent ministry, Economic, quality, Environment regulators, NGOs	Parent ministry, Economic, quality, Environment regulators, NGOs	Parent ministry, Economic, quality, Environment regulators, NGOs
Financing fixed assets	Public	Public	Public	Public	Public	Public	Private	Private	Private	Private/Common
Working capital	Public	Public	Public (Revenues)	Public (Revenues)	Public (Revenues)	Private	Private	Private	Private	Private/Common
Operations and maintenance	Public	Public	Public	Private	Private	Private	Private	Private	Private	Private/Common
Managerial authority	Public	Public	Public	Public	Private	Private	Private	Private	Private	Private/Common
Bearer of commercial risk	Public	Public	Public	Public	Public	Private	Private	Private	Private	Private
Basis of private compensation	n.a.	n.a.	n.a.	Fixed Fees	Incentive contract	Incentive contract	Incentive contract	Incentive contract	Incentive contract	Incentive contract
Typical duration	No limit	No limit	No limit	Less than 5 years	Less than 5 years	Less than 15 years	Less than 30 years	Between 25 and 30 years	No limit	No limit

Figure 10.1: Regulatory formats and the pattern of European institutional choices

of the industry was owned and operated by private undertakings.[14] Currently, most European countries utilize a combination of these formats to deal with issues of operational efficiency and asset management, water pricing and funding, as well as broader stakeholder and regulatory concerns. On the one hand, privatization in England and Wales resulted in ten integrated private corporations that follow central economic, quality and environmental regulation and guarantee most of the water supply; local authorities commonly have no role to play. On the other hand, Denmark, with around 2,900 private, non-profit cooperatives, affords the largest degree of regulatory decentralization and industry fragmentation. In between these extremes, France and Germany both treat water supply as a largely municipal affair but differ in terms of regulatory "precautions." While French municipalities are not permitted to install their own private law corporations and must identify the most competitive independent private contractors, mandatory tendering is far less common in the German system that largely relies on semi-autonomous municipal enterprises and prices subject to cost-plus municipal standards or federal cartel monitoring. These distinct patterns of industrial organization may explain differences in tariffs and consumption levels, infrastructure conditions and financing requirements, and the willingness of domestic water service providers to expand their geographic and service base. In each case, EU reforms, investment requirements and the need for politically acceptable water prices cause fundamentals to be reassessed.

Germany

Europe's largest drinking-water reserves, lowest leakage level, second-lowest *per capita* consumption, and leadership in the development of ecological water technologies and integrated river-basin management are the main characteristics of the German water industry. For some, Germany offers "a modern model of public infrastructure provision" reflecting its "tradition of subsidiarity and municipal and associational self-government," that is "possibly the best counterpoint to the (domination) of large private enterprises as in the case of France or England and Wales".[15] For others, the concomitant fragmentation of the sector causes inefficiencies in operations, resource allocation and investments that are sustained by a "new form of municipal

---

[14] EUREAU (1997) *Water management systems in the EU*, Brussels.
[15] Barraque, B., (1998) Europäische Antwort auf John Briscoe . . . , *gwf Wasser-Abwasser*, No. 6, 360–66, at p. 360.

feudalism" run by bureaucracies, associations and lobbies with no incentive to reduce costs or promote privatization to meet tighter budgets.[16] Both perspectives interpret identical data about the industry's structure, current performance and future challenges.

Industry structure

According to German federal water legislation,[17] water supply and waste-water treatment, although physically and administratively separated, are the responsibilities of municipalities. Municipalities may delegate operations to independent service providers but will always retain supervisory responsibility. Since the early 1970s, (West) German water supply has been consolidated from about 15,000 undertakings to presently around 6,000 companies with broadly different ownership and management structures.[18] With the exception of large, cooperative waste-water organizations covering the vast urban zones along the river Ruhr – the *Ruhrverband* – sewage treatment in West Germany is dealt with by nearly 7,000 municipal building departments (*Stadtwerke*). By comparison, the fifteen *Wasser- und Abwasserbetriebe* (WAB), which were in charge of water-related services in the former GDR, have since then been privatized and split up along the Western model to form limited liability service providers to municipalities. Yet, infrastructure costs and the economics of resource management favor further consolidation of supplying areas beyond the legal boundaries of public administration.[19]

Performance and challenges

Water supply companies determine water charges in conjunction with supervisory bodies to cover total costs. Prices set by public utilities, in accordance with the *Kommunalabgabegesetz*, cover water consumption, an appropriate return on own and outside funds, and a reserve to maintain the real value of

---

[16] Briscoe, J., (1995) The German water and sewage sector, *World Bank Report*, February 1995.

[17] See "Gesetz zur Ordnung des Wasserhaushalts," "Abwasserabgabegesetz," and "Trinkwasserverordnung."

[18] More than 35% are part of the public administration with independent budgets, (*Eigen–und Regiebetriebe*); 30% are public sector entities incorporated as joint stock or limited liability companies (*AGs or GmbHs*) with open access to capital markets. 15% are organized on the basis of performance and service contracts; 20% are supra-municipal cooperatives that operate their own facilities as a pool (so-called *Zweck-, Wasser- und Bodenverbände*).

[19] Sauer (2005) shows that the optimal firm size in the German water industry is on average about three times higher than the existing one. Sauer, J. (2005) Strukturelle Ineffizienz im Wassersektor, *Schmollers Jahrbuch: Zeitschrift für Wirtschafts- und Sozialwissenschaften*, 125(3), 369–403.

assets. Water prices charged by utilities subject to private law are controlled by means of company law contracts and are subject to price monitoring by the Federal Cartel Office. Water prices for industrial users may be lower than for private households if lower delivery costs can be reflected in volume discounts or preferential time-of-use rates. Given the principal of cost-based pricing, the costs of water supply, varying with hydrological, topographical and demographic conditions, differ up to 1,200% within Germany. Furthermore, cost-based pricing and the need to balance budgets each year have traditionally pushed German utilities to demand the highest water charges within the EU; they have also allowed the utilities to raise capital on the open market to fuel investments. Conversely, waste-water authorities depend solely on tight municipal funding, which is possibly one of the reasons why sewage treatment has been far less open to technological innovations, new products, methods and suppliers.

Currently, around 98% of the West German population is connected to fresh water and 92.1% to public sewer treatment; in the eastern *Länder*, only 70% of the population is connected to sewers, which provide a generally lower level of waste-water treatment. Given the level of future investments required, the poor financial conditions of most municipalities and the limits to further increases in water charges, observers expect a rise in functional outsourcing, public-private partnerships as well as in the number of Build, Operate, Own, and Transfer (BOOT) schemes. To facilitate this, the federal government would need to further liberalize water supply and deal with unresolved concerns over how to assess efficiencies, compare prices and establish effective regulatory controls. Yet, industry associations[20] reject mandatory performance benchmarking, call for decentralized self-regulation and central governmental involvement largely limited to supporting a harmonious set of domestic standards and its uploading to the EU.

France

By early 2000, the estimated share of the French population receiving drinking water and sewage services from private undertakings was 75% and 40% respectively.[21] To some, the French system provides a compelling model of delegated regulation, localized adaptation of a national approach to

---

[20] See Bundesverband der deutschen Gas- und Wasserwirtschaft BGW (2005) Wasserprogrammatik, at www.bgw.de.

[21] This compares to a 30% private-sector share in French drinking water supply (per volume) in the mid-1950s. Haarmeyer, D., (2000) *Privatizing infrastructure*, www.rppi.org/ps1515.

integrated water resource management and effective, market-led infrastructure provision. To others, decentralization has weakened economic and environmental regulation and diffused enforcement powers *vis-à-vis* the three major private water companies jointly "organizing competition" of 95% of the private water supply and sanitation services.[22] With water prices growing six times faster than the consumer price index between 1991 and 1996, and private companies charging up to 44 times the water price of comparable public service providers,[23] French consumer organizations and public authorities called for the introduction of a "water observatory" and strengthened regulatory control. In October 2001, a largely diluted legislative bill, proposing a shortening of concession contracts and an "*haut conseil des services publics de l'eau*," had its first reading in parliament but was of little consequence. More recent initiatives by the French Ministry for Ecology and Sustainable Development aim to retain existing governing structures while enhancing the role of the state and water agencies.[24]

Structure

At present, the decentralization laws of 1982 and 1983 limit the role of the State to water law enforcement (withdrawal and discharge authorizations) and the assurance of public health and safety and compliance with technical standards and budget and competition control. Beyond this, the state employs two principal redistribution mechanisms to achieve "user solidarity." At the national level, the National Fund for Rural Water Supply (FNDAE) levies taxes to subsidize water infrastructures in sparsely populated areas. At the level of each of the six large river basins, a self-financing water agency (*Agence de l'Eau*), linked to the Ministry of the Environment, implements policies decided by regional River Basin Committees and levies charges on water withdrawal and discharge to subsidize municipal investments in water resource management. While the pollution tax currently is still a flat fee and not levied on agricultural runoffs, legislation has been proposed to increase the agricultural sector's share of costs.

The actual provision of water services is governed by around 36,000 communes, which either manage operations themselves as local *Régies* or inter-municipal water associations, or contract out varying degrees of

---

[22] Cour des Comptes (1997) *La gestion des services publics locaux d'eau et d'assainissement*, January.
[23] *The Economist, Profit stream*, March 29, 1997, p. 70.
[24] Grainge, Z., (2004) Spain and France bid to clean up acts, *Utility Week*, 22(6), 10.

management responsibility to private operators. Close to 75% of water resources are privately managed as concessions[25] under twelve- and thirty-year contracts, subject to the required investment volume. The municipalities own facilities, including the assets financed by the concessionaire as part of the arrangement. Water charges are fixed by contract, subject to automatic adjustment rules and re-negotiation possibilities. Typically, French water prices are set as a flat rate plus a connection charge (potable water) based on fresh-water volume (sewage services), or the amount of industrial effluents that require above-average processing (industrial sewage).

Performance and challenge

French franchise-bidding procedures are forever under scrutiny. In some cases, mayors have been accused of charging private companies high "entry fees" to bolster municipal budgets and avoid raising taxes, while in turn allowing concessionaires to overcharge over the duration of the contract (usually beyond the mayor's electoral mandate).[26] These findings led to the passage of legislation in 1993 forbidding the transfer of money between the water service budget and the general commune budget. In other cases, it was found that incumbent companies had abused their dominant positions at contract renewal.[27] However, decisions by the French *Conseil de la Concurrence* have been hampered by a lack of comparable data and the fear that case-based judgments would increase centralized regulatory discretion and legal uncertainty and thereby complicate local contract negotiations. The current recognition of the need for closer supervision and more effective competition[28] comes at a time when France's compliance with stricter EU water norms calls for massive investments in clean water and sewage treatment facilities and inconspicuous tariff increases to fund them.

---

[25] Given to local, mixed-capital companies (SEML), or to fully private operators.

[26] One controversy erupted in St. Etienne, where a court disallowed a thirty-year deal between the commune and a consortium of Vivendi and Suez, which included a FFr1.13 bn "entry fee" and a 76% water price increase.

[27] Refusing to communicate wholesale prices to other companies bidding for parts of the concession, Suez, for instance, had effectively prevented competitive tendering and forced a renewal of the arrangements in thirteen communes in 1997.

[28] See Garcia, S., Alban, T., (2003) Regulation of public utilities under asymmetric information: The case of municipal water supply in France, *Environmental and Resource Economics*, Special Issue, September 2003, 26 (1), 145–62. See also Menard, C., Saussier, S., (2002) Contractual choice and performance: The case of water supply in France. In Brousseau, E. *et al.* (eds.) *The economics of contracts*, Cambridge: Cambridge University Press, pp. 440–62.

England and Wales

In the UK, Northern Irish public-sector water services coexist with the Scottish state-owned water authority and privatized water and sewage undertakings in England and Wales. In the latter case, integrated river-basin management employs privatized assets under centralized but shared industry regulation. The country's water experience has received reviews similar to those of other UK utility reforms. To some, the Conservative party's privatization policy had succeeded in reversing Labour's nationalization of utilities, using them to provide cross-subsidies and hide taxes. Regulators had followed governmental guidance in channeling entrepreneurial behavior and, through "light-touch" price-cap regulation, had mimicked market incentives to reduce monitoring needs, boost productivity and infrastructure conditions, and broadly cut user tariffs.[29] To others, Labour's recent reforms merely added "bells and whistles" to a system in need of fundamental overhaul, if not a complete retreat from privatization. In this view, UK utility privatization has been plagued by severe "design failures" resulting in inadequate industry structures, limited market references, regulatory inconsistencies and vague statutes that shelter excessive regulatory discretion from legal challenge and agency supervision. Problems of anti-competitive and fraudulent abuse of price-cap regulation were unlikely to be overcome by extending data to boards or wider appellate review.[30] Clearly, these positions mark the opposite extremes in a long-standing debate on UK utility regulation.[31] The discussion has recently been rekindled by proposals to mutualize the ownership of water assets and thereby possibly trigger the most drastic reorganization of the water industry since its privatization in 1989.

Structure

The Water Act 1989 led to the privatization of ten regional water and sewerage companies (WaSCs) to undertake integrated water-related activities[32] and

---

[29] See National Economic Research Associates (1998) *Incentives and Commitment in RPI-X Regulation*, London.

[30] Kay, J., (1996) The future of UK utility regulation. In Beesley, M. E. (ed.) (1996) *Regulating utilities*, London: IEA.

[31] For earlier but rather similar discussions see Keynes, J. M., (1927) Liberalism and industry. In Keynes, J. M., (1927) *Collected writings*, Vol. XIX, pp. 644–46; Bussing, I., (1936) *Public utility regulation and the so-called sliding scale*, New York: Columbia University Press.

[32] In addition, twenty-nine water-only companies (WoCs) were given statutory responsibility to supply nearly 20% of the total fresh water to areas not covered by "integrated river-basin management" (IRBM).

entrusted the Drinking Water Inspectorate, the National River Authority and the Office of Water Services (OFWAT) with the quality, environmental and economic regulation of the sector. The Act however did not detail their respective tasks, methods, or patterns of interaction. Like other utility regulators, the Director General of OFWAT opted for price-cap regulation. He did so, on the basis of initial price limits set by Ministers for a sector whose aggregated market value, established around the time of privatization, reflected merely 10% of the replacement value of underlying assets. In addition, he was given a rather unique primary regulatory duty: "to secure that companies are (. . .) able (in particular by securing *reasonable* returns on their capital) to finance the proper carrying out of their functions."[33] Only subject to this, OFWAT was to concern itself with the interests of customers and ways to *facilitate* (rather than promote) competition. Clearly, the privatization of waterworks was meant to privatize responsibility for substantial and uncertain investment requirements. For nearly a decade, this had led to concerns regarding the balance of utility bills and capital returns and the broader sharing of benefits and costs.

Performance and challenges

By the year 2000, a total of £36bn had been spent to tackle a sizable backlog of capital investments built up under public ownership to improve deteriorated infrastructure and environmental conditions in line with EU commitments. Financing primarily had come from increased water charges amounting to an average household bill of £245, i.e. 40% in real terms above the 1989 level. Companies' efficiency improvements, to the extent projected at periodic price-cap reviews, had contributed to share the burden. However, companies' "out-performance" of the regulatory targets agreed upon had generated exceptional returns on capital and dividends. Relative to the regulatory target rate of 7% p.a., the sector had earned an average annual return on regulatory assets of 11.5%.[34] Relative to a 3–5% p.a. real dividend growth anticipated in the 1989 privatization prospectus, the industry's average growth had slowed to around 14%.[35] Still, the real value transfer – in terms of cross-subsidizing

---

[33] Water Industry Act 1991, restated in National Audit Office (1996) *The work of the directors general*, p. 226.
[34] Based on OFWAT's out-turns for 1993–1997.
[35] The 1996–1997 average real dividend growth for the industry was 15%; Thames Water and Yorkshire Water share repurchasing drove growth up to 22%.

diversification or bolstering executive pay – can only be presumed.[36] And yet, by February 2000, leaking pipes continued to cause environmental hazards and a loss of around 3,500 mega-liters of water a day, or 25% of total distribution inputs.

Reacting to this, OFWAT's 1999 five-year price determination trimmed average charges to customers by 12.3% reducing annual household bills by £30. A large share of the industry's £15bn investment program was to be financed by reduced operating expenditures. Unless companies outper-formed the underlying efficiency targets, operating profits would be cut by €800–850 m. Anticipating regulatory change, share prices had already fallen by an average 30% during the period 1998–1999, causing the once attractive water sector to under-perform the FTSE All Share index by 55% and to trade at about 40% discount to its combined regulated asset base.

In response, during 2001 nearly all of the ten water and sewage companies in England and Wales were considering options for separating the running from the owning of their infrastructures. Even though the previous regulator Sir Ian Byatt had rejected plans by Kelda, owner of Yorkshire Water, to sell its water assets to a customer-owned mutual company, his successor, Mr. Philip Fletcher, later cleared a fairly similar restructuring plan for Dwr Cymru and initially expressed his hope that this type of restructuring would not set a precedent.[37] Facing a growing number of proposals for debt-financed buy-outs, restructurings or acquisitions,[38] at year end, Mr. Fletcher appeared less committed to his previous position and stated that "it is not up to the regulator to dictate the structure of the industry."[39] At the same time, however, OFWAT, troubled by the uncertain impact of changed financing on management incen-tives, called on the government to introduce legislation to promote trading in abstraction licenses and competition among actual and potential operators. More recently, OFWAT and a Parliamentary Select Committee have commis-sioned independent reviews of the policy and regulatory frameworks asking for

---

[36] For a discussion of self-administered pay raises/boardroom packages see Ogden, S., (1997) Corporate governance in the privatized utilities. In Keasey, K. *et al.* (eds.) (1997) *Corporate governance*, Oxford: Oxford University Press, pp. 252–78.

[37] M2Press WIRE, November 10, 2000, see www.presswire.net. Clearly, proponents of the approach argued that selling assets to companies entirely funded by debt promises lower costs of capital in meeting the stringent investment targets and tough price limits set by OFWAT in 1999. But it also appeared that once an increasing share of the sector is financed almost entirely by debt, the rest would have to follow, because, at price reviews, OFWAT would have to set allowable returns against the cost of debt rather than a blend of debt and more expensive equity. See Boscheck, R. (2002) Asset mutualisa-tion and governance – the case of Dwr Cymru, Lausanne: IMD Working Paper.

[38] See, for example, the cases of Portsmouth Water, AWG (owner of Anglian Water) or Mid-Kent Water.

[39] Taylor, A., (2001) Water regulator to allow funding from debt, *Financial Times*, November 28.

opportunities to fine-tune or drastically overhaul the system.[40] At the time of writing, Mr. Fletcher, considering EU regulatory requirements, preparing asset management plans for 2005–10 and the next price review in 2009, announced his intention to spread the costs of full compliance with the EU WFD over three six-year cycles – provided this is acceptable to consumers. Had the regulator's contract changed?

Governance concerns

Clearly, Europe's largest water systems do not offer any simple reference. Operational and regulatory practices in Germany, France, and England and Wales raise concern about the *a priori* efficacy of associational self-administration, competitive concessions contracting or price-cap regulation. But any judgment requires a reference – ideal, counterfactual or otherwise. Broadly different institutional contexts, diverse policy objectives and the lack of comparable data prevent any meaningful benchmarking and relegate the often-suggested competition among regulatory models to the realm of economic modeling. In fact, the absence of common standards to compare crucial performance indicators such as operating efficiency or pricing casts in doubt the viability of national regulatory and managerial supervision, let alone a given system's ability to serve an example for others.

Assessing a water system's level of *operating efficiency* presupposes some understanding of technology choices, investment and employment levels, as well as optimal ranges of capacity utilization in line with maintenance, reinvestment and service standards. But these standards barely exist within – let alone across – European countries. With the resulting level of data insulation interpreting performance amounts to a near-pointless citing of circumstantial data that discredits the "uninitiated" and quiets critique. Along these lines, a recent World Bank review of the German water sector, admonishing excessive staffing and investment levels, the absence of a discussion about the relative costs and benefits of high environmental standards and the therefore extremely low leakage rates, was easily pushed aside as largely "impressionistic," "ill-informed" and "grossly exaggerated."[41] Similarly, facing France's

---

[40] See Hobson, S., (2005) Regulating the regulators, *Utility Week*, 13565532, 11/18, 2005. 24(114).

[41] See Briscoe (1995), reporting for the World Bank, who showed that German water works employ ten (rather than seven) employees for 1,000 connections; use high-quality, lined vitrified clay sewerage pipes (rather than simply standard plastic pipes) and achieve leakage levels as low as 12.8%, (compared to 25% in France for example). For a critique see Linden, U., (1996) Stellungname zur Veröffentlichung von J. Briscoe "Der Sektor Wasser & Abwasser in Deutschland", *gwf- Wasser-Abwasser* 137, No.1, pp. 41–2; see also Barraque, B., (1998).

tightly oligopolistic market and largely non-transparent bidding processes, observers may have no other way than to ineptly "impute" efficiencies from consolidated global earnings rather than from operations.[42] It is therefore immensely sensible for OFWAT to intend to use bidding processes to directly market-test capital and operating expenditure as data inputs for its price-cap regulation. One may only be concerned how the regulator will frame the bidding contest if crucial productivity and performance criteria are not widely shared. To be sure, a list of technical and financial performance measures has recently been recommended by the International Water Association (IWA).[43] But the fact that such a list would create the necessary level playing field may indeed limit its chance for pan-European adoption.

Water prices, in theory, should reflect costs in line with usage. In practice, pricing policies often address much broader concerns, including the financial sustainability of operations, economic and regional development objectives as well as the realization of some level of social equity. Hence, comparing water prices requires differences in costs, subsidies, profits, taxes and charges to be identified and traced to objective drivers and causes. Cost conditions alone will vary based on, first, the origin, quality and quantity of raw water and the responsibility for protection of source water; second, the state of the infrastructure and the resulting leakage rates; third, the cost of labor and procured materials; and fourth, the quality of water and the level of service (interruptions and pressures) provided. Financial charges to be considered depend on sources of finance and policy objectives (for example, the level of cost recovery, renewal rates, depreciation methods). Finally, price quotes may reflect metered unit consumptions, some estimated average consumption per household, or various methods and reasons for tariff differentiation. Ultimately, in each case the community pays for maintaining the water infrastructure. Yet, given that the choice is when (now or in the future), how (user charges or taxes) and to whom (extent of cross-subsidization) to present the bill, national systems are not easily compared.

Hence, while German prices for water and sewage disposal continue to be the highest in Europe, the question is how to judge this. The World Bank traces these prices to the alleged absence of any public discussion about the merits of very high environmental standards, and a presumed general lack of

---

[42] See Haarmeyer, D., (2000).
[43] Lambert, A., Hirner,. W., (2000) Losses from water supply systems – standard terminology and recommended performance measures, *The Blue Pages*, IWA October, pp. 1–13.

attention to economic efficiency and costs. The industry itself defends its charges as active demand management based on full costing decreed by law, reflecting lower capacity utilization levels of high fixed cost operations relative to many international comparators, the absence of subsidies, and broadly higher service levels.[44] Neither side furnishes a yardstick for comparison. Yet, international benchmarking, for example with France or England and Wales, is also only of limited value.

Since 1991, the typical French household's water bill has increased by 87%, 6½ times faster than the consumer price index. Similar to the German case, prices vary significantly although not subject to location but depending on whether suppliers are public or private. Yet, the fact that at any given time private supply is nearly up to 50% more expensive than the public one may be interpreted in very different ways. It could be either due to collusive bidding practices driving up private companies' cost estimates, or reflect the concessionaire's enhanced service levels, actual accounting for depreciation or its inability to continue the politically motivated under-pricing of its public predecessor/comparator. Reform initiatives, intended to create the needed national reference, are held up in the French Parliament. Similarly, the evolution of water prices in England and Wales largely reflects the mechanics of price-cap regulation, operators' informational advantages relative to regulators and the opportunity for external price-reviews. OFWAT's renewed interest in making appointments more contestable and setting up a new econometric benchmarking tool signals the regulator's need for better references – if only to deflect public criticism. Incidentally, a recent comparison of profit margins of the ten integrated water companies in England and Wales with international players found profit margins in the UK typically to be three or even four times higher than the margins of private and public water companies in France, Spain, Sweden or Hungary.[45] And yet, by which standard is one to judge this suggestive use of data? Or more broadly, how would all of the above affect or be affected by the introduction of a unified EU water framework?

---

[44] With 80% fixed costs, Linden (1998) traces differences in operating scale and costs to differences in e.g. US and German consumption levels of 300 vs. 40 litres/day respectively. Baraque (1998) compares German and French water prices for equal size municipalities and reasons the resulting 15–20% premium of the former with reference to general living expenses, higher treatment costs due to higher pollution and higher population density.

[45] Hall, D., Lobina, E., (1999) *Employment and profit margins in UK water companies: Implications for price regulation proposals.* Public Services International Research Unit, November 1999.

2. The EU Water Framework Directive

Different from what a first reading may suggest, the 2000 EU Water Framework Directive does not merely concern itself with issues of water quality and the environment. It rather affects much wider areas of EU industry, policy and governance. As a framework directive it aims to establish integrative water management by replacing pre-existing, fragmented EU water regulations with one unifying legislative Act that commits Member States to deliver towards mandatory, time-bound and measurable targets on a river-basin scale. Its preamble spells out that this will require (a.o.) preventive actions, linking emission values to environmental quality standards, insisting on the polluter pays principle and the recovery of total costs of water use, and decentralizing decisions as close as possible to the location where water is used or affected. The directive clearly impinges not only on all aspects of water management. It directly calls for coordinating pan-European policies related to agriculture and fishery, navigation and transport, regional policy and tourism, as well as energy. But the WFD's ambitious agenda presents only one of the reasons why the directive has become famous amongst analysts for its tortuous evolution and still highly uncertain future. Another is that the legislation emerged during a fundamental shift in EU governance aimed at increasing public involvement partly by means of granting co-decision power to the EU Parliament[46] and partly by seeking broader involvement of un-elected non-governmental organizations. At the end, neither objective was achieved.

Stages and issues of policy formulation[47]

During the four years between the Commission's initial communications on European water policy in 1996 and the publication of the WFD in the Official Journal of the EU in December 2000, discussions about the directive turned from a broadly shared appreciation of an important ecological initiative into

---

[46] Introduced by the Maastricht Treaty (Art. 189b) and amended by the 1997 Treaty of Amsterdam, the European Parliament, as the locally elected body in the Union's decision-making structure, was elevated to equal legislative standing with the Council of Ministers.

[47] Kaika and Page (2003) trace both the ways in which internal changes in the EU's decision-making process have influenced the shape of the final WFD and the ways in which the increasing participation of NGOs has influenced the final text. Kaika, M., and Page, B., (2003) The EU Water Framework Directive: Part 1: European policy making and the changing topography of lobbying, *European Environment*, 13(6) 314–27.

an intense confrontation among stakeholders realizing the proposal's implications. Reacting to the economic costs of tightening existing regulations vs. the ecological risks of diluting them, EU institutions sided with their respective constituencies to frame particular issues, review timescales and voting rules and either limit or expand the directive's impact and binding nature. In dealing with the key concerns – economic pricing, emissions standards and the legislation's binding nature – the Commission acted as arbiter between the Council of Ministers, representing Member State governments and typically focused producer interests, and the EU Parliament, acting on its direct mandate and in response to diffuse citizen demands and broader ecological objectives. Three stages may be distinguished.

Council initiative and response

In Spring 1998, the Council of Ministers, keen to settle issues before having to share relevant legislative responsibilities with the EU Parliament as part of the impending co-decision procedure, tabled a draft directive, which in the eyes of many not only diluted the WFD's environmental credentials but amounted to a provocation.[48] For one, the draft had no mention of cost-efficient water pricing; in addition, it nearly tripled the permitted time of derogations on implementing the directive to thirty-four years. Next, the Council proposal was presented as a final version even before the EU Parliament had given the directive a first reading and without considering the views of special interests, particularly environmental NGOs, that the Commission had decided to informally involve to ensure that any new obligation would not lower substantive and enforcement standards. Reacting to this, the majority of the EU Parliament decided to revert to the original position of the Commission, calling for full-cost pricing for all consumers, including agriculture.[49] Following conciliation talks, that version received its first reading in the European Parliament in February 1999 which resulted in 200 amendments to the text.

Defying parliamentary proposals

Reviewing the document from Parliament, the Commission rejected Amendment 1 as purely rhetorical. This amendment read "water is not a commercial product like any other, but instead is a part of Europe's heritage

---

[48] For a discussion see Scheuer, S., (2001) The NGO perspective, *The Freshwater Framework*, Globe EU Fimenel.

[49] Socialist Members of Parliament (MEPs) with southern European agricultural constituencies sided with the Council.

which belongs to the peoples of the European Union and therefore ought to be protected." The Council, reacting more strongly, reverted to most of its previous position and thereby contravened the EU Parliament in four major areas: *First*, while both the Parliament and the Commission had insisted on full-cost pricing, the Council eliminated this obligation once again; *second*, the Ministers maintained their view on thirty-four years of derogation and added a range of derogations effectively exempting many European waters from the directive; *third*, while the EU Parliament held that the directive "obliged" Member States to achieve "good water status" the Council suggested that the directive "requests that Member States make an effort" to that effect. Finally, the Council proposed to abandon the zero-emission approach for substances covered under the Groundwater Directive (80/68) and to eliminate zero-emission requirements for 60% of the list of 129 dangerous substances. In effect, binding legislation of the 1970s and 1980s was to be replaced by a suggestion of voluntary undertakings.

Co-decision with a fixed deadline

In December 1999, following the introduction of co-decision-making in line with the Amsterdam Treaty, the strengthened EU Parliament re-tabled most revisions previously rejected by the Council, including alterations with regard to water pricing, the elimination of hazardous substances and execution timetables. In addition, concerns about the unenforceability of the directive's language caused the EU Parliament to insist on clear-cut wording so as to eliminate opportunities for non-compliance. At that stage, Spain claimed that water resource management was not part of qualified decision-making according to paragraph 1, Art 175 of the EU Treaty, but instead required unanimous support in the Council of Ministers. It took two months and a European Court of Law decision to do away with single-country veto power in environmental affairs. But the risks to the Parliament's agenda had not been completely eliminated by that. While the Amsterdam Treaty upgraded the role of the Parliament, it also stipulated that Council and Parliament had six weeks to reach a written agreement on any contending issue or else abandon it. Expectedly, the final agreement on the WFD, achieved on the June 30, 2000, after long and exhausting talks, had all the trappings of a forced compromise.

Results and reactions

Whilst it is not possible to predict the outcome of EU institutional bargaining merely on the basis of the types of constituencies that are being served, the

EU's WFD, on a superficial level, offers at least an illustration of a fundamental regularity of public choice. The EU Parliament and the Council of Ministers, catering to diffuse and focused interests respectively, delivered apposite results: Parliament succeeded in reinserting its avowal that "water is not a commercial product like any other, but rather a heritage which must be protected, defended and treated as such." The Council won the rest.

First, even though some subordinate phrases in the latter parts of the directive assert that member states "shall" protect, enhance, or prevent water from deteriorating etc., Articles 4(1)(a) and 4(6)(a) and (b) require Member States only to "aim to achieve" good water status. There may be an obligation to try but, whenever steps are considered "not practical," "not reasonable" or "disproportionately expensive", there is no need to achieve a "good status" of ground and surface water.

Second, whereas the Parliament's implementation plan had a ten-year time horizon, the WFD stipulates fifteen years, one year less than the Council's original bargaining position.

Third, whilst a combined approach of environmental quality standards and emission limits is to be used in controlling pollution discharges by 2012, the prohibition of discharging radioactive substances has been dropped as has the obligation to prevent groundwater pollution.

Fourth, Article 9.1 of the WFD outlines the objectives of water pricing as (1) the implementation of the EC polluter pays principle (Art 174(2) of the EC Treaty); (2) the provision of adequate incentives for users to utilize water resources efficiently; and (3) the contribution towards a good "quantitative groundwater status," i.e. a balance between supply and demand, water abstraction and a "good ecological status of surface water." Also, in its communication on "Pricing Policies for Enhancing the Sustainability of Water Resources,"[50] the Commission has given further guidance on appropriate, effective and efficient pricing mechanisms. But both documents, for the sake of subsidiarity and flexibility, leave fundamental issues of cost recovery and usage-based pricing up to be interpreted by Member States.

Fifth and finally, whilst water prices are to incorporate environmental costs, the EU Parliament permitted an opt-out clause which allows Member States to ignore this requirement completely.

Hence, while the EU Parliament managed to enshrine the notion of water as a non-commodity, the Council's determination of virtually all economically and operationally significant aspects of the directive reveals the hollowness of

---

[50] COM (2000) 477, Brussels, July 26, 2000.

this rhetoric and weakens the framework's binding character, substantive impact and practical relevance. Even worse, the attempt to negotiate a common ground not only lowered regulatory standards but substituted previously enforceable commitments by an appeal to voluntarism, common sense and long-term views. In the words of an observer, "(i)t all depends on the goodwill and the seriousness of all players to fully use the opportunities of this directive for enhanced water protection and to prevent the abuse of the legal ambiguities of the agreed text".[51] Yet in light of the EU's record in engendering regulatory compliance – particularly in the area of the environment – this comment sounds at best naïve.

Recent studies, analyzing the lack of observance of EU environmental law, identify the 2000 Water Framework Directive (WFD) as one of the least implemented of all environmental internal market directives.[52] The EU reasons this with respect to the directive's complexity, the cost of legislative integration and the non-transparency of local environmental conditions.[53] To deal with this, the Commission suggests a combination of implementation advice and legal actions against non-complying Member States. Yet, the problem with the first is that the WFD effectively leaves vague substantive and procedural rules for decentralized policy makers to specify. Interjecting central guidance at this stage defeats the purpose of subsidiarity and regulatory delegation, is administratively inefficient and conceivably illegitimate as it amounts to changing legislative content – *ex post*. The problem with the second is that Arts (4) – (7) outline conditional grounds for exemptions that ultimately require cost–benefit analyses or proportionality tests to establish non-compliance, begin prosecution and determine the remedies and fines required. Yet to do so, local conditions would need to be transparent, EU monitoring and benchmarking viable or regulatory delegation to national authorities realistic. In which case, of course, non-compliance would be no issue. But non-compliance is also a potentially growing concern in the cases of England and Wales, France and Germany.

In the UK, WFD requirements are currently being addressed separately for the water regimes of Scotland, Northern Ireland and England and Wales. While Scotland and Northern Ireland had no licensing regime of water

---

[51] Statement by the Secretary General of the European Environmental Bureau (EEB), quoted from Page, B., and Kaika, A., (2003) The EU Water Framework Directive: Part 2, *European Environment*, 13(6) 328–43, at 338.

[52] Grimeaud, D., (2004) The EC Water Framework Directive, *RECIEL*, 13(1), 27–39.

[53] EU Commission (2004) Water Policy – Commission Acts against Eight Member States, Press Release, January 13, 2004.

abstraction and impoundment and therefore started from a clean slate when designing their water regulation,[54] a large number of elements of the WFD were already contained in the existing water legislation in England and Wales. But public criticism of OFWAT's regulatory performance has triggered a number of high-profile reviews of the current system of governance and the need to manage the acceptability of potential price increases. While the industry body, Water UK, promotes the need to tackle unregulated pollution, it also cautions that investment demands must be squared with consumer debt and affordability. Meanwhile, Mr. Fletcher in preparing his next five-year price review in 2009 intends to ask consumers about their willingness to pay for environmental improvements in line with the WFD.

In France, integrated river-basin management was established by the 1964 Water Law and undertaken in line with the 1992 Water Law by *Comités de Bassin*. But neither the *Agences de l'Eau* nor the *Comités de Bassin* ever concretely dealt with water management and economic analysis; in addition, public participation is restricted. While the French Ministry for Ecology and Sustainable Development proposes to increase the agricultural sector's share of water clean-up costs, it suggests that curtailed investment plans would allow consumer prices to remain stable. But investment needs to increase to comply with EU standards. There is clearly a need to develop the political will to handle a thorny question of whether and how to finance WFD requirements.

Germany's two main industry associations point out that meeting the 1998 EU standards alone cost €150bn and, at annual investments of €6 to 8bn, will take twenty to thirty years to accomplish. Still with the level of investment today and going forward, it is estimated that 52% of the German ground-water bodies are unlikely to reach WFD quality standards by 2015.[55] Nevertheless, the BGW/Deutsche Vereinigung des Gas-und Wasserfaches (DVGW) call for a harmonious transposition of EU law into national law and the translation of WFD terminology into measurable standards as long as cost recovery contines to be ensured. However, facing growing public discontent and the political use of international "reference" data, the latter would require the uploading of German standards on pollutants and price calculation on the EU level. In view of the recent WFD experience this seems highly unlikely.

---

[54] The Water Environment (Controlled Activities) Regulations 2005 set up a system of controls via authorization by the Scottish Environment Protection Agency (SEPA) and came into force in April 2006.

[55] BGW/DVGW (2006) *Comments for the second reading of EU groundwater guidelines*, February 2, 2006.

3. EU Water Infrastructure Management – governance concerns

Current efforts to identify transferable solutions to an unsustainable use of water resources also focus on European resource management, particularly on national approaches to operating and charging for water and infrastructure investments as well as the EU's Water Framework Directive (WFD). But Europe does not offer any simple answers either. Europe's national or regional water systems reflect the particular cultural, political and social fabric of the society they serve; governance structures are rather idiosyncratic and share hardly any common references.

In the absence of any comparable performance data, assessing the effectiveness and efficiency of a given water supply system or even suggesting its emulation amounts to expressing an unfounded opinion (e.g.) about the presumed merits of price-cap regulation, the benefits of self-administration by associations, or the efficacy of decentralized private concessions based on continuous bidding. Such difficulty in making credible and legitimate inferences however can only partly be explained by Europe's diversity in policy objectives and, presumably related, fundamentally different tariff structures and charging methods. Rather a lack of central data collection and incompatible measurement practices shelter national systems from market testing, offering potential windfall gains across the broader regulatory community, and may therefore be self-sustaining.

The EU's Water Framework Directive (WFD) did not create the necessary set of common denominators either. Its evolution and final shape rather reflects the impact of a protracted power struggle among EU institutions, Member States and stakeholder groups. The result is a political compromise that dilutes pre-existing regulatory norms and invokes national discretion to close EU legislative gaps. It is for all practical purposes largely unenforceable as the Commission, lacking standards, will find it difficult to assess a Member State's capacity to comply with already low-level regulatory requirements.

But sliding towards non-coordination is no option either. With more than 4,000 river basins crisscrossing 46 countries, Europe's waterways link the rich and the poor, the drought-ridden and flood-prone, regions with safe and unsafe drinking water conditions, and with optimal and non-existing sanitation. As natural watersheds rarely coincide with political borders, cross-border cooperation is an integral part of European water management. In addition, the pervasive impact of water on other sectors and aspects of society requires coordination for far-reaching economic and political reasons.

Hence, searching for the best model of water resource management or creating a proper EU framework for integrated water management may actually have to begin with establishing a neutral third-party reference, empowered to set up common statistical methods, collect and evaluate data, and to provide a broader informational base to national political and regulatory decision-makers and interested parties. The structure may be modeled after the French National Water Data Network, intended to inform France's approach to integrated water resource management, and may benefit from OFWAT's unparalleled modeling experience. Statutory reporting requirements would ensure the availability and quality of data and could be partly motivated by feeding back anonymous benchmarking reports. However, to ultimately benefit from more decentralized regulatory control, it is of the atmost importance to maintain institutional independence and neutrality and the broadest level of stakeholders' data access.

Only then will European systems be able to tackle the three principal issues identified by the World Bank as typically contributing to the poor performance of water supply facilities: inadequate data on operation and maintenance, poor management of water supply facilities, and unclear patterns of political interference.[56] Only then will stakeholders have the basis to discuss the costs and benefits, and therefore, the desirability of various policy objectives – from ensuring efficient supply, sustainable infrastructures, long-term efficient and equitable resource management, to broader social goals. And only then could these systems be potentially considered for emulation elsewhere.

---

[56] World Bank (1993) *Water resource management*, Washington D.C.: International Bank for Reconstruction and Development. See also World Bank (1997) *Water allocation mechanisms*, Washington, D.C: World Bank.

11 Market-testing healthcare: Managed care, market evolution and the search for regulatory principles

Ralf Boscheck

With 30% of the OECD's GDP projected to be spent on healthcare by 2030, numerous Member States attempt to market-test healthcare by tying demand and supply to fixed-price, prospective contracts. Hence, the 2003–4 Bush Administration's Medicare bill offered $500bn prescription drug benefits to motivate pensioners to join for-profit health maintenance plans that manage costs by substituting closed budgets for fee-for-service arrangements. The same year, German healthcare reforms proposed sickness funds to pool chronically ill patients in specialized disease management programs, replacing itemized reimbursement by global budgets. Finally, the reforms of the UK National Health Service (NHS), intended to improve the system's overall capacity to respond to patient needs, employed fixed-price performance contracts to stimulate competition in primary and hospital care. In each case, determining cost-effective therapies as a condition for coverage amounts to "managing care" and continues to raise concerns about the legitimacy and constestability of results and standards. Governance concerns related to treatment guidelines, patient rights and the legal status of various stakeholders are covered elsewhere.[1] This chapter deals with market reactions to regulatory changes and vice versa.

Following a brief introduction to healthcare systems and the convergence towards "managed care", section 1 focuses on the most recent developments in the UK NHS and the transformation of US managed care towards what President Bush in his 2006 State of the Union address called consumer-driven healthcare. Section 2 discusses US antitrust rationales for curbing specialty hospitals and upholding apparently anti-competitive settlements between generic and branded drug producers. Section 3 concludes.

---

[1] For a review see Boscheck, R., (2005) Healthcare reforms and governance concerns: The cases of the United States, the United Kingdom, and Germany, *Intereconomics*, 40(2), 75–88; Boscheck, R. (2004) Healthcare rationing and patient rights, *Intereconomics*, 39(6), 310–13.

1. From the convergence towards "Managed care" to the common loss of cost control

For healthcare markets to ensure efficient and equitable supply,[2] demand-side and supply-side distortions have to be overcome. On the demand side, insurance contracts blur the link between consumers' price and treatment cost and thereby may artificially fuel demand; they may involve a screening of enrollees based on risks (rather than income) or result in differentially priced or otherwise uneven coverage. On the supply side, patients' and payers' difficulties in judging the need for and the quality of treatment may trigger "supplier-induced" services, unwarranted premium-priced therapies, or conversely, the unjustified exclusion from vital cures. Countries apply different means of healthcare governance to regulate patient access and provider and payer performance. Figure 11.1, sorting arrangements based on types of funding method and supply contract, offers a first albeit crude perspective.

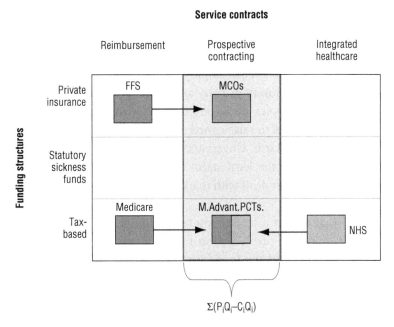

Figure 11.1: Convergence towards prospective contracting

[2] For a review see Rothschild, M, Stiglitz, J. E., (1976) Equilibrium in competitive insurance markets, *Quarterly Journal of Economics*, 90(4), 629–49; Newhouse, J. P., (1996) Reimbursing health plans and providers, *Journal of Economic Literature*, 34(3), 1236–63.

No OECD country fits neatly into any one class, and no category by itself, warrants any *a priori* judgment on healthcare performance.

The *vertical axis* identifies the three principal sources of healthcare finance, which differ in terms of coverage, choice, degree of risk selection and the process of fund allocation: *private insurance* charges premiums typically based on age and health status at time of enrolment; *statutory sickness funds* pool occupational risk classes, have premiums that are independent of individual health risk, and draw payroll taxes into dedicated funds governed by social partners; *tax-based healthcare systems* use centrally or de-centrally collected funds subject to political decisions. All three mechanisms may involve co-payment depending on the type of service rendered. The *horizontal axis* lists medical supply arrangements that differ in terms of payer–provider relations and degree of patient choice. *Reimbursement* facilitates complex contracting between multiple payers and providers as well as patient choice (rather than cost control). *Prospective contracting* limits the catalog of eligible suppliers to a small number of pre-qualified providers willing to accept cost containment based on budgets, funding caps and fixed-price contracts. *Integrated healthcare* combines funding and service provision in one organization in an attempt to internalize uncertainties arising from costs and contractual complexities.

Analyzing the original healthcare reform projects pursued by President George W. Bush and former Prime Minister Tony Blair shows the US and UK systems set to converge towards cost-effective prospective contracting. In both cases, however, actual market developments led to quite different outcomes and calls for policy adjustments.

UK healthcare reform – original intent and status 2006

A tax-financed, integrated system, the UK's NHS links public sector providers with self-employed general practitioners (GPs), who are compensated based on a mix of fee-for-service and capitation and act as "gatekeepers" for non-emergency hospital services. Strict enforcement of budget limits helped to contain national healthcare expenditure to 7.6% of GDP in 2001, a level much lower than in other northern or central European countries. But it also caused understaffing and waiting lists and positioned the UK in terms of capacity and perceived – not actual – quality close to the bottom of the OECD. Responding to this, most recent reforms, spearheaded by former Prime Minister Tony Blair, try to use markets to improve services while centrally containing costs.

More specifically, GPs, as independent contractors, were led to form regional, primary care groups (PCGs) and own and operate so-called primary care trusts (PCTs) offering community health services including chronic disease management and managed self-care. Hence, the role of the GP changed from a gate keeper to be part of an integrated service provider under annual agreements and budgetary responsibility with health authorities. To expand the range of services on offer, new contracts for general practitioners offered pay rises of up to 50% from 2004 onwards. Next, to address capacity and efficiency concerns in non-ambulatory healthcare services, top-performing hospitals were selected to operate as autonomous, locally run "foundations" permitted to raise private finance and set staff pay. In addition, hospital consultants, typically maintaining private offices while being paid by the NHS, were offered more lucrative contracts in return for accepting tighter government control over their working practices.

Markets reacted. From 1997 to 2005, the NHS headcount swelled by over 300,000 to nearly 1.4 m, including 80,000 additional hospital and community nurses and 31,000 additional hospital administrators. During that period, the number of hospital consultants increased by 49%. Next, primary care services reorganized: top practices turned into franchise operations to compete head-on with global players such as US United Health or GlaxoSmithKline disease management operations; private diagnosis and treatment centers (DTCs) were set up to offer walk-in ambulatory care – from speedy analytical procedures to day surgery. In May 2006, for instance, Care UK won a contract to run a practice for 4,000 patients employing three GPs and seven nurses. Competition and performance pay also transformed hospital services; as of spring 2006, hospital revenues are closely tied to the number of services rendered and patients have a choice of four acute hospitals for outpatient appointments and operations.

But results are mixed – at best. Markets give choice, stimulate and sort out practice innovations and cut the number of patients waiting over six months for an operation from 12,000 in 1997 to 3,000 in 2006. Today, thirty-one of the thirty-two NHS trusts holding foundation status report a combined surplus of £20m. Still, only fifteen out of twenty-six health targets, established by the ministerial committee on NHS reform, have been achieved so far. Official productivity statistics, tracking annual changes in the health-service output-to-input ratio from 1999 to 2004, vary between −1.5% and 1.6% subject to the format of input calculation or the weighting of case mixes.[3] What is worse, in 2005–6, the NHS accumulated a deficit of £536 m, more than twice

---

[3] For a discussion see also www.reform.co.uk/website/pressroom/bulletinarchive.aspx?o=83.

its shortfall of the previous period, and a total debt in the hospital sector of £1.1 bn. Even though the Department of Health admitted to overspending £610m on new contracts for nurses, consultants and GP, with budget caps and after all permissible adjustments, the system can react only in one way: in April 2006, the NHS announced 7,000 jobs were to be cut. Capacities will be tighter once again.[4]

Curiously, in mid-2006, two years prior to the official completion date of NHS reform, the UK public debate united Tories and traditional Labour supporters in rejecting the Blair reform agenda as principally flawed. For the first group, it adds "layer upon layer of bureaucracy," for the second, it amounts to "privatization by stealth." And yet, there are obvious parallels to other UK regulatory reform experiences where the combination of underestimated efficiency potentials and performance incentives caused "overshooting."[5] In this particular case, it resulted in the stimulation of supplier-induced services and fee-for-service contracts. Unconstrained markets beating performance targets cause the loss of central cost control. Put differently, UK reforms unwittingly generated a situation similar to the one encountered by the US just prior to the beginning of its managed care journey.

US healthcare – from managed care to consumer-driven healthcare

Figure 11.2 tracks the transformation of the US healthcare system over the last ten years as an interaction of different players along the extended healthcare business system – from the pharmaceutical and device industry, drug distribution, and health plans to hospitals, specialists and general practitioners to employers and employees. Three phases may be distinguished:

1995–1999[6]

US employers, encouraged by the tax treatment of insurance premia to offer health plans, cover around 85% of the American working population and

[4] *The Economist*, (2006), *Blot on the landscape*, June 8, 2006.
[5] Helm, D., Jenkinson, T., (1998) Introducing competition into regulated industries. In Helm, D., Jenkinson, T. (eds.) *Competition in regulated industries*, Oxford: Oxford University Press, pp. 1–22. For earlier, but rather similar discussions, see Keynes, J. M., (1927) Liberalism and industry. In Keynes, J. M. (1927) *Collected writings*, Vol. XIX, pp. 644–46; Bussing, I., (1936) *Public utility regulation and the so-called sliding scale*, New York: Columbia University Press.
[6] Reviewers set slightly different time lines. Compare Boscheck (2005); Ginsburg, P. B. *et al.* (2006) *A decade of tracking healthcare system change*, Washington D.C.: Center for Studying Health System Change; Medicare Payment Advisory Committee (2003) *Variations and innovation in Medicare*, at www.medpac.gov/publications/congressional_report.

their dependants. Yet, throughout the 1990s, a combination of low-cost competition, relative labor surplus, high healthcare costs and severe rate increases not only caused firms to reduce benefits for workers as well as retirees, but also to replace conventional fee-for-service plans by cost-optimized managed care contracts. Traditional insurance companies, learning to manage care either through the acquisition of health maintenance organizations (HMOs) or their key personnel, grew market share through mergers, premium discounts or the participation in the then still-less-cost-focused Medicare market. The resulting scale gave bargaining leverage in exacting rate concessions from healthcare providers. Seeing their margins squeezed, numerous hospitals reacted by entering the insurance business to offer integrated delivery systems, consolidated through acquisitions, or tied up GPs and specialists in physician hospital organizations (PHOs) to jointly negotiate with plans. Similarly, physicians entered independent practice associations (IPAs) as well as specialist groups. With the gateways to markets tightening, many pharmaceutical and device suppliers integrated forward. Some offered fixed-priced treatment-outcomes as disease and device management packages; others took over pharmacy-benefit managers (PBMs), a new form of bulk-buying pharma distributors that rank alternative drug-device combinations in terms of efficacy and price.[7] *In sum*, during the second half of the 1990s, the US shift towards managed care, driven by employers and plan providers, triggered a chain reaction of horizontal and vertical coordination to ensure fixed-price commitments, control costs and market choice. But the situation did not last.

1999–2003

By the turn of the century, specific cost-saving practices and cases of abuse had sufficiently alienated providers and patients to trigger regulatory and market reactions against them. Class-action suits drew on common-law theories of breach of contract, fraud and nondisclosure to invalidate the entire range of cost containment methods. Employers reacted to media pressures and contracting labor markets by moving away from tight plan management. In the process, original, integrated staff HMOs, employing full-time medical professionals to strictly enforce treatment guidelines, lost out to more arm's-length preferred-provider organizations (PPOs) offering more

---

[7] Boscheck, R., (1996) Healthcare reform and the restructuring of the pharmaceutical industry, *LRP*, pp. 629–42.

	1995–1999	1999–2003	2003–200?
Pharma/ Device	Disease and device management	Patent disputes and financial settlements	Hatch-Waxman review Supreme Court decision
Distribution	Pharmacy benefit managers (PBMs)	Pharmacy benefit managers (PBMs)	Consolidation
Health Plan	Consolidation; Market-share race	Abolition of authorization/ capitation; PPOs	Consumer-driven plans, administrative controls
Hospitals	Integrated delivery systems (IDSs), Mergers	Joint-hospital-physician contracting, mergers	Retailing services FTC: "Roll-back" reviews
Specialist	Specialist networks	New medical arms race Single-specialty hospitals	Single-speciality hospitals – medicare reimbursement
GP	Gatekeeper	Loss of gate-keeper function	Networked
Employer	Labor surplus	Labor squeeze and media pressure	Buy-down of service levels
Employer	Cost reduction	Concerns about quality and wrongful denial	Patient cost sharing

Figure 11.2: From managed care to consumer-driven healthcare

patient choice albeit at higher and increasing costs. In 2003, these new networks together enrolled more than 70% of all insured US employees, but with largely dismal financial results. Shifts in bargaining power in favor of informed and price-sensitive payers had slowed premium growth at a time of rapidly rising, non-controllable costs. Even though the broad-based elimination of authorization requirements and capitation had reduced the demand and pay for primary-care physicians, mergers, broadening provider networks and the perception of tighter capacities gave hospitals and specialists an occasion to increase rates.[8] At the same time, both groups began to diversify into ancillary diagnostics and screening services as well as ambulatory surgery, stepping up the level of non-price competition in a reemerging and costly medical arms race. Insurers either consolidated further or exited the market. *In sum*, the backlash against managed care, driven by employers and employees, shifted the power from plans to providers.

2003–200?

At present, with healthcare costs again growing at an accelerated rate, employers refocus on cost savings. But instead of going back to tightly

---

[8] See Strunk, B. C. *et al.* (2005), Tracking health care costs *Health Affairs*, June 21, 2005.

managed care, new contracts increase patients' share of the costs through higher deductibles, co-payment and co-insurance. These so-called consumer-driven plans typically involve an employer-paid healthcare-reimbursement account and an employee-paid top-up and offer patients information on providers, prices and qualities. They are based on the assumption that, in general, Americans are over-insured, consumers will spend their *own* health-care dollars more wisely, and that "feeling the price-pinch" will improve health behavior. They are also expected to benefit US employers by reducing the average health insurance premium by 2% to 3% annually.[9] In a parallel development, conventional health plans apply reestablished administrative controls such as authorization requirements for high-price, and in particular ancillary, services,[10] or pay-for-performance contracts with service providers.[11] Their margins remain tight as healthcare providers, above all hospitals and specialists, continue to grow bargaining power with scale or segment dominance,[12] and GPs attempt to leverage networks and opportunities for collective bargaining. Upstream of the extended healthcare business system, the pharmaceutical industry just "has been given a break" by the Supreme Court upholding market-entry agreements between branded and generic drug producers, which will impact healthcare costs.

In sum, by mid-2006, consumer-driven healthcare, the new focal point of US managed care, settled the consumer with the opportunity and risk of optimizing his or her global healthcare budget. While this practice has been criticized for "down-streaming" the risk to patients, one may, alternatively, interpret the concept as delegating decisions to consumers for optimal market benefits. Yet, next to obvious concerns regarding consumer sovereignty in healthcare markets and the legal limits to enforcing patient rights, one may wonder whether patients as payers can truly resist a rebounding supplier drive. While in the UK, similar supply-led developments are ultimately curbed by NHS budgetary limits and policy controls, the more market-based US system requires more competitive checks and balances. But, as section 2 explains, US healthcare markets and competition law may not be ready to deliver the necessary restrictions.

---

[9] Trude, S. *et al.* (2004) Patient cost-sharing innovations, *Issue Brief* No. 75, CSHSC, January 2004.

[10] G. P. Mays *et al.* Managed care rebound? Recent changes in health plans cost containment strategies *Health Affairs*, August 11, 2004.

[11] Bodenheimer, T. *et al.* (2005) Can money buy quality? *Issue Brief* No. 102, CSHSC, December 2005.

[12] Casalino, L. P. *et al.* (2004) Growth of single-specialty medical groups, *Health Affairs*, 23(2), 82–91.

2. US antitrust enforcement in healthcare – markets beyond regulation?

Seen by many analysts to signal a revival of antitrust scrutiny in healthcare, a 2003 joint report by the US Federal Trade Commission and the Department of Justice[13] focused on three main topics: (a) the licensing and joint contracting of physicians; (b) the impact of consolidating hospital networks on group purchasing, labor contracting, plan-provider bargaining, and the bundling and pricing of services; (c) the pricing, distribution and advertising of pharmaceuticals and the competition between branded and generic drugs. Yet, developments in two key areas suggest that the recovery of antitrust is far from complete.

Checking hospital market power – can compounding regulatory failures finally be overcome?

According to Centers for Medicare and Medicaid Services (CMS), payments to hospitals for inpatient care currently account for approximately 31% of the $1.7 trillion in US healthcare spending; 60% of this amount is paid by the federal and state governments.[14] Although hospitals are typically categorized as publicly-owned, nonprofit or for-profit private entities, distinctions are blurred as many nonprofit hospitals own for-profit institutions and for-profit systems manage nonprofit and publicly owned facilities. Grouping hospitals based on the level and complexity of the care as primary, secondary, tertiary, and quaternary can also be misleading as institutions are not restricted to only offer the services associated with one category. Irrespective of the type of classification that is used, however, the majority of hospitals face a shortage of nursing staff and other hospital personnel, increased regulatory requirements, payer demands for information, as well as rising cost of liability premiums and prescription drugs. But do these pressures alone explain recent increases in hospital rates?

While prospective payment systems under Medicare and their adoption by private payers managed to constrain growth of hospital expenditure until the end of the 1990s, recent analyses predict a 55% to 75% real increase in *per capita* hospital expenditure up to 2013.[15] Studies abound that link hospital

---

[13] At www.ftc.goc./reports/healthcare/04072healthcarerpt.pdf.   [14] See www.cms.hbs.gov.

[15] Heffler S. *et al.* (2004) Health spending projection through 2013, *Health Affairs*, (web exclusive) and Shactman D. *et al.* (2003) Outlook for hospital spending, *Health Affairs*, Nov./Dec. 2003.

consolidation, ostensibly reasoned in terms of efficiency increases and the need to deliver full-fledged, cross-subsidized community services, to the creation of market power for the sole purpose of increasing prices.[16] But regulatory and market controls remain muted.

Whereas in 1979, only 31% of US hospitals were affiliated, by 2001, 66.7% of them operated as part of a system with different degrees of financial and operational integration.[17] Weighing potential efficiencies against likely anticompetitive effects, the FTC and Department of Justice formulated "safety zones" for presumably innocuous hospital mergers and were initially quite successful in taking legal actions against obvious outliers. However, from 1994 to 2000, at a time of around 900 hospital mergers, both agencies and state antitrust enforcers lost all seven cases they litigated.[18] Courts accepted broader market definitions, offsetting consumer benefits and special community commitments of nonprofit organizations. Regulatory controls were basically blocked, but market challengers did not fare much better.

In the second half of the 1990s, a rather new breed of physician-owned single-specialty hospitals (SSHs), focusing mostly on cardiac, orthopedic and general surgery, had set out to compete with general hospitals and ambulatory surgery centers. Specialists joined an SSH to share capital costs, specialize further within a recognized specialty group, and leverage scale and professional management in dealing with health plans and ever more regulatory environments. Market reception was expectedly mixed.

Advocates argued that SSHs – as focused factories – provided higher quality care at, at times, significant price discounts. Critics contended that specialty hospitals fed on self-referral and concentrated on relatively profitable conditions and less severely ill patients. As a result, general hospitals were seen in need to either compensate for the loss of cross-subsidization by raising the average price of service, sign lower-priced full-line supply contracts with plans or suffer a loss; at any rate, their ability to provide emergency care and other essential community services was likely to be impaired. In this situation,

---

[16] Katz, M, Shapiro, C., (2003) Critical loss: Let's tell the whole story, *Antitrust Bulletin*, Spring 2003, 49–56, Danger, K. L., Frech, H. E., (2001) Critical thinking about "critical loss", Antitrust, *Antitrust Bulletin*, 340–42.

[17] Bazzoli, G. J., (2003) *The US hospital industry*: www.ftc.gov/ogc/healthcarehearings/docs/0305 29bazzoli.pdf.

[18] *California* v. *Sutter Health Sys.*, 84 F. Supp. 2d 1057(N.D. Cal.); *FTC* v. *Tenet Healthcare Corp.*, 17 F. Supp. 2d 937 (E. D. Mo. 1998); *United States* v. *Long Island Jewish Med. Ctr.*, 983 F. Supp. 121 (E.D.N.Y. 1997); *FTC* v. *Butterworth Health Corp.*, 946 F. Supp. 1285; *United States* v. *Mercy Health Services*, 902 F. Supp.968 (N.D . Iowa 1995); *FTC* v. *Freeman Hosp.*, 911 F. Supp. 1213 (W.D. M o.); *Inre* v. *Adventist Health Sys.*, 117 F.T.C. 224 (1994).

some responses of general hospitals seemed justified even if questionable from a competition policy point of view:

Reacting to physicians involved with SSHs, some general hospitals removed their admitting privileges, de-listed them from on-call rotations, or limited their access to operating rooms. In other cases, hospital networks entered into managed care contracts with health plans that precluded the use of any SSH or lobbied regulators to apply certificate of need laws to encumber specialty hospital entry altogether. At the height of the "specialty hospital backlash," the Medicare Modernization Act of 2003 (MMA) imposed an eighteen-month moratorium on new physician-owned heart, orthopedic and surgical specialty hospitals to temporarily stall the rapid growth of SSHs. Under the moratorium, physicians may not refer Medicare patients to a specialty hospital in which they have an ownership interest, and Medicare may not pay specialty hospitals for any services rendered as a result of a prohibited referral. Oddly enough, an in-house referral within a dominant hospital network is obviously considered part of a necessarily bundled service as it fetches the full rate.

And yet, there are signs of change. Since August 2002, a new FTC task force has been in place to establish more robust and narrow market definitions[19] and conduct retrospective assessments of certain hospital mergers. Rather than trying to contest good-faith commitment of merging parties before the act, the new "look back" approach makes use of hard evidence to determine whether the merger has caused smaller hospitals to close, service charges to rise, and whether the efficiencies promised in the Hart-Scott-Rodino filing in fact have been realized. Negative findings can lead to forced divestitures.

In 2005, an FTC administrative law judge ruled that the three-hospital Evanston Northwestern Healthcare (ENH) illegally raised prices after the merger and ordered the system to divest Highland Park Hospital.[20] Payers provided daunting evidence: in 2000, Evanston Northwestern, among others, raised prices to UnitedHealthcare's HMO by 52% at its Evanston facility and Glenbrook (Ill.) Hospital and 38% at Highland Park and raised its rates to UnitedHealthcare's PPO by 190% for Evanston and Glenbrook and 20% for Highland Park.[21] The administrative law judge rejected alternative remedies suggested by ENH and was not concerned about the consequences of

---

[19] For a discussion see Boscheck, R., (2008) *Healthcare and antitrust*, forthcoming.

[20] The not-for-profit system challenged the decision before the full commission. A ruling is expected by May 17, 2007.

[21] The system is said to have also raised prices to Humana in 2000 by nearly 60%, Aetna by 15%, and Cigna's HMO by 15% to 20%, and 30% to its PPO. Private Healthcare Systems saw a 40% increase by the Evanston and Glenbrook hospitals. See Taylor, M., (2006) Antitrust watchdog, *Modern Healthcare*, June 26, 2006, 36(26).

"unscrambling of the eggs." Even though the case is still under review by the full commission, whose decision can also be appealed, US hospital networks are preparing themselves to defend the competitive impacts and pro-competitive justifications of their recent mergers. They also better be ready to face revitalized market tests.

In August 2006, the CMS announced that specialty hospitals will be allowed to re-enter Medicare.[22] The policy shift has been linked to a recent study,[23] commissioned by the CMS, which compared thirteen physician-owned specialty hospitals with acute-care competitors in terms of physician referral patterns, clinical quality, patient satisfaction and community benefits. The results show that physicians did, in fact, refer more of their patients to their own facilities than to competing hospitals. But clinical care was at par, patients were very satisfied and specialty hospitals provided more community benefits than their not-for-profit competitors when taxes were taken into account. One may expect the strengthening specialty hospitals, together with the revival of regulatory scrutiny, to provide a check on hospital market power. In another important healthcare area, however, recent court decisions may well end up damaging consumer welfare.

Reviewing Hatch-Waxman – making drug supplies contestable or collusion look good?

According to the Government Accountability Office, "(p)rescription drug spending as a share of national health expenditures increased from 5.8 percent in 1993 to 10.7 percent in 2003 and was the fastest growing segment of health care expenditures."[24] In 2001, the US spent $140.6bn on pharmaceuticals, three times more than a decade earlier, chiefly due to an increase in drug utilization, increased retail prices and the more intensive use of more expensive drugs. During the same period, the annual R&D spending in the pharmaceutical industry swelled from $8bn to $30bn. By 2004, the average drug development cost per compound, pre-approval, was estimated to be around $1.4bn and the average new drug required $0.5bn sales to earn a return just above the industry cost of capital.[25]

---

[22] CMS (2006) Addressing specialty hospitals, *Report on Medicare Compliance*, August, 14 2006.

[23] Burda, D., (2006)A bottom-line debate: opposition to doc-owned hospitals comes down to money, March 20, 2006, *Modern Healthcare*, 36(12).

[24] Government Accountability Office, (2005) *Prescription drugs: Price trends for frequently used brand and generic drugs from 2000 through 2004*, (August).

[25] Marakon Associates (2004) "What crisis?" A fresh diagnosis of pharma R&D productivity crunch. Company material.

Patents provide incentives for companies to undertake risky research by temporarily excluding followers from competing away supra-normal profits; they also entail the disclosure of information that may allow others to circumvent the original functional mechanism and thereby stimulate innovation and diffusion. The 1984 Hatch-Waxman Amendments to the Food, Drug and Cosmetic Act (FDC Act),[26] regulating the generic drug approval process, lowered barriers to competition and product prices significantly. But the law also created incentives for branded and generic producers to settle patent disputes in ways that may delay the entry of generics and reduce consumer welfare.

The FDC Act offers generic drug producers an Abbreviated New Drug Application (ANDA) upon demonstrating that their new drugs are "bio-equivalent" to the approved pioneer product and after providing "Paragraph IV" certifications that assert that any patent surrounding the original compound is either invalid or not infringed. Once the information is filed, the patent holder has forty-five days to bring an infringement suit, which automatically delays the FDA's ANDA approval and hence the generic's chance to reach the market by thirty months. If the patent holder does not bring suit, the ANDA may be immediately approved. The first successful filer of an ANDA containing "Paragraph IV" certification is granted a 180-day period of exclusivity, calculated from the day of the first commercial marketing of the generic drug, during which no second ANDA filer may enter the market. In the prevailing interpretation of the Hatch-Waxman Amendments, the first filer can substantially delay the commencement of the exclusivity period.[27]

A review of all relevant patent litigation initiated between 1992 and 2000 found that generics prevailed in 73% of the disputes; in the cases of Prozac, Zantac, Taxol and Plantinol alone, bringing generics to market before patent expiration saved US consumers more than $9bn.[28] For brand-name manufacturers and generic producers, it would be clearly more lucrative to settle patent disputes, agree to defer entry and share the avoided profit loss. But a

---

[26] Congress passed the Hatch-Waxman Amendments to the Food, Drug and Cosmetic Act ("FDC Act") in 1984. Drug Price Competition and Patent Term Restoration Act of 1984, Pub. L.Ko. 98-417, 98 Stat 1585 (1984) (codified as amended 21 U.S.C. §355 (1994)).

[27] Leibowitz (2006) points out that a second filer will only be able to overcome the generic bottleneck if a court decides that the patent supporting the 180-day exclusivity period is invalid or not infringed. This however requires that the brand-name company sues the subsequent ANDA filer and thereby allows it to obtain a favorable court decision. If the branded product manufacturer does not do this, generic entry may be forestalled. See Leibowitz, J. (2006) *Barriers to generic entry*. Prepared Statement of the FTC before the Special Committee on Aging of the US Senate, July 20, 2006.

[28] Federal Trade Commission (2002) *Generic drug entry prior to patent expiration: An FTC study*, at www.ftc.gov/os/2002/07/genericdrugstudy.pdf.

presumption is no proof. Between 1992 and 1999, eight out fourteen settlements involved payments from the brand-name manufacture to the generic first filer. All cases were investigated by the FTC and its learning was passed on to Congress. As a result, the 2003 Medicare Modernization Act amended the Hatch-Waxman Act to ensure that patent settlement agreements are filed with the FTC and the Department of Justice and that only one thirty-month stay per branded product can be granted. But courts seem unwilling to follow the Commission's presumption that financial settlements pay for deferred entry, are anti-competitive, and should be illegal *per se*.

In 2003, the FTC considered that Schering-Plough Corporation, Upsher-Smith Laboratories, Inc., and American Home Products had settled patent litigation on terms that included substantial payments by Schering to its potential rivals in return for agreements to defer introduction of low-cost generic substitutes for Schering's prescription drug K-Dur20. Regarding these provisions to be unfair methods of competition, the FTC entered an order that would bar similar conduct in the future. The Eleventh Circuit set aside the Commission's decision finding that "a payment by the patentee, accompanied by an agreement by the challenger to defer entry, could not support an inference that the challenger must have agreed to a later date in return for such payment."[29] The Commission sought but was denied a *certiorari* review by the Supreme Court in June 2006.[30]

Both courts were apparently swayed by an economic analysis, prepared on behalf of Schering-Plough Corporation, of the "perhaps dramatically socially counterproductive" consequences of a *per se* condemnation of financial agreements under conditions of uncertain market entry and significant litigation costs. It argues that financial agreements may be necessary for settling patent disputes, where incumbents and entrants hold different expectations on the patent's remaining market value, the probability of litigation success and the likelihood of third-party entry.[31] Where such settling the dispute results in entry earlier than with litigation, consumer welfare *may* be

---

[29] See Leibowitz (2006), pp. 15–16.

[30] Federal Trade Commission, Petition for a Writ of *Certiorari*, *FTC* v. *Schering-Plough Corp.*, No. 05-273 (June 26, 2006) (denying cert. petition); *Schering-Plough Corp.* v. *F.T.C.*, 402 F.3d 1056 (11th Cir. 2005); *Schering-Plough Corp.*, No. 9297, 2003 WL 22989651 (F.T.C.) (December 8, 2003) (Commission decision and final order).

[31] See Willig, R. D., Bigelow, J. P., (2004) Antitrust policy towards agreements that settle patent litigation, *Antitrust Bulletin*, Fall 2004, 655–98. The authors point out that their research was begun in connection with work performed on behalf of Schering-Plough Corporation. For a contrarian view see Shapiro, C., (2003a) Antitrust analysis of patent settlements between rivals, *Antitrust*, Summer, 2003, but also Shapiro, C., (2003b) Antitrust limits to patent settlements, *Rand Journal of Economics*, 34(2), 391–411.

improved. But the question is how does one know when litigation results would have otherwise occurred, and whether pre-entry arrangements do not shape post-entry conduct? The supporting analysis in the Schering case is far from formulating a needed *rule of reason*.[32] There is a danger that conditional economic arguments are interpreted in ways that could even make collusion look good rather than as contributing towards identifying bright-line, efficient rules, i.e. principles that allow for efficient law enforcement while limiting the costs of taking wrong decisions. Also, considering financial settlements illegal *per se* may be a rough guideline but in some high-profile cases it has in fact sped up rather than delayed litigation and entry.

In 2001, Eli Lilly rejected an offer by Barr Laboratories to settle a patent dispute over Prozac in exchange for $200m and Barr's commitment not to produce a generic version of the drug until 2004, when Lilly's patent was set to expire. Sidney Taurel, Lilly's CEO, "felt that settling violated antitrust laws and it isn't morally right."[33] Barr won a court ruling and, within two weeks of putting its own anti-depressant on the market, took over 50% of Lilly's sales of Prozac. In the final analysis, US consumers saved an estimated $2.5bn in line with Hatch's and Waxman's original intent. Yet, with the Supreme Court's decision of June 26, 2006 consumers may see more financial settlements and less generic competition.

Is a revival of antitrust sufficient?

During its evolution from managed care to consumer-driven healthcare, parties across the US healthcare system adjusted first to ensure fixed-price commitments, then to offer a broader choice among providers, and now to enable consumers to optimize their individual healthcare budgets. Throughout, the balance of market power shifted in line with competitive success and coordination, but only lately seems to have rekindled regulatory concerns. In their 2003 joint report, the FTC and DoJ committed themselves to vigorously enforce competition in healthcare markets, relying wherever possible on individual rather than coordinated decisions and markets rather than organized countervailing powers to offset dominance. As the above sections suggest, there is a need to refine these principles in line with specific contexts

---

[32] It rather suggests that to speculate "whether the amount that was found to be paid could, as a matter of plain logic, purchase a significant postponement of competition?" See Willig and Bigelow (2004), p. 678.

[33] Kirchgaessner, S., Waldmeir, P., (2006) Drug parent payoffs bring scrutiny of side-effects, *Financial Times*, Monday, April 24, 2006.

and changing market realities; both agencies are inviting inputs. Ultimately, however, consumer-driven healthcare puts patients at the end of a line of coordination decisions that they may or may not be able to assess. What type of competition policy can guarantee that healthcare providers compete on relevant as opposed to merely patient-observable performance parameters and that consumers face proper incentives and have adequate information to take self-responsible decisions? And with all of it in place, would this ensure an efficient, market-tested healthcare delivery or simply overload an emotionally involved, but otherwise rationally ignorant, consumer?

3. Options going forward – once again!

In mid-2006, two years prior to the official completion of the UK NHS reform, the stimulation of supplier-induced services had resulted in a £0.5bn annual deficit and the need to reverse critical capacity expansions. Unconstrained markets beat performance targets but also central cost control. In the US, fixed-price performance contracts for providers are being substituted by consumer-managed healthcare budgets; healthcare competition has intensified but focuses on increasing service volume rather than efficiency. Antitrust principles are being reviewed to roll back provider concentration and regulatory gaming, but one may question whether this is sufficient to empower patients as consumers to take adequate, self-responsible decisions. In either country, users and the public at large reject blunt administrative controls and restricted provider choice, characteristics of tightly managed plans. But in either country, payers are confronting affordability problems. Still, before rejecting prospective contracting as principally flawed, one may want to recall the fundamental characteristics of its alternatives.

On the one hand, a publicly-financed healthcare minimum may provide the foundation on which to establish *decentralized healthcare coordination*, with tax credits for both employers and employees contributing to health plans, unfettered competition in healthcare and insurance markets subject to harmonized minimum quality standards and vigorous and unbiased antitrust enforcement. On the other hand, a full-fledged publicly financed, *single-payer national health system* requires centrally set payment rates, macro-budgets and micro-treatment decisions that rely on outcome data and limited incentive contracts. Whereas in the first case, one may doubt whether one can rely on patients acting as sovereign consumers, the second asks how to instill trust in the efficiency of centralized coordination and the innovativeness of cost center management?

Put into context, the middle ground, based on *prospective contracting*, may not look too bad. It attempts to delegate treatment decisions to knowledgeable service providers closest to a case, but is clearly hampered by providers' conflict of interest and lacking regulatory controls. Incentives need to be constantly redesigned to align public interests with private profit motives in ways that limit the need for external monitoring. Still, considering the alternatives, current setbacks in the US and the UK may be just the price to be paid for ultimately improving the system. Either way, failure is no option. With 30% of OECD GDP projected to be spent on healthcare in 2030, there is an urgent need to find a system that rations healthcare in the most efficient, effective and politically acceptable way.

12 On governing natural resources

Ralf Boscheck

Issues and barriers to adjustment

Environmental degradation, defined by the UN as one, and possibly *the* main, threat facing mankind,[1] apparently meets with little effective response.

For one, according to the Intergovernmental Panel on Climate Change, (IPCC),[2] avoiding levels of CO_2 concentration that would make current global warming trends irreversible requires the industrialized world to cut emissions to 25% of the current level by 2050, i.e. the immediate and full implementation of the Kyoto protocol by all countries including the US. In addition the fast-rising emission levels in the industrializing world need to be curbed. But the Kyoto-follow-up conference in Montreal in 2005 broke down as the US maintained its unilateral stance and developing countries rejected any "eco-colonial" restraints on their legitimate desire to catch-up. *Next*, melting polar ice caps, which drastically cut the level of deflected solar radiation, redirect the Gulf Stream, raise sea levels and dramatically transform flora and fauna in coastal and lower inland areas, were the main reason behind the creation of the Arctic Council in 1996. But eleven years on, the US, Canada and Russia are still unable to agree on even one countermeasure.[3] *Also*, rising seas and – as a result of overstocking or over-ploughing land and deforestation – advancing deserts are shrinking the areas that are capable of supporting human habitation. Currently, China alone loses 1,400 square miles to deserts annually; in northern Africa, the Sahara pushes the populations of Morocco, Tunisia, and Algeria northward toward the Mediterranean; in the south, Nigeria, whose human and livestock population during the second half of the twentieth century grew 4-fold and 11-fold respectively,

---

[1] The UN High Level Threat Panel also lists poverty, infectious disease, interstate war, civil war, genocide, proliferation of weapons of mass destruction, and trans-national crime as threats: www.un.org.

[2] The IPCC currently projects a substantial increase in greenhouse gas concentration driving temperature increases up to 1.4 to 5.8 degrees in between 2000 and 2100. See www.ipcc.ch as well as www.unfccc.int.

[3] See www.arctic-council.org; for a discussion of arctic climate impact assessment see www.acia.uaf.edu.

loses more than 1,300 square miles of rangeland and cropland to desertification per year. Populations are being squeezed into denser urban areas and fuel the growing stream of so-called eco-refugees.[4] The Food and Agriculture Organization (FAO) reckons that population growth and increased prosperity will more than double current global demand for meat and milk production by 2050. The global livestock sector not only represents a major source of land and water degradation, but generates almost 20% more CO_2-equivalent greenhouse gas emissions than transport.[5] Clearly, human population and consumption growth threatens ecosystems and their ability "to provide for human consumption." As per the World Wildlife Fund's (WWF) biodiversity index, tracking the rate of habitat loss and related extinctions, terrestrial, freshwater and marine species have declined by 31, 28 and 27% respectively in the past thirty-three years. On December 14, 2006, only two weeks prior to the beginning of the UN's "year of the dolphin," the Yangtze River Dolphin, a 20-million-year old species and one of the oldest mammals in the world, had been declared functionally extinct. Scientists blame the destruction of dolphin habitat, and the effects of over-fishing and pollution. By 2025 at least 3.5bn people, or 48% of the world's population, will live in "water-stressed" conditions, i.e, experience severe water scarcity and gravely strained aquatic ecosystems.[6]

How can man master his self-selected task of managing nature?

Discussions about environmental sustainability are often heated and seldom rational. Analysis mixes with cynicism, denial with defeatism. Issues are intricate, forces interacting and findings hopelessly conditional. Any attempt to express a vital concern in its entirety and complexity is necessarily abstract, indirect and therefore often deemed irrelevant by the intended audience; catchphrases, however simplified, assumptions and statistics are quickly discredited by skeptics.[7] Yet even if hype were to be avoided and concerns concisely presented, acting on crucial issues often requires agreement on policy instruments, institutional contexts and enforcement mechanisms that may not be forthcoming if adjustment costs are prohibitive or freely shifted onto others. Continued inaction in the face of critical concerns is often justified based on some overarching principle that ultimately blocks any progress.

The following chapter offers a perspective on some of these issues. Section 1 sketches the plight of global marine fishery as a case study of non-adjustment;

---

[4] See Brown, L. R., (2001) *Eco-economy: Building an economy for the earth*, New York: W. W. Norton.
[5] OECD-FAO, (2005) *Agricultural outlook 2015*, Paris: OECD.
[6] See www.unesco.org/water, www.worldwaterforum.org.
[7] See Lomborg, B., (2001) *The skeptical environmentalist*, Cambridge: Cambridge University Press.

Section 2 identifies the key issues underlying that case as constituting the main challenges in managing natural resources and discusses issues of globalizing environmental standards and challenges the need for economic growth.

1. The case of global marine fishery

The 2006 outlook for global fishery was bleak. 44% of the world's commercial fish stocks were fully exploited; 29% had collapsed.[8] Lobster, pollock, striped and black sea bass, haddock, blue crab, and whiting were acutely overfished in most regions around the world. Atlantic cod and halibut, five varieties of tuna, and yellowtail flounder, fish that once furnished the livelihood of fishermen worldwide, were included in the IUCN Red List of threatened species.[9] Technological change, fiscal incentives, governmental regulation, and the industrial extension of a tough fishing culture appeared to have triggered overexploitation, resource waste, and the destruction of large marine ecosystems. Environmental and social impacts were massive. Adjustment required coordination among stakeholders facing substantial investment and income risks, unclear legal jurisdictions and enforcement conditions and hardly any universally accepted data to substantiate opinions about the sustainability of a common, wild resource. In fact, there was no common understanding on whether overfishing was a true concern, and if so, how it had come about, what impact it had and what type of adjustment it required. Were public and private initiatives trying to conserve fishing cultures and employment, or biodiversity and maritime habitats, or both?

A vital concern?

During the second half of the twentieth century, global marine fish and shellfish production had increased sixfold from 17m metric tons in 1950 to 105m metric tons in 1997. By 2015, total world consumption was predicted to reach 179m metric tons.[10] Although, particularly in the last two decades, this rapid growth had been fuelled by the expansion of aquaculture, world marine capture still accounted for more than four-fifths of the total harvest.

---

[8] Worm, B. *et. al*, (2006) Impacts of biodiversity loss on ocean ecosystems, *Science*, Vol. 314, 787–90.
[9] See www.redlist.org .
[10] FAO (2004) The State of World Fisheries & Aquaculture (SOFIA), www.fao.org/sof/sofia/indexen.htm.

But since 1989, the catch had declined by roughly 2% annually. In addition, its composition had been changing. Over time, the percentage of the global catch made up by small, low-value species, such as anchovies, pilchard or sardines, many of which were reduced to fish-meal or livestock feed, had risen to more than 30% in 2002. This "fishing down the food web", substituting top predators like cod or hake by plankton eaters, masked the true extent of resource depletion. It also reflected changes in marine ecosystems, particularly increased water temperatures and nutrient levels that stimulated plankton growth, but cut big fish reproduction levels. Continued deterioration of marine habitats and the fish stocks they supported were likely to impinge on future production and consumption.

By the turn of the century, more than 30 million people depended directly or indirectly on fisheries for their employment and income; 95% of these fish-related jobs were in developing countries. Their harvest provided 16.5% of the total animal protein and 6% of all proteins consumed by humans. Approximately 1 billion people, predominantly within the developing world, relied on fish as their primary source of animal protein. In view of the expected demand increases, the FAO had warned early on that only under the most optimistic scenario – with aquaculture rapidly growing further and overfishing eliminated to permit stocks to recover – would there be enough fish to meet global requirements.[11] But also fish farming had its price. Its installation in coastal deltas and mangroves often involved the destruction of natural fish habitats and spawning grounds; it also required to either fish to feed high-price carnivores like salmon or to feed grain to lower-priced species like carps at a biomass conversion rate of 2:1.

An avoidable crisis?

Already recognized in the early 1900s, the danger of overfishing had long been confined to a small number of species in the North Atlantic, the North Pacific and the Mediterranean Sea, and remained limited by the type of equipment used. This changed with the introduction of the steel-hulled fishing trawler, on-board processing and the innovation of frozen foods. Replacing sailing vessels and the hook and line, factory trawlers, dragging nets across the ocean floor in search of high-priced, bottom-dwelling fish, massively increased a crew's catch and territorial reach. The required refrigeration for record catches drove the emergence of strong post-harvest operations, vastly

---

[11] FAO (2001) *The state of the world fishery and aquaculture*, Rome.

Box 12.1: Threatened by over-fishing?

King Crab
Northeastern Pacific
depleted

Bluefin Tuna
Atlantic
depleted

Atlantic Cod
Northeastern Atlantic
depleted to overfished

Haddock
Northwestern Atlantic
depleted to overfished

Salmon
Northeastern Pacific
overfished to steady

Shrimp
East central Pacific
overfished to steady

Atlantic Redfish
Northeastern Atlantic
overfished to steady

Pacific Halibut
Northeastern Pacific
overfished to steady

Alaska Pollock
Northeastern Pacific
overfished to steady

Atlantic Mackerel
Northeastern Atlantic
overfished to steady

Albacore Tuna
Pacific
overfished to steady

Silver Hake
Northwestern Atlantic
abundant

Illustrations © Tim Phelps

enlarged geographic markets and stimulated the continuous use of ever more powerful vessels and efficient gear ever farther from shore. In the process, fishing lost its seasonality, fish was often harvested prior to spawning, and twenty-four hour trawling operations combed and destroyed ever wider feeding grounds, nurseries, and shelters of their prey. The amount of by-catch, the unintended catch of non-targeted and hence discarded species, rose to an average of 40%.

By the mid-1960s, the accelerated degradation of marine ecosystems was undeniable. However, fishing nations responded by protecting fishermen not fish. A decade later, most nations had laid claim to exclusive fishing rights up to 200 miles from their shores and reports over violent disputes between, for example Canadian and Spanish fishermen, or Icelandic and British trawlers were frequent. The 1982 UN Convention on the Law of the Sea (UNCLOS), codifying the introduction of 200-mile exclusive zones (EEZs) resulted in the departure of foreign vessels and redundant capacities in large distant-water fleets. But it also caused domestic operators to fill the void. Using grants and other forms of assistance for fleet modernization, domestic fleets grew in size, technological sophistication and productivity until, by the late 1980s, the decline of the fish population reached catastrophic proportions and fish stocks began to collapse.[12] By end of the century, the global harvesting capacity needed to be reduced by 40% to bring it into balance with the remaining fish supply. Fishing communities bore the economic brunt of the ecological crisis.

The context for adjustment?

The experience of Gloucester and New Bedford, the two largest fishing ports in Massachusetts, was representative of many around the globe: between 1990 and 2000, unemployment consistently exceeded, sometimes nearly doubled, the state-wide average. However, local fishery households – as owner-operator, family member or share worker – not only suffered loss of income, but tended to hold purely diversified investments, mostly consisting of the ship-ping vessels and associated gear as the principal asset. The average age of owner-operators was typically greater than that found in the working popu-lation at large, while the average age of the hired workers was younger. Levels of formal education were generally below the statistical average. For these

---

[12] See FAO (2001).

Box 12.2: The United Nations Convention on the Law of the Sea

UNCLOS endeavors to govern all aspects of ocean space including environmental control, scientific research, fishing and other economic and commercial activities, technology and the settlement of disputes relating to ocean matters. With the establishment of Exclusive Economic Zones (EEZ), (Arts 55–75), a coastal state enjoys "sovereign rights for the purpose of exploring and exploiting, conserving and managing the natural resources, whether living or non-living" (Art. 56). The coastal state has the right to set a total allowable catch on the basis of the best scientific evidence available to it (Art. 61), and effectively limit access to its fisheries. In the early 1990s, the interest among countries in conserving and managing high seas fisheries resources led to the 1995 UN Fish Stocks Agreement, which builds on two UNCLOS provisions. All states have a duty to ensure that their nationals comply with conservation measures adopted for high seas stocks (Art. 117). Secondly, on the high seas, states have jurisdiction over vessels flying their flag (Arts. 90–98). The Agreement provides for the establishment of regional fisheries management organizations to undertake scientific research, stock assessment, monitoring, surveillance, control and enforcement (Art. 10). The organization can limit participation by new entrants according to a set of criteria listed in Art. 11. Various multilateral agreements have since evolved. The Code of Conduct for Responsible Fishing (1995) *inter alia* spells out flag state responsibilities for the activities of fishing vessels flying its flag and seeks to advance management measures, by agreement among states that improve the optimal and sustainable use of fisheries resources. The Agreement to Promote Compliance with International Conservation and Management Measures by Fishing Vessels on the High Seas (Resolution 15/93), known also as the Compliance Agreement, similarly builds on flag state responsibility for fishing vessels flying its flag (Art. III) and operating on the high seas. Other agreements affecting the management of fisheries resources are the 1992 Biological Diversity Convention, the 1982 Convention on the Conservation of Antarctic Marine Living Resources, and the 1972 World Heritage Convention. (See www.oceansatlas.org.)

---

reasons, but also because of family and community obligations, adjustments were often either delayed or undertaken half-heartedly.

But continuing against all odds was equally difficult. Traditional structures of credit, whereby fishers could fuel, operate and maintain their vessels based on the return of future voyages, were deteriorating. In 1994, Gloucester's fishing population was 20% of its mid-century size, and yet the US National Marine Fisheries Service estimated that the Gloucester fishing fleet was twice the size that existing fish stocks could sustain. In May 2000, the New England Fishery Management Council concluded that fish populations were well below the targets necessary for rebuilding stocks and recommended further reductions in both fishing effort and fleet capacity.

Responding to calls for diversification, Gloucester opened the region's first herring and mackerel processing plant in August 2001. Mass Development along with the Boston Archdiocese invested about $5 m to build the fish-processing site and create thirty new jobs. Products were destined for West African, Middle Eastern, European and Japanese markets. Due to the lack of local demand, only 100,000 tons of herring, i.e. one-third of the permitted catch and less than 3% of the estimated local stock, had been harvested the year before. Commentators remembered a 1996 plan to process herring off the New England coast in a giant 369-foot factory trawler. This had been blocked by a coalition of fishermen, environmentalists and politicians who feared the operation would decimate the region's already precarious fishing stocks – cod and pollock. Clearly, some form of structural adjustment was required.

Adjusting towards maximum sustainable yield?

Measuring the yield that could potentially be extracted from fish stock in a stable environment, the notion of a "maximum sustainable yield" provides a widely used policy objective for managing renewable natural resources. Its attainment, subject to given environmental, economic and capacity conditions, requires the management of three principal adjustment costs: opportunity costs, for fishermen and consumers from yields foregone from the fishery due to its depleted state; costs incurred by the fishing industry in the transition process, while a depleted stock is being rebuilt; and uncertainty costs due to constantly changing catch opportunities that often characterize depleted fish stocks and efforts to rebuild them. Choosing among demand-side and supply-side measures requires balancing the need for smooth economic and social impact against the risk of fostering a culture of dependency.

Supply-side measures typically affect harvesting efforts and cushion adjustments of labor and capital providers. Harvesting may be managed through output limits, e.g. catch restrictions subject to sex and size, or input limits, e.g. efforts or gear restrictions or limited area access subject to timing and zone size. Quotas and total allowable catch (TACs) limits may be given to harvesters or processors, individually or for a region, and may be non-transferable or tradable and stacked. Input and output measures tend to have different impacts on the length and stability of the season, and the productivity of catch and employment. Workforce adjustments, subject to age and alternative employment opportunities, may involve anything from job counselling and retraining to outward job creation through wage-cost subsidies, venture aid or public employment programs. Passive programs involve income transfers to

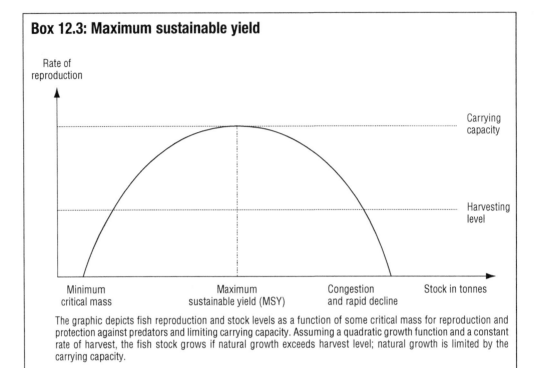

Box 12.3: Maximum sustainable yield

Rate of
reproduction

Carrying
capacity

Harvesting
level

Minimum   Maximum   Congestion   Stock in tonnes
critical mass   sustainable yield (MSY)   and rapid decline

The graphic depicts fish reproduction and stock levels as a function of some critical mass for reproduction and
protection against predators and limiting carrying capacity. Assuming a quadratic growth function and a constant
rate of harvest, the fish stock grows if natural growth exceeds harvest level; natural growth is limited by the
carrying capacity.

the unemployed with the amount and duration usually related to the recipient's age, his or her level of earnings before becoming unemployed and the contribution to a government-run unemployment insurance scheme. Also, unemployment benefits may be related to financial compensations, such as vessel, gear or license buyback. In devising active and passive labor market and compensatory measures for the harvest and the post-harvest sector, there is a need for coherent signals to fishery workers that link concerns for resource management, social protection, and labor market efficiency.

Demand-side measures affect distribution and consumer decisions and have an effect on the harvesting community. They may involve demand management through eco-labelling and promoting sustainable species and the imposition of common marketing standards and/or market access rules for international competition. In addition, market fluctuations may be cushioned through various forms of price support that, among others, allow quantities to be withdrawn based on reference prices linked to total catch in present and previous years. Measures need to account for changing environmental and economic conditions, be non-discriminatory to avoid abuse and reflect stakeholder interests. Yet while theoretically straightforward, demand-side and supply-side adjustment in practice is often cumbersome.

The Marine Stewardship Council, (MSC), for example, was created in 1996 as a demand-managing eco-labelling scheme for seafood products that maintained three "sustainability criteria": a healthy target fish population, the integrity of the marine ecosystems and effective fishery management. Founded by Unilever, one of the world's biggest buyers of frozen fish, and the WWF, the scheme soon became autonomous and certification was carried out by an independent third party, chosen by a fishery seeking the label. But observers were wondering whether a market-oriented organization could be trusted with ecological stewardship. After all, production volumes of the New Zealand hoki, a species which had been approved by the MSC and quickly substituted for cod in Europe's fast-food chains in the late 90s, had come under pressure as weather conditions had affected spawning grounds.[13] Had MSC set biomass baselines too low to be able to guarantee sustainability? Other MSC certificates were challenged by environmentalists for confusing consumers with unjustified blanket approvals across different species and large numbers of locations – as in the case of the British Columbia salmon – or for not recognizing spill-overs across the wider eco-system – as in the case of the Eastern Bering Sea pollock fishery that jeopardized endangered Steller sea-lions.

On the supply side, issues were equally troublesome. In 1997, OECD countries had spent $6.3bn in government financial transfers to the fishing industry, 77% of which was devoted to fisheries infrastructure and activities to ensure the sustainable use of fish stocks and the aquatic ecosystem. A further $1.4bn had gone into direct payments and cost-reducing transfers (e.g. modernization grants, income support and tax exemptions) intended to boost profitability, reduce dependency on fishery and thereby pressure on stocks. By 2006, however, subsidies to the fishing industry totalled more than $15bn a year worldwide – nearly 20% of industry revenue.[14] In some cases, transfers effectively encouraged the build-up of additional capacity – in the developed and the developing world. The latter supplied nearly 50% of the total world fish exports, almost half stemming from so-called low-income food-deficit countries. Here the objectives of fishery management often focused on intensifying rather than reducing fishing efforts, which, it appeared, needed to be taken into consideration when discussing supply management within the OECD. But steps did not seem to go in the right

---

[13] Ensuring fishing will have a future? *New Zealand Herald*, October 7, 2001.
[14] See www.globefish.org/index.

direction – not even in countries formally committed to partnership agreements with "Southern countries" and presumable benefiting from supranational policy coordination as in the case of the European Union.

A 2001 Green Paper had outlined the EU's future common fishery policy that was to involve proactive planning, community-wide coordination, and effective structural adjustment oriented towards long-term solutions. In particular, "openness, transparency, non-discrimination and compatibility with the Community's institutional framework" were to be the guiding principles. Wherever possible, "powers to deal with problems in the Member States' own waters" were to be delegated "to national levels without discriminating however against the fishermen and infringe the right of initiative of the Commission. Scientific advice (was to be) better integrated into the decision-making process and Community financial assistance concentrated on reducing overcapacity."[15]

In December 2006, however, EU fisheries ministers rejected pleas by the EU Commission for capacity cuts as well as proposals by scientists and environmental campaigners calling for a total ban on cod fishing and drastically reduced time at sea. They instead opted to lower the cod catch by 14%, increase quotas for hake, prawns, mackerel and monkfish and trim the number of permitted fishing days by 8%. While ministers suggested the need for further voluntary reductions they were "unwilling to impose more severe cuts in an effort to protect the fishing industry."[16] Greenpeace merely staged a symbolic funeral for the "last cod;" its "Save Our Seas" campaign had already shifted focus onto the Mediterranean, where spotter planes tracked bluefin tuna for the Japanese market, contributing to an estimated total catch of around 40% above the TAC set by international quotas. Apparently, the General Fisheries Commission for the Mediterranean (GFCM), and International Commission for the Conservation of Atlantic Tuna (ICCAT) had been unable to stop misreported catches and illegal boats. For the time being, Greenpeace's activists maintained a non-interventionist, observer status.

2. Beyond fish: Environmental degradation and regulatory response

Discussions of the above case material typically focus on the adjustment costs of the various stakeholders involved, the lack of universally accepted data on

---

[15] EU News Release on the Green Paper on the Future of the Common Fisheries Policy, May 28, 2001.
[16] *The Guardian*, Thursday December 21, 2006.

the status of the resource, and the ambiguous jurisdiction and enforcement conditions surrounding any agreement. Parties are facing a Prisoner's Dilemma that requires some form of coordination lest the common resource is over-exploited. This "tragedy of the commons,"[17] underlying many vital resource management problems, has been a key concern of economic analysis. Yet while economic theory offers a range of fairly clear-cut policy responses,[18] their effectiveness presupposes institutional structures and regulatory processes, which in many areas of global environmental concern are either not available or are distorted in line with dominant interests. Hence, addressing regulatory responses to environmental degradation in general, the interest lies less on the specific policy but the process of policy-making. Who sets regulatory standards and how are they being globalized? What determines the stability and the level of regulatory control? Is there a need for coordinating sectoral standards and centralizing environmental regulation globally? And, given its vast distributional effects – what adjustments would be required?

Globalizing environmental standards?

To say that "(t)he failure of globalization is that markets are global but regulation is not"[19] is simply wrong. In the area of the environment alone, there are in excess of 1,000 multilateral or bilateral international legal instruments that not only affect national environmental standards but stimulate and shape national regulatory developments. Hence, the important question is "whose/which standard wins?"

A standard reflects a fundamental design principle and spells out operational rules to be locally applied; it is adopted if expected benefits outweigh broadly defined switching costs. Successful standard setters promote the emulation of their model by compensating switching costs and suggesting growing benefits in line with increased adoption; they capture and spread local enhancements of their operational rules to the extent that they reflect the fundamental design principle. Dominant but obsolete standards are often sheltered by mass inertia rooted in network benefits; exit barriers avert progress. This intuition is also reflected in the history of globalizing environmental norms.[20]

---

[17] Hardin, G., (1968) The tragedy of the commons, *Science*, Vol. 162, pp. 1243–48.

[18] Helm, D., (2005) Economic instruments and environmental policy, *Economic & Social Review* 36(3), 205–28.

[19] Hauchler, I *et al.* (eds.), (2003) *Global Trends 2004/2005*, Frankfurt A.M: Fischer Verlag, pp. 179–93, at p. 180.

[20] See Braithwaite, J., Dahos, P., (2000) *Global business regulation*, Cambridge: Cambridge University Press.

For one, major economies and corporate players set out models for emulation by others. The US National Environmental Policy Act of 1969, for example, outlined the method of environmental impact analysis which was adopted by the majority of industrialized countries. In drafting current EU environmental rules, Austria, Denmark, Finland, Germany, the Netherlands and Sweden tend to "set the pace," using their combined voting powers and national expertise in dealing with the Commission. Operating from a less developed regulatory base, Greece, Portugal and Spain typically "drag their feet" and accept more stringent measures only if compensation can be obtained. Belgium, France, Ireland and the UK "sit on the fence" – playing the "environmental card" in negotiating unrelated issues or scape-goating Brussels for inconvenient policy decisions.[21] At corporate level, 3M set up its 'pollution prevention pays' program in 1975. Over the next thirty years this has not only resulted in close to 6,000 "eco-efficiency" projects, currently reducing emissions across 3M's extended supply-chain by 1m tons annually, but inspired the global search for "eco-effectiveness," e.g. reusable or completely biodegradable products.[22] The Forest Stewardship Council (FSC) provides an example for how these concepts inspire and upgrade globalized regulatory standards. A network of producers and retailers of wood products and NGOs, the FSC requires eco-effective, lifecycle thinking beyond the requirements stipulated by ISO norms, before it grants its sustainable forests label.[23]

However, once emerging regulatory standards are feared to distort competition, impose substantial adjustment costs, or be of marginal interest to potential adopters and broader stakeholder groups, mere "role modelling" is likely to be insufficient. Here, adoption and compliance often require third-party involvement, the provision of rewards or the broadening of the regulatory agenda.[24] For instance, following up on a US initiative, the OECD Environment Committee in 1971 established test guidelines for chemicals endorsing the principles of national treatment and non-discrimination, according to which imported and domestic services were to be treated

---

[21] For a detailed assessment see Börzel, T. A., (2002) Pace-setting, foot-dragging, and fence-sitting: Member state responses to Europeanization, *Journal of Common Market Studies*, 40(2), 193–214.

[22] Assadourian, E., (2006) International agierende Unternehmen im Wandel. In Worldwatch Institute (ed.) *Zur Lage der Welt 2006*, pp. 286–313.

[23] See Braithwaite, J., Dahos, P., (2000), p. 282.

[24] See Koehane, R. O. *et al.*, (1993) The effectiveness of international environmental institutions. In P. M. Haas *et al.* (ed.) *Institutions for the Earth: Sources of effective international environmental protection*, Cambridge MA: MIT Press.

equally as long as they reflected the same underlying methodology.[25] Next, US-initiated "debt for nature swaps" or the Global Environmental Facility (GEF), pursuant to the 1992 Rio Summit, channel funds into developing countries to facilitate investments into environmental protection and compliance with raised regulatory requirements. Finally, the EU Water Framework Directive represents an attempt to bundle regulatory agendas and involve more stakeholders early on to improve commitment, enhance bargaining opportunities and thereby ultimately the chance of promoting a new set of environmental standards.[26]

Taken to the extreme, broadening the regulatory agenda and using compensation under some central, third-party auspices, would effectively replace national or corporate regulatory leadership by some world organization of environmental affairs. In 1970, UN General Secretary U Thant proposed an International Environmental Organization to pursue an integrated strategy; in 1987, the World Commission called for a change in the UN Charter to set up a World Environmental Security Council able to enforce global environmental policies determined by the majority of UN members; in 1997, UN General Secretary Kofi Annan proposed a World Environmental Fiduciary Council as part of his UN reform program. A world organization may be tied into the Bretton Woods system, to coordinate overlapping institutions, foster the North-South dialogue and build the capacity to act.[27] It may also result in protracted institutional bargaining. But if effective, it would cut out forum shopping and channel regulatory competition based upon a generally agreed direction of environmental regulatory reforms, its "design principle." A shared commitment to pursue regulatory reforms that "race to the top" rather than seeking to profit from diluting regulatory standards would help overcome the global tragedy of the commons. It may or may not require a global leviathan, but it definitely requires a fundamental change of mind.

Changing the chip?

As of October 1999, the world houses more than 6 billion people; in 2010 it will be 7 billion; by 2050 the number may climb to 9bn; if the global economy

---

[25] The EU's principle of subsidiarity requires harmonized not mutually recognized environmental norms.
[26] See Chapter 10 in this volume.
[27] Biermann, F., Simonis, U. E., (2000) Institutionelle Reform der Weltumweltpolitik? Zur politischen Debatte um die Gründung einer Weltumweltorganisation, *Zeitschrift für Internationale Beziehungen*, 7:15, pp. 163–83.

maintains an average annual growth rate of 2.5%, by then it will be more than three times its current size. Economic growth easily outpaces population numbers; for neither to dramatically strain ecosystems, decoupling requires significant technological advance. Yet, with the exception of rather isolated improvements, particularly in the area of energy efficiency, there is little evidence of this.[28] But why grow the economy? What are the demand-side and supply-side implications of a stationary situation? Could an environmentally efficient catch-up of the developing world be facilitated in a global no-growth environment? Would no growth kill progress? The literature on each question is vast; its impact on policy discussions is limited.

While standard micro-economics assumes that people are endowed with unlimited wants, it takes significant marketing efforts to "uncover latent demands," motivate and aggregate consumers and make production cycles predictable. While x% of the world population is unable to properly feed itself, substantial funds are spent to create demand for personalized Christmas jingles on mobile phones. Consumerism, that is consumption completely divorced from needs and Maslow's "creature comforts," significantly contributes to global production and shows up in national competitiveness indicators. Corporate growth drives bonuses just as GNP growth gets politicians re-elected. Growth – at least in the industrialized world – has become valuable in itself – a fetish.[29]

"No growth" in the affluent world could mean improving quality and productivity but also the need to assume responsibility for life. On the demand side, "voluntary simplification," as an alternative to a consumerist life-style, may translate into looking out for contentment rather than consumption, for self-expression, for less is more.[30] On the supply side, "no growth" would unleash hyper-competition, rationalize production, eliminate "me too" offers, drive productivity and restructure labor relations. It would mean managing under tight resource constraints to maximize quality not quantity, substituting capital for labor wherever possible. Unemployment and other forms of hidden income distribution would give way to a redefinition of work, job sharing and unpaid occupations. What would people do with their free time in this scenario? Possibly join what Nomura Securities

---

[28] For reviews of recent sightings of technological decoupling see the World Resource Institute, at www.wri.org.

[29] See Galbraith, J. K., (1968) *Die moderne Industriegesellschaft*, München; Hamilton, C. (2003) *Growth fetish*, London: Pluto Press.

[30] Etzioni, A., (1999) Voluntary simplification. In W. E. Halal *et al.* (eds.) *21st Century Economics*, New York: St. Martin's Press.

already in the 1970s projected as an unavoidable "information society," in which people learn as much as they can as long as they can. According to research financed by the Merck Family Fund, this is at least what most Americans would do today, if given the chance.[31]

"No growth" for the developing world today is no option. Tempted by the sheer level of affluence achieved by the First World, all other countries want to catch up. The question is whether replication is feasible, desirable and which political implications this may entail. In 1998, it took roughly 5 ha of productive ecosystem to support the average US citizen's consumption of goods and services versus less than 0.5 ha to support consumption levels of the average citizen in the developing world;[32] annual *per capita* CO_2 emissions were more than 11,000 kg in industrial countries; in Asia it was less than 3,000 kg. But the gap in both absolute and relative terms is closing fast. In November 2006, China and India ranked second and third after the United States, in terms of the WWF's ecological footprint index.[33] On December 2, 2006, the deputy head of China's State Environmental Protection Administration estimated environmental damage at 8 to 13% of China's national income per year.[34] Put differently, the cost of pollution, if it were internalized, would offset almost all of China's economic gains since the late 1970s. However, given that similar assessments have been around for more than a decade,[35] one should not expect China to quickly discard its "grow now, clean up later" program of economic development. Similarly, the government-run Indian Council of Agricultural Research (ICAR) has just acknowledged research results by a study team of the University of California at Berkley claiming that brown clouds or "Asian haze" – layers of air pollution, which contains soot and other fine particles – cut growth-rates in the Indian rice-harvest by 11% annually. ICAR announced that it was not immediately concerned with the findings but supported the development of new strains of staple crops, including rice, which would be tailored to changing environmental conditions.[36]

---

[31] The Harwood Group, Yearning for Balance: Views of Americans on consumption, materialism, and the environment, at www.iisd.ca/linkages/consumer/harwood.html.

[32] See Wackernagel, M., Yount, J. D., (2000) *Environment, development and sustainability*, New York: Springer.

[33] The index measures the consumption and waste patterns of natural resources by nations as well as the amount of carbon dioxide they release into the atmosphere due to the burning of fossil fuels.

[34] In a letter to the *South China Morning Post*, December 2, 2006, reported by Reuters.

[35] See assessments by the World Bank and the World Resource Institute under www.usembassy-china. org.cn/sandt/CostofPollution-web.html, last visited January 4, 2007.

[36] See www.insnet.org/insheadlines.rxml?id=3729, last visited January 4, 2007.

Westerners, alarmed about such a nonchalant attitude, need to be reminded that countries like China and India merely continue a conventional pattern of environmental (ab-)use,[37] except possibly faster and at a larger scale, and that concern for the environment is a rather recent phenomenon – a good that is cherished as income rises and conservatism grows. Rather, such information should drive home the message that is for the affluent world to accommodate the rest to catch up fast, with the lowest possible impact on the environment and to dress up "no growth" as the new model to emulate.

Human history is sometimes recounted as man's struggle to circumvent basic environmental constraints and the impact on nature of doing so. While the transition towards agriculture and settled communities has largely been consummated around the world, the transition from pre-industrial to an industrialized society – with its use of hydrocarbons, long-distance transportation, fast communication, globalized production and the invisibility of its impact to the final consumer – has not. However, the developing world's legitimate demand to catch up and the Western unquestioned insistence on continued economic growth need to be coordinated to avoid straining the natural ecosystem even further. In discussing the globalization of environmental standards, the underlying design model needs to be made explicit: growth or sustainability? Questioning growth is a starting point that could lead to a more meaningful definition of progress and the role of man in nature.

---

[37] The pattern: selectively destroying mixed woodlands allowed the intensive cultivation of crops; bringing water to dry areas boosted plant productivity; replacing wild, fickle species, the bison, by more resistant, domesticated ones, cattle, enhanced meat output. As human population numbers spiralled beyond the levels sustained by the natural ecosystem, more intensive methods were developed to drive up output even further. Man's control of the environment, his increased use of capital and better husbandry are signs of progress; yet, for some ecologists, they signify little more than an increasingly intrusive and technologically ever more complex way of meeting the same basic human needs. See Ponting, C., (1993) *A green history of the world – The environment and the collapse of great civilizations*, New York: Penguin.

Part IV

Country/International level

13 Governing oil supply: Fiscal regimes, NOCs and the steering of resource-based economies

Ralf Boscheck

Current oil price speculations – broadly concerned with fuel substitution or technological supply constraints – hardly ever seem to account for the role of national oil companies (NOCs). This may be because NOCs, habitually secretive and subject to political discretion, typically do not render information in any timely, market-relevant way. Or it may reflect the perception that NOCs simply operate outside the realm of conventional market, corporate and regulatory controls. But it is the NOCs that, by some measure, control roughly 90% of the global hydrocarbon reserves[1] and whose operating and investment decisions affect prices, demand adjustments, and also their own country's policy options. Recent endeavors to substitute analysis for prevailing economic and political clichés, clarify important but largely unconnected questions. This chapter charts an integrative approach. By way of introduction, section 1 ties current oil price discussions to conceivable supply adjustments and the importance of NOCs. Section 2 looks at NOCs – conceptually, historically and in current market contexts. Section 3 discusses NOC governance. Section 4 links NOCs to the challenges of steering resource-based economic development. Section 5 sums up.

1. Oil market evolution, supply-side adjustments and NOCs

In its 2005 forecast,[2] the International Energy Agency (IEA) predicted a 51% growth of energy consumption over the next two decades up to the year 2030; oil is expected to remain the energy source of choice. Back-of-the-envelope calculations show that by 2050 the world will require double its

---

[1] Marcel, V., (2006) *Oil titans*, London: Chatham House.
[2] IEA (2005) *World energy outlook*, Paris.

current level of energy.[3] In the absence of substantial, medium-term demand adjustments,[4] and if all currently known reserve capacities are included – i.e. existing reserves are developed, oil recovery is enhanced, non-conventional oils are brought forward and new discoveries are made – the world will be short of roughly 62 million barrels per day (MMbpd) (+/−25%) by 2020. Put differently, there is a need to find the equivalent of one additional UK North Sea – annually. Of course these numbers are contested and hence the necessity and feasibility of supply-side adjustments; but the very discussion may easily block the view on the real issues.

Since the early 1970s, "peak oil" scenarios, predicting that the world was running out of oil, have consistently been proved wrong by new discoveries and technological advance. But optimists, pointing to geological surveys and investment schedules to suggest a potentially vast and available global hydrocarbon base, have also often overlooked the fact that resource access and capacity expansion merely create options to increase supply. Their use depends on a country's stance on accelerating reserve depletion in view of current and future economic and political conditions; its impact reflects the effectiveness of coordinating producers with broadly different interests. It is not technology but the political economy that matters.[5]

Table 13.1 gives a quick overview of the geographic base, the cost and the coordination of oil supply. According to the *Oil and Gas Journal*, in 2005, 84% of the world's 1.1 trillion barrels of proven conventional reserves were held by OPEC and its total crude oil production of 29.9 MMbpd represented 35.5% of total supply. At 2004 crude oil production rates, OPEC's overall reserve-to-production ratio translated into 83 years of remaining reserves; non-OPEC producers held a stock lasting 26 years. While throughout the 1980s and 1990s low, volatile prices inhibited investments, both OPEC and non-OPEC producers are expected to increase capacity. Yet whereas OPEC

---

[3] Assuming that the world population increases by 1.4% annually, the global economy expands by 3.5% and technological progress reduces energy intensity by 2% on average, global energy demand will rise by 1.6% annually.

[4] For such caution see Hall, K. (2006) Challenges on the pathway to a hydrogen economy; Demers, D. (2006) Natural gas vehicles in China – An answer to high oil demand?, and Bockamp, S., Kruhl, J. (2006) Emissions trading chapters in Boscheck, R., (2006) (ed.) *Energy futures*, Basingstoke: Palgrave Macmillan at, pp. 157–75, 176–83, and 208–18 respectively.

[5] For a pessimistic view see Hubbert, M. K., (1949) Energy from fossil fuel, *Science*, 109(2823) 103–109; Campbell, C. J., (2004) *The essence of oil and gas depletion*, Multi-Science Publishing. For an optimistic perspective see the United States Geological Survey that predicts that only one-third of the world's 3 trillion barrels of recoverable oil have been used (see www.usgs.gov/pubprod) and Cambridge Energy Research Associates (CERA) who extrapolate from 360 ongoing upstream projects a 15MMbpd increase by 2010 (see www.cera.com/home, last visited September 7, 2006).

Table 13.1: Geographic base, coordination and cost of oil supply

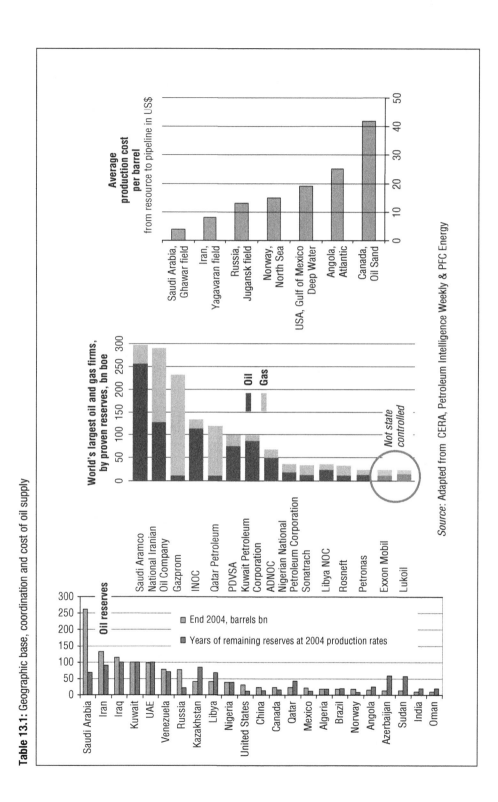

Source: Adapted from CERA, Petroleum Intelligence Weekly & PFC Energy

members are anticipated to raise crude capacity by about 5 MMbpd to 37.9 MMbpd by 2010,[6] increases in non-OPEC production, most importantly from countries like Angola, Brazil, Russia and the states bordering the Caspian Sea, are likely to have only a limited, short-term market impact. At the end of the decade, total non-OPEC oil production is projected to plateau and gradually decline. This will further increase OPEC's global market share and create a production shortfall that upcoming Middle Eastern capacity expansion will need to meet. But how will the necessary decisions be taken? Are changes in domestic agendas likely to undermine investments and further increase the output gap? How can the outside world judge supply-side adjustments?

Ten of the thirteen oil companies overshadowing Exxon-Mobil's proven reserves are North African or Middle Eastern, all are NOCs. NOCs not only control 72% of proven oil and 55% gas reserves but, based on six operational criteria – oil and gas reserves and production, refining capacity and product sales – represent five of the top ten oil producers. Facing such economically powerful actors, with operating modes and political contexts often quite distinct from conventional references, even learned observers are quick to substitute truisms for insight. Hence, The *Economist*, freely bunching Iran with Venezuela, Statoil with Saudi Aramco, and NOCs with their home countries' interests, proclaims that "(n)ationalisation has failed" and derides NOCs as "badly run" symbols of "resource nationalism" that "should be privatized."[7]

For Ali Al-Naimi, Saudi Arabia's Minister of Petroleum and Mineral Resources and former CEO of Saudi Aramco, "(t)he onslaught against NOCs in recent years is largely due to generalizations, lack of knowledge and appreciation of their role."[8]

What then is their role? What explains their origin and what are the alternatives? How are they governed and when and how can policies effectively direct their growth? How do they respond to or even drive the demands of resource-based economies? And when are political and macroeconomic conditions indicative of national output decisions?

---

[6] In the Gulf, the largest additions will come from Saudi Arabia, (+1.5 MMbpd), the UAE (+0.9 MMbpd) and Kuwait (+0.6 MMbpd). Libya is courting international oil companies (IOCs) to raise its current capacity of 1.7 MMbpd back to the its pre-sanction 3.3 MMbpd level; Algeria is planning to add one-third to its current 2 MMbpd by 2010.

[7] The Economist (2006) Big oil, August 10, 2006.

[8] Al-Naimi, A., (2004) *The role of national oil companies in a changing world's economic and energy relations*, OPEC International Seminar, Vienna, September 16, 2004.

2. Superseding the market: Fiscal regimes and NOC benefits

Governments, evaluating the extent of their direct involvement in exploiting their country's oil and gas resources, face a range of choices – from entirely outsourcing to completely "internalizing" operations in the hands of a stand-alone, state-owned, state-run enterprise. If there is *a priori* no reason why private or governmental control would result in different views on the attractiveness of the resource and options for operations, why would any country set up its own import-competing NOC rather than create a regulatory and fiscal regime which is able to attract global specialists?

The answer must lie in the perceived inability of the resource and the fiscal/regulatory regime to attract an adequate suitor, overcome differences in views on the value of the resource and the content of development plans, engender trust in the enforceability of the contracts, allow for the promotion of related, indigenous industries, capture spill-overs in infrastructure and skill-building or simply make use of existing but idle capacities. Yet, even if all of these requirements were met, NOCs may still serve a broader economic and political purpose. Put differently, NOCs are chosen to respond to or create market failures.

Playing the market – competing on prospectivity, fiscal and regulatory terms

Governments are expected to structure their hydrocarbon tax to attract investments, attain a fair share of profits and an assured periodic income plus a range of the above benefits. Regulation is to ensure efficient resource use. International oil companies seek profitable prospectivity, resource and market access, low transaction costs, maximized shareholder return and a diversified portfolio. Both groups face each other in markets. *Ex ante*, resource owners may have to compete for investments by offering the most favorable terms, or, given superior levels of prospectivity, may not need to do this and still induce a feeding frenzy among investors. *Ex post*, committed investors are concerned about the stability of the fiscal regime. But requiring strictly stable fiscal regimes is equal to asking for a long-term contract without an adjustment clause; in fact, it may be in neither party's interest to insist on it. Over time, changes in global commodity prices, investment activities, or the relative prospectivity of the region are likely to change as much as the country's economic policy and view on foreign participation. Systems are

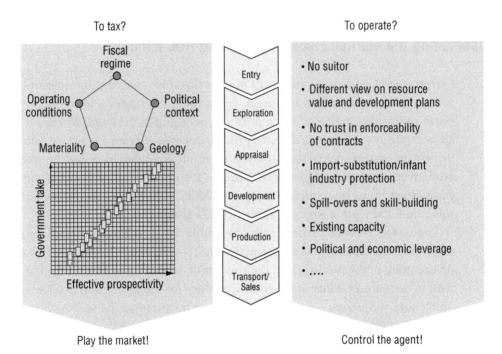

Figure 13.1: The choice of resource owners: Play the market or control the agent?

necessarily in flux and fiscal adjustments can keep a basin competitive. Consider the evolution of the UK continental shelf (UKCS) fiscal regime.[9]

In 2003 and 2004, the UKCS – the ninth most important oil and gas province in the world in production terms – recorded the largest oil production decline of all basins in the BP annual review – approximately 230 MMbpd. A year later, the basin also had the highest level of exploration, appraisal, and development activities (as measured by number of well starts) since 1998. According to a recent Wood Mackenzie benchmarking analysis of oil and gas basins,[10] the UKCS ranked 47 out of 58 in both development and finding costs and 42 out of 58 in terms of commercial success with a chance of 10%. Yet, it ranked 5 out of 63 in terms of exploration wells drilled from 1994 to 2003 and 2 in terms of expenditure. The fiscal regime had evolved to maintain a high level of interest – "against all odds."

---

[9] For a review see Earp, M. (2003) *Review of UKCS tax policies*, London: Department of Trade and Industry.
[10] Quoted from Hall, R. (2005) *Living with fiscal instability – the UK Experience*. Presentation given at the IQPC conference "Stabilizing Fiscal Terms in Upstream Oil and Gas", London. August 17–18, 2005.

Reacting to the 1973 oil price hikes, the Oil Taxation Act 1975 introduced the first sophisticated fiscal regime for the UKCS. It involved a 45% Petroleum Revenue Tax (PRT) charged on profits arising from individual oil fields; (2) various methods for tax relief, particularly in view of smaller and marginal fields; and (3) a ring fence for corporate tax purposes to prevent intra-company rent shifting. In the following year, however, PRT hikes and a supplementary Petroleum Tax, resulting in a 90% marginal tax rate, discouraged investment, despite record oil prices of over $80 a barrel. The pendulum had to swing back.

In 1983, a reformed PRT allowed new exploration and appraisal costs to be set against existing field profits, doubled oil allowances and abolished the royalty for new developments; a new Oil Taxation Act incentivised the sharing of infrastructures and corporate taxes were cut from 52 to 35%. Exploration activity picked up again, but the total PRT income fell as companies optimized their tax burden. The Treasury reacted in 1993 and 1997 by cutting the PRT rate on old fields and abolishing it on new ones. Hence, opportunities for tax shifting were eliminated and activity levels and the tax yield were raised. This did not change even after Labour added a 10% non-deductible surcharge to the hydrocarbon corporate tax in 2002.

At present, with high oil prices and the growing appeal of other oil regions, various initiatives aim to prop up mid-size independent oil producers, rejuvenate dormant fields and encourage new entrants. As the UK primary energy demand is projected to grow by 10% to 255 tones in 2020, accepting maturity and decommissioning of around 40% of assets by then would cut production to 0.5 m barrels of oil equivalent per day (boepd) and require 90% of demand to be covered by imports at an estimated cost of £25bn. Conversely, delaying decommissioning by ten years, and producing 1.5–2 m boepd would meet 50% of total UK oil and gas needs. The difference between the two scenarios in cumulative tax receipts at 2004 oil prices would amounts to £60bn by 2020.[11]

Clearly not a NOC, but the UKCS fiscal regime and the Department of Trade and Industry (DTI) have sustained the success of this very mature basin. But to take the UK's market-driven accomplishment and wonder why 90% of the world's hydrocarbon resources are controlled by state-owned enterprises means being agnostic about history.[12] For markets to work

---

[11] See Earp (2003).

[12] The complex history of most NOCs is widely documented and does not need repeating here. See Clark, J. G. (1990) *The political economy of world energy*, Boston: Prentice Hall Harvester Wheatsheaf; Mommer, B. (2002) *Global oil and the nation state*, Oxford: Oxford University Press; Yergin, D. (1991) *The prize: The epic quest for oil, money, and power*, New York: Simon & Schuster.

efficiently certain legal conditions must hold. Historically they often did not
and political contexts changed. Consider the cases of the National Iranian Oil
Company (NIOC) and Saudi Aramco.

Superseding the market – the quest for national political control

In 1918, seventeen years after the first oil concession in the Middle East had
been granted by the Shah of Persia to what became the Anglo-Persian Oil
Company,[13] the Ottoman Empire collapsed and Britain, France, Russia and
the US began to restructure the region's geopolitical landscape and hydro-
carbon base. In 1925, Ahmad Shah Qajar was toppled by Britain's protégé
General Mohammed Reza Khan – the first Pahlavi Shah. Unexpectedly,
however, the Shah soon set out to cancel earlier agreements, cut Anglo-
Iranian's concession area and increase the government take. In 1951, the
Shah was ousted. The incoming Mosaddeq government – reacting to cumbersome profit-sharing negotiations and encouraged by similar moves in
Central and Latin America – nationalized the Anglo-Iranian concession.
Following British protests, Britain and the US conspired to reinstate the
Shah in 1953, reestablished the concession with a 40:60 split between BP
and US companies, and reduced the role of the NIOC from an operator of
previously nationalized assets to a central contractor with foreign concessionaires. Meanwhile, in Saudi Arabia, a sixty-year concession, granted in 1932
by King Abdulaziz to Standard Oil of California, had expanded to include
Texaco and been incorporated in 1944 as Arabian-American Oil Company
(Aramco). By 1950, Standard Oil of New Jersey and Standard Oil of New
York joined Aramco and the concession entailed a 50:50 profit-sharing
arrangement and increased royalties for the kingdom.

President Nasser's nationalization of the Suez Canal and the ensuing Suez
crisis in 1956 not only highlighted Britain's and France's fading regional
resolve and fueled nationalist sentiments but came at a time when increased
oil supplies cut the price of crude, fees and tax revenues. In response,
government officials of Iran, Iraq, Kuwait, Saudi Arabia and Venezuela met
in Baghdad and formed OPEC, the Organization of Petroleum Exporting
Countries. The stated goal was to control and coordinate oil production to
the benefit of the producing economies. But the cartel's cohesion was soon to
be challenged.

---

[13] The Anglo-Persian Oil Company of 1909, Anglo-Iranian Oil Company as of 1935, turned British
Petroleum in 1954.

1901 1918 1925 1932 1944 1948/50 1951   1953   1956 1959 1960/61 1967 1968/71 1973 1979 1980 1997

Iran: 1st Oil Concession In Middle East		Mosaddeq's Nationalisation Anglo-Iranian Oil Company	Suez Crisis	Shah/Iranian Concession Struggles	Iranian Revolution: NIOC, NIGC, NPC, NIDC takeover
First Pahlavi Shah		NIOC (1948)	Oil Glut/ Cairo: Arab Oil	Six-Day War/ Oil Embargo	Yom Kippur (October)
Collapse of Ottoman Empire		Ousting of Mosaddeq, Reinstatement of Shah;	Conference: OPEC		First Oil Shock	Second Oil Shock	OPEC/ Non-OPE
Kingdom of Saudi Arabia		NIOC main Contractor with foreign concessions	UEA	Saudi Arabia/ Abu Dhabi: Participation Agreements	Saudi Arabia 100% participation in Aramaco
SOCAL ARAMCO concession					(1988 NOC: Saudi Aramco)
		+SO.NJ/SO.NY PSA: 50:50			

Figure 13.2: The quest for political control: NIOC and Saudi Aramco

During the 1967 Six-Day War, the oil embargo by Arab OPEC members against the US and the UK failed as Venezuela and Iran simply increased production *and* international oil companies were freed from antitrust constraints to jointly circumvent restrictions. Clearly, sustaining cooperation among cartel members was already challenging enough, even without US and European concessionaires effectively undermining output and market controls and thereby the use of oil for political purposes. As a result, by the mid-1970s, Libya had expropriated BP assets, Algeria and Kuwait had fully nationalized hydrocarbon infrastructures, the War of Yom Kippur of 1973 had seen a more effective use of the oil weapon and the world suffered the First Oil Shock. Meanwhile, Iran and Saudi Arabia continued to pursue very distinct strategies albeit with broadly similar results. While the Shah had managed to control contractors' assets and to convert concessions into renewable five-year contracts, the revolution in 1979 effectively annulled these agreements and the NIOC, with associated national enterprises, assumed operational responsibilities. At the same time, the Saudi government began to formally participate within Aramco, compensating for the book value of production assets, and in 1988, eight years after it had acquired a 100% interest, established the Saudi Arabian Oil Company (Saudi Aramco) to replace it. Relative to the Iranian struggle, Saudi Arabia had not only avoided directly challenging the global majors and their oil market controls, but, assuming the position of a junior partner, had accumulated valuable know-how and goodwill for future use.

In either case, attaining control over national resources and assets – through nationalization or participation agreements – was more than a straight response to failing arm's-length coordination with IOCs. NIOC and Saudi Aramco emerged as symbols of political emancipation and vital tools for the national steering of resource and infrastructure development, the management of economic, sectoral and financial balances, and the international coordination of economic and political producer interests. For most NOCs these rationales remain intact today – even in the face of competition.

According to a 2005 review of fiscal regimes by the *Oil & Gas Investor*,[14] numerous countries had switched to or improved existing production sharing regimes in terms of investment allowances, performance terms, effective royalty, tax and tariff rates as well as customs exemptions. But only a few considered noticeably reducing or even abolishing state participation. In fact, some countries did exactly the opposite. In 2004, Venezuela unilaterally increased its royalty on contracts to develop and produce heavy oil from the Orinoco region from 1 to 16.67%; the Bolivian draft hydrocarbon law provided for mandatory conversion of existing E&P agreements into service contracts stripping contractors of their share of production. Likewise, in April 2003, the Russian government stalled international E&P investment by not signing off on thirty already-negotiated production-sharing agreements (PSAs) and two months later issued a law which rendered new PSAs virtually inaccessible to investors. By auctioning off most of YUKOS's assets to a shell company and then transferring these to state-owned Rosneft, the Russian government has effectively moved towards *de facto* nationalization of its oil and natural gas resources.

Clearly, in line with the above argument, the Russian government – and with it those of many other oil exporting countries – appears convinced that a fiscal and regulatory system is unable to capture all economic value and to provide additional economic and political leverage. *But* superseding the market and, in the extreme, putting the exploitation of a country's oil and gas resource into the hands of one stand-alone, state-owned, state-run enterprise raises efficiency and broader regulatory concerns. Section 3 discusses issues of NOC governance and problems of controlling the "state within a state."

---

[14] Major shifts in global oil and gas industry, *Oil & Gas Investor*, March, 1 2005.

3. Controlling the "Agent": The governance of NOCs

Recent analyses of NOC regulation, mostly as part of an assessment of the broader political context or the specific incentives affecting a given company, are typically wedded to one, implicit or explicit, model of "best governance." Hence, the IMF, intending to identify the political system that "best" manages oil wealth, starts from a classification of five political structures to deduce typical institutional and economic implications to which an NOC would have to respond. Yet, while the typology that results barely suffices to characterize the cases it summarizes, the process of policy making and its impact on the sector and the NOC are left unclear.[15] Likewise, research, currently undertaken by Chatham House and the Centre for Energy, Petroleum and Mineral Law Policy (CEPMLP),[16] aims to provide a first and much needed comparative assessment of NOC regulatory structures. It sets out from a list of five "universal principles of good governance" – such as "clarity of roles" – to establish detailed questionnaires for case-by-case analysis. Yet, even if they are intuitively obvious, one may doubt the universality of these principles. The notion of *clarity of roles*, for example, assumes near predictability of any potential vagary, the absence of which results in the very challenge of governance – the need to deal with discretion.

Trying to avoid any implicit normative language, this section *first* introduces the conceptual apparatus of institutional economics to identify options for regulating NOCs at interrelated levels of governance. It *then* presents three cases highlighting specific events during the regulation of three rather distinct NOCs: Statoil, Saudi Aramco and the Nigerian National Petroleum Company (NNPC). *Finally*, the conceptual apparatus is used as an audit trail to structure common regulatory concerns and remedies.

Institutional economics and NOC governance

Institutional economics[17] provides a rich set of perspectives for discussing the formation, structure and economic impact of various institutions of market

---

[15] See Benn, E. *et al.* (2003) Managing oil wealth, *Finance and Development*, IMF, March, 40(1).

[16] The principles include (1) clarity of goals, roles and responsibilities; (2) enablement to carry out the role assigned; (3) accountability of decision-making and performance; (4) transparency of information and (5) sustainable development for future generations. See Chatham House (2006) Good Governance of the National Petroleum Sector, Interim report, at www.chathamhouse.org.uk/pdf/research/sdp/GGagenda010606.pdf.

[17] For a review of institutional economics – old and new – and a restatement of its original methodology see Boscheck, R., (2002) *Market drive and governance*, New York: Routledge, particularly chapter 1.

and non-market governance. Aggregating this work, one may conceive of six levels of regulations from operational control and company management via regulatory control and agency supervision to political direction and global governance. At each level, control is executed by markets, relational controls and/or direct central supervision.

In the ideal, markets afford the most efficient means for handling dispersed information and decentrally coordinating economic and political activities. But when information is incomplete and specific investments create exposure to potential abuse, markets fail to work efficiently and other levels of non-spot-market governance emerge and reduce the sum of all coordination or transaction costs incurred. Hence *operational control* based on spot markets, at some level of transaction risk, will be superseded by relational contracts or in-house budgets. *Managerial control*, based on labor-market rates, is likely to be replaced by incentive pay or equity participation. *Regulatory controls* of company performance in competitive product and factor markets will be superseded by regulatory contracts, or, in the extreme, by public budget control and asset ownership. *Agency supervision* may be left to the contests among officers and stakeholders, subject to the right of regulators to target reviews or call for direct ministerial oversight. *Political direction* may be based on electoral outcomes, parliamentary agreements, stable constitutional decree or autocratic rule. *Global governance* built on competition in factor and commodity markets, gives way to contingent rules, or global accords.

Figure 13.3 depicts the resulting reference that helps illustrate the evolution and limits of institutional solutions to the principal problem of governance – distrust. At each level, implicit contracts supplant explicit ones; fiat replaces market contest and triggers concerns over accountability, fairness and inevitable discretion. Obviously, there is very limited scope for any *a priori* judgment on the efficiency and fairness of patterns of economic and commercial coordination; rather, an integrative view on the interaction of multiple levels of governance is required for discussing the specifics of a case at hand.

Applied to the governance of oil supply, "nationalizing the control" over a country's hydrocarbon industry to avoid transaction costs when dealing with external parties comes at the price of governing the NOC, monitoring its regulators and adjusting the system over time. The costs increase with the complexity of the role that the NOC is expected to take.

Already for the relatively narrow task of upstream exploration and production, ensuring an NOC's efficiency may be achieved in a number of ways. At the level of operations and management, it may involve the partial or

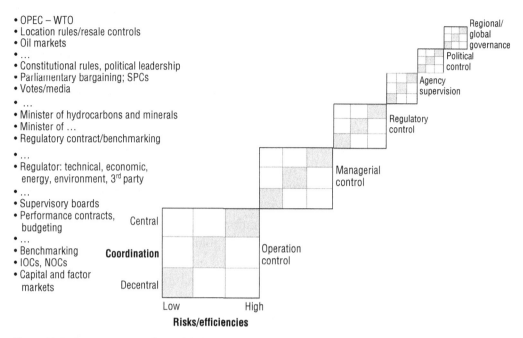

- OPEC – WTO
- Location rules/resale controls
- Oil markets
- ...
- Constitutional rules, political leadership
- Parliamentary bargaining; SPCs
- Votes/media
- ...
- Minister of hydrocarbons and minerals
- Minister of ...
- Regulatory contract/benchmarking
- ...
- Regulator: technical, economic, energy, environment, 3rd party
- ...
- Supervisory boards
- Performance contracts, budgeting
- ...
- Benchmarking
- IOCs, NOCs
- Capital and factor markets

Figure 13.3: The governance of the NOC: Operational and regulatory options

complete outsourcing of operations or its benchmarking *vis-à-vis* others, national or international, public or private, undertakings in a given resource base. In the absence of these, it may require the monitoring of performance and investment indicators, the use of incentive-based budgets and performance pay or the "shadowing" of all NOC operations based on some input-output plan. At the level of regulatory control, product markets, even if subject to OPEC or non-OPEC supply constraints, may still provide competitive checks depending on the hydrocarbon grade, supply conditions and delivery contracts. Labor and financial markets can perform this function only if NOCs are permitted to raise capital and capital and labor markets are sufficiently liquid, i.e. suppliers have a choice. Regulatory tasks, proper, may be combined or broken up subject to technology, resort or activity base and their effectiveness benchmarked nationally *vis-à-vis* other sectors, or across the industry on a global level. Where such comparison is deemed futile, regulators themselves may be subjected to career tournaments or other forms of incentive-based assignments and ministerial reviews. National political control may involve public discourse and even issue-based voting on depletion or geographic expansion programs, parliamentary reviews, or be limited to presidential veto or absolute rule. Ultimately, a given combination of governance arrangements – the national institutional structure – must survive product and factor market competition or may be sheltered by regional or international market arrangements from global market review.

But in reality, matters are often more complicated than this. Most NOCs were initially given, or grew into pursuing, a much broader set of tasks. These may include contracting or undertaking infrastructure development, awarding and monitoring licenses, collecting hydrocarbon-related taxes, subsidizing energy and non-energy consumption, creating and maintaining employment and skill-building in related and less related areas, as well as representing the country in international fora. As its remit broadens, the distinction between operation and policy making begins to blur and the NOC gradually resembles a "state within a state." As a result, conflicts of interests seem "unavoidable", bear on operational and regulatory efficiency and raise concerns about the true location of political power. Now, who should monitor the NOC and, ultimately, based on what? Will multiple regulators and stakeholder groups deliver effective monitoring or be divided and conquered by the state-owned operator? Which level of transparency is required for supervision but potentially detrimental to commercial operation? Will the time horizon of regulatory and political contracts underpin or defy operational imperatives? Who decides whether, when and how to adjust the system? What is the link between the NOC's governance structure and the country's macro-economic status and what is the role of the outside world? Three cases identify different issues with regard to retaining regulatory control; the subsequent discussion identifies common governance challenges.

Statoil – the evolution of the Norwegian model

Reacting to a request by IOCs for oil and gas concessions in 1962, the Norwegian government was initially unwilling, and even openly discouraged Norwegian investors, to commit resources to an ostensibly highly risky venture. The resulting legislative framework gave the government overall control but relied on foreign companies to undertake exploration and production.[18] In 1970, after oil had been found and OPEC countries had insisted on equity participation, the Norwegian concession system shifted to include local content requirements and state participation with "carried interests" until commercial discoveries were made. Also the system of individual applications made ample information available to the Norwegian

---

[18] See Claes, D. H., (2003) *Statoil – between nationalisation, globalisation and Europeanisation*, ARENA Working Papers WP 02/3; Al-Kasim, F., (2006) *Managing petroleum resources: The Norwegian model, in a broad perspective* Oxford: Oxford Institute for Energy Studies.

bureaucracy. By 1972, the Storting had agreed to "ten oil commandments" emphasizing Norway's national control over all activities related to petroleum resources, its use in new industrial activities and the need for one state-owned, one para-statal and one private national player. The Ministry of Industry was charged with effecting legislation and concessions; the Oil Directorate with general administration and regulation, and Statoil with the government's commercial interest. Norsk-Hydro and Saga were the para-statal and private operators, respectively.

The creation of the NOC increased the state's participation with IOCs, in addition to the carried interest clause, ultimately by a sliding scale of between 50 and 80% direct share to be granted to Statoil. As of 1974, Statoil, using its voting rights, effectively controlled all production leases and field development decisions, capping the IOCs' long-term outlook to acting as "consultants or possibly minority shareholders."[19] Also, as nexus of all contracts, Statoil had an informational advantage in pursuing particularly promising concessions and in advising policy makers and regulators. By 1980, Norway's NOC had grown to more than 1,000 employees, and it invested annually in excess of 2.5bn Norwegian kroner and made substantial direct, and via local content requirements, indirect contributions to the country's GNP.

Statoil had reached a level of economic power and independence most likely unforeseen by original regulators. At any rate, in 1984, the conservative minority government sought out opportunities to limit the company's future growth potential. The approach that was finally taken kept earnings from operations with Statoil while channeling tax revenues, with the exception of the earnings of the large Stratfjord field, directly to the public treasury. Stratfjord's earnings helped Statoil to finance developments elsewhere; the state's direct share of economic involvement (SDOE) exposed the government to changes in economic returns.

Two years after the reform, the concurrent collapse of oil price and dollar value cut Norwegian hydrocarbon exports from one year to another by 32bn NOK resulting in a nearly equal-size current account deficit and a 1988 hydrocarbon tax revenue of just 22% of its 1985 value. The public treasury still had to finance the state's share of new hydrocarbon investments. The Norwegian government reacted by devaluing the krone by 12%, fixing the dollar exchange rate, cutting governmental expenditures and halving aggregate demand through a series of interest rate hikes. Also as of 1990, any fiscal

---

[19] See Claes (2003) p. 5; footnote 7 makes reference to Report to the Norwegian Parliament No. 25, 1973–4, p. 13.

surplus was set aside in the Government Petroleum Fund, managed by the central bank in cooperation with external money managers, to preserve some share of the oil revenues for future generations and insulate the economy from inflationary shocks and adverse oil price and exchange rate changes.

At the same time, around the world, new areas of exploration opened up giving IOCs opportunities to play the market. To stay competitive Norway had to reduce its government take, abandon the sliding scale as well as the provision guaranteeing the State and Statoil a 50% share. But despite calls for complete liberalization, the Ministry of Oil and Energy insisted on maintaining the overall level of state involvement and Statoil's participation in all licenses. This situation was only partly challenged by Norway's gradual acceptance of EU internal market rules and the eventual move towards privatization.

EU internal market provisions affected Statoil's activities and its role in the Norwegian energy sector in two ways. For one, Statoil's 50% share, the "carried interest" and the "sliding scale," had always been in clear violation of the EU anti-discrimination standards; their abolition in response to increased regional competition improved EU relations. A second concern was however more difficult to handle. The Norwegian gas selling committee, (GFU), headed by Statoil, was intended to offset downstream market power and excluded foreign companies because of their alleged downstream stakes. Yet, after having defended the GFU against EU discrimination and market power charges for more than ten years, the Norwegian government abolished the GFU in 2001 and formally proposed the adoption of the EU gas directive in February 2002. Statoil had been prepared for partial privatization and internationalization.

Already, since the mid-1990s, opponents to state ownership had identified it as a potential drawback when accessing capital and hydrocarbon resources around the world. Privatization, in contrast, provided financing, added capital market controls and made shares available for exchange in alliances and partnerships. But it was not until June 2001 that the necessary parliamentary majority had been formed and Statoil was listed on the Oslo and New York Stock Exchanges. At the time, 15% of the SDOE had been sold to Statoil and 6.5% to Norsk Hydro and foreign companies; shortly thereafter Saga Petroleum was split up between Norsk Hydro and Statoil. Also, at the time of the public listing, two new 100% state-owned companies had been set up. *Petoro* began to manage the State's direct financial interests while leaving the sales of physical hydrocarbons and reserves to Statoil; *Gassco* was charged with operating the gas grid in the Norwegian continental shelf and managing capacities in the interests of all shippers. By 2005, 30% of Statoil's shares had been acquired by private interest and a new operating model focused on shareholder value, performance contracting and strict corporate controls.

Saudi Aramco – A state within a state?

Responsible for 99% of the Kingdom's proven crude oil reserves, roughly one-fifth of the world's total, and for about 10% of global oil production, Saudi Aramco owns domestic refineries and distribution assets, one of the world's largest and newest tanker fleets and operates a network of marketing and refining partnerships. The company's international status – as the No.1 oil producer – is matched by its domestic importance. Hydrocarbons contribute 88% to Saudi Arabia's exports and 79% to its government revenues.[20] Saudi Aramco runs hospitals and airlines, builds infrastructures and schools, trains and finances studies abroad, and offers home-ownership programs, quality rental and recreational facilities for Saudi and expatriate professionals. The company ensures that no less than 90% of material purchases are supplied by Saudi vendors and manufacturers. With a workforce of 54,000, Saudi Aramco is not only the single largest employer in Saudi Arabia, but it has increased the share of Saudis in its ranks from less than 60% three decades ago to currently 85%. A job at Saudi Aramco comes with relatively high salaries, interest-free home loans and a westernized environment – the company language is English and female employees are allowed to wear western clothing and to drive – on company property. Ali I. Al-Naimi, who had started with Aramco at age eleven, became the company's first Saudi President and CEO in 1984 and in 1995 moved on to be named Saudia Arabia's Minister of Petroleum and Mineral Resources and the Chairman of Saudi Aramco. Still, with all of this, the company's present CEO Abdallah Jumah insists that "(w)e are not a state within a state."[21]

Although Saudi Arabia's Kings hold absolute legislative and executive powers, it is widely recognized that they let key decisions reflect broader family, business and tribal interests as well as the demands of powerful clergies.[22] In this context, Saudi Aramco has been granted more autonomy and a system of regulation that combines western governance practices with some reliance on a strong professional ethos.

[20] EIU (2006) Saudi Arabia, London.
[21] *The Washington Post* (2004) *Saudi Aramco is not a state within a state*, March 16, 2004.
[22] See Abir, M., (1993) *Saudi Arabia: Society, government and the Gulf Crisis*, London: Routledge; Netton, R.(ed.) (1986) *Arabia and the Gulf,: From traditional society to modern states* Barnes & Noble and Allen, M., (2006) *Arabs*, London/New York Totowa: Continuum.

At the policy level, the Supreme Petroleum Council, with the King and the Crown Prince as chair and deputy chair respectively, and Saudi Aramco's CEO as one company representative, governs the petroleum policy process and approves Saudi Aramco's five-year strategy plans as presented by its board of directors. The board of directors, on the side of the government, includes the Minister of Petroleum and Mineral Resources as chair, the secretary general of the Supreme Economic Council, two ministers, and the vice president of King Abdul Aziz City of Science and Technology. Company and non-government board members are Saudi Aramco's CEO, three of the company's VPs, the former minister of state and president of the seaport authority, as well as the retired presidents of Marathon and Texaco and the former vice chairman of J. P. Morgan & Co.

At the operational level, governance is largely financial and budget based. The company's royalty and dividends amount to around 93% of its profit and leave it with the rest to finance investments but possibly little explicit inducement to minimize costs. But restraints are implicit. Company executives openly profess to be proud of being part of *the* elite, professional organization in the country, but one that operates largely free from political interference and in pursuit of more than just short-term objectives.[23] That freedom and high-level trust had been earned as the company continued to prove itself to be the best for the job. (To be sure, the General Petroleum and Mineral Organization [Petromin], a public corporation wholly owned by the Saudi government and established in 1962, had originally been earmarked to become the country's national oil company. But repeated exploration failures and operational deficiencies triggered restructuring and its absorption into Saudi Aramco in 1993.)[24] And yet, in at least one recent incidence, Saudi Arabia's Gas Initiative,[25] Saudi Aramco's interests appeared to conflict with those of the political sovereign, allegedly caused the NOC to interfere with politics and triggered thorough institutional reforms.

In late 1998, at a meeting attended mostly by US IOC executives, Crown Prince Abdullah invited US corporations to invest in Saudia Arabia. Interpreted as potentially reversing the national upstream monopoly, was this

---

[23] See Marcel (2006) for supporting interviews. For economists this resembles the notion of an efficiency wage.

[24] During restructuring, Petromin's responsibility was focused on controlling the domestic and joint-venture refining capacity and the overall responsibility for marketing and refining the kingdom's oil handed over in 1988 to Samarec – the Saudi Arabian Marketing and Refining Company. By mid-1993, both companied were merged with Saudi Aramco.

[25] For a detailed account see Robins, P., (2004) Slow, slow, quick, quick, slow: Saudi Arabia's gas initiative, *Energy Policy*, 32(3), 321–33.

invitation a mere diplomatic gesture, a proper change in policy, a hint towards Saudi Aramco, or all of the above? The following emerges from scattered information.

Largely for economic reasons, gas had hardly ever been the focus of Saudi Arabia's hydrocarbon policies. But priorities changed with the need to diversify the Kingdom's income base, and with opportunities for downstream developments in refining and petrochemicals as well as expected domestic and foreign fuel substitution. As a result, Saudi Aramco was charged with establishing a $12bn Master Gas System (MGS) to collect, process and utilize gas. But, by 1998, market downturns and their impact on the Kingdom's foreign exchange position called into question Saudi Aramco's ability to finance the project. In addition, there was growing concern about the company's level of efficiency, its alleged lack of interest in downstream investments, and its substantial political power, which it purportedly used to cement the *status quo* even at the expense of other, public or private, interests.

In this context, Saudi Aramco most likely perceived Crown Prince Abdullah's pitch for foreign direct investment to open upstream oil and gas to IOCs investments, thereby ending the company's control over the exploration and development of hydrocarbon resources and severely reducing its institutional status. Linking motive to means, analysts identified a range of developments during the initial preparation period of the Gas Initiative that effectively delayed or redirected the reform to the benefit of the NOC.[26]

First, soon after the initial invitation to invest, the project's geographic scope was widened to include all foreign oil majors; this added technical and regulatory complexity and required specialist knowledge available only at Saudi Aramco. Second, at the outset, the project had been focused on downstream initiatives – from petrochemicals to water desalination – which the NOC's supporters presented as focusing Saudi capital upstream, but, in effect would have thrown IOCs into a complex tangle of having to deal with multiple bureaucracies and inter-agency relations. Third, in numerous announcements and government listings, the oil sector was explicitly excluded from the catalog of sectors inviting foreign investments. Fourth, all along, Saudi Aramco was seen to be rather slow to cooperate, particularly when asked for information.

The government reacted by rolling out high-level and far-reaching institutional reforms. A ministerial oil committee, headed by the foreign minister and previous deputy oil minister Prince Saud al-Faisal, was set up to evaluate

---

[26] See Robins (2004), Marcel (2006).

IOC proposals and, in a later stage, reestablished, with a minor involvement of Saudi Aramco, to negotiate with foreign majors. The commission's work was complemented by a technical committee, chaired by the undersecretary of petroleum affairs in the ministry, Prince Abdul Aziz bin Salman bin Abdul Aziz, but had to rely on Saudi Aramco for technical expertise and was, due to "the obstructionist nature of the committee's performance . . . soon bypassed in the decision-making process."[27] Crown Prince Abdullah himself chaired the Supreme Economic Council (SEC), set up in August 1999 to stir the overall institutional and economic reform process and create a broader forum for consultation. Six months later, the SEC was complemented by the Supreme Petroleum and Mineral Affairs Council (SPMC) that replaced the Supreme Petroleum Council and was given "the final word on all affairs of petroleum, gas and other hydrocarbon materials."[28] More specifically, the SPMC was empowered by royal decree to supervise the activities of Saudi Aramco, take over from the NOCs, the responsibility for all gas activities, and to deliver final decisions on contract awards recommended by the ministerial oil committee. SPMC's remit and institutional set up, financed out of the general cabinet budget and physically located within the Council of Minister's court, have been interpreted to clearly signal a reduction in the policy import of Saudi Aramco and the oil ministry.

Still, while the precise roles played by other bureaucratic players, such as SABIC or the Saudi Electricity Company, remain uncertain, it is clear that both the oil ministry and Saudi Aramco were decisive in shaping the further evolution of the Saudi Gas initiative. Participating in the projects, Saudi Aramco maintained insights and, in later stages of negotiations, acted as a regulatory tool when confronting IOCs on issues such as expected returns, project duration, and negotiation style. Also, as the initiative progressed from discussing macro objectives to detailed project work, observers noted that it was much "harder for Abdullah's reformers to monitor its progress and maintain its momentum."[29] Clearly, implementing the King's structural reforms required the cooperation of "the state within a state."

---

[27] See Robbins (2004) at p. 329.

[28] *Ibid*, Robbins comments "The presence of Al-Naimi and of his successor as Aramco chief executive, Abdullah bin Saleh Jumaa, among the SPMC membership was more than counter balanced by the inclusion of Prince Saud, Assaf and an array of reform-minded ministers, including Hashim Yamani (industry and electricity) and Khalid bin Muhammad al-Gosaibi (planning and telecommunications)."

[29] See Robbins (2004), at p. 332.

NNPC – regulatory opportunities – avoided by whom?

Commercially exploiting its oil reserves since the late 1950s, Nigeria's first petroleum tax system of 1959 introduced a 50:50 profit split between the government and international operators. The government sought equity stakes, but did not exercise its options until April 1971, partly as a prerequisite for joining OPEC that year, partly as a response to certain IOCs sponsoring the Biafran war of succession.[30] Decree 18 of 1971 established the Nigerian National Oil Corporation (NNOC) to "participate in all aspects of petroleum including exploration, production, refining, marketing, transportation, and distribution." More specifically, NNOC was charged with training indigenous workers; managing oil leases and refineries; encouraging native participation in infrastructure developments; ensuring domestic price uniformity; developing a tanker fleet; constructing pipelines; and investing in allied industries, such as fertilizers.

By 1976, NNOC held 55% stakes in the Nigerian operations of Elf, Agip/Philips, Shell-BP, Gulf, Mobile and Texaco and its finances were monitored by the Commissioner of Mines and Powers and the Federal Executive Council. The permanent secretary of the Ministry of Mines and Power chaired the company's board, which included representatives from the Ministries of Finance, Economic Development and Planning, the director of Petroleum Resources, the general manager of NNOC, and three other industry experts. Yet, as was made public only during the 1980 Crude Oil Sales Tribunal, NNOC had not produced audited accounts from 1975, and during 1975–1978 had "failed to collect" some 182.95 m barrels of equity oil, owed to it by three IOCs and amounting to an estimated revenue loss in excess of $2bn.

Reacting to this, on April 1, 1977, Decree 33 vested all NNOC assets and liabilities in the Nigerian National Petroleum Corporation (NNPC), kept the previous board structure and lifted the ceiling on contracts that it could award fifty-fold. In addition, the NNPC housed the Petroleum Inspectorate, issuing licenses and overseeing pipeline access, ultimately responsible only to the commissioner for petroleum. Following the 1977 Indigenization Decree, the NNPC's equity stakes in the Nigerian businesses of Elf, Agip, Gulf, Mobil, Texaco, and Pan Ocean had risen to 60%, by 1979 – 80% in the Shell venture. BP lost its 20% stake following disagreements with the Nigerian government over South Africa. Finally, in 1986, a Memorandum of Understanding set a profit limit of $2 per barrel.

---

[30] Biafra held more than two-thirds of the country's then known oil reserves.

Problems with record-keeping, the non-collection of equity oil, and speculatory hoarding continued even after the Ministry of Petroleum Resources had been charged with directly controlling NNPC operations in 1986. In 1989, Petroleum Resources Minister Rilwanu Lukman restructured NNPC as a "financially autonomous, commercially integrated" oil company, consisting of eleven subsidiaries that span the entire hydrocarbon-chemical cluster.[31] Reshuffling of key personnel raised public concern.[32] Also, to underpin its commitment to expand reserves and output (to 2.5MMbpd) by 1995, in 1989, the NNPC sold 20% of its holding in the Shell joint venture for around $2bn to Shell (10%), Elf (5%) and Agip (5%).

During the 1990s, Nigeria continued to exemplify poor governance, high-level corruption, political instability and civil unrest; NNPC reforms were largely ineffective, IOCs stayed interested and public cynicism grew. By 2000, Nigeria had received an estimated total of $280–330bn[33] from oil income, but successive governments had squandered money on numerous 'infrastructure' projects that had never been completed, or had simply helped themselves.[34] All along, future production had to secure a spiraling foreign debt. Whenever commodity markets weakened, Nigeria was quick to undercut OPEC accords. And the economy grew ever more oil-dependent and poor.

Whereas in 1960 oil had accounted for 1% of federal government revenues, four decades later it had risen to 95%. In 2005, Nigeria's oil sector accounted for 46% of GDP, 98% of exports by value and 85% of its foreign exchange earnings. The country's level of GDP per capita, approximately $260, was below the level at independence 40 years previously and income inequality was widening. While the middle-income oil-producing economy of 5 million people had a per capita income of about $2,200, 115 million people in the non-oil producing economy had an average per capita income of $200. With official unemployment around 40%, the shadow economy constituted 77%

---

[31] These included the Nigerian Petroleum Development Company, the Warri Refining and Petrochemicals Company, the Kaduna Refining and Petrochemicals Company, the Pipeline and Products Marketing Company, the Hydrocarbon Services of Nigeria Company, the Engineering Company of Nigeria, the Nigerian Gas Development Company, the LNG Company, the Port Harcourt Refining Company, the Eleme Petrochemicals Company, and Integrated Data Services.

[32] Aret Adams, appointed as the group managing director in the beginning of 1989, and his counterpart at the LNG Company, were suspended late the same year, apparently for refusing to accept government appointees to the LNG Company; in 1990, the former Petroleum Resource Minister Tam David-West was jailed.

[33] Data varies by source; see *The Economist* (2000) *The tale of two giants*, January, 13; Turner, B. (2006) *The statesman's yearbook 2006*, Houndsmill: Palgrave Macmillan and www.nigeriabusinessinfo.com/fos.htm.

[34] For detailed accounts see www.globalintegrity.org; www.nigeriabusinessinfo.com.

of the country's official GDP – one of the highest in the world. The World Economic Forum's most recent Environmental Sustainability Index, measuring a country's ability to maintain favorable environmental conditions and sustainable natural resource management, ranked Nigeria 133 out of 142 countries.

But there may be also signs of a potential turnaround: President Olesegun Obasanjo, whose democratic election in 1999 had ended sixteen years of military rule, set out to reform Nigeria's oil and gas sector, and public finance and administration. Promoting environmental clean-up and the banning of flaring gas, his administration aimed to build up Nigeria's gas production to equal its oil revenues by 2010. To that effect, it directed NNPC to cooperate with Chevron Texaco, AGIP, Total Fina Elf, and Shell to develop offshore production, liquification for the overseas markets, and a West African pipeline to supply Ghana, Benin, and Togo. Economic and institutional reforms were strengthened with the appointment of Ngozi Okonjo-Iweala, a senior World Bank staffer, to head the finance ministry.

In October 2005, Ms Okonjo-Iweala achieved a debt relief of 60% of the $31bn owed by Nigeria to international lenders (the Paris Club) in return for its commitment to use the recent oil windfall ($28bn of reserves in 2005) to repay $12bn over a one-year period. Next, successful anti-corruption and transparency campaigns were recognized by the World Bank and succeeded in removing Nigeria from the blacklists of international money-laundering task forces. In June 2006, and before her fiscal responsibility bill was presented to Parliament, Ms. Okonjo-Iweala was promoted to the foreign office. On August 3, 2006 she resigned.

With the Nigerian Senate rejecting a constitutional amendment, which would have allowed Mr. Obasanjo to seek a third term in office, and the next election scheduled for April 21, 2007, the president's remaining time in office may bring order or spell havoc to national governance. In September 2006, Nigeria's anti-corruption agency set out to prosecute more than half of its governors, yet no high-level arrests were made. In view of the continued interest of IOCs and the decision of the Paris Club, one may wonder about the role of international markets in enforcing the proper governance of national oil supply.

Discussion

The discovery of hydrocarbon reserves has brought enormous benefits to some countries; to others it spelled "waste, corruption, debt and the collapse of public services."[35] It is reasonable to assume that the governance of the NOCs has some impact on this, but comparing countries' respective set-ups does not result in one "right" answer. In fact, such comparisons are contentious. When oil was struck, the three countries discussed had very different physical and institutional infrastructures, industrial and educational bases, and levels of income. Their proven reserves per capita differ significantly. Some led, and some followed developments. Each case would open up very distinct governance discussions (see Figure 13.4), and yet, each points to several regulatory concerns that, in the end, seem common to all.

With hindsight, the role of Statoil, part of the Norwegian Model of managing a hydrocarbon base, evolved from risk-aversion and the leveraging of IOC know-how, via carried interests, increased equity participation and E&P control, resulting in sectoral dominance and large-scale economic impact. Whereas the state initially had used Statoil for operation, skill-building and tax collection, it eventually assumed direct economic risks and used markets to govern and facilitate the growth of the NOC. Political control had been maintained through retained shareholdings, the strengthening of Statoil and Norsk Hydro, the creation of the petroleum fund, and a licensing process, with which Norway, even under EU internal market rules, retains its power over output, natural resource and market management decisions. The latter made it a viable partner to OPEC in governing global oil supply. *But* is limiting an NOC's growth necessary to stay politically in charge? Could the same outcome be achieved by strengthening other national players subject to different forms of government direction? Is privatization the only way to attain something akin to capital market control? Is there an NOC bonus in international markets? How is one to ensure that the internationalization of an NOC does not dilute its concern for the home base? When does this concern lose relevance?

Emerging from participating in IOCs and absorbing national benchmarks, Saudi Aramco's very success in building and consolidating physical and institutional infrastructures, as well as technological know-how, crowded out opportunities for third-party involvement and heightened the need for government control. Saudi Arabia's Gas Initiative, however motivated, focused attention on the process of introducing or maintaining competitive checks; it also illustrated the power of incumbent NOCs to set, refocus and

---

[35] In 1975 Juan Pablo Pérez Alfonso, co-founder of OPEC, called petroleum "the devil's excrement . . . it results in waste, corruption, debt and the collapse of public services." The *devil's excrement*, *The Economist*, May 22, 2004.

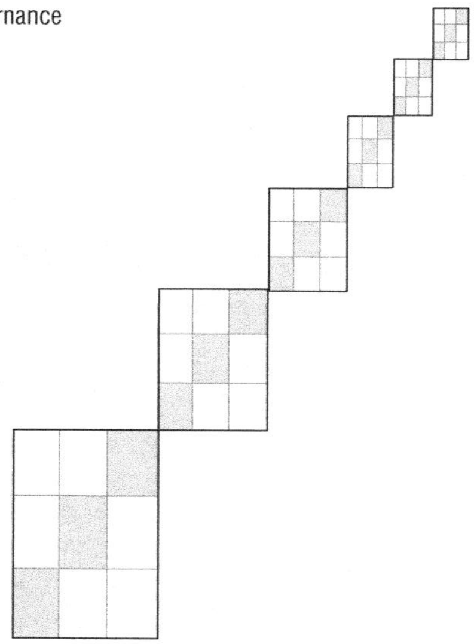

Regional / global governance

- How to involve lenders, OPEC and others in performing a broader global governance function?
- Where, how and for which reasons to shelter the national regulatory set-up?
- How to maintain a competitive check on the national institutional regime?

Political control

- How to decouple sectoral decisions from macroeconomic imperatives? How to manage the economy's hydrocarbon exposure (see section 4)?
- How to allocate political responsibilities to ensure sectoral needs for long-term stability?
- How to ensure that inter-generational concerns are adequately taken into consideration?

Agency supervision

- How to ensure that political supervision can cooperate with regulatory institutions without being captured by them?
- How to create a sufficiently deep and broadly held sector understanding that allows for viable inter-agency competition, effective supervision and makes replacement viable?
- How to formulate regulatory contracts that allow for simple benchmarking of the regulator?

Regulatory control

- How to ensure that the NOC's internationalization does not compromise its national function?
- How to unbundle NOC tasks without incurring inefficiencies and loss of information?
- How to formulate incentive-compatible performance contracts and structure effective regulatory reviews?
- How to leverage possible market-checks while avoiding inefficient entry?

Management control

- How to formulate tasks, assess performance and utilize private sector incentives within a state-owned enterprise serving a broader and more diffuse set of policy objectives?
- How to capture the benefits of being the recognized preferred employer while avoiding crowding out the external labor market?

Operation control

- How to decide on the operational scope of an NOC – balancing outsourcing opportunities, learning needs or industrial policy objectives?
- How to balance/combine reliance on fiscal and regulatory competition with NOC benefits?
- Whether, when and how to transfer NOC capacities and to whom?

Regional/ global governance

Political control

Agency supervision

Regulatory control

Managerial control

Operation control

Figure 13.4: Governing the NOC – Common operational and regulatory concerns

dilute policy agendas and to slow down institutional reforms and the process of deregulation. *But* when and how does one best transfer NOC capacities – hydrocarbon or otherwise – and to whom? How does one unbundle NOC operations without diluting efficiency and learning? Can reporting and documentation requirements effectively limit the regulators' information gap? What are the roles of the media and NGOs? How to can NOC operations be made contestable, i.e. open to potential market review? Is there a need to protect the NOC and the economy against "ruinous," "cherry-picking" competition? When are incumbent concerns about inefficient entry legitimate? How can fiscal regimes be structured to mitigate these risks up front?

Since its inception, the control of the Nigerian National Petroleum Company appeared to be doomed by the vast and ever-increasing scope of its assignment, the lack of separation between policy and executive tasks, imprecise regulatory mandates and their ineffective use. But where and how does specialization increase the effectiveness of supervision? How can transparency be increased on issues directly affecting the system's perceived legitimacy? If corporate liability ultimately relies on political accountability, how can national and global governance be effective in enforcing it? Which political system seems best in (re-) introducing and maintaining institutional structures that allocate resources to their originally intended use? As IOCs respond to fiscal and regulatory competition, which regulatory levers need to be in place to supersede market-driven considerations and enforce sustainable national structures? How is financial leverage of single or multilateral lenders used? And how can debt-relief be used to encourage positive change and avoid letting a corrupt system off the hook? Giving its broader mission, how could OPEC be involved in improving the national governance of oil supply?

Figure 13.4 lists some common operational and regulatory concerns emerging from the discussion of the Norwegian, Saudi Arabian and Nigerian experience in governing their respective NOCs. NOCs emerge when fiscal and regulatory regimes appear to be insufficient to capture all the economic and political benefits of a given hydrocarbon base. In the language of institutional economics, they are set up to respond to, but also to cause, market failures. Once the market is superseded, NOCs give rise to internal and external governance concerns. Assessing regulatory combinations and their adjustments is necessarily case-specific and requires more information than the descriptions above are able to suggest. Figure 13.2 simply presents a graphical guide to structure the task. And yet, that analysis remains incomplete unless it considers the macroeconomic imperatives of any broadly resource-based economy to which the NOC and its governance may need to respond.

4. Steering the resource-based economy – Hydrocarbon exposure and structural adjustment

The production and export of hydrocarbons adds to employment and the build-up of skills and physical and institutional infrastructures. Most importantly, however, it contributes to an economy's level and distribution of income, and trade and currency positions in ways that may need to be managed.

Identifying the hydrocarbon exposure

Massive and to some extent sudden revenue inflows, typical of larger project starts or oil-price swings, can drive up real exchange rates and distort domestic prices. This affects income distribution and could harm or "crowd out" import-competing and exporting non-hydrocarbon sectors of the economy. They also distort public and private budgets and investment decisions. Smoothing the income stream, for example by delaying developments, may mitigate these problems and buy time to ramp up domestic institutions, infrastructures and infant industries. But it may also be unacceptable to either domestic stakeholders or IOCs interested in faster paybacks. The alternatives, NOC operations and limited transparency, raise governance and efficiency concerns. Borrowing against expected revenues, or, conversely, channeling these into stabilization funds, smoothes or delays the fund flow and reduces its impact, but, as seen in the cases of Nigeria (above) or Alaska[36], may trigger overspending and rent-seeking behavior.

A country unable to control the relative size of its booming hydrocarbon sector may find itself entirely dependent on its hydrocarbon sales to pay for the cost of delivering imports and public services to the non-hydrocarbon

[36] Alaskan oil provides jobs, makes state taxes unnecessary and provides everyone with an annual check from the oil-financed $29bn Permanent Fund ($900 for each resident at the end of 2004). As a result check seekers, estimated to be around 10% of the state population, are attracted by the annual check and an additional $900 family incentive. Given that citizens pay no taxes, Alaskans are presumably unaware about the costs and needs of government. Infrastructure investments are said to be pushed aside because they would come out of the Permanent Fund and cut annual checks. See *The Economist* (2005) *The paradox of plenty*, December 20, 2005.

sectors. Where hydrocarbon sales face resource limits and oil prices have some upper bound, managing the economy's fiscal and current account balances requires structural adjustments. A non-hydrocarbon fiscal deficit may be overcome by (1) introducing or increasing taxes on non-hydrocarbon products; (2) reducing (or privatizing) government expenditure in the non-hydrocarbon economy; (3) increasing non-hydrocarbon income, through a combination of import substitution, export promotion and general upgrading. The latter strategy would also help to mitigate a balance-of-payment deficit in the current account of the non-hydrocarbon economy.

The alternative, increasing hydrocarbon sales and tax revenues through a combination of increased production and efficiency, domestic fuel substitution for export expansion, increases in prices, royalties and fees, pays for both fiscal and trade imbalances. But it deepens the economy's dependency on hydrocarbons, and fails to create proper governance processes, and creates the need to accept an NOC playing the role of a "state within a state." While a given resource base sets natural limits on this strategy, competition among fiscal regimes and oil suppliers provides market checks. Consider Saudi Arabia's current options.

Managing structural adjustment: Saudi Arabia

According to the 2006 BP Statistical Review, Saudia Arabia's proven oil reserves, roughly one-fifth of the global total, if exploited at current extraction rates, will last another sixty-six years. Saudi Arabia's oil policy traditionally pursued three objectives: (a) avoiding fuel substitution and ensuring demand through stable, moderate international oil prices; (b) maintaining sufficient excess capacity to stabilize oil markets short-term and position the Kingdom as a stable long-term supplier to the West; (c) receiving sufficient oil revenues to promote the economy and avert fundamental changes in the domestic political system. What are the challenges affecting the Saudi political and economic context today? In view of its hydrocarbon exposure, which are Saudi Arabia's production/depletion scenarios? Which price assumptions would relax constraints? What does this entail for Saudi Arabia's position within OPEC and Saudi Aramco's corporate agenda?

Political and economic context

Saudi rule not only predates the formal origin of the Kingdom of Saudi Arabia and the reign of King Abdul Aziz, the father of the current King

Abdullah, but has imprinted on it some rather idiosyncratic characteristics. While formally the monarchy bestows absolute legislative and executive powers, key decisions reflect broad-based consensus. The political and judicial apparatus is based on Islamic principles, with the Koran functioning as the constitutional reference and Saudi *majlises* – public receptions – as fora of interest articulation. Although the Kingdom's history is closely linked with Hanbalism, a conservative school of Sunni Muslim thought, in practice, Saudi Arabia has been more pragmatic than other Islamic states in terms of, for example, openly dealing with interest-bearing accounts or in settling commercial disputes in front of public trade commissions rather than in *Sharia* courts. Also, institutional reforms initiated by King Fahd and King Abdullah resulted in the first basic law and created institutions such as citizen petitions and national consultative councils that formalize elements of direct representation, albeit with limited mandates. Still, most observers tend to agree that Saudi Arabia is unlikely to move towards anything resembling a western conception of representative democracy. They also agree that it has been remarkably stable – in terms of leadership and policy direction – even in the face of rather massive economic challenges. But will the Kingdom cope with current concerns?

Between 1980 and 2000, a constant and fast population growth in parallel with economic cycles halved Saudi Arabia's GDP per capita.[37] In the 1980s, the Saudi economy endured the oil price explosion of 1979–80, the collapse of oil prices in 1986, and the need to rebuild global market share and the depletion of foreign reserves to contribute to the first Gulf War. During the 1990s, fiscal tightening and oil price and volume changes stabilized the non-hydrocarbon deficit, mainly due to constant reduction in personal consumption.[38] It also provided the context for government restructuring, the Saudi Gas Initiative as well as the total or partial privatization within 200 sectors following the 2000 Foreign Investment Act. Also during that time, the key policy issues going forward were becoming increasingly apparent: educational reform to bring standards and output in line with labor market requirements; tackling unemployment, which is officially at around 9.4%

---

[37] From \$15,999 in 1980 to \$8,373 in 2002.

[38] During that time Saudi Arabia's non-oil budget deficit remained more or less constant at just below 200bn riyals (\$53.4bn) in real terms. Still, by 2002–3, the non-hydrocarbon deficits as a percentage of non-petroleum GDP were around 41% (highest of all except for Kuwait). Meanwhile, population growth was 2.7% between 1990–2003 p.a. Government expenditure grew by 3.7% and capital expenditure – around 20% of GDP – grew by (only) 2.7.% Personal consumption fell by 1.5% annually up to 2005. Source: Mitchell, J. V., (2006) *Economic background*. In Marcel (2006). pp. 235–65.

but unofficially often estimated to be close to 15%; nationalizing the workforce; improving income distribution; improving infrastructures.

The rebounding oil price might have stifled the urge to reform: oil exports, at a mere $35bn in 1998, have since recovered to reach a record $160bn and translated into a current account surplus of nearly $100bn in 2005. The central bank's net foreign reserves rose to $135bn, a jump of $90bn in just three years. But these windfall profits of course do not address the initial concern that hydrocarbon production is expected to level off and adjustments are required.

Hydrocarbon exposure, the Kingdom's role in OPEC and Saudi Aramco's positioning

Mitchell (2006) simulates Saudi Arabia's non-hydrocarbon fiscal deficit in line with currently known expansion plans, depletion policies, expenditure levels and oil price assumptions. Accordingly, Saudi Arabia is likely to reach a production plateau between 2016 and 2034. At oil prices of $25 a barrel, the Kingdom will be unable to continue its current non-hydrocarbon fiscal deficit and subsidized domestic fuel prices; at $35 a barrel, a daily production of 12MMb would allow the continuation of "unchanged" policies; at 15MMb, the non-hydrocarbon fiscal deficit could grow 4% annually until 2025.[39] But current oil prices are much higher and coffers are full! If structural adjustments could deal with macroeconomic challenges, output could be reduced to defer depletion and maintain or possibly increase oil prices to meet revenue requirements. Overshooting oil prices would promote more serious fuel substitution, ultimately require production increases at reduced prices and devalue Saudia Arabia's resource base. The Kingdom's options for structural adjustment are conditioned by global market discipline or the lack of it. What are the implications for Saudi Arabia's role within OPEC? And is there an alternative to policy-based market management?

In the mid-1980s, Saudi Arabia's adherence to OPEC's official price system, which most other cartel members had abandoned, left the Kingdom in the role of the swing producer and its capacity utilization cut by more than 70%. Finally switching to the market price, and using its excess capacity and foreign financial reserves, precipitated an oil price crash and established a new OPEC discipline: a guaranteed quota of approximately 25% of the total output ceiling, correlated to a US$18 per barrel price objective. Since then, income requirements and production short-falls in the wake of the two Gulf Wars, reshuffled quota systems and pricing objectives denied the Kingdom its

---

[39] Mitchell (2006).

long-term objective of obtaining a agreement on Saudi Arabia's 35% market share of all future output ceilings within OPEC. The Kingdom added another dimension to its oil policy: using Saudi Aramco to capture value downstream.

In Junc 2006, addressing the Center of Strategic and International Studies, Abdullatif Al-Othman, Senior Vice-president Finance of Saudi Aramco, outlined the company's international activities.[40] It appears that by broadening its international footprint and partnership network in refining, petrochemicals, transport, storage and retail, Saudi Aramco aims to capture additional value, tie up customers for crude, and control prices, terms and market access. In addition, failing to control the markets at the level of OPEC, Saudi Arabia through the means of Saudi Aramco continues to pursue a bilateral, commercial approach offering consuming countries "reciprocal security measures," under which the Kingdom guarantees supply, through capacity additions or stockpiling, in return for importing countries' elimination of taxes and import restrictions on oil. Saudi Aramco adds an additional dimension to the above NOC characteristics: it supersedes the market, it provides the vehicle for political coordination, but now, with its downstream approach, it sets out to substitute for non-viable political market management. One can expect that consumers will respond in line with projected market developments.

5. Summary and conclusion

Recognizing the importance of, but also the common lack of understanding of NOCs, this chapter explored three main questions: (1) What is their role, i.e. why have them at all? (2) How are they governed and when and how can policies effectively direct their growth? (3) How do they respond to, or even drive, the economic imperatives of resource-based economies?

In addressing the first question, section 2 juxtaposed the option of competing on fiscal and regulatory terms in attracting IOCs, illustrated with the development of the UKCS tax regime, with the historical evolution of the two largest NOCs in terms of total proven hydrocarbon reserves: Saudi Aramco and NIOC. NOCs are institutional responses to failing market coordination with IOCs but also facilitate the coordination among producer countries in exerting political and economic interests. But superseding the market and, in the extreme, putting the exploitation of a country's oil and gas resource into

---

[40] At www.csis.org/component/option,comcsisevents/task,view/id,1021/

the hands of one stand-alone, state-owned, state-run enterprise raises efficiency and broader regulatory concerns.

Addressing these, section 3 first introduced the conceptual apparatus of institutional economics to identify options for regulating NOCs at interrelated levels of governance. It then proceeded to present three cases highlighting specific events during the regulation of three rather distinct NOCs: Statoil, Saudi Aramco and the Nigerian National Petroleum Company, (NNPC). Assessing regulatory combinations and their adjustments is necessarily case-specific and requires more information than the descriptions are able to suggest. In any event, the conceptual apparatus, depicted in Figure 13.2, ought to be used as a graphical audit trail to structure any in-depth analysis. Figure 13.4 lists some common operational and regulatory concerns emerging from a cursory discussion of the Norwegian, Saudi Arabian and Nigerian experience.

Still, any analysis of a NOC would be incomplete unless it considered the macroeconomic imperatives of the broadly resource-based economy to which it and its governance may need to respond. Section 4 first identified the sources of the economic hydrocarbon exposure that an exporting nation would need to manage, and then reviewed Saudi Arabia's need and options for structural adjustment, its leverage over oil prices and the resulting implication for Saudi Aramco. The kingdom's NOC, set up to supersede IOCs, develop the economy and facilitate the political coordination of producer interests, now sets out to complement political coordination at the level of OPEC by capturing customers and value downstream. It is a vital extension of the Kingdom's national resource management and hardly a representation of "resource nationalism."

14 China – External imperatives and internal reforms*

Jean-Pierre Lehmann

1 China and reform in the global era

Supachai Panitchpakdi, formerly Director General of the WTO and now Secretary General of UNCTAD, and Mark Clifford, Editor of the *South China Morning Post* and long-time Greater China observer, set the tone for the implications of China's resurgent entry into the global political and economic environment in a book published at the dawn of this century.[1]

Whether it's looking out over the next few years or the next quarter-century, how the world's most populous country handles the many developmental challenges it faces will go a long way toward determining what kind of world we inhabit. Pick an issue – the environment, the military, international affairs or the global economy – China's choices will have a major impact on Asia and the world. If China makes the wrong decisions, the result will be chilling, not only for the country's 1.3 billion citizens but for many people beyond its borders as well. Conversely, a China that successfully makes the transformation to a relatively affluent, open society will be both an inspiration to other countries and a locomotive that will help to power the world's economies.

The decisions of course are not just China's to make. Much also depends on how the rest of the world, and especially the US, reacts to China's apparently inexorable ascendancy. We have seen often in the past century the coming and going of potential new "great powers" that turned out to be mirages. "I have seen the future and it works," remarked the American journalist Lincoln Steffens, upon returning from the Soviet Union in 1931. In the 1960s the focus was on the emergence of Brazil, which then collapsed

---

* According to Chinese practice, family names precede given names. Thus Mao Zedong comes from the family called Mao, whose parents gave him the personal name Zedong. The common Pinyin system of transcription is used throughout the text, hence Mao Zedong and not Mao Tse-tung, the latter corresponding to the Wade-Giles system of transcription.
[1] Panitchpakdi, S., Clifford, M., (2002) *China and the WTO: Changing China, changing world trade*, Chichester: John Wiley & Sons Ltd, p. 1; See also Lehmann, J. P., (July 2002) The stakes are very high in China's latest gamble, *Open Democracy*.

under debt and hyper-inflation; in the 1970s there was much talk about the impending Iranian economic power, which was brutally dashed by the revolution of 1979. More recently there was the Japan mania. The twenty-first century, it was confidently predicted, would be the "Japanese century."[2] Hardly had the prediction been made than the Japanese economy tanked and is only now hesitatingly re-emerging. So, what about China? Is there not also a possible phenomenon of China hype?

The answer is yes and no. In the business and popular media the power of China's economy tends to be highly over-rated. This feeds into the anxiety felt in some quarters that China poses a threat, not just economic, but also political, military and in what is termed "soft power,"[3] which might be loosely defined as the power of cultural seduction. Things must be put in perspective: China is still a comparatively poor country. While its total GDP now ranks it among the two, three or four (depending on how you calculate) largest global economies,[4] in GDP per capita terms it is very much towards the bottom, about one hundredth. As Chen Siwei, the Chinese political leader and academic, has put it: "if you take any number and multiply it by 1.3 billion, it is bound to be very big; but take any number and divided it by 1.3 billion and it is bound to be very small."[5]

The leading economist Fan Gang strikingly illustrates the dual challenge of the Chinese economy; China, he states, is both a transition economy and a developing economy.[6] In other words, like other former socialist countries, China is seeking to transition from a central command-based economy to a market economy. This is in itself a huge challenge. Unlike the other transition economies, however, China is underdeveloped and poor. Poland, Russia, the Czech Republic, Latvia, even Romania have higher GDPs per capita than China and also have a much more advanced industrial base. Hence China also faces the challenges of poor developing countries.

---

[2] The "Japan as global juggernaut" prediction generated a great deal of literature; the pioneer work that established the genre was by the Harvard Professor Ezra Vogel (1979) *Japan as number one: Lessons for America*, Cambridge MA: Harvard University Press.

[3] American commentators are especially concerned that as the US soft power has greatly decreased as a result of the Iraq war, Abu Ghraib, Guantanamo, etc, China's soft power has correspondingly greatly increased. This view does tend to be borne out by surveys. See Kohut, A., Stokes, B., (2006) America against the World: How we are different and why we are disliked, New York: Times Books (2005) Attitudes to China are mostly positive, *Oxford Analytical Policy Brief*.

[4] In 2005, the IMF ranked China as the fourth largest economy behind the US, Japan and Germany in GDP on the basis of market exchange rates and second after the US in purchasing power parity (see Emerging at last, *The Economist*, September 16, 2006.

[5] Quoted in The Evian Group I China Meeting, (September 2005) A Global Economic Order for the 21st Century.

[6] Gang, F., (May 25, 2005) Reform and the Chinese economy. Presentation given in Shanghai.

China's position therefore is unique. There is no historical model to draw from. Not only is China in uncharted territory, so are academics seeking to analyze the Chinese phenomenon and the country's future prospects.[7] This is all the more the case in that the Chinese phenomenon refers not just, as Fan Gang states, to the challenges of transition and development, but also because China has, for now, opted to undertake a policy of quite dramatic economic opening within the framework of a closed political system. To the Cartesian mind, this is unsustainable. It certainly is, without doubt, bringing numerous contradictions and tensions to the fore. The Chinese government's somewhat schizophrenic attitude to information technology is revealing. Though IT is seen as a major driver of growth – and growth is an absolute imperative for China – it is also seen as a major potential source of spiritual and political pollution.[8] Policies in respect to the internet, therefore, tend to be of the three-steps-forward-two-steps-backwards-four-steps-sideways variety!

The point that can be made is that reform is crucial to the whole enterprise. It is, I believe, difficult to argue with the proposition that China in the course of the last decade-and-a-half has undergone the most radical reform process in the shortest period of time the world has ever seen. The results and consequences have been remarkable. Not only has China maintained an average double-digit growth rate over the last fifteen years, but it has also transformed its economy – or, more precisely, the urban/manufacturing part of its economy – in such a way that, at the risk of two clichés, China has redefined the basis of global competition and it has redefined the global trade paradigm.[9] The latter has been driven, as Jim Rollo has stated, by the deepest and most extensive unilateral trade liberalisation that the global economy has experienced in over half-a-century, arguably more.[10]

China is both a global export power and a global import power. This was never the case with Japan or with any of the other Asian "tigers," which

---

[7] Though China has no model to draw from, it is becoming a model in its own right. Vietnam has recently embarked on a Chinese-style "market-Leninist" (!) revolution. See Templar, R., (1998) *Shadows and wind: A view of modern vietnam*, London: Little Brown.

[8] For the Chinese government's policies and attempts in controlling the internet, see Internet Filtering in China in 2004–2005: A Country Study, www.opennetinitiative.net/studies/china/.

[9] Garrett, M., Lehmann, J. P., (2005) The China challenge, *European Business Forum*, Winter, 24–9; How China runs the world economy (2000) *The Economist*, July 28 Story, J., (2003) *China: The race to market*, London: FT Press; Cass, D. Z., Williams, B. G., Barker, G. (eds), (2003) *China and the world trading system: Entering the new millennium*, New York: Cambridge University Press; Martin, W., Manole, V., (2007) China's emergence as the workshop of the world. In Fleischer B and Hope N (eds.) Policy reform and Chinese markets: Progress and challenges. Cheltenham: Edward Elgar (forthcoming).

[10] China has undeniably assumed the role of driver of unilateral trade liberalization, quoted in Lehmann, F., Evian Group X Plenary Report: Sounding the clarion call, November 2005.

tended to focus on exports and greatly limit exports, or what Daniel Yergin has labelled "compete out/protect in."[11] Thus, while China's economy in nominal terms is less than half that of Japan's, its contribution to global growth and especially growth in trade is infinitely higher.[12] China's voracious appetite for energy and raw materials has resulted in a dramatic increase in commodity prices – reversing a historical trend of falling prices of over half a century. Not only have China's Asian neighbours seen the Chinese market as their biggest and/or fastest growing export market, but so have countries as far afield as Chile, Brazil, Argentina, South Africa, Nigeria, and the UAE.[13]

The Chinese economy has also developed a very "symbiotic" relationship with the American economy in what has been referred to as "one economy – two systems."[14] The Chinese produce, save and lend (to the Americans), while the Americans consume, spend and borrow (from the Chinese). There has developed a quite extraordinary interdependence between the two economies on opposite sides of the Pacific.[15] American policy has vacillated in response, from defining China as a "strategic competitor" to a partner. More recently, US Secretary of the Treasury Henry Paulson has recognised how sustained reform of the Chinese economy is vital for the sake of the American economy.[16]

The stakes, therefore, as Supachai Panitchpakdi and Mark Clifford have argued, are extremely high. What happens inside China will have an immense impact outside China, not least on the United States. The world can only hope, therefore, that the process of reform will be continued so that the Chinese economy's growth and development over the course of the next decades will be sustained. That, however, is not a given. There are two potential opposing forces, one internal, the other external.

The Chinese reform process has been in many respects breathtakingly successful, but also in others terribly brutal. The brutality includes immense inequality – Chinese scholars worry about the "Latin-american-isation" of the Chinese

---

[11] Yergin, D., Stanislaw, J., (2002) *The commanding heights: The battle for the world economy*, New York: Simon and Schuster.

[12] According to the IMF, in the period 1995–2002 China's contribution to global growth amounted to 25%, against 20% for the US, 13% for the EU and just 2% for Japan.

[13] This phenomenon of the "hungry dragon" boosting commodity prices has various consequences, both positive and potentially negative; see Thirlwell, M., (2006) The high price of feeding the hungry dragon, *Financial Times*, April, 27.

[14] I am grateful to Lyric Hughes who provided this very neat description at a discussion during the China Summit of the World Economic Forum, September 9, 2006. See also Stokes, B., (2006) US needs Chinese investment, *National Journal*, vol 38, 56–7.

[15] Hufbauer, G., (August, 2006) *US-China trade disputes: Rising tide, rising stakes*, Washington D.C.: Peterson Institute for International Economics.

[16] Paulson decides to be the good cop, *Financial Times* September 15, 2006.

economy as the Gini coefficient has seen a dramatic increase[17] – especially the urban-rural divide; there has also been great poverty, rising unemployment, crime and other social ills, rampant corruption and what could become an environmental disaster.[18] Even though a dictatorship, China has not been immune to the rise, impact and influence of NGOs, which, on issues ranging from environment, peasants' rights, and labor standards, have become increasingly vocal.[19]

Furthermore, however, some of what has been generally seen as part of the "success" has come under increasing scrutiny. In the last decade China has been recipient to a phenomenal amount of foreign direct investment (FDI), in the neighbourhood of $60 bn per annum. China has also become, as noted earlier, a tremendous export power, having come from literally nowhere to being the world's third biggest exporter.[20] Sounds good, except, argue critics, that in fact the FDI + export formula underlines China's dependence and backwardness. The contention is that in fact China has become no more than a vast screwdriver factory, that it has become highly reliant on the import of technology, components and capital goods on the one hand, while, on the other, all the value added in branding, marketing, distribution, etc, accrues to foreign investors and not to Chinese.[21]

There are three strands of internal opposition to the reform process. The three are not necessarily discrete, independent elements, and two or indeed all three may be present in any particular individual, group, faction or school.

The first is ideological. It is true that it is absolutely amazing that two policies, which may be termed Maoism and Dengism, that are 180° apart, should exist within the same political framework. One cannot think of any parallel. While the reform has been driven by highly educated, pragmatic and indeed quite visionary party intellectuals and technocrats, there is in the party the old rearguard and the provincial cadres who oppose change. Deng Xiaoping got away, so to speak, with his reforms, because after the death of

---

[17] See Becker, J., (2000) *The Chinese*, London: John Murray and Kynge, J., (2006) *China shakes the world: The rise of a hungry nation*, New York: Weidenfield and Nicholson.

[18] Economy, E., (2004) *The river runs black: The environmental challenge to China's future*, Ithaca, NY Cornell University Press.

[19] Jiang, W., (2006) The dynamics of China's social crisis, *China Brief* 6(2); Kelly D., (2006) Social movements in urban China; Fan L., (2006) Unrest in China's countryside, available at: www.msnbc.msn.com, Mooney, P., How to deal with NGOs – China", *Yale Global Online*, August 1, 2006.

[20] China's share of world trade is estimated to reach 10% this year, up from 4% in 2000, surpassing Japan making China third only to the EU and the US (September 16, 2006). A survey of the world economy, *The Economist*.

[21] Chen, K., (April 11, 2006) Amid tension with the US, China faces protectionist surge at home, *Wall Street Journal*.

Mao in 1976 and the ensuing struggle with the "Gang of Four," the Chinese economy was in freefall and the Party feared anarchy might break out and it would lose its power. Paradoxically, the reforms were, initially, driven primarily by a perceived imperative to bolster the Party's power.[22] Having let the genie out of the bottle, however, a momentum sprang up that has caused the rearguard great concern: Deng Xiaoping's incantation that "to be rich is glorious" and Jiang Zemin's more recent "theory" of the "three represents," whereby capitalists and entrepreneurs are to be admitted into the Party, are seen (not unjustifiably!) as ideological blasphemy.[23]

Along with the rearguard, in very recent years there has also arisen, especially in universities, what is termed the "new left". Their concerns are not so much driven by any nostalgia for past ideology, but by what they see as the forces of capitalist exploitation that have become rampant in the country.[24] Their position would not be radically different from that of the Western so-called protest community, notably that of ATTAC. They would halt the current reforms, redirecting them by stressing the distribution, rather than the accumulation, of wealth. This, they argue, requires state control. The differences within the party have become so acute that some believe, indeed advocate, that the Party should split.[25]

The second internal force of opposition is nationalist. From a general political perspective, while there is, apart from the single fact of the rule of the party, hardly anything left that one might term communism in China, and certainly not any of the ideals contained in Marx-Lenin-Maoist thought, a national spiritual and ideological vacuum has been filled mainly by nationalism. Though China's ascension in world affairs and as an economic power should hearten patriots – and there is no doubt that national pride is a prominent feature of contemporary Chinese society – nationalists nevertheless bristle at what they see as national humiliations. The most extreme case of course is Japan, which has resulted in the occasional outbreak of quite violent riots,[26] but also included is the perception of foreign economic domination mentioned above.

In this respect, however, it has to be said that China is not in any way *sui generis*. There has been a resurgence of economic nationalism generally, in

[22] Gittings, J., (2005) *The changing face of China: From Mao to market*, Oxford: Oxford University Press.
[23] Pei, M., (2006) *China's trapped transition: The limits of development autocracy*, Cambridge MA: Harward University Press.
[24] Pocha, J. P., (May 9, 2005) Letter from Beijing: China's New Left, *The Nation*.
[25] (June 2006) Interviews with Chinese party officials.
[26] Chellaney, B., Japan-China – Nationalism on the rise, *Yale Global Online*, August 16, 2006.

Europe, the US, Japan, and elsewhere.[27] Thus, while the US bombing of the Chinese embassy in Belgrade was seen as a huge slap on the political cheek of the face, the blockage by Washington of the attempt by the Chinese petroleum company CNOOC to acquire the American company Unocal was seen as a huge slap on the business cheek.[28] The government has to be very careful how it manages this increasingly strong emotional force. The very violent anti-Japanese riots of April 2005 were, it appeared, condoned by the government, at least for a while, as a means of allowing steam to be let off. In China, as elsewhere, the forces of globalism have generated a counter-reaction of nationalism and indeed chauvinism.[29]

The third internal force of opposition is cultural. This aspect I shall develop a bit more below. Suffice it to say here that for Chinese polity to dance to a foreign tune is not part, to put it very mildly, of the Chinese tradition. In the 1970s, the Scottish political scientist and China specialist, Jack Grey, used to say that to understand the dynamics of Chinese politics, economics and society, it was necessary to recognise three of its basic existential features: China is communist, China is poor, China is Chinese.[30] Thirty years later, though China is no longer communist, and, while residues of poverty remain, the country and some of its inhabitants have becoming increasingly rich, on the third dimension, one can say that China is still Chinese.

What this means, whether in the 1970s, when China was in the throes of the cultural revolution, or in the early twenty-first century, when it is in the throes of the capitalist revolution, is that the country does not lightly dispose of its 5,000 years of historical baggage.[31] China's self-perception is not so much that it is a country, but that it is a civilisation and, unlike its giant neighbor India, it is not a composite of heterogenous civilisations, but a quite homogenous unity.[32] Thus, while the usage by Party officials and ideologues of terms such as "market socialism with Chinese characteristics" may sound to foreign ears like so much gibberish, in fact it is a quite subtle

---

[27] Wruuck, P., Economic patriotism: New game in industrial policy?, *Deutsche Bank Research*, June 2006.

[28] China bashing – Giving China a bloody nose, *The Economist*, August 4, 2005.

[29] Zheng, Y., (1999) *Discovering Chinese nationalism in China: Modernization, identity and international relations*, Cambridge: Cambridge University Press.

[30] Grey, J., (1972). Lectures on China at Glasgow University.

[31] Spence, J., (1990) *The search for modern China*, New York: WW Norton & Co

[32] There are of course minorities in China and since China is huge, individual "minorities" can add up to the equivalent in numbers to a large European state. For example, there are an estimated 45 million Muslims in Western China, i.e. the equivalent of Italy, making China one of the ten biggest "Muslim" countries. Comparatively speaking, however, with about 85% of the population Han Chinese and with a sense of a common history, China possesses a homogenous unity.

attempt at balancing all the different strands and forces propelling China into the very choppy seas of reform and globalisation.

China's social, ideological, political, economic and military trajectory in the twenty-first century will be determined not only by internal forces – both accelerators and brakes – but also by external forces. In respect to the impact and consequences of the emergence of a new great economic power – especially in so short a time – the history of the previous century does not provide much encouragement. The forceful entries in the global arena of the United States, Germany, Japan and the Soviet Union all precipitated wars and imperialism. There are no historical examples of the massive entry of a new power generating peace and prosperity.

There is the view, therefore, that China will be a twenty-first century variation on a twentieth-century theme. This, in turn, leads to the view that China must be contained, not only geopolitically, but also economically. In this perspective, China's economic rise is seen, not as the emergence of a great new market for the world's exports of goods and services and a source of capital, but as the means by which China will be able to obtain the sources of energy and military hardware to pursue its inexorable policy of expansion. In this scenario, war between China and the US is seen as the great showdown of the twenty-first century, as war between the US and Japan was the showdown of the previous century.[33]

The Chinese have sought to provide an alternative scenario, one which has been especially articulated by the prominent intellectual leader of Chinese reform, Zheng Bijian, notably in his article entitled "China's Peaceful Rise".[34] China, this school of thought argues, has to put all its eggs in the development basket. It has still a huge effort to accomplish in providing a decent livelihood to its 1.3 billion people. It has an enormous challenge especially in respect to the 800 million or so who live in the countryside, roughly one-third of whom will have to be urbanized in the course of the next couple of decades. China needs to build infrastructure and develop a social framework that will be conducive to achieving these ends. Diverting resources away from these crucial tasks would be suicidal. Furthermore, Chinese well recognize that the country's integration into the global market is a national imperative.

---

[33] The specter of a US–China confrontation gave rise to a new genre of alarmist literature straddling political science and science fiction, e.g. Hawksley, H., Holberton, S., (1997) *Dragon strike: The millennium war*, London: Sidgwick & Jackson Ltd; for a more sober analysis, see Terrill, R., (2003) *The New Chinese Empire – and what it means for the United States*, New York: Basic Books.

[34] Bijian, Z., (2005) China's peaceful rise to great power status, *Foreign Affairs* 84(5) 18–24.

For both China and the rest of the world, however, the process of adjustment is not easy. It requires very sensitive strategic management. These are not qualities – sensitivity and strategy – that are particularly conspicuous in the current global environment. A clash, therefore, of one form or another, cannot be dismissed as a total impossibility.

In terms of assessing how external global imperatives may impact on China's internal reforms, as suggested above, it is necessary to understand the historical patterns and dynamics of China's view of its place in the world and the backdrop of the modern age that hangs over China's contemporary rise.

2. Chinese historical dynamics and resistance to reform

From a traditional Chinese perspective, the title of this chapter, *China – External imperatives and internal reforms*, is incongruous. A title in conformity with the traditional perspective could be: China – Internal imperatives and external adjustments. China, the Middle Kingdom, has for millennia had a view of its place in the planet that stands at the opposite end of the Westphalian system of the equality of states and national sovereignty according to international law. China's view of its place in the world was based both on geography and on cosmology.

Geographically, China was the central empire surrounded by vassal states, such as Manchuria, Korea, Annam (the central Vietnamese kingdom with its capital in Hue), Thailand, Burma, etc. China had an emperor; the other states had kings, who, as vassals, owed fealty to the Chinese emperor. Cosmologically, China was the center of civilisation; all surrounding states were, by definition, barbarian. The world was divided into concentric circles. The further the circle from Beijing, the more barbarian.

As with the history and cosmology of all nations, there is a strong element of myth. As China's history is long and mighty, the myths tend to be proportionately greater. The system never actually functioned in reality as it was meant to according to Chinese cosmology. What is true, however, is that throughout history until the modern era, beginning with the American, French and Industrial revolutions of the late eighteenth century, China civilized its neighbors. Thus, for example, though China never succeeded in actually invading Japan militarily – the greatest attempt at which was the aborted invasion ordered by Kublai Khan in the late thirteenth century – Japan "borrowed" virtually all aspects of its own culture from China. In the course of the second half of the first millennium, Japanese scholars and monks undertook a series of "study tours" to China, returning to Japan laden with multiple elements of civilization. In East Asia, in contrast to Europe, there was no passing of the torch of civilization. Thus if we envisage "Western" civilization beginning in Mesopotamia, passing on to Greece, then to Rome, and subsequently spreading out to Western and Eastern Europe, no such phenomenon occurred in East Asia. China was the cradle of civilization and remained the centre of civilization. Vietnamese, Mongolians, Koreans and Japanese learned from China. Not the other way around.

What today would be described as China's "soft power" – all aspects of its cultural reach and influence – remained powerful and constant through the ages, even when any particular dynasty's "hard power" – military, economic and political might – declined. China was regularly invaded by "barbarians" from the North, Mongols and Manchus, but never did the invaders make any attempt to alter China's cultural and administrative essence; on the contrary, "foreign" dynasties often undertook a Sino-centered cultural renaissance with a view to restoring, increasing and strengthening China's glory. This was true of the early Manchu Qing dynasty (1644–1911) which succeeded the Han Chinese Ming dynasty (1368–1644). Hence, however much the Chinese might have been weak militarily, including times leading to very prolonged foreign occupation, Chinese culture as such was never undermined. The Chinese had nothing to learn or to gain from the outside world.

Contrasts can be drawn between the Chinese great Western Ocean voyages of the fifteenth century with the emergence of the Portuguese, Spanish and Dutch seaborne empires of the late fifteenth and early sixteenth centuries. Chinese fleets under the command of the great admiral Zheng He circumnavigated a good deal of the world in the period 1405 – 1422, including South East Asia, the Persian Gulf, Africa down to the Cape of Good Hope, and possibly the Americas, though this remains a matter of academic dispute.[35] Zheng He's exploits preceded by a century those of the great Portuguese seafarer Vasco da Gama. The period in European history that the Portuguese inaugurated has been called "The Age of Discovery".[36] One of the key European goals was to gain direct access to the spices, silks and other goods that hitherto Europe had imported through Arab traders and agents who travelled by land across Central Asia. The discovery was meant to identify

---

[35] A recent book, Menzies, G., (2003) *1421: The year China discovered America*, London: Bantam Press claims that Zheng He in fact was the first to "discover" America.

[36] See Boxer, C., (1965) *The Portuguese seaborne empire: 1415–1825*, London: Hutchinson, (1966) *The Dutch seaborne empire*, London: Hutchinson

those products that could be useful or simply enjoyable for Europeans and to learn about other societies, ultimately all the better to subjugate them. The Chinese voyages, on the other hand, could be better described as an exercise in ostentation[37] – representing the desire to show off China's great power and glory. China had the notion – that persisted well into the 1970s – that it was in every way self-sufficient, whether in terms of products or ideas.[38]

The early phases of the Chinese-European encounter were marked by European awe and admiration.[39] The annals of Marco Polo first inspired a Western image of great Chinese wealth and luster. This was reinforced by the writings of missionaries, especially the Jesuits, about China in the sixteenth and seventeenth centuries. In eighteenth-century Europe, as political philosophers sought a new form of political rule and legitimacy, China was seen as a model not only for its material wealth, but also for its wisdom and governance, especially the Confucianist principle that related to legitimacy being conferred by the "mandate of heaven" in contrast to the European principle of the divine right of kings.[40] The great perceived wealth of China further enthused British traders in the late eighteenth and early nineteenth centuries with the vision of great gains to be had from the Chinese market, epitomized by slogans such as, "if every Chinaman adds one quarter-of-an-inch to his shirttails, Lancashire mills will be kept in production for centuries!".

Indeed China's global power continued into the early nineteenth century. In 1820, according to Angus Maddison,[41] China accounted for 33% of world GDP. Within less than two decades, however, the great Chinese empire was about to experience collapse and humiliation. Chinese leaders had totally failed to recognize that the world had dramatically changed. Having been a pioneer of science and technology in the past, innovation, for whatever reason, ceased and China fell dramatically behind. While China, along with most of the rest of the northern hemisphere, experienced a demographic boom in the eighteenth century, the Chinese, unlike the Europeans, failed to

---

[37] Landes, D., (1998) *The wealth of poverty of nations: Why some are so rich and some so poor*, New York: Norton. Ascribes a good deal of China's comparative fall and the West's rise to the lack of curiosity of the former and specifically cites the voyages of Zheng He as evidence.

[38] An excellent and succinct analysis of Chinese cosmology and China's place in the world can be found in Cranmer-Byng, J., (1973) The Chinese view of their place in the World: An historical perspective, *China Quarterly*, pp. 67–79; for a penetrating historical analysis of China and the outside world, see Lovell, J., (2006) *The Great Wall: China against the World: 1000 BC to AD 2000*, London: Atlantic Books.

[39] Spence, J., (1998) *The Chan's great continent: China in Western minds*, New York: W.W. Norton.

[40] Shackleton, R., (1965) Asia as seen by the French Enlightenment. In Raghavan Iyer, (ed.) *The glass curtain between Asia and Europe*, London.

[41] Maddison, A., (2002) *The world economy: A millennial perspective*, Paris: OECD.

introduce new agricultural technology and patterns of land-holding. The peasants became ever more numerous, but productivity and output remained constant. The result was over a century of peasant risings, culminating in the Chinese "communist" peasant revolution under Mao Zedong from 1927 to 1949.[42] The contrast between China and Japan is striking.[43] Japan underwent radical reform in the face of the "Western challenge"; China met the Western challenge with staunch resistance, punctuated by occasional half-hearted reform. From the first Opium War (1839–1842) until 1949, China was subject to almost constant foreign wars, invasions, occupations and humiliations.[44] Although China as such was never colonized, as was India, Sun Yatsen, the revolutionary nationalist leader of the early twentieth century, described China as a "poly-colony".[45] All the Western powers along with Japan just went ahead and helped themselves to Chinese resources and territory by obtaining what were known as "spheres of influence", whereby the country that obtained one had exclusive rights on activities such as mining and railway construction.[46] This was known in imperial parlance as "slicing the melon".

By the second half of the twentieth century, China's continuous precipitate decline had brought the figure of 33% of world GDP down to 5%.[47] Though the world economy had greatly expanded during that period, China's population had also dramatically increased from an estimated 200 million to over one billion. Whichever way you want to look at it, the Chinese were dirt-poor.

China was further weakened, humiliated and exploited by the war waged by Japan from 1937 to 1945. This was followed by a rampant civil war from 1946 to 1949 pitting the communist Red Army against the army of the American supported Chiang Kaishek. In October 1949, the Red Army won and Mao entered Beijing, ascended the great balcony of Tienanmen Square and proclaimed, "The Chinese people have stood up. Never will China be humiliated again."

Although Mao certainly brought dramatic radical change to China's economy and society, in some respects he conformed to Chinese historical

[42] Chesneaux, J., (1973) *Peasant revolts in China 1840–1949*, New York: W.W. Norton.
[43] Lehmann, J. P., (1982) *The roots of modern Japan*, London: Macmillan.
[44] See Lovell, J., (2006). As Shanghai epitomised China's fall and humiliation, highly relevant to this topic are: Dong, S., (2001) *Shanghai: The rise and fall of a decadent city 1842–1949*, London: HarperCollins and Wood, F., (2000) *No dogs and not many Chinese: Treaty port life in China 1843–1943*, London: John Murray
[45] Sharman, L., (1934) *Sun Yat-Sen: His life and its meaning*, Stanford CA: Stanford University Press.
[46] Chesneaux, J., Bergère, M.C., (1970) *China from the Opium Wars to the 1911 Revolution*, New York: Pantheon Books
[47] See Maddison, A., (2002).

patterns of governance and indeed was known to be a very keen student of Chinese history.[48] The continuity was especially marked in respect to attitudes to the outside world. Mao is said to have only gone abroad once, to Moscow to attend Stalin's funeral. While leading the "permanent" revolution in China – which included the 100 Flowers movement, the Great Leap Forward and the Cultural Revolution – Mao also projected himself as a great intellectual and political leader of the global revolution and wars of independence. This corresponded to a time when many developing countries were both going through decolonization and establishing statehood. The Chinese model was one of the most prominent. No third-world leader failed to call on the great helmsman. China's nationalist-revolutionary credentials were further strengthened by the open and deep split with Moscow. Chinese policy under Mao was emphatically home-grown! Also, throughout most of the period of Mao's leadership, from 1949 to when he died in 1976, China was isolated from much of the industrialized world. Nixon made his famous journey to renew ties in 1972 and in 1978, Carter established diplomatic ties with Beijing, thereby abandoning American policy which had been to recognize the renegade government of Chiang Kaishek in Taipei as the legitimate government of China. It was only under Deng Xiaoping, however, that China was brought back into the globe, albeit under dramatically different conditions than those that characterized its 5,000-year history!

3. China, reform and globalization

In his seminal article, "China's Peaceful Rise to Great Power Status", Zheng Bijian wrote:

The most significant strategic choice the Chinese have made was to embrace economic globalization rather than detach themselves from it. In the late 1970s, when the new technological revolution and a new wave of economic globalization were unfolding with great momentum, Beijing grasped the trend and reversed the erroneous practices of the Cultural Revolution. On the basis of the judgment that China's development would depend on its place in an open world, Deng Xiaoping and other Chinese leaders decided to seize the historic opportunity and shift the focus of their work to economic development. They carried out reforms meant to open up and foster domestic markets and tap into international ones.[49]

[48] Schram, S., (1967) *The political thought of Mao Tse-Tung*, New York: Simon and Schuster.
[49] Bijian, Z., (2005) p. 20.

The Chinese leadership's decision to reform and to open the economy was based on a perceived absolute imperative and to a very considerable extent driven by national goals. This was based both on internal forces, primarily the dismal economic situation of China in the wake of the devastating cultural revolution, and on external "models". China anticipated global trends and the need for domestic adjustments at least a decade ahead of Russia, India, Brazil and all other countries that embarked on reform in the 1990s. One reason for this is China's geographic location. By the late 1970s not only was Japan's economy well on its way to greater growth and stellar performance – having skilfully managed the oil crisis of the early part of that decade – but the 1970s also witnessed the emergence of the four "Asian tigers" or NIEs (newly industrialized economies), Singapore, Hong Kong, South Korea and Taiwan. Marx's theory that Asian societies were incapable of growth and development due to what he called "the Asiatic mode of production" seemed quite evidently to be contradicted by what increasingly came to be called the "Asian model".[50] China, therefore, did not just embrace globalization, but it also embraced Asian Pacific regionalization, developing, in particular, a very close economic relationship with Taiwan and Hong Kong. The combination of Taiwan's advanced technologies, Hong Kong's capital and know-how in international trade, with the People's Republic of China's vast labor pool has been a fundamental driving force of the global economy in the late twentieth and early twenty-first centuries.

Critical to this development was the recognition by China that its own development depended greatly on globalization both in respect to foreign trade and to foreign investments. Foreign trade required that Chinese products should be competitive on global markets, demanding not only that they be manufactured cheaply, but also shipped, distributed, priced, marketed, of reasonable quality, etc. To achieve this, the quickest and surest means was to attract foreign investors.[51] To this day, foreign companies are estimated to account for over 60% of Chinese exports. Thus, foreign investment would help bolster China's position in global trade, it would provide technology and know-how, and it would create employment. The policy has proved eminently successful, as foreign investment has poured into China throughout

---

[50] Lehmann, J. P., (2003) China and the East Asian Politico-Economic Model. In Buzan, B., Foot R., (eds) (2003) *Does China matter? – A reassessment*, Oxford: Oxford University Press. *The East Asian Economic Miracle: Economic Growth and Public Policy*, (1993) World Bank Publications, Oxford: Oxford University Press.

[51] Rosen, D., (1999) *Behind the open door: Foreign enterprises in the Chinese market place*, Washington D.C. Institute for International Economics, Council on Foreign Relations.

the last twenty years, only briefly interrupted by the Tienanmen massacre of June 4, 1989. Although China was naturally attractive to foreign investors in view of its size, efforts still had to be made to sustain the attraction and ensure the continued flow of direct foreign investment. The process has not been entirely smooth. China lacks many of the institutional underpinnings of a modern market economy, in particular the rule of law. China's capital markets and banks are notoriously inefficient and riddled with cronyism, as SOEs (state-owned enterprises) treat them as their piggy-banks.[52] Though the manufacturing sector is increasingly dominated by the private sector, the party retains control of the banking sector. A very fundamental problem, as Stephen Green has argued, is the absence of transparency, which, he alleges, is the principal reason why the Chinese stock market remains backwards and anachronistic.[53]

Notwithstanding the weaknesses, on balance China's reform process has been quite profound and remarkably successful. It is not, however, over. As noted earlier, there are internal forces that are quite hostile to reform. The political base on which reform rests is more fragile than people realize. The policy constraints are also not negligible. It is not unreasonable to be pessimistic.[54] It is this realization that has led US Treasury Secretary Henry Paulson to argue that the real threat to the US is not Chinese competitiveness, but the prospect that reform might cease.

A key element in China's reform process was the WTO.[55] China first applied to join the GATT in 1986. China's application was at the time strongly supported by Washington, as Beijing was perceived as a potential counter-weight to the still (at the time) ongoing rivalry with the Soviet Union. Three years later, however, the Berlin Wall collapsed, soon to be followed by the implosion of the Soviet Empire, while China was temporarily ostracized due to events in Tienanmen Square. By the early 1990s, Beijing was again actively pursuing negotiations to gain accession to the GATT/WTO. Membership of the WTO was presented to the Chinese people as a key means for China to be part of the global community and to influence its policy agenda. In other words, the WTO was a matter of national pride. For its part, the Chinese leadership recognized that accession to the WTO was a very important means of carrying out domestic reforms that otherwise could well

[52] Lardy, N., (1999) *China's unfinished economic revolution*, Washington D.C. The Brookings Institute

[53] Green, S., (2003) *China's stock market: The players, the institutions and the future*, London: Profile Books.

[54] See Pei, M, (2006).

[55] Lee, K. T., (ed.) (2001) *China's integration with the World Economy: Repercussions to China's accession to the WTO*, Korean Institute of International Economic Policy; See Panitchpakdi, S., Clifford, M., (2002).

have been unpalatable.[56] In 2001, at the Doha Ministerial Conference, China was finally admitted to the WTO. This has been seen as arguably one of the greatest historical landmarks of the last half-century or more.[57]

By the 1990s, virtually all countries had embarked on reform. This was either voluntary or as a requirement for meeting conditions laid down by the IMF, hence the imposition that countries conform to the so-called Washington consensus.[58] The fact that China has pursued reforms with greater zeal than many other countries in the same situation, notably India, has been ascribed to the fact that China had to reform in order to gain accession to the WTO (which, as was pointed out, was a national goal). Whereas both China and India were signatories to the establishment of the GATT in 1947, China then left, which India did not. Although it is very difficult to gain accession to the WTO, no country has ever been expelled. If all countries, including industrialized ones, had to go through the arduous process undertaken by China to gain accession to the WTO, the world economy would be a far better place as it would be resting on a far more level playing field! American and European agricultural subsidies would, *inter alia*, have to be scrapped, hence the main obstacle to the completion of the Doha Development Round would have been removed!

Although China has been an eager new member of the WTO, reaction to China among WTO members and especially industrialized country members has been often less than enthusiastic. In Washington there is a rising chorus demanding vigorous action against China in light of the US massive trade deficit with China and the perception that this is in good part due to unfair practices, notably manipulation of the exchange rate giving Chinese products a huge advantage because of the undervaluation of the renminbi. The EU's reaction has been more concentrated on certain sectors, notably textiles, garments and shoes, leading to what was referred to as the "bra wars" of the summer of 2005.[59]

The international climate so far as China is concerned could therefore hardly be described as unreservedly bright and sunny. As other global economies fail to undertake reforms comparable to China's, there is always the risk

---

[56] Moore, T., (2002) *China in the world market: Chinese industry and international sources of reform in the post-Mao era*, New York, Cambridge University Press; Nolan, P., (2001) *China and the global economy: National champions, industrial policy and the big business revolution*, Houndsmill: Palgrave Macmillan.

[57] Ianchovichina, F., Martin, W., (December 2005) *Economic impacts of China's accession to the WTO*, Washington D.C, World Bank.

[58] See Naïm, M., (1999) Fads and fashion in economic reform: Washington consensus or Washington confusion?, *Foreign Policy*, Fall, 80–93.

[59] Elliott, L., Bra wars: Europe strikes back, *The Guardian* August 26, 2005; Kanter, J., Aiming to avert a 'bra wars' sequel, *International Herald Tribune*, July 3, 2006; Bersten, F., A clash of titans could hurt us all, *Financial Times*, August 24, 2005; Hubauer, G., (2006) Lieberthal, K. Why the US malaise over China?, *Yale Global Online* January 19, 2006.

that it will be seen and used as a scapegoat. This is true of Washington, Brussels and Tokyo, but also of Brasilia, Pretoria, Delhi, and many, many other developing countries' capitals, which see Chinese competition devastating their manufacturing industry, notably in textiles and garments. Indeed Pretoria, in spite of being one of the quartet of leaders of the G-20, is proposing to impose an import ban on Chinese textiles.[60] Mexicans hold China responsible for the collapse of their electronics industry.[61]

The global economy in this first quarter of the twenty-first century would probably be facing a good deal of turbulence in any case, resulting from demographic, technological, and social forces. There is no doubt, however, that China has greatly contributed to the turbulence.

4. Prospects

Paradoxically, while European free-traders were bitterly critical of EU policies during the "bra wars," some Chinese economists warmly welcomed the EU assault on the grounds that if China is forced to cease competing globally simply on price in low-value-added goods, it will then be forced to move up the value-added chain and enhance productivity. This theorem has proved to be true in other comparable circumstances. Import restrictions on cheap Japanese automobiles in the European and American markets in the 1980s forced Japanese auto makers to make more expensive and higher-quality cars.

Certainly the mantra of the Eleventh Five Year Plan, which has recently been publicized, places enormous emphasis on innovation. The pressures on China in trade and the internal pressures on gaining higher value-added have led the government, among other things, to commit to a much higher level of expenditure on R&D.[62]

Thus, inadvertently, Western protectionist reactions to China could accelerate the transformation of China into a far more devastatingly competitive economy in areas, especially of high-technology, that are much closer to where Western competitiveness currently lies.

Whether this will be the case remains, of course, to be seen. One key determinant will be foreign policies and attitudes, especially from Washington. Economic nationalism may generate economic nationalism. The prohibition

---

[60] Hazelhurst, E., Import quotas – the great leap backwards, *Business Report*, September 16, 2006.
[61] Luhnow, D., China stealing jobs from Mexico, *Wall Street Journal*, March 5, 2004.
[62] Ten features in China's Eleventh five year plan, *People's Daily Online*, March 8, 2006.

by Congress of the acquisition of Unocal by CNOOC (China National Offshore Oil Corporation) has led Chinese nationalists to urge for far more restrictions to be imposed on foreign companies operating in China. A backlash against China would almost certainly result in a Chinese anti-globalization backlash.

However, even in a reasonably positive global environment, things could still go wrong in China. There are immense social pressures and increasing social unrest, as has been noted. There is also the fact that while the Chinese economy is open, the political system is closed. Liberal Chinese advocates have imperatives for reform to sustain growth and development in the years ahead.[63] The first is reform of the government. They do not necessarily call for "democracy" in the sense of one-person-one-vote, but even within the one-party state, cleaner, more accountable and more transparent government is crucial for sustained socio-economic growth and development. The second is reform of party-industry relations, especially in the financial sector, where the government hand is not invisible, but far too conspicuous. In particular, capital markets must become far more open to private entrepreneurs. Currently 90% of bank lending goes to the state sector. Private entrepreneurs must rely on their own resources, frequently those of their families and friends. This situation may change once liberalization in the financial sector is undertaken. The third is an imperative for reform in social security, especially pensions. The collapse of the "iron bowl", whereby virtually all Chinese, especially in the urban industrial sector, were guaranteed income, employment and social amenities, has resulted in great social uncertainty. Public goods, such as education and health, have suffered considerably as a result. This, among other things, accounts for the very high savings rate and the fact that domestic consumption in China is weak. Social security and pension reform will become all the more critical as the Chinese population, as a result of the one-child policy adopted in 1978, is rapidly aging.[64]

Pundits have referred to the twenty-first century as the Chinese century. This will be true insofar as the greatest challenge of this era will be whether China does succeed in transforming itself into a viable, dynamic and robust society. It is certainly going in that direction, but there is still a very, very long way to go. If China continues to grow at an average annual rate of 9%, by 2030 Chinese per-capita GDP will be the same as that of Japan in 1973.[65] China has a long way to go down the road of reform.

[63] Interviews carried out with Chinese reformers in June and September 2006. See also Jinglian, W., (2006) The road ahead for capitalism in China, *The McKinsey Quarterly*, Special edition.

[64] Qiao, H. H., (2006) Will China grow old before growing rich?, *Goldman Sachs Global Economics Paper No 138*, February 14.

[65] See Gang, F. (2005).

15 EU constitutional governance: Failure as opportunity!?

Ralf Boscheck

On June 17, 2005, the European Union summit broke up in a bitter dispute over the EU's budget and the future of its constitution. Arguments about the union's financial plans, even sullen accusations of national egoism, have been a frequent element of European politics for years. But the popular rejection of the proposed EU constitution by France and the Netherlands, two major advocates of European unity, just prior to the meeting had raised deep questions about the Union's legitimacy and purpose. Hopes by some that successful ratifications in the remaining EU countries would change the French and Dutch stance were soon dispelled. Already at the summit, the Dutch prime minister announced that his country would not vote again on the same, unamended document; Denmark, Portugal, Ireland, Britain and the Czech Republic put their referendum schedule on hold. Nearly fifty-five years since the beginning of the European voyage, attempts to reach the EU's "final and natural constitutional destiny"[1] appeared to have thrown the Union off course and into "one of the deepest crises in its history."[2] Or, is Europe facing a unique opportunity for political, economic and institutional renewal?

By way of introduction, section 1 of this chapter briefly sketches some elements of the EU's current economic status, its institutional aspirations and *Realpolitik*, and the range of challenges that a European constitution was envisioned to meet. Section 2 outlines key considerations for assessing the origin and performance of constitutional governance and the political economy of federalism. Section 3 applies these to a critical review of EU constitutional efforts resulting in the Draft Treaty, which was published by the Convention for the Future of Europe in July 2003, accepted in its final version

---

[1] In the words of Germany's foreign minister Joschka Fischer, in Fischer, J., (2000) From confederation to federation: Thoughts on the finality of European integration, *Federal Trust – European Essay*, No 8, 2000.

[2] Jean-Claude Juncker, Prime Minister of Luxembourg, chairman of the Brussels summit. Europe's identity crisis deepens, *The Economist* June 18, 2005.

by the leaders of the EU-25 in June 2004,[3] and eventually rejected by the French and Dutch referenda in May 2005. Section 4 invites readers to speculate about alternative strategies for "re-engineering" EU governance based on a review of European regional economic activity and a growing interest in the devolution of political control.

1. The contours of Europe's "crisis" in 2005 – symptoms and causes

Robert Schuman and Jean Monnet, the founding fathers of the EU, tried to lay the institutional foundation for economic prosperity to stabilize a war-ridden, disunited continent. Current constitutional initiatives also respond to pressing needs. But this time, they arise from growing popular discontent with the EU's economic and institutional achievements, perceived democratic deficits and calls for political reforms.[4] Clearly, whether one deems the EU's record of attainment and future priorities satisfactory or legitimate largely reflects one's own historical perspectives, economic interests and political biases. But there can be little doubt that, as Europe's overall economy is waning and stakeholders grow in numbers and diversity, the EU in its current set-up will be hard pressed to sustain cohesion.

Europe's economic performance

Consider the region's ailing macroeconomic record. As the world economy was projected to expand by 4.4% in 2005, the EU-25 and €-area were only likely to grow by a mere 1.9% and 1.2% respectively. While in 2004 world merchandise trade expanded at twice the rate of world output, Europe, accounting for about 46% of global trade, recorded the lowest real merchandise import growth of all regions and saw its exports increase by less than global trade. Whilst US unemployment fell to 5.1% in May 2005 and Japan's unemployment rate appears stabilized at around 4.4%, the €-area unemployment rate grew to 9%. *Yet* the concern for aggregates blocks the view on vital differences. Europe is but a label. It covers nations with GDP growth rates ranging from 8.6% to −1.2%; export expansions varying from 38.4% to −15.9%,

---

[3] European Convention for the Future of Europe (2003), *Draft Treaty establishing a Constitution for Europe*, www.european-convention.eu.int.

[4] See EU Commission's White Paper on Governance, COM 2001, 428; Menéndez, A. J., (2005) Between Laeken and the deep blue sea, *European Public Law*, 11(1), 105–44; Skach, C., (2005) We, the peoples? Constitutionalizing the European Union, *Journal of Common Market Studies*, 43(1), March 149–71.

and national unemployment rates stretching from 3.1% to 18.1%. Europe houses economies with an industry/agriculture share of more than 65% of GDP and others whose economic activities are more than 80% service-related. In terms of labor productivity in 2004, a European employee generated as much US$56.44 or as little as US$9.11 worth of output per hour; hourly manufacturing wages ranged from $35.37 to $0.53. In addition, while disparities among European nations are pronounced, regional differences within them are becoming economically and politically even important.[5] In 2004, the productivity per capita in Bavaria ranked $10,100 above the German average; a Catalan added $5,200 more to the Spanish GDP than his average countryman. Among the Union's 250 regions, GDP per capita was almost three times higher in the ten wealthiest locations than in the ten at the bottom of the scale.[6] Differences in skills and infrastructures explain patterns of economic activity and rising income polarization – the coexistence of regional growth magnets and poverty traps. Enlargement adds to this.

Figure 15.1 presents an array of European socioeconomic indicators. Some of the underlying data is often aggregated to suggest patterns of economic performance and common political interests. But delineations, such as "€-bloc", "old" and "new" Europe, "Anglo-Saxon pragmatists" and "Continental welfare idealists", even if useful to incite an argument, often prove too crude to predict any consistent political behavior. Indeed, the growing diversity in economic capacity and policy preference at national and regional levels presents the single most important challenge to the pursuit of the EU's core objectives of market creation, policy coordination and cohesion. Past efforts to speed up decision-making and enhance the EU's management role have largely failed. France's threat to withdraw from the Council had maintained national veto powers on all matters of "vital national interests" until the adoption of the Single European Act (SEA) in 1986. Since then, consultation and cooperation procedures were to centralize the policy-making power in the Commission, and qualified majorities were to replace unanimity in taking substantive policy decisions. But many of the resulting policies were simply not executed. Today, after twenty years, the most crucial SEA directives are still not implemented in the former EU-15 Member States; distortions in markets and political representation continue and unmet policy challenges frustrate the public and require fundamental reforms.[7] To consider a few:

---

[5] Maza, A., Villaverde, J., (2004) Regional disparities in the EU, *Applied Economic Letters*, 11(8), 517–23.

[6] Second Report on Economic and Social Cohesion, Brussels: EC Commission.

[7] Kassim, H., (2002) Internal policy developments, *Journal of Common Market Studies*, 40(1), 53–73.

Indicator	Maximum score		Minimum score	
GDP growth, Percentage change, based on national currency in constant prices, 2003/4	Romania	8.59	Portugal	0.04
Industry % GDP	Romania	41.90	Ile-de-France	16.70
Service % GDP	Ile-de-France	83.10	Romania	44.60
Productivity, GDP (PPP) per person employed, US$	Luxembourg	96,456.77	Romania	18,232.89
Labor Productivity: GDP (PPP) per person employed per hour, US$	Ile-de-France	56.44	Romania	9.15
Total hourly compensation for manufacturing workers (wages + supplementary benefits), US$	Denmark	35.37	Romania	0.53
Unemployment rate (% of labor force)	Iceland	3.10	Poland	18.80
Long-term unemployment	Norway	0.28	Slovenia	11.00
Exports of goods – real growth, % change based on US$ values, 2004	Poland	38.41	Ile-de-France	−15.89
Balance of trade, US$billions, 2004	Germany	197.30	UK	−116.40
Terms of trade index, Unit value of exports over unit value of imports (2000 = 100), 2004	France	111.62	Scotland	64.43
Government final consumption expenditure, % of GDP	Hungary	10.51	Sweden	28.20
Government budget surplus/deficit, % of GDP	Norway	9.63	Greece	−6.85
Dependency ratio: (Population under 15 and over 64 years old, divided by active population (15 to 64 years))	Rhone-Alps	63.20	Slovak Republic	40.42
Social cohesion is a priority for the government, 0–10	Poland	2.65	Denmark	8.06
Income distribution – Percentage of household incomes going to lowest 20% of households	Portugal	5.80	Czech Republic	10.30
Income distribution – Percentage of household incomes going to highest 20% of households	Portugal	45.90	Slovak Republic	34.80

Source: IMD World Competitiveness Yearbook 2005 based on national statistics and survey data

Figure 15.1: European socioeconomic indicators

Demography and productivity

In its Green Paper "Confronting Demographic Change,"[8] the EU succinctly outlined the challenge ahead: With an average EU fertility rate of 1.48 and a mean increase in life-expectancy of around 4-5 years since the 1960s, Europe's working population will have shrunk by almost 20.6 m in 2030 but it will have to shoulder an increased dependency ratio (currently 49%, predicted 66%). In addition, aging will not only halve Europe's GNP growth potential from currently 2–2.25% to 1.25% in 2040, but the demographic profile of their electorate may make it impossible for a range of EU states to reform their un-funded pay-as-you-go pension systems. Three policy responses could, in principle, be combined: (a) increase labor supply, (by means of immigration, family policies, increase in employment rate, hours worked per day and over life-time); (b) increase productivity (through improved education, R&D, technology and infrastructure investments); (c) cut claims. Pros, cons and respective feasibilities of these strategies have been widely discussed.[9] What is of interest here is how the EU approached the issue.

In March 2000, heads of EU states and governments adopted the so-called Lisbon strategy. They intended to end the EU's high level of structural unemployment and widening skill and technology gaps, principally by committing their countries to a 70% employment rate and national R&D expenditure of at least 3% of GDP. The strategy involved an "open method of coordination, (OMC)" – an informal, non-binding approach to build consensus among peers – as well as regular checks of targets and half-yearly reviews by the EU Council. Regrettably, the novel soft-law approach gave rise to a proliferation of non-operational objectives, process fatigue and cynicism. Within a year, the scope of the Lisbon strategy had been extended to capture the attainment of competitiveness, social cohesion and environmental sustainability; sixteen actions plans had formulated twenty-eight main objectives, 120 sub-objectives and 117 indicators. In the words of one observer "(w)ith the enlargement of the Union no less than 300 annual reports are to be produced in order to check progress. ... There is an obvious technocratic attempt to replace ... trial and error processes inherent in the functioning of markets in general and in the fostering of innovation in particular."[10] Disappointingly, by 2004 only two Member States had spent 3% of their

---

[8] EU Commission (2005), *Green Paper: Confronting Demographic Change*, Brussels, March.
[9] See Ederveen, S. *et al.*, (2005) Growth and jobs: A different approach to each, *Intereconomics*, 40(2), 66–9.
[10] Csaba, L., (2005) Poetry and reality about the future of the Union: Reflections on the dimensions and nature of the re-launch of the Lisbon Strategy, *Intereconomics*, March/April 2005, pp. 61–5.

GDP on R&D, and the EU had lost even more ground in international benchmarking exercises, particularly in the area of productivity and technology adoption.[11]

Based on this, the reaction of the Barroso Commission in March 2005 is noteworthy for two reasons. First, it re-launched "the Lisbon Strategy (as) – a key priority of the Commission."[12] Second, it renewed the OMC process without however addressing its lack of operational clarity, incentives, and sanctions. Why prescribe a general 70% employment rate irrespective of productivity differences? Why does the EU's most important policy to date receive a mere 0.1% of the EU's GNI as financial backing? Why are there no effective controls on Member State implementation? No wonder therefore, that on the level of practical politics, the "Lisbon strategy" – the EU's key strategy to ensure competitiveness – is increasingly sidelined relative to more salient issues such as budget rebates, the Common Agricultural Policy or the management of enlargement. No wonder also, that recent reviews of this policy – discussing the appropriate allocation of tasks between the Commission and Member States as well as process concerns[13] – compare it unfavorably with the EU's more structured working in areas such as the Stability and Growth Pact. But particularly with regard to the latter, these reviewers may give more credit than is due.

Stability and growth

There is still no free lunch! The benefits of a European Monetary System – deeper capital markets, better risk allocation, enhanced contestability and trade creation – come at a price: the recognition that Europe is not an optimum currency area and for that reason has an even stronger need for fiscal constraints. Unsynchronized business cycles, inflexible product and factor markets and little practice of fiscal solidarity make Europe susceptible to asymmetric shocks.[14] Fiscal rules, like those enshrined in the Maastricht Treaty's Stability and Growth Pact (SGP) should lessen pressures for more expansive monetary policies and the risk of crowding out the private sector or, in a common financial market, smaller-country borrowers. In addition,

---

[11] Denis, C., et al., (2005) The Lisbon Strategy and the EU's structural productivity problem. In EU Commission European Economy, *Economic Papers*, No. 221, Brussels, February.

[12] Barroso, J. M., (2005) The Lisbon Strategy – a key priority of the EU Commission. Talk delivered to the ETUC conference, Brussels. Reprinted in *EurActiv*, 1 March 2005.

[13] See Csaba (2005), Denis (2005), and Ederveen et al. (2005).

[14] See Mundell. R., (1961) A theory of optimum currency areas, *American Economic Review*, 51(3), 657–65; McKinnion, R., (1963) Optimum currency areas, *American Economic Review*, 53(4), 717–25.

fiscal restraints limit national discretion and may be sought as a form of self-restraint to curb domestic rent-seeking behavior. But this theory has two problems: First, painful fiscal consolidation may attain the targets in the short term, but may be difficult to sustain thereafter. Second, simple rules, such as a budget deficit limit of 3% and a debt ratio of maximum of 60% of GDP, can be gamed. Hence, the question is how to monitor and enforce the arrangement?

None of the market and non-market mechanisms currently available seem sufficient. Interest rate differentials for government bonds within the EU are negligible,[15] suggesting that financial markets may not be able to distinguish the offers of various EMU members. On the other hand, national ministers drafting national budgets possibly should not be relied upon in deciding whether they are in breach of the Treaty. Recent discussions therefore focus on how to involve national central banks, the European Court of Auditors or some central refinancing mechanism in monitoring a country's fiscal perfor- mance and on how to sanction non-compliance. But that discussion seems academic in view of the fact that the EU finds it difficult to punish big offenders, and recently suggested reforms dilute standards to the point that they turn the SGP on its head and disregard basic principles of fairness.

The Commission's recent proposal to accept a breach of the 3% deficit limit given "exceptional circumstance,"[16] has come just after the Union's decision to sanction Portugal's but not France's and Germany's violation of fiscal commitments. This has led to debates about the likely economic rationale for treating different stakeholders differently – depending on size, timing of entry, or generational membership. Is special treatment for larger countries justified based on presumably larger adjustment costs and slower turnaround time or simply because of the fear that their hardship may spill over into smaller neighbors? Is the two-year waiting period prior to EMU membership, the Exchange Rate Mechanism II, truly necessary to facilitate macroeconomic convergence and structural change in accession countries, even if some – like Estonia, Lithuania and Slovenia – have a long-term record of fulfilling the very SGP criteria which several EU-15 members fail to meet? Finally, and in view of the demographic challenge discussed above, should both the debt and deficit limits not be much tighter, rather than looser, to ensure inter-generational justice and avoid that current generations live at the

---

[15] Boonstra, W., (2005) Proposal for a better stability pact, *Intereconomics*, January/February, 4–9.
[16] For a discussion see Hefeker, C., (2005) Will a revised stability pact improve fiscal policy in Europe? *Intereconomics*, January/February, 17–21.

cost of future ones? Clearly, as in the previous case, it is difficult not to become concerned about the EU's methods of stakeholder representation.

Stakeholder representation and policy games

EU decision making processes are highly intricate and, with expanding membership, will grow in complexity. But will legitimacy improve? Concerns about national representation and policy adoption serve as an illustration here. On several occasions following the enlargement of the EU, larger member countries demanded a re-weighting of the EU Council votes to avoid minorities blocking decisions that require a qualified majority (i.e. in nearly 80% of all cases). But such adjustments often came at a high political cost and at the expense of operational efficiency. For instance, in 2000, the European Council meeting in Nice established the provision that a qualified majority must include a majority of states and represent at least 62% of the EC's population. Yet, the formula not only reduced the passage probability in an enlarged EU-27 to 2.1%, thereby effectively deadlocking decision making,[17] it also required concession in operating another EU institution. The Nice Council meeting sought to establish fair methods for redistributing seats in the EU Parliament to facilitate the ultimate enlargement to EU-27 without (greatly) increasing the number of seats. However, in the final hours of negotiations "complications arose" and so "seats were thrown around like loose change" in order to make Belgium (and later Greece and Portugal) accept the new voting weights. (As a result) "the Czech Republic and Hungary, with the same population as Belgium, were given fewer seats."[18] Clearly, political representation within the EU is a major cause for concern; but so are Member States' strategies for setting policy agendas, shaping legislation or obstructing implementation.

All Member States have, in principle, an interest in "uploading" their policies to the European level, but they differ in their willingness and capacity to drive standards.[19] In drafting EU environmental rules, for example, Austria, Denmark, Finland, Germany, the Netherlands and Sweden tend to

---

[17] Baldwin, R., Berglöf, E., Giavazzi, F., Widgrén, M., (2001) *Nice try: Should the Treaty of Nice be ratified?* CEPR Paper MEI 11, London: Centre for European Policy Research.

[18] Moberg, A., (2002) The Nice Treaty and voting rules in the council, *Journal of Common Market Studies*, 40(2), 259–82.

[19] For a detailed assessment see Börzel, T. A., (2002) Pace-setting, foot-dragging, and fence-sitting: Member State responses to Europeanization, *Journal of Common Market Studies*, 40(2), 193–214; Liefferink, D., Andersen, M. S., (1998) Strategies of the "green" Member States in EU environmental policy-making, *Journal of European Public Policy*, 5(2), 254–70.

"set the pace," using their combined voting powers and national expertise in dealing with the Commission. Operating from a less developed regulatory base, Greece, Portugal and Spain typically "drag their feet" and accept more stringent measures only if compensation can be obtained. Belgium, France, Ireland and the UK "sit on the fence" – playing the "environmental card" when negotiating unrelated issues or scapegoating Brussels for inconvenient policy decisions. Clearly, preferred strategies change with topics. The level of regulation that is finally obtained reflects the composition of the winning coalition and the voting method applied. However, with stakeholders growing in numbers and diversity, how likely is it that centralized institutional bargaining within the EU will result in adequate, economically efficient and legitimate policy?

In sum, recent EU policy experiences illustrate three points. First, soft-law methods, as in the case of the Lisbon Strategy, tend to end up in a proliferation of objectives and monitoring mechanisms, cause process fatigue and cynicism and drag on long after their failure has been established. Second, structured approaches to European market regulation, as in the case of the Single European Act or the Stability and Growth Pact, often suffer from a mix of non-compliance and under-enforcement, ultimately leading to the discriminatory application of ever more diluted standards and the acceptance of effective defiance by some. Third, both outcomes reflect the EU's mode of operation, its set of responsibilities and type of stakeholder representation. The public expresses its frustration in voter turnouts and opinion polls.[20]

More broadly, however, these three issues represent the fundamental challenges faced by any union, political or otherwise. Alliances are viable only to the extent that they create and maintain procedural and substantive consensus and deference to it. They tend to expand to some point of saturation and disintegrate once membership grows further in numbers and diversity, its leadership is closed to participation or does not deliver benefits, and necessary reforms are delayed or not pursued by all.[21] The EU faces a typical alliance problem and is forced to review the scope of policy making at and in between different levels of government and to establish efficient rules of

---

[20] The voter turnout in the elections for the European Parliament in June 2004 reached an all-time low of 45.7%. In a spring 2004 Eurobarometer opinion poll, taken in the fifteen countries that made up the EU before enlargement, 21% of the respondents said that they had a negative image of the EU and 26% that they considered it "a waste of money."

[21] For a review of classical perspectives see Dougherty, R., Pfalzgraph, J., (1984) *Theories of international relations*, New York: Harcourt Brace.

engagement and adjudication. It is a matter of institutional and constitutional reform.

In fact, the current debate on the EU's constitution emanates from institutional reform initiatives that were intended to improve performance and re-establish operational consensus. These were inspired by Member States calling, at the Nice Summit, for a debate on the delineation of competence between the EU and the Member States, the principle of subsidiarity and the role of the national parliaments in the EU's institutional architecture. They were furthered by the Prodi Commission's White Paper on Good Governance, which proposed to open up the EU Commission to national, regional and local consultation and accountability while giving it more direct powers to speed up the implementation of legislation. Finally, they were channeled by a Committee of "wise men," conveyed *ad hoc* by the Belgian government, in the Laeken Declaration in December 2001. Yet, relative to previous initiatives, which concentrated on improving the functioning of EU decision processes, the focus of the Laeken Declaration was on *democracy* and *legitimacy* – it resulted in an explicit process of constitution making. But was the process and outcome of trying to constitutionalize the EU democratic and legitimate? Does the proposed constitution fix the alliance problem? Which conceivable alternatives ought to be considered and which standards apply?

2. Some perspectives on constitutional governance and the economics of political union

Before assessing the EU's recent constitutional efforts a number of questions ought to be clarified. What is the role of a constitution and what makes it legitimate? Who should set norms and implement policies for the purpose of efficiency? What are the costs and benefits of alternative methods for allocating responsibilities across different levels of government?

On the legitimacy of constitutional order

Political systems not only differ in terms of who articulates and aggregates interests and who makes, implements and adjudicates policy decisions, but also in terms of the focus and extent of regulatory output, the level and distribution of income and the forms and expressions of political culture. The predictability of a given system relies on its underlying rules to be understood and stable in guiding cases of unavoidable discretion. To this end, constitutions provide the highest-ranked, legally justifiable definition of powers and duties among governmental organizations, societal actors and citizens.[22] The fact that they can only be amended by special procedures not applicable to ordinary legislation provides a stable basis for assessing issues of accountability. But it also poses questions about a constitution's own legitimacy – *a priori* and over time.

Some recent reviews of EU constitutional efforts apply some notion of "output-oriented" authority.[23] Accordingly, a constitution may be considered legitimate if it is believed that "for that particular country at that particular historical juncture no other type of regime could assure a more successful pursuit of collective goals."[24] But without counterfactual evidence and any clarification of process and performance objectives how is one to judge? Clearly, output-oriented authority is a pragmatic shortcut into a blind alley. A deontological discussion of legitimacy is required and necessarily broader.

Normative theories of constitutionalism – from classical natural law foundations to current perspectives on "deliberative democracy"[25] and constitutional economics[26] – link legitimacy to voluntarism, participation and efficiency. Reasonable people escape the brutish state of nature by handing over certain individual liberties to a state that monopolizes the power of coercion and from there on in guarantees their private autonomy. Put differently, bottom-up delegation "constitutes" the original state. What legitimizes its evolution thereafter hinges on citizens' right to limit state activity and participate in deliberating and monitoring laws and policy.

In Continental European and common law tradition, with their respective emphasis on legislative and judicial norm development, public rules are, for all practical purposes, legitimized through either direct or representative democracy or the election of constitutional courts.[27] Requirements for "deliberatively democratic" legitimacy are stronger, calling on citizens to have the opportunity, in principle, to participate in identifying problems, selecting alternative responses for analysis and deliberation, formulating and

---

[22] For a detailed discussion see Raz, J., (1998) On the authority and interpretation of constitutions: Some preliminaries. In L. Alexander (ed.) *Constitutionalism*, Cambridge: Cambridge University Press, pp. 152–53.

[23] See Skatch (2005).

[24] Linz, J. J. (1978) Crisis, breakdown and re-equilibration. In Linz, J., Stephan, A. (eds.) (1978) *Breakdown of democratic regimes*, Baltimore: Johns Hopkins University Press, p. 18.

[25] For a review see Nino, C., (1996) *The constitution of deliberative democracy*, New Haven and London: Yale University Press; Habermas, J., (2001) Constitutional democracy, a paradoxical union of contradictory principles, *Political Theory*, 29(6), 766–81.

[26] For a review see Mueller, D. C., (2003) *Public Choice III*, Cambridge: Cambridge University Press.

[27] For reasons of the separation of power, they are not seen to create new law but to interpret norms to execute legislative intent.

reviewing norms, and screening reviewers and judges. Direct political parti-cipation not only protects individual rights but is also seen to educate citizens and make them aware of and respect the positions of others; it is the source of civic virtues. In the words of the classical theory of democracy, the "delib-eratively democratic" ideal is a *polyarchic* constitution, which results from full "popular inclusion" in providing legislative inputs and complete "popular contestation" of legislative results.[28] Real-world rule-making, however, often falls into three other categories, which limit citizen involvement to either providing inputs or ratifying outputs, or exclude the public entirely from any legislative participation.[29] In the latter case, *hegemonic* constitutions result, which attempt to impose a central design on decentral circumstances. As such, this mode not only conflicts with any "deliberatively democratic" ideal but also falls short of central efficiency concerns espoused by the economic analysis of law.

On efficient governance and inter-governmental coordination

Constitutional economists and public choice theorists argue for the devolu-tion of legislative and regulatory powers and the need to constrain political discretion through markets. Setting norms decentrally is seen to better reflect local conditions and citizen preference, increase legal innovation and limit the negative impact of policy discretion or corruption. Issue-based voting best sanctions the process. From this perspective, aggregating issues into political platforms, harmonizing rules, extending the reach of constitutional cover or centralizing the making of a constitution amounts to colluding in the market for political control. Yet, it is also clear that for lower-level regulatory and legislative competition to work at all, some market-creating constitu-tional norms are nevertheless required. The challenge is to balance the benefits of decentralization against potentially foregone efficiencies of central scale and coordination. How can the trade-off be managed?

Most of the literature on federalism, discussing the comparative efficiency of alternative mechanisms for inter-governmental coordination,[30] abstracts

---

[28] Dahl, R. A., (1973) *Polyarchy: Participation and opposition*, New Haven: Yale University Press.

[29] Skach (2005) presents a positioning map along the dimensions of public inclusion and public con-testation, with "polyarchic" and "hegemonic" presenting full and no score on each dimension respec-tively. "Full oligarchic" constitution-making has no public input but full public contestation, the reverse is labeled "inclusive hegemonic."

[30] For a review see Inman, R. P., Rubinfeld, D. L., (1997) The political economy of federalism. In D. C. Mueller (ed.) *Perspectives on public choice*, Cambridge: Cambridge University Press, pp. 73–105; See Mueller (2003).

from two classical models. On the one hand, there is Montesquieu's view of the *confederate republic*. It allows small city-states to pursue democratic rights and civic virtues while linking with others to further pursue common objectives based on unanimous decisions and the right to exit at any time. On the other hand, James Madison, appreciating the city-states' ability to efficiently produce in line with local demands, links them up in a *compound republic* under a central government that receives its legitimacy from the majority approval of all its citizens rather than from the unanimous consent of all city-states. The executive implements the laws approved by the legislature. Juxtaposing both perspectives is sometimes meant to illustrate a presumed impasse between pursuing political and economic objectives, between civic virtues and efficiency. However, analyses on the political economy of federalism do not appear to support this.

Models of federalism typically explore the interaction of four sets of variables: levels of governmental hierarchy (local, state, central); levels of local representation in the center (from town-meetings sending one representative to the central legislature to presidential formats in which all city-states elect one representative in a single central election); assignments of policy responsibilities for supplying national or particularistic, local public goods; and decision making by unanimity or some form of majority rule. Even at the risk of oversimplifying, some broad patterns emerge from these studies:

Under unanimity, increasing representation at the central level increases spending for both national and particularistic goods. Under majority rule, increases in spending on national public goods requires an increase in the representation of the coalition favoring that particular good, while spending on particularistic goods increases depending on who ultimately pays for building up the political demand for it. A strong central executive office may check on the potential risk of increased spending through increased representation but would itself need to be balanced by some representation of local interest. Alternatively, changing the assignment of responsibilities may lessen the need for adding layers of controls to deal with deep-seated distrust. In fact, modeling the impact of assigning policy responsibilities to local authorities for the above cases demonstrates that local provision of particularistic goods is most efficient as long as inter-state free riding can be avoided. The rule of thumb is: national public goods are efficiently assigned to the center; the provision of particularistic goods is better left to locals. Hence, there may not be a need to choose between civic virtue and efficiency as long as economies of scale and spillovers of governmental activities can be clearly identified, assignment principles are constitutionally pronounced and adequately applied. In practice, this is where the problem starts.

In sum, constitutions present the highest-ranked, stable legal definition of societal organization. They are legitimate as long as they reflect the principle of voluntarism and the public's participation in providing legislative input and contesting results. Hegemonic constitutions not only conflict with any deliberatively democratic ideal but, from an economic perspective, amount to monopolizing the market for regulatory and political control. In general, devolving legislative and regulatory powers is best to capture local conditions, fuel regulatory innovation and efficiency but finds its limits in potentially foregone efficiencies of central scale and coordination. Seeking to combine democratic benefits and civic virtue with the need for efficient public office, constitutional assignments of public responsibilities must reflect the economics of the given service. Where changes in underlying economic conditions blur decisions about assignments, political choice needs to be made contestable, principally by involving delegated, decentralized controls. Section 3 applies these ideas to assess the *process* and *outcome* of the EU's recent constitutional efforts.

3. Assessing the EU's Recent Constitutional Efforts

The Draft Treaty establishing a Constitution for Europe, as accepted in its final version by the leaders of the EU-25 in June 2004, is divided into four parts, all of equal rank. Following a Preamble recalling the history and heritage of Europe and its determination to transcend its divisions, Part I is devoted to the principles, objectives and institutional provisions governing the new EU. Part II comprises the European Chapter of Fundamental Rights. Part III includes the provisions governing the policies and functioning of the Union. Part IV groups together the general and final provisions of the Constitution, including entry into force, the procedure for revising the Constitution and the repeal of earlier Treaties. A number of protocols have been annexed to the Treaty establishing the Constitution, in particular the Protocol on the role of national parliaments in the EU; the Protocol on the application of the principles of subsidiarity and proportionality, the Protocol of the Euro Group, the Protocol amending the Euratom Treaty, and the Protocol on the transitional provisions relating to the institutions and bodies of the Union.

In the words of the EU Commission, the Draft Treaty establishes the EU as a single legal personality and "provides a clearer presentation of competences" and "a simplified set of legal instruments" to act. Moreover, it is seen "to confirm in one fundamental text a number of provisions aiming at more democratic, transparent and controllable EU institutions that are closer to the citizen."[31] The following assesses the *process* that led to the formulation of the Draft Treaty and its rejection by the French and Dutch referendum in May 2005, and the *outcome*, i.e. the relationship between the EU, Member States and citizens that is being proposed.

Process

Before discussing the democratic credentials of the process that led to the formulation of the Draft Treaty it is necessary to pinpoint its beginning. This is important as it has been argued that the Draft Treaty neither requires any broad-based "public inclusion" nor "contestation" as it merely elaborates an already existing constitutional order based on the Treaties, the European Court of Justice doctrine and the language used in it.[32] Already in 1963, the European Court of Justice's position on *Van Gend* spoke in terms of the Communities creating a "new legal order of international law for the benefit of which the states have limited their sovereign rights."[33] And in *Les Verts*, 1986, the Court described the Treaty as the basic constitutional charter of the Community.[34] However, judicial norm setting is typically limited to expressing legislative intent. Yet, since the Treaties are merely diplomatically negotiated international contracts they do not provide any direct democratic foundation for constituting the Union. EU constitutional efforts are clearly more recent and their democratic legitimacy ought to be discussed.

The initial thrust – emanating from the announcements of Member States during the Nice Summit, the Prodi Commission's White Paper of Good Governance, the *ad hoc* meeting of "wise men" and finally the "selection" of the Convention's chairman and co-vice-chairmen – reflected political entrepreneurship and secretive, bureaucratic maneuvering rather than any direct democratic involvement. However during the Convention,

---

[31] See htpp://europa.eu.int/constitution.

[32] For a detailed discussion of this point see Craig, P., (2001) Constitutions, constitutionalism and the European Union, *European Law Journal*, 7(2), June, 125–50.

[33] Case 26/62 N.V. *Algemene Transporten Expeditie Onderneming van Gend en Loos* v. *Nederlands Administratie de Belastingen* (1963) ECR 1, 12.

[34] Case 294/83 *Parti Ecologiste 'Les Verts'* v. *Parliament* (1986) ECR 1339, 1365.

representation, at least formally, improved. All but two members of the Convention of the Future of Europe were elected representatives appointed by national and European parliaments. In addition, the Economic and Social Committee and the Committee of the Regions, the social partners and the European Ombudsman were allowed to send observers.[35] Still, the agenda had been broadly set upfront, and most effort was spent on process deliberation, with little time left for concrete discussion of final proposals. In addition, voting had been excluded to drive consensus on key issues. Given that the Convention often failed to document why certain decisions had been taken, a voting record would have lent outcomes at least some modicum of normative authority.[36]

The Convention concluded its work at the end of July 2003, which drastically shrunk any opportunity for in-depth public debate prior to the intergovernmental negotiations that began in the fall. The Intergovernmental Conference, shrouded in secrecy and hampered by drafting complexities, gave no chance for the general public to bring divisive issues, like those surrounding "Social Europe," to the fore. During the European Council Meeting in December 2003, Poland and Spain vetoed the principle of double majority, thereby blocking an agreement, and gave rise to at least six major modifications of the original Draft. It was only due to the dismissal of both countries' incumbent governments in the spring of 2004 that the final agreement was reached in June 2004. In the eyes of an observer "(t)he failure of the Brussels Summit in December 2003 and ... the dilution of the Draft put forward by the Convention ... entrenched the perception that the process of writing primary Union law was a matter of cruel bargaining and pork-barrel politics."[37]

Arguably efforts to initiate and develop an EU constitution did not include the general public in any direct way. In fact, one may question whether it was at all possible for elected politicians, national and European parliaments and the Convention to capture the mind of the EU public, let alone its common constitutional will. In an opinion poll, taken in the fifteen countries that made up the EU before enlargement, only 43% of the respondents said they had a positive image of the Union, 21% said they had a negative image and

---

[35] Still, it has been argued that already the composition of the Convention might have tilted the balance towards a centralized outcome. See The European Constitutional Group, (2004) The constitutional proposal of the European Convention: An appraisal and explanation, *IEA Economic Affairs*, March 2004, pp. 22–7.

[36] Menédez, A. J., (2005) Between Laeken and the Deep Blue Sea, *European Public Law*, 11(1) 105–44.

[37] See Menédez, pp. 119–20.

26% considered it "a waste of money."[38] The voter turn-out in the elections for the European Parliament in June 2004 had reached an all-time low of 45.7%; in the Netherlands, for instance, it had dropped to less than 30% compared to almost 80% in 1979. With very little "public inclusion" in the origination of the Draft, maintaining some democratic legitimacy required involving the general public in "contesting" the outcome.

In September 2004, eleven of the 25 EU countries – Belgium, Britain, the Czech Republic, Denmark France, Ireland, Luxembourg, the Netherlands, Poland, Portugal and Spain – had promised or all but promised to hold a referendum on the constitution. To be clear, citizens were not asked to vote, let alone comment, on parts of the text, but to either endorse or reject it *en bloc*. Yet, following the French and Dutch rejection of the Draft Constitution in May 2005, Denmark, Portugal, Ireland, Britain and the Czech Republic put their referendum schedule on hold. But this reaction was not unexpected. Already a year earlier, the Intergovernmental Conference had adopted a "Declaration on the ratification of the Treaty establishing the Constitution" providing for a "political solution" to be found if a Member State failed to ratify the Treaty. This sheds a sobering light onto a process that had been started by interpreting the public's discontent with the EU as "an unarticulated will to enact a constitution for the Union"[39] and was to celebrate democracy and legitimacy. Did the French and the Dutch reject the Constitution or the method used to attain it? With the process lacking democratic credentials, is the result more in line with the outlined normative reference?

Outcome

The following comments on the Draft Treaty relate to: (1) its constitutional character; (2) aspects of institutional representation; (3) the Commission's roles and the concepts of subsidiarity and proportionality; (4) the Council voting rules; (5) concerns for regulatory competition viz. harmonization; and, finally (6), the logic of tasks assignment.

First, for constitutions to provide the highest-ranked, stable, legally justifiable definition of powers, duties and rights in society, there are necessarily meta rules, at the top of any other legislation, requiring lower-level laws to spell out specifics. They need to cover vital principles to avoid

---

[38] See Eurobarometer.
[39] See Menédez, A. J. (2005), p. 122.

under-constitutionalization but must refrain from over-specifying lest they stifle the discretion necessary to deal with specific circumstances. The Draft Treaty comprises four, in various ways, highly interrelated parts of different level of detail but equal constitutional standing. To avoid the evident danger of over-constitutionalization, inevitable reforms require simplified procedures. But this drastically diminishes the constitutional role that the Draft Treaty can play.

Second, the Draft Treaty only slightly modifies the EU institutional framework. The European Council continues to operate as an advisory body to define general directions and priorities, largely based on consensus, with no legislative authority and now headed by a president elected for two-and-a-half years. Art. 29 clarifies the judicial system as "the European Court of Justice, the General Court and specialized courts." The High Representative for Common Foreign and Security Policy and the Commissioner for Foreign Relations are merged into a Union Minister of Foreign Affairs. The European Central Bank is identified as an EU institution. The Council of Ministers together with the European Parliament exercises legislative and budgetary functions by means of an extended co-decision procedure. The Commission continues its task of "inter-institutional programming," performs executive functions and (except for foreign and security policy) external representation.

In this context, the role of the European Parliament, as the only directly elected representation of European citizens, is said to be enhanced by extending the co-decision procedure into the "ordinary legislative procedure," making it the "co-legislator in almost all cases, with the exception of a dozen acts, where it will only be consulted." But, the Council's veto power qualifies the Parliament's position, and both institutions will continue to merely react to the Commission, thus maintaining its near monopoly of legislative initiative. Also, the EU Parliament, part of the EU institutional framework, has no existence outside, and therefore has a vested interest in maintaining the center's role. European citizens have the right to submit legislative proposals to the legislator if they manage to submit one million signatures from a "significant" number of Member States. But the Draft Treaty does not commit the EU to any reaction. Finally, national parliaments are mere bystanders, entitled to receive information and to guard national competences based on the principle of subsidiarity. But here also, the required process is far from clear-cut.

Third, Art. I-11 states that competences not conferred upon the Union in the Constitution remain with the Member States; Art. I–13 specifies those areas in which the Union has exclusive competence. Art. I–14 contains a non-exhaustive list of shared competences, in which both Union and Member States may act in parallel. Art. I–17 specifies areas, in which the Union will have competence to support, coordinate or supplement the actions of the Member States. Art. I–18 provides a "flexibility clause" that allows the Union to expand its reach based on the Council's unanimous endorsement of a Commission proposal and with the consent of the European Parliament. The exercise of any of these competences is governed by the principle of subsidiarity and proportionality.

Art. 11–3 states that "(u)nder the principle of subsidiarity, in areas which do not fall within its exclusive competence, the Union shall act only insofar as the objectives of the proposed action cannot be sufficiently be achieved by the Member States, either at central or at regional and local level, but can rather, by reason of the scale effects of the proposed action, be better achieved at Union level." And Art. 11–4 holds that "under the principle of proportionality, the content and form of Union action shall not exceed what is necessary to achieve the objectives of the Constitution."

What are the options for Member States to resist? National Parliaments have six weeks to send a reasoned opinion to object but that period may – in urgent cases – collapse to ten days.[40] To respond in time, national Parliaments need to continuously monitor EU activities and be able to change their legislative calendars to react. In any case, the Commission must review its proposal only if one-third of national Parliaments consider that a Commission proposal does not comply with the principle of subsidiarity. Hence, for any specific item affecting only a small number of Member States, coordination costs may be substantial and may move the competence to the EU center. Which raises the general issue of EU decision-making procedures, particularly voting rules, and is thereby perhaps the most significant change proposed by the Convention.

Fourth, the scope of unanimous decision making in the EU framework is broadly reduced. Laws on the Union's own "resources" and "financial perspectives" must be adopted unanimously, as must any revision of the Constitution itself. Also, in addition to some specific provisions, unanimity is retained in the field of taxation, partially, in the field of social policy and common foreign and security policy. However, so-called *passerelles* allow a unanimous decision to be (partially) transformed into a qualified majority.

---

[40] See both "Protocol on the Role of National Parliaments in the European Union" and "Protocol on the Application of the Principles of Subsidiarity and Proportionality" Annex I and II to the Draft Treaty.

The new Council voting system repeals the weighting of votes and bases the qualified majority on only two criteria – majority of Member States and the population of the Union. Double majority is seen as an expression of double legitimacy. Different from the Convention's proposal, Art. I–25 of the Draft Treaty raises the threshold, requiring (1) a qualified majority to be supported by 55% of the Member States representing 65% (rather than 60%) of the population, and (2) a blocking minority to comprise at least four Member States. Council members representing three-quarters of a blocking minority – whether based on Member States or population – can demand a vote to be postponed and the discussion to continue for a reasonable time to reach broader consensus within the Council.

The changes will move the probability of acceptance above the level resulting from the Nice Treaty but lower than the calculated 22% in line with the original proposal by the Convention. This will limit the risk of blockage and speed up decision making. But clearly, operational speed is not the sole objective in deciding on constitutional standards. To quote an observer "(e)ven more than before, a majority of highly regulated Member States could impose their regulations on the less regulated Members States. … As competition from the less regulated Member States diminishes, the intensity of regulation will increase in the highly regulated Member States."[41] Seen this way, EU constitutional reform may speed up operational efficiency, but by reduced regulatory competition and, ultimately, competitiveness. Other indicators point in the same direction.

Fifth, already Art. I–2 lists a set of common values, which are thought to be shared by Member States, and therefore are also reflected in the criteria for accession and suspending membership, Arts. I–58 and I–59. Art. I–3 covers the Union's internal and external objectives, including "the promotion of a highly competitive social market economy," which, refined in Art. III–115 – Art. III–122, implies fulfilling "requirements relating to employment and social policy." Art I–15 states: (1) "Member States shall coordinate their economic policies within the Union. To this end, the Council of Ministers shall adopt measures, in particular broad guidelines for these policies." (2) The Union shall take initiatives to ensure coordination of the employment policies of the Member States, in particular by defining guidelines for these policies. (3) The Union may take initiatives to ensure coordination of Member States' social policy." "The Member States shall facilitate the Union's tasks

---

[41] European Constitutional Group (2004) A Proposal for a European Constitution, *European Policy Forum*.

and refrain from any measure which could jeopardize the attainment of the Union's objectives" (Art. I–5, para 2, line 3). Despite its frequent assertions to the contrary, the EU clearly aims to create cohesion based on harmonizing policies rather than benefiting from internal regulatory competition. What is the economic rationale for the EU's broad-scale involvement?

Sixth, the sections above point to the need to clearly identify economies of scale and spillovers of governmental activities as the basis for task assignment. Research on fiscal federalism offers a host of considerations for how to determine at which level of government to allocate the responsibility for various tasks.[42] But there is no evidence that the EU's constitutional effort is inspired by any attempt to assess the economics of public service provision. The Draft Treaty, through the notions of subsidiarity and proportionality, merely establishes a process that Member States may follow to contest any further encroachment by the EU. The relevant protocols define the need to consider quantitative and qualitative evidence only at that review stage. In addition, contrary to the principles outlined in the Prodi White Paper on Good Governance, there has been no attempt to market test the need for the public provision of specific services or the allocation of tasks to local or regional levels of government. Any argument for or against specific task allocations is therefore bound to reflect the observer's (de-)centralization biases rather than economic evidence.

In sum, contrary to the Commission's intention to bring more democratic EU institutions closer to citizens, efforts to initiate and develop a EU constitution did not allow for public inputs and resulted in a document that the general public was to either endorse or reject *en bloc*. However, it is not only for process reasons that the rejection by the Dutch and the French referendum should be welcomed. Rather, the outcome of the process is simply unacceptable. Formally, the Draft Treaty's comprehensiveness requires simplified adjustment mechanisms that cancel out the constitutional role that it could play. Institutionally, the relationship between the Commission, the Councils, and citizen representation are largely maintained. The value of co-decision procedures has not been upgraded; citizens may provide input but its impact is unclear; national Parliaments are largely in a reactive role. Finally, utilizing the principles of subsidiarity and proportionality requires an economic assessment of public service provision that should have taken place at the outset of the constitutional effort. This might not have resulted in a completely different allocation of tasks and responsibilities, but it would

---

[42] See Oates, W. E., (1999) An essay on fiscal federalism, *Journal of Economic Literature*, 37(3), 1120–49.

have at least helped to address the EU's need for attaining deference and procedural and substantive consensus. But this would have required a dispassionate constitutional initiative able to side-step Europe's conventional patterns of political organization.

4. Re-engineering Europe – including regional and local perspectives?

Devising a constitution for Europe is also about finding the right scale at which to coordinate a competitive European economy. The current discussion focuses almost entirely on the interaction between the EU and nation states and thereby neglects important regional, or even urban dimensions. In fact many commentators now see city regions as motors of the European economy and as useful political vehicles to manage EU enlargement. Others advocate devolving power from national to regional and local governments simply because traditional state benefits – such as free trade among regions, the efficient provision of public goods, or access to national infrastructures and standards – could be made available within a broader and possibly more efficient, supranational framework.[43]

At present, European regions and metropolitan areas differ in their constitutional set-up, degree of autonomy and fiscal and plan-making powers. But they share an ambition that inadvertently challenges formal regional and national boundaries and the competencies of adjacent levels of political hierarchy. Already a cursory view suffices to show that issues surrounding the need for inter- and intra-regional coordination mirror those involved in constitutionalizing Europe. The ultimate response in either case must be the same.

At the regional level, a location's economic base and performance drives its choice between cooperative and competitive coordination. While cooperation within and among the EU's waning objective II regions appears motivated by the need to coopt competition,[44] urban growth areas are often observed to be single-mindedly pursuing their individual growth objective and to look outside their "home" base for economic leverage and political clout. The Region Urbaine de Lyon, for example, accounts for 80% of the GDP of the Rhone-Alps region but reportedly sees its economic interests more closely linked to its vibrant cross-regional partnership with Montpellier and

---

[43] Newman, P., (2000) Changing patterns of regional governance in the EU, *Urban Studies*, 37(5)(6), May.

[44] Amin, A., (1999) An institutionalist perspective on regional economic development, *International Journal of Urban and Regional Research*, 23(2), 365–78.

Marseilles and its own interaction with the European Commission. A host of issues may arise from this. But whether one debates the extent to which regional cooperation delays adjustments, or the need for strong regional centers to support ailing peripheries, in the final analysis, the question is who should decide and which process coordinates best?

National responses to growing regional demands reflect different views on policy aims and means. Italy and Spain granted more fiscal autonomy to regions, which allowed those with a strong tax base to compete with equally powerful European centers, while it kept others more closely tied to state transfers. Conversely, German *Länder*, in spite of having large responsibilities and resources, have no autonomy over taxation and, for reasons of social cohesion, see their tax revenues largely equalized. Following reunification, an initiative of the federal government has led to the review of regional and urban structures in an attempt to promote metropolitan areas for global competition. French regions, which contrary to the common view of French centralism had enjoyed substantial freedom to fix tax rates, recently lost some of their fiscal autonomy. In addition, Paris controls budgets and EU funds to hold regions accountable for infrastructure investments and forge competitive links between them. Here one may challenge the merits of fiscal competition in a federal system or any government's ability to outsmart markets in determining growth centers. But the key concern should be, who should decide and which process coordinates best?

Finally, the EU Commission's view on regions is at best ambivalent. On the one hand, the EU's Committee of Regions, set up in 1994 under the Maastricht Treaty, is an advisory body composed of the EU's regional and local authorities to ensure that regional and local prerogatives are represented. On the other hand, the Commission avoids antagonizing powerful Member States and therefore does not overtly encourage regional ambitions. For that reason, the Committee of Regions presents only a weak form of grassroots representation, and the constitutional convention rebuffed any effort by Catalonia, Scotland, Flanders or the German *Länder* to have a bigger role for regions written into the Draft Treaty. In addition, a European Parliament resolution of 1999 called on the EU to avoid uneven growth, which translated into initiatives by the EU's Structural Funds and the Cohesion Fund to achieve regional uniformity of factor incomes. Of course, one may question whether the EU should represent Member States, regions or citizens or whether any EU policy should aim for equity or efficiency as a means to sustain cohesion. But also here the key concern should be, who should decide and which process coordinates best?

In each case the response must be the same. Devolving legislative and regulatory powers in line with economic efficiency and deliberatively democratic ideals calls for unanimous decisions on (1) the centralization of only a few key functions necessary for the provision of truly large-scale public goods, (2) the creation and enforcement of simple, market-creating norms, and (3) the delegation of authority on all other issues to the most decentralized level of governance. This not only drastically limits the need for procedural and substantive consensus and deference to it, and so contributes to solving the EU's alliance problem, it also links civic virtues and efficiency and calls on citizens to self-select. What is the implication for the European constitutional efforts? Go back to the drawing board!

16 One competition standard to regulate global trade and protection?

Ralf Boscheck

On August 1, 2004, the WTO General Council's decision to implement the Doha Work Program[1] fell notably short of the "breakthrough" they were proclaimed to achieve. To be sure, only two years after quarrels over including competition policy in the "millennium trade negotiation round" had brought the WTO Seattle summit to a sudden halt, the Doha Declaration of 2001 put the issue back on to the agenda. But already at the Fifth Ministerial Conference at Cancun in September 2003, competition policy concerns were separated from central deliberations, making it easy to exclude them altogether from the 2004 WTO implementation plan. By November 2005, WTO ministerial declarations no longer identified respective liberalization targets, but clearly reflected reduced ambitions.[2] The significance of these events is often missed.

For nearly a decade, the EU and Japan had argued for an extension to the scope of GATT/WTO law, from its focus on public border measures to those domestic policies and private actions threatening to foreclose markets and distort competition. In their view, WTO members needed to enforce competition rules in line with shared principles for cases with an international dimension and to agree to agency cooperation and binding dispute settlement.[3] All along, US trade representatives accepted the need for collaboration among authorities but saw no merit in a trade-focused forum setting competition standards, or "second-guessing complex national prosecutorial decisions."[4] They held that, in the absence of a global consensus on economic, legal and procedural principles, efforts to harmonize diverse national regulations would create lowest-common-denominator rules, politicize national

---

[1] WTO (2004), *Doha Work Programme*, General Council Meeting, WT/L/579.
[2] Agence Europe (2005) Reduced ambition draft ministerial declaration for Hong Kong submitted by Pascal Lamy.
[3] For an early presentation see Brittan, L., (1992) *A framework for international competition*, World Economic Forum: Davos.
[4] Klein, J. I., (1999) *A reality check on antitrust rules in the WTO*, Paris: OECD.

antitrust enforcement, and overburden the WTO system. Negotiators of developing countries, while typically impartial about the subject, as of late, also began to support the separation of competition and trade policy matters. To some, this change reflected the need of developing countries to avoid linking trade concerns to issues in which their technical expertise remained limited; to others it was better explained by the massive increase in contingent protection applied by developing countries themselves. And yet, at the beginning of 2007, it became increasingly difficult to deny the need for some statutory mechanism lest discriminatory trade measures continued to undermine the integrity of international trade accords and their constraining impact on domestic protectionism. Antidumping (AD) presents *the* case in point.

Today, 103 years after the first antidumping law was passed in Canada, and with ninety-eight countries enacting such rules to potentially cover more than 90% of worldwide imports,[5] antidumping proceedings only rarely live up to domestic competition standards or general economic principles. Rather, with tariffs, voluntary export restraints or safeguards drastically reduced, banned, or enjoining compensation, WTO-condoned antidumping action has turned into a powerful trade weapon. Its threatened use alone can cause international competitors to raise prices and effectively agree to collude at consumers' expense. Mounting welfare losses are only topped by the cost of corrupted global trade.

Reform initiatives abound – ranging from the promotion of unilateralism to diverse models of multilateral coordination, often involving the use of common, centrally or decentrally applied competition standards. Yet, while the drawbacks of the former are sufficiently clear, the latter usually presuppose that broadly diverse regulatory criteria can be harmonized and objective enforcement, review and arbitration institutionally ensured. But multilateralists typically don't answer the question of why national authorities, in reality, would limit their discretion over the domestic allocation of trade protection and which preconditions would be required for this outcome to be achieved. This chapter aims to do just that.

By way of introduction, section 1 applies concepts of constitutional economics to discuss *the political economy of trade and protection,* the domestic foundation of international trade commitments, and the interest in broadening the scope of the WTO to address competition policy concerns. Section 2

---

[5] Zanardi, M., (2006), Does antidumping use contribute to trade liberalization? Working Paper, University of Tilburg.

tackles the processes and standards for *judging injurious trade*, particularly dumping, and calls for institutional reforms in pursuit of long-term efficiency and consumer benefits. Section 3 discusses various initiatives towards creating the prerequisite *global competition code*. Section 4 evaluates *conditions for change* that would motivate a switch from current practice. Section 5 presents a *summary and conclusion*.

1. The political economy of trade and protection

Trade theories – old and new[6] – trace gains from trade to productive specialization based on some advantageous factor endowment. But they also recognize that necessary adjustments to any given or to-be-created comparative advantage may trigger calls for temporary protection. Such interventions may take the form of active interference, or entail the simple condonation of what otherwise would be considered anti-competitive practice. They may be considered to be blatant "beggar-thy-neighbor" policies, legitimate forms of domestic income redistribution, or simple expressions of a sovereign choice of an economic or cultural model. Either way they distort international production and exchange relations and call for common rules to stabilize the global trading system and constitutionally restrain intra- and international protectionist free riding. But any regulatory intervention is itself the outcome of a rent-seeking and rent-shifting process.[7]

Politicians broker between those who demand protection and those who are unable to efficiently organize protest and therefore pay for it. Typically, regulatory outcomes are bent in favor of domestic constituencies and focused producer interest at the expense of foreigners and dispersed consumer demands. Producer interests receive an additional boost due to the fact that the immobility of factors creates sector coalitions across differences based on

---

[6] For a synthesis of the arguments in favor of or against compromising the free trade ideal see Bhagwati, J. N., (1971) The generalized theory of distortions and welfare. In Bhagwati, J. N. *et al.*, (eds.) *Trade, balance of payments and growth*, Amsterdam: North Holland. For an overview of modern, strategic trade theory see Brander, J. A., Spencer, B. J., (1981) Tariffs and the extraction of foreign monopoly rents and potential entry, *Canadian Journal of Economics*, 14(3), 371–89; Krugman, P. R., (1984) Targeted industrial policies: Theories and evidence. In *Industrial change and public policy*, Kansas City: Federal Reserve Bank of Kansas City, pp. 123–56. For a critique see Dixit, A., (1984) International trade policy for oligopolistic industries, *Economic Journal*, Conference Papers, 94, 1–16.

[7] See Buchanan, J. M., (1987) The constitution of economic policy, *American Economic Review*, 77(3), 243–50; Hauser, H., (1986) Domestic policy foundation and domestic policy function of international trade rules, *Aussenwirtschaft*, 41(II/III), 171–84; Petersmann, E.-U., (1986) Trade policy as a constitutional problem, *Aussenwirtschaft*, 41(II/III), 405–39.

factor-income and because the benefits of protection may be more visible than its cost. Yet, there are substantial costs besides the immediate effects on income distribution. Protectionism means free riding on the benefit of an open international trading system and is likely to result in a loss of goodwill and trust.[8] As a result, a government's intervention into free trade in response to a particular interest may end up reducing the attractiveness of its entire citizenry as an international trading partner. International trade commitments, from promises of national treatment to the automatic, non-discriminatory extension of most-favored nation treatment, can limit governmental discretion in domestic political affairs provided the chosen monitoring and enforcement mechanisms are effective.

Two classes of enforcement methods may be briefly compared. *Trade retaliation* in response to non-compliance is seldom found to directly harm the responsible perpetrator or to be limited to an adequate tit-for-tat response.[9] Rather measures are easily corrupted to further offensive rather than defensive aims; brinkmanship spills over and destabilizes broader commercial relations. Alternatively, a nation's trade commitments can be *internally enforced*. To do so, trade obligations need to be covered by national legislation, and, as private rights, domestically enforced against the imposing government. This presupposes that trade policy actions and their impact are made transparent, and citizens and foreigners have equal standing and access to the law. In addition, replacing "trade diplomats" with "nation-blind" judiciaries is apt to make trade commitments at once more predictable and effective. Still, the complexity of regulatory obligations will require broad discretion to be held by national authorities, which may compromise the consistency and legitimacy of national enforcement as seen from outside. To deal with this, complexity may be reduced by restricting the subject matter and the heterogeneity of parties involved; conversely, national adjudication of international agreements may be made subsidiary to, or replaced by, central, third-party monitoring and arbitration. Obviously, the latter option not only poses questions regarding the capacity and objectivity of that international body, but allegiance to it sacrifices national legal sovereignty for the benefit of sustaining

---

[8] Kindleberger, C. P., (1986) International public goods without government, *American Economic Review*, 76(1), 7.

[9] See Richardson (1986) for discussions of retaliatory responses to non-compliance, Richardson, D. J. (1986) The new political economy of trade policy. In Krugman, P. (ed.) *Strategic trade policy and the new international economics*, Cambridge MA: MIT Press; Kaempfer, W. H., Lowenberg, A., (1988) The theory of international sanctions: A public choice approach, *American Economic Review*, 78(4), 786–93.

international trade and deeper systemic integration. What is the institutional record to date?

Both the GATT and the WTO present rather incomplete responses to intra- and international protectionist free riding. The original GATT specified principles of reciprocity, non-discrimination, tariffication,[10] and legitimate safeguards but provided no framework for implementation and, as an institution, had no independent right of initiative to investigate, censure or impose penalties. The WTO replaced the provisional treaty that created the GATT with a permanent international trade organization that in a legal sense is equivalent to the IMF and the World Bank. Whereas the GATT committed members to a set of common principles, but allowed for "individualized" application, the WTO's Final Act binds signatories to both specific, in the sense of measurable and scheduled, as well as general commitments to reduce protectionism. Whereas under the GATT, a member's veto of panel formation or panel decision blocked dispute settlement, the WTO provides time schedules for arbitration and requires consensus of all members of the dispute settlement body to obstruct the process. In addition, the Trade Policy Review Body surveys member countries' policy making in an effort to: (1) enhance domestic transparency of governmental decisions; (2) promote member compliance with multilateral trade commitments; and (3) assess the impact of member policies on the functioning of the multilateral trade system. Still, although the WTO improves the GATT in matters of governance and dispute settlement, major challenges remain.

Vital obligations regarding services, intellectual property, trade-related investment measures, subsidies, technical barriers and antidumping rules have all been kept general. Although the WTO recognizes the "inherent value" of making the effects of trade policy-decisions transparent, the Trade Policy Review Mechanism neither quantifies the costs of protectionism nor provides a basis for dispute settlement. The organization insists that transparency is voluntary.[11] Next, enforcement has improved only slightly and the producer bias is maintained, as, just like under the GATT, individuals and private parties have no significant legal and procedural standing. Although WTO commitments may be given "direct effect", as in Article XX challenge procedures, the scope of international agreements overriding national law is still very limited. Moreover, as the WTO can only authorize another

---

[10] Tariffs are preferable to NTBs as they are price-based, transparent and precisely measurable.

[11] See WTO Agreement, Annex 3 § B. See Bronckers, M. C. E. J., (1996) Rehabilitating antidumping and other trade remedies through cost–benefit analyses, *Journal of World Trade*, 30(2), 5–37, for a critique along these lines.

country to take retaliatory counter-measures, rather than impose a fine, trade distortion is systemic. Therefore, the WTO may increase the visibility of trade violations but compliance remains essentially voluntary. In fact, members that have lost arbitration proceedings occasionally chose to "note" rather than "adopt" arbitration rules or threatened to leave the organization altogether.[12]

But then, can one expect an organization that systematically under-enforces minimalist commitments to deal with an expanded agenda of "new trade issues", especially if these reach deeply into particularistic dimensions of societies and challenge national standards and legislation? Will an expanded trade agenda reduce regulatory segmentation, improve integration and thereby strengthen the WTO?[13] Or will new concerns overburden the agenda, dilute multilateral agreements and promote bilateral understandings and unilateral actions? One of these "new trade issues" involves the need to devise common standards for dealing with the rise in contingent protection and injurious trade.

2. Judging injurious trade

Since the signing of the GATT in 1947, 136 countries have bound themselves to multilateral trade concessions growing the world trade volume 16-fold, at three times the rate of global output.[14] Today, the WTO endeavors to commit signatories to *one* common set of rules whose application may be challenged in the course of a dispute settlement process. It is this control and the elimination of significant barriers to trade that may explain the sharp increase in various forms of contingent protection, as yet not subject to multilateral trade agreements. The prime example, antidumping action, is to relieve domestic producers from "unfair" and "injurious" low-price imports.

---

[12] Petersmann (1994) finds that throughout the 1980s a dramatic increase in non-compliance occurred, notably by the US, Canada and the EU. See Petersmann, E.-U., (1994) The dispute settlement system of the World Trade Organization and the evolution of the GATT dispute settlement system since 1948, *Common Market Law Review*, 31(6), 1157–244. Already at the outset, the US warned that it would pull out of the WTO if it were to suffer three adverse, "unfair" rulings within five years. The US was to determine what constitutes "fairness". (Rapid, January 28, 1995).

[13] Zampetti and Sauvé (1996) discuss potentially beneficial economies of scale and scope in rule making that will strengthen the WTO and improve enforcement. Zampetti, A. B., Sauvé, P. (1996) Onwards to Singapore: The international contestability of markets and the new trade agenda, *The World Economy*, 19(3), 333–43.

[14] OECD (1998) *Open markets matter: The benefits of trade and investment liberalization*, Paris: OECD.

At the beginning of the 1990s, a *total* of 405 antidumping orders were globally in place, roughly two-thirds of which had been brought by developed countries. At the beginning of the year 2000, the number of investigations initiated by *per year* had risen to 328 from an annual average of 232 for the preceding three years, and traditional users (the US, EU, Australia, Canada) accounted for only 46% of all the filings. Clearly, WTO-condoned antidumping action has spread to become *the* global trade remedy of choice – but in the process, its use and impact changed. While, during the last two decades of the twentieth century, the US topped the list of antidumping initiations, it ranked rather lowly in terms of intensity, i.e. the number of petitions divided by the real value of imports. New users, such as South Africa and Argentina, with intensity scores fourteen times higher than that of the US,[15] more easily resorted to AD filing and increasingly directed their actions against developing countries. From January 2002 to April 2003, India initiated sixty-six antidumping cases against China alone, imposing countervailing duties on forty-four products.[16] Between July and December 2005, China faced thirty-three such allegations resulting in the imposition of duties in twenty-two cases; during the same time, China itself launched thirteen antidumping investigations antidumping, more than any other country.[17]

In any case, however, the use of antidumping procedures, commonly justified with reference to some unfair private anti-competitive conduct or discriminatory governmental policy, only rarely lives up to domestic competition standards or broader economic principles.[18] They are the outcome of domestic policy-making processes that discount broadly spread gains from freer trade to react to focused protectionist demands. Given their massive welfare costs, the increased use of antidumping can only be explained by a combination of murky assessment practices and deficient institutional restraints.

Just consider the direct impact on the US economy. Totaling the direct costs of restricting imports and maintaining such protection, the net economic loss to the US economy due to antidumping and countervailing duty actions at the beginning of this century was estimated to be $4bn per annum.[19] This does not cover related costs of business closure, industry

---

[15] Zanardi (2006) presents an in-depth discussion of AD filing statistics.

[16] *Hindustan Times*, April 22, 2003.

[17] The Economist (2006) *Emerging market indicators: Antidumping*, May 11, 2006.

[18] Willig (1998) concludes that less than 10% of international antidumping petitions in the US, the EU and Canada in the 1980s could be justified on competition policy grounds. See Willig, R., (1998) *Competition policy and antidumping*, Brookings Trade Policy Forum.

[19] Gallaway, M. P., Blonigen, B. A., Flynn, J. E., (1999) Welfare costs of the US antidumping and countervailing duty laws, *Journal of International Economics*, 49(2), 211–44;

relocation and long-term skill loss. Of the about 250 antidumping petitions filed by US steel producers since 1980, around 100 were still enforced twenty years later "protecting" less than 0.1% of the US labor force at an estimated 40% cost-penalty to steel-consuming sectors employing more than 50 times as many workers.[20] Similar efforts in the 1980s to protect the US car industry cut consumers' real incomes between US$3.50 and US$5.50 for each dollar of added profit; each job saved cost consumers between US$93,000 to US$250,000 per year.[21] Although average US antidumping duties have been reduced from 50.6% during 1992/3 to 41.9% for 1997/9, the value of imports affected has increased substantially. While $8.34bn worth of US imports were covered by antidumping duties between 1983 and 1993, the respective value for the next ten years until 2003 nearly doubled to $14bn.[22] Comparable figures can be found for most economies delaying adjustments while seeking to "benefit" from free trade.[23] The explanation for this general state of affairs is equally universal: imprecise antidumping standards and inadequate stakeholder representation.

The original Article VI, para 1 of the GATT condemns export sales below normal value when they "cause or threaten material injury to an established industry in the territory of the contracting party or materially retard the establishment of a domestic industry." Yet, the Kennedy, Tokyo and Uruguay Rounds of trade negotiations left evident issues surrounding industry definition and the links between dumping and injury unclear, causing a *de facto* relaxation of causality and injury standards and a perversion of the underlying economic rationales.[24] In assessing the fairness of import prices, for example, some national authorities compare these either with an importer's domestic price levels or its cost of production. Technically, the former requires a comparison of like products/markets, but authorities, upon finding price differentials, do not judge them for what they are – a sign of maximizing profit and welfare. The latter amounts to *ordering* an acceptable margin on a product level and thereby bans typical market entry strategies like cross-subsidization and penetration pricing. Either way, the often applied "constructed average cost approach" systematically penalizes efficient

---

[20] Boscheck, R., (2000) Managing structural adjustment in the global steel industry!? *IMD Industry Note*.

[21] OECD (1987) *The costs of restricting imports: The automobile industry*, Paris: OECD, p. 38.

[22] According to Mankiw N. and Swagel P. L. (2005) Antidumping: The third rail of trade policy, *Foreign Affairs*, 48(4), 107–19.

[23] See e.g., Coppel, J., Durand, M., (1999) Trends in market openness *OECD Working Paper* No. 221.

[24] For a discussion see Boscheck, R., (2001) The governance of global market relations, *World Competition*, 24(2), 1–18; and Trebilcock, M. J., Howse, R., (1995) *The regulation of international trade*, London: Routledge.

importers. Similarly, standards for establishing injury in the sense of "not inconsequential, immaterial or unimportant," cannot but lead to a near general acceptance of injury claims, irrespective of alleged causes or impacts on sales, capacity utilization, profits or cash flow.[25]

This is not to say that dumping remedy is conceptually flawed. But of the three types of economic rationales commonly advanced in favor of antidumping – international price discrimination, intermittent dumping, and predatory pricing – only the latter provides a cogent, but largely theoretical justification. Charging different prices in different markets may lead to a total increase, rather then reduction, in output and value creation, which limits welfare concerns to the costs of sustaining segregated market segments – but these are borne by the exporter, not the importer. Next, long-term systematic, or intermittent, dumping may injure consumers only if domestic supply is unable to adjust, which relates to concerns for efficient factor markets rather than trade remedies. Finally, predatory pricing is defined as "systematically pricing below cost with a view of intimidating and/or eliminating rivals in an effort to bring about a market price higher than would otherwise prevail."[26] But for predatory pricing to be viable, the exporter's home market or some third country must provide a source of cross-subsidy. Given that insight into these markets is vital for establishing predatory conduct, the question is which agency seems best positioned and most likely to judge the case in line with broader welfare objectives rather than particular protectionist demands?

If policy is to be institutionally constrained to promote trade as the means for an efficient, global specialization of production, there is a necessary case to substitute antitrust for antidumping and delegate the assessment of dumping charges to the exporter's competition authorities. To some, this amounts to "putting the fox in charge of the hen house".[27] To others it means limiting the inconsistent application and potential abuse of trade remedies, and avoiding double standards for dealing with domestic vs. international competitors. This proposal requires the decentralized application of harmonized competition principles and assessment practices subject to arbitration. In addition, it calls on national authorities to switch from seeking trade relief to

---

[25] From January 1980 to July 1997, such claims were rejected only 12% of the time after the preliminary investigation and 17% of the time after the final investigation. See Klitgaard, T., Schiele, K., (1998) Free versus fair trade: The dumping issue, *Current Issues in Economics and Finance, Federal Reserve Bank of New York* 4(8), August.

[26] Compare with the Sherman Act, 15 U.S.C., para 2 (1988).

[27] See Morgan, C., (1996) Competition policy and antidumping, *Journal of World Trade*, 30(5), 61–88;

pursuing antitrust remedies and, by that, to limit their discretion in dealing with the needs of domestic protectionists. So what are the options for harmonizing international antitrust principles and what are the conditions for change?

3. A global competition code?

The link between international trade and national competition rules has been a focal point of academic and policy debates for more than fifty years.[28] Recently, the topic has regained wider public attention with the formation of a WTO working group to explore multilateral disciplines relating to competition law and the respective, conflicting views held by the heads of the US and EU antitrust authorities. While the need to coordinate is broadly shared, the way to do this is not.

Clearly, inconsistencies in national competition rules and law enforcement burden international commerce through uncertainty and transaction costs, or worse, may give rise to market access barriers, abuse of dominance, concerns over reciprocity and retaliatory trade sanctions. Hence, countries stand to gain from putting institutional limits to the temptation of systematically under-enforcing or discriminatorily applying legal standards. But, as in any conventional Prisoner's Dilemma, the question is how to coordinate in a way that avoids a universal adoption of a free-riding strategy which would render each party worse off.

Should coordination be limited to mere procedural cooperation, or should it involve substantive agreements on the aims and means of competition policy? Should such efforts lead to a binding list of methods that a country ought not to adopt rather than which it must adopt; and would these commitments link a small/large number of fairly homogenous/heterogenous economies with more/less developed competition policies? Next, how would all of this affect the standing of those who could bring a case, against whom and under which jurisdiction? Finally, which forum would be suited for this effort?

In principle, coordination options range from seeking a comprehensive and centrally administered competition policy – a "one world view"[29] – to

---

[28] For complementary reviews of the literature see Scott, A., (2005) Cain and Abel? Trade and competition laws in the global economy, *Modern Law Review*, 68(1), 135–55; Fox, E., (2003) International antitrust and the Doha Dome *Virginia Journal of International Law* 43, 911, 930; Cadot, O., Grether, J.-M., de Melo, J., (2000) Trade and competition policy, *Journal of World Trade*, 34(3), 1–20.

[29] For an exposition of this view see Fox and Ordover (1996).

rejecting any direct cooperation and insisting on liberalized trade and investments to effect regulatory harmonization.[30] In between these nodes, an array of coordination opportunities extends from mere bilateral, procedural collaboration via focused sector- or issue-based agreements, to multilateral accords on minimum or broader antitrust standards.

Obviously, pure reliance on unilateral, extra-territorial enforcement of national competition principles is apt to meet resistance among trading partners.[31] In its simplest form, coordination may be achieved through bilateral accords, such as those negotiated by the US with Canada, Australia, Germany and the EU, merely to notify of pending enforcement actions. Over time, these have been expanded to the extension of investigation powers and to the obligation to consider the welfare consequences on others – the principles of positive comity.[32] Still, bilateral, procedural cooperation does not automatically result in "soft harmonization" of substantive law.[33] Variances in national competition laws may relate to broadly different conceptions of the respective ends and means, procedures and processes, and relations to other economic and non-economic policies.[34] Yet even if a purely bilateral, substantive agreement was attainable, it is unlikely to be desirable if it sustains global market distortions and discriminatory practices. Harmonizing substantive standards on a much broader, multilateral base, however, requires simpler rules to be applied with broader discretion to national enforcement and commensurate concerns with free riding. How can one ensure the objectivity of national enforcement agents, especially in areas that relate to international transactions and may even involve the state as actor? How can one motivate national enforcement to be subordinated to international, objective third-party

---

[30] For a presentation of this position, see Lall, A. (1996) Competition policy in Singapore: There is none. In Green, C. J., Rosenthal, D. E. (eds.) *Competition regulation in the Pacific rim*, New York: Oceana Publications.

[31] With the exception of US antitrust law, national competition rules do not claim jurisdiction over national firms in outside markets. Yet most national trade laws do not directly cover purely private business practices, so some limited form of cooperation is unavoidable. For evidence of the growing appreciation of the need to coordinate, even among more unilaterally inclined parties, like the US, see WTO (1997) *Annual Report*, 1, Geneva: WTO, p. 85.

[32] See the 1991 US-EU Antitrust Cooperation Agreement and its revised form of June 1998. For a practical application of the notion to interagency cooperation, see Hoekman, B. M., Mavroidis, P. C., (1996) Dumping, antidumping and antitrust, *Journal of World Trade*, 30(1), 27–52 and see section 4.3 below.

[33] For a suggestion of "soft harmonization" see Janow, M. E., (1999) Contribution to the antitrust and trade policy roundtable. In Hawk, B. (ed.) *International antitrust law and policy*, New York: Fordham Corporate Law Institute.

[34] Consider the important differences between the US and the EU regarding which business practices are deemed illegal per se and which are conditionally justifiable, and which size and concentration thresholds trigger welfare concerns, or whether and how to deal with so-called non-economic interest or the acts of the State.

review, or even establish a supra-national authority that could command allegiance?

The answer given by the WTO on various occasions presumes that national authorities, realizing that enforcement of national competition law can lower global welfare, will not pursue their short-term interest.[35] But by asking national authorities to apply a *world-welfare-view*, the WTO essentially restates the case of free trade, which, if generally accepted and acted upon, would largely obviate the need for third-party intervention including that of the WTO. This ideal does not stand up to the reality of political economy and rent-seeking behavior. Unfortunately, numerous policy initiatives – past and present – equally fail to answer the original question.

Already the International Trade Organization (ITO), outlined in the 1948 Havana Charter, was to investigate member countries, permitting private practices in restraints to trade and market access, and recommend and monitor remedial actions. But the ITO did not pass US Congressional approval over concerns for US legal sovereignty. Similarly, competition standards embedded in the UNCTAD's Code on Restrictive Business Practices and the UN's Code of Conduct for Transnational Corporations were thrown out during debates on how to deal with multinational versus state-owned enterprises. Only the OECD Agreement on Restrictive Practices, essentially a notification requirement, was accepted by all member countries. In all but the latter case, parties' concerns with national legal sovereignty and corporate interest reflected a primary interest in protecting national competitors rather than the global competitive process.

The only case where competition standards have been completely harmonized and have in fact replaced trade policy – the EU – continues to require deeper systemic integration and cohesion measures. No other major regional agreement, such as the Australia New Zealand Closer Economic Trade Agreement (ANZCERTA), the Canada-US Free Trade Agreement, or NAFTA, attempts to harmonize competition laws, allowing governments, in principle, to retain their second line of protectionist defense. Responding to this, academic proposals have kept the debate on harmonizing competition rules alive.

The Munich Group of competition law experts, for example, proposed a set of mandatory competition rules to be incorporated into the GATT

---

[35] See WTO (1997) Chapter 4, III.2, for an exposition of the argument see Bachetta, M., Horn, H., Mavroidis, P., (1997) Do negative spillovers from nationally pursued competition policies provide a case for multilateral competition rules, Geneva: WTO Working Paper.

and directly invoked by private parties before national courts. Implemented by an International Antitrust Authority operating through the offices of national competition agencies, the code, its interpretation as well as findings may be challenged before a permanent antitrust panel as part of the WTO dispute settlement process. As a plurilateral treaty, the International Antitrust Code would be applicable only to those WTO members that sign it.

Similarly, Scherer (1994) proposed the creation of an International Competition Policy Office (ICPO) within the ambit of the WTO, holding both investigative and enforcement powers. Signatories would submit to common rules regarding import and export cartels, abuse of dominance, and mergers and initially would be allowed to cushion adjustment by exempting three sectors from the ban of export cartels. The broad language of "monopolistic practices" is purposely used "to cover many complex practices upon which a general international consensus would be difficult or impossible to achieve. It limits signatory nations' ability to engage in aggressive unilateralism, ... (that may) evoke retaliation ... and a breakdown of harmonious trading relationships."[36]

More recently, Fox (2003) reassesses the continuum of global antitrust governance ranging from a stand-alone world antitrust enforcement system to mere technical assistance and peer-review. Halfway between, national authorities are seen to be networking to resolve truly international concerns and issue framework directives based on a basic consensus over substantive antitrust principles. Cooperation is to be channeled by incorporating principles of non-discrimination, transparency and due process into a binding WTO agreement, so as to "economically democratize a still balkanized world in a global economy."[37]

All proposals stress voluntary commitments, phased adjustments, and the plurilateral nature of the agreement, but while the first two foresee central third-party arbitration under the auspices of the WTO, the third discusses a broader range of coordination mechanisms. But neither one provides a rationale for why rent-seeking political parties would want to promote any scheme that would tie their hands in the domestic political process. From the point of view of public choice, the immediate answer is because governments see it in their best interest to do so. What is required to achieve this?

---

[36] See Scherer (1994), chapter 5, especially proposals 10 and 11.   [37] Fox (2003), p. 930.

4. Conditions for change

For one, there is a need to expose the differences in trade and competition policy objectives and the constituencies they serve. Next, antitrust principles and trade commitments must be directly enforced in national courts with citizens and foreigners having equal standing and subject to international third-party arbitration. Direct enforcement, however, is not sufficient unless it includes enforcement against the offending government, which would require acts of state to be included, for example, into US antitrust law. Also, given problems of collective action, private parties are more likely to enforce their rights if the costs and benefits of policy decisions were transparent. This in turn requires that all affected interests have access to institutions and information and that their views are being timely and systematically solicited. In that situation, the question still remains whether the WTO seems best in housing such an initiative and how to roll it out. To assess the preconditions for an international coordination of competition-related trade issues, antidumping provides a useful reference.

Exposing differences in policy objectives and constituencies

Trade and antitrust laws typically differ in objectives, patterns of influence that shape enforcement policies, procedures and institutions, as well as crucial injury and pricing standards. US trade and competition laws serve to illustrate this.

The administration of US trade law follows the trade policy objectives as set by the President, the US Trade Representative, the Department of Commerce and Congress. Although trade law action may be reviewed by the US Court of International Trade and the US Court of Appeals, US trade law as such is typically not bound by adjudicative rules. It pursues trade remedies, i.e. duties or restrictions on imports and market access, in case harm is "not inconsequential, immaterial or unimportant" but does not require evidence of predatory intent or case-specific economic analysis.

Conversely, US antitrust enforcement is carried out by the Department of Justice and the Federal Trade Commission subject to congressional oversight, the Administrative Procedure Act (APA) and reviewed by the US Court of Appeals. US antitrust laws primarily focus on the competitive process and outcome as assessed by measures of consumer welfare and require a demonstration of unreasonable restraints to trade or a substantial lessening of competition to establish injury. Put differently, while US trade law provides a broadly discretionary and fairly blunt executive tool "to pursue the competitiveness of domestic competitors vis-à-vis foreigners . . . rather than competitive processes or consumer welfare,"[38] US antitrust policy is much more tightly constrained and guided by principles of predictable enforcement and economic efficiency. It is largely for that reason that both Canada and Mexico but also ABA's Antitrust Sections argued for substituting antitrust for trade law in NAFTA. The US resistance to this does is not surprising and sheds light on the structure of interest representation.

Giving consumers access to institutions, information and legal standing

Articles 6 and 12 of the WTO Antidumping Agreement outline procedural rights of interested parties but limit consumers and users to present information on dumping, injury and causality rather than on the broader public interest. In fact, the WTO does not prescribe any cost–benefit analysis of antidumping relief. The United States Antidumping Code also does not contain any public interest provision. Canadian and EU authorities, however, are held to assess the broader impact of antidumping, at least in principle. Yet, while the Canadian International Trade Tribunal professes concern that "concentration on producer interest alone is too narrow a focus and consumer interest must be considered, . . . in practice, only a few public interest hearings have been convened since the provision was enacted in 1985, and consumer groups did not initiate or participate in any of these hearings."[39] Similarly, while Art. 21 of the EU Antidumping regulation[40] denies relief unless it is in the broader community interest, and for that reason explicitly asks consumer organizations to submit written views at the beginning of an investigation,[41] consumers or user groups have no right of disclosure or

---

[38] For reviews see Applebaum, H. M., (1987) The interface of trade/competition law and policy: An antitrust perspective, *Antitrust Law Journal*, 56(2), 409; and in (1998) The interface of the trade laws and the antitrust laws, *George Mason Law Review*, 6(3), 479–92.

[39] Trebilcock and House (1995), p. 111 and Chapter 5, footnote 99.

[40] Regulation No. 3283/94, O.J. 1994, L 349/1, revised O.J. 1995, C319/10. Another mitigating factor is the lesser duty rule. Antidumping duties will not equal the dumping margin if the EU authorities considered that a lesser duty would suffice to remove the injury suffered by the European industry as a result of dumped imports, Arts. 7(2) and 9(4).

[41] Upon receipt of such comments, parties have access to non-confidential files and the right to request an oral hearing whose content is to be taken into consideration in the final decision. See Regulation No. 3283/94, Article 6(5), 6(7).

to request an interim review of antidumping measures.[42] EU authorities do not need to verify any information other than from producers and traders and are not obliged to publish the results of any cost–benefit analysis. Furthermore, community interest does not figure during sunset reviews. Hence, although there is marked improvement in the procedural position of user and consumer interest relative to earlier rulings,[43] their standing still does not equal that of producers. Art. 21(1) points to "the need to eliminate the trade distorting effects of injurious dumping and to restore effective competition," but antidumping relief will be rejected only when relief is clearly *not* in the Community's interest. Clearly, the EU's definition of "Community interest" seems to include producers first, then users, but does not aspire to the world-welfare view proposed by the WTO; the latter is true for the US and Canada as well.

Exposing the constituencies and welfare effects of trade protection and improving institutional access for consumers would drive policy makers to institutionalize the application of harmonized competition standards to domestic – private and public – distortions of trade. This would mean a switch from current practice. So far, however, governments have effectively avoided publishing comprehensive assessments of the costs and benefits of protection or extending the WTO Trade Policy Review Mechanism to evaluate trade remedies and domestic policy processes. Already in the 1980s, trading nations greeted, but never effectively adopted, similar suggestions. The Leutwiler Group, for example, proposed a "protection balance sheet" with which a government was to identify annually all trade restrictions and subsidies benefiting particular industries.[44] Twenty years later, Baldwin (2004) recommended that the administration of antidumping law should be based on detailed and fact-based demonstration of causality and supported by policy-oriented studies reflecting diverse stakeholder interests.[45] Clearly, any international commitment and institution will be unable to constrain domestic policy processes and guarantee the advantages of an open, rule-based international policy, unless it is backed by transparency and appropriate domestic representation. What would make governments change their views?

---

[42] Regulation No. 3283/94, Art. 20.
[43] For decisions on data access and presentation see *BEUC* v. *Commission*, Case C-170/89 (1991) ECR I-5709, paras 18–23; see also Regulation No. 2423/88, Art. 7(4)a9, O.J. 1988, L.209/88.
[44] See the GATT (1985) *Trade policies for a better future*, Annex II, Geneva.
[45] Baldwin, R. E., (2005) The political economy of reforming antidumping laws, *World Economy*, 28(5), 745–47.

Addressing this question, Jan Tumlir, the former head economist of the GATT, proposed the introduction of self-executing treaty provisions, giving citizens legal rights against governments that violate the principles of open, non-discriminatory trade.[46] Building on this, Petersmann (1999) detailed its foundation in international law by referring back to the Kantian notion of international constitutionalism based on three types of linked pledges: interlocking guarantees of individual civil rights within a nation, international rights of states in relations with one another, and cosmopolitan rights pertaining to the relationships of states and individuals in external affairs.[47] The resulting arrangement does not depend on rule enforcement by international organizations, but on self-enforcement. International guarantees of freedom and non-discrimination reinforce equivalent national commitments. For Petersmann, EC law provides a model. It grants citizens the right, in principle, to enforce their market freedoms against protectionist interests, calls for the progressive replacement of national policies by common commercial and monetary policies, and links the evolution of EC law and institutions to international laws and agreements.[48] Man, pursuing his cosmopolitan rights in international affairs, constrains and legitimizes national policies. The universal pursuit of individual self-restraint balances unbridled self-interest, governs and constitutes market relations, and provides the foundation for any public rules and coordination.

But Petersmann also does not fail to notice that in practice the system is frequently hollowed out. National and international institutions "collude" to evade domestic constitutional restraints and thereby lower the legal and judicial protection of equal citizen rights. Hence – while for public consumption the WTO General Council's decision to implement the Doha Program on August 1, 2004 was displayed as a breakthrough – in reality it was a step back to serve focused stakeholder interests. It reflects the assumption that it is possible to benefit from global markets without any global market governance. Facing that attitude, one cannot but agree with the tenor of recent WTO ministerial declarations cautioning against any ambitions on further substantive liberalization.

---

[46] Tumlir, J., (1983) International economic order and democratic constitutionalism, *ORDO*, 34, 82.

[47] See Kant, I. (1971) Perpetual peace. In Reiss, H. (ed.) (1971) *Political writings*, Cambridge: Cambridge University Press; Petersmann, E.-U., (1999) How to constitutionalize international law and foreign policy for the benefit of civil society, *Michigan Journal of International Law*, 20(1), 1–30.

[48] Petersmann, E.-U., (1994), p. 28.

5. Summary and conclusion

Exposing the constituencies and welfare effects of trade protection and improving institutional access for consumers would drive policy makers to institutionalize the application of harmonized competition standards to domestic – private and public – distortions of trade. National authorities, unwilling to limit their discretion over the domestic allocation of trade protection, resist this switch from current practice. A liberal constitution, granting cosmopolitan citizen rights, would facilitate a deeper, self-enforcing systemic integration and provide the foundation for the governance of global market relations.

Part V

An observation in closing

17 Addressing the market paradox

Ralf Boscheck

The question is: what are the values that are built into the dominant contemporary economic theories that specialists generate, managers and policymakers use, popular movements turn into slogans, ethicists try to investigate and philosophers and theologians seek to understand and subject to normative criticism?

Max L. Stackhouse, Princeton Theological Seminary[1]

Dealing with governance concerns at the firm, industry and international level, the chapters included in this volume shed light on the benefits and limits of market-based coordination. Structural conditions permitting, markets are recognized to be efficient in allocating resources and stimulating their adept and innovative use as long as market participants pursue their self-interest. At the same time, for markets to work, strategic behavior, in its modern, Websterian definition, may be problematic as the pursuit of interest should not extend to forms of opportunistic behavior, misrepresentation and guile. In other words, market coordination requires the vigorous pursuit and clear limitation of self-interest. To deal constructively with this apparent *market paradox*, successful, capitalist economies rely on habits and behavioral norms to buttress more formal institutions in sustaining system trusts and dependable, decentralized coordination. Conversely, institutional deficiencies cause market failures, legitimacy concerns and the loss of faith in economic and even political liberties; they are ultimately linked to economic backwardness. While, none of this is new, its importance is often not recognized by both proponents and critics of market-driven life.

1. Lost in translation

While proponents and critics of market-driven life like to refer to Adam Smith's conceptualization of the "invisible hand", they typically do not realize

---

[1] Stackhouse, M. L., (2001) *Forward*. In Nelson, R. N. *Economics as religion*, University Park: Penn State University Press, p. xii.

that they are quoting out of context. Smith sought to develop a fully-fledged theory of man in society. He outlined his anthropology and view on societal construction in his "Theory of moral sentiment" and discussed conditions for implementation in "An inquiry concerning the nature and causes of the wealth of nations." A third exposé on the legal system was planned but never completed.[2]

The "Theory of moral sentiment" introduces two axioms: "self-love" and "the need of man to live in society".[3] The potential conflict between them is not mitigated by a rational, utilitarian calculation[4] but by man's sentiment – his sympathy for others, which is based on his ability to "feel how others feel."[5] This ability, man's "inhabitant of the breast,"[6] allows him to assume the role of an objective observer, and build consciousness and moral guidance. Given that "feelings of moral acceptance and rejection are based on the strongest sentiments of human nature,"[7] it is only prudent that man has a strong need to follow his moral intuition. But there are observational limits. At the level of the economy, where the identity of the other is not known, it is impossible to "feel the way he feels;" hence, competitive market adjustments need to step in, take the role of the objective observer and prevent abuse in exchange. "An inquiry concerning the nature and causes of the wealth of nations" provides the program. Beyond the assurance of competitive market exchange, man's "self-love" and "the need of man to live in society" require him to agree to some abstract ethical standard and impartial conceptions of the good and the right as well as some processes to enforce these. Exploring the legal structures and decision rules of this minimalist state was to be the culmination of Smith's work and remains the missing link.

Obviously, Smith did not propose a mono-causal market ideal. His classical conception of societal regulation relies on individual ethics, competitive markets, and legal structures as *complementary and only partially*

---

[2] The closing paragraph of the sixth and final edition of *The theory of moral sentiment* announces an upcoming account of the general principles of law and government. Fragments of this are published under the title *Lecture on jurisprudence* in the 1978 Glasgow edition of Smith's writings.

[3] Smith, A., (1963) *The works of Adam Smith – In five volumes*, D. Stewart (ed.) London, 1811–1812, (1963), Vol. I: Theory of moral sentiments; Vol. II–IV: Inquiry into the nature and the causes of the wealth of nations; Vol. I, p. 1.

[4] This originates only later with the work of Jeremy Bentham (1789) who argued for a calculus of pain and pleasure, and was traced further by John Stuart Mill (1861). See Bentham, J. (1988) *An introduction to the principles of morals and legislation*, (1789) Buffalo New York: Prometheus Books, reprint; and Mill, J. S (1861) Utilitarianism. In Alan Ryan (1987) (ed.) *Utilitarianism and other essays: J. S. Mill and J. Bentham*, New York: Penguin Books.

[5] See Smith, A., (1963) Vol. I., pp. 24 and 541.   [6] *Ibid.*, p. 231.   [7] *Ibid.*, p. 347.

substitutable means for efficiently coordinating economic and social life. This interpretation, based on the recent "Glasgow edition" of his complete work,[8] contradicts earlier commentaries that, solely rooted in *The Wealth of Nations*, held that Smith abolished moral concerns by requiring "individuals to act egoistically for the good of all to be attained."[9] Captured by the notion of "private vices, public benefits", "the good of all" was seen to rely purely on self-interest and on markets to eliminate dysfunctional behavior.[10] This view not only inspired tomes of sometimes trite polemics on the need to constrain or complement market processes,[11] but can only be understood in the context of the evolution, or better, reduction of Smith's political economy to economics.

Smith was interested in understanding the interaction among different governance institutions rather than modeling their isolated working. Market models, assuming perfect information, competition and a legal system that enforces property rights, can do without contracts, firms, or virtuous behavior. In fact, given these assumptions, one attains the neoclassical socio-economic optimum based on pure market adjustments where common and individual interests converge and society is in an overall state of Pareto optimality. Rooted in the writings of W. S. Jevons and Alfred Marshall, the model of perfect competition[12] gave economics the scientific justification to manifest itself as one of numerous specializing social sciences. The model is attractive as it seems to dissolve ethical and institutional concerns with reference to competitive market exchange. But its moral underpinnings are quite different from those of Smith.

---

[8] See also Tribe, K., (1999) Adam Smith: Critical theorist? *Journal of Economic Literature*, Vol. 37, June 1999, 609–32; Muller, J., (1993) *Adam Smith in his time and ours: Designing the decent society*, New York: Free Press; Pack, S. J., (1991) *Capitalism as a moral system. Adam Smith's critique of the free market economy*, New York: Edward Elgar.

[9] Robinson, J., (1964) *Economic philosophy*, Harmondsworth: Penguin, p. 53.

[10] Mandeville, B., (1924) *The fable of the bees: Private vices, Public benefits*. F. B. Kaye, (ed). 2 vol., Oxford: Claredon Press.

[11] Stigler, G., (1976) The success and failures of Professor Smith, *Journal of Political Economy*, 84, 1199–213; Hirschman, A. O., (1977) *The passions and the interests: Political arguments for capitalism before its triumph*, Princeton: Princeton University Press; Friedman, M., (1978) Adam Smith's Relevance for 1976. In *Adam Smith and the wealth of nations, 1776–1976 Bicentennary essays*, F. R. Glahe (ed.) Boulder Colorado Association University Press, pp. 7–20; Johnson, H. G., (1978) The individual and the State: Some contemporary problems. In *Adam Smith and the wealth of nations, 1776–1976 Bicentennary essays*, F. R. Glahe (ed.) Boulder Colorado Association University Press, pp. 21–34; Heilbroner, R. L. (ed.) (1986) *The essential Adam Smith*, Oxford: Oxford University Press.

[12] For the first comprehensive formulation of model conditions of perfect competition see Knight, F. N., (1921) *Risk, uncertainty and profit*, Boston and New York: Houghton Mifflin Company, pp. 51–6.

Whereas Smith's "enlightened self-interest" is based on a moral that is established *a priori*, irrespective of consequence, the neoclassical model derives its optimality from the calculative pursuit of self-interest, a utilitarian principle that judges means by their ends, *a posteriori*. Hence, a transaction that constitutes a Pareto improvement is morally good. When all external costs of production are internalized, a firm's profit maximization maximizes the difference between social benefits and social costs; utilitarianism co-incides with the pursuit of self-interest and makes it the social responsibility of business to maximize profit – nothing else.[13] Market competition and "consumer sovereignty" replace self-regulation through the "inhabitant of the breast". The problem is that in reality markets fail and are made to fail. Once complexities and investments create exposures, contracts are incomplete and relationships durable, institutional structures are needed to supersede and constrain market coordination and deal with problems of collective action. Does superseding the market mean superseding market rationality? Is there a need to discard self-interest to ensure cooperation?[14]

2. From the invisible and visible to the conventional hand

Coordination failures are sometimes likened to a Hobbesian "State of Nature" – a situation in which the absence of assured cooperation drives even "limited" egoists to single-mindedly pursue their self-interest. Given that markets and regulation are forever incomplete, how do real-life people avoid getting stuck in such Prisoner's Dilemmas?

Modern rational choice theory explains that opportunistic but learning players deal with inevitable discretion and the resulting uncertainty by switching from purely "self-serving" to broader "society-centered" reasoning and, as a result, create "limited conditional good will" to support cooperation.[15] These outcomes are self-enforcing, provided reciprocity is systematic and concerns

---

[13] For an elaboration of the argument see Friedman, M., (1970) The social responsibility of business is to increase its profits, *The New York Times Magazine*, September 13, 1970, 32–3.

[14] For representations of non-self-interest approaches to understanding institutions see Quirk, P. J., (1990) Deregulation and the politics of ideas in Congress. In J. J. Mansbridge (ed.), *Beyond self-interest*, Chicago: University of Chicago Press, pp. 183–99; Elster, J. (1989) *The cement of society. A study of social order*, Cambridge: Cambridge University Press.

[15] Casting cooperation in terms of a Prisoner's Dilemma allows coordination rules to emerge endogenously as equilibria of non-cooperative games. Calvert (1993, 1995) presents a repeated Prisoner's Dilemma played by randomly matched pairs of players, with or without the facilitation of a "director" or "communication round". His models show that rules of the game are endogenously created to shape the institution and that repetition, adaptive learning and communication improves chances for

for equity and compensation are broadly addressed by parties that are fairly unsure about their own future but know that there is a chance/risk of continued interaction and response.[16] Far from implying any form of altruism, the motivational base here is sheer self-interest – but it is *long-term* self-interest. Given uncertainty, long-term self-interest necessarily implies concern for the broader context and its translation into general operating principles. Conventions emerge.

Yet, the use of the "conventional" in support of the "visible" and "invisible" hand does not guarantee efficiency or equity *per se*.[17] It merely reflects the dominant preference of the parties involved, based on salient patterns of behavior or accepted leadership,[18] historically grown and embedded into the

cooperation. Complications arise in "public good" or "collective action" cases that involve many players simultaneously and where withholding cooperation as a means of punishment is harmful not just to the defector but the entire group. Here, too many incompatible ways to enforce an *n*-player collective action militate against the emergence of one specific system. Yet, to efficiently "ensure" continued success in repeated rounds, players would have to agree on the same solution each time around. Put differently, coordination must be focused, possibly by means of some convention. Schelling's theory of *focal points* does not explain the origin of conventions. But more recent coordination games, allowing players to adjust their stage strategies based on observations in previous rounds, illustrate how "learning in games," "cheap talk" and sound communication reduce coordination efforts, establish norms, *and* create "values" that supersede short-term self-interest to sustain cooperation among egoists. See also Frohlich, N. *et al.*, (1971) *Political leadership and collective goods*, Princeton, NJ: Princeton University Press; Schelling, T. C., (1960) *The strategy of conflict*, Cambridge, MA: Harvard University Press; Farrell, J., (1987) Cheap talk, coordination and entry, *Rand Journal of Economics*, 18, (1) 34–9. Calvert, R. L., (1995) Rational choice theory of social institutions: Cooperation, coordination, and communication. In Banks, J. S., Hanushek, E. A. (eds.) *Modern political economy*, Cambridge: Cambridge University Press, pp. 216–67. Baier, K. (1995) *The rational and the moral*, Open Court, Peru, I., pp. 157–73, and 186–93.

[16] See Banks, J. S., Calvert, R. L., (1992) A battle-of-the-sexes games with incomplete information, *Games and Economic Behavior*, 4, 347–72. Axelrod, R., (1984) *The evolution of cooperation*, New York: Basic Books, especially pp. 126–41.

[17] See Sugden, R., (1998) Conventions. In *The New Palgrave Dictionary on Law and Economics*, London: Palgrave Macmillan pp. 453–60. He illustrates this point with reference to two simple coordination games. In *Stag hunt*, a story following Rousseau (1755), deer hunting requires cooperation to be successful, hare hunting is less productive but does not require any cooperation. Yet, although the Deer equilibrium is Pareto-superior to the Hare equilibrium, both players will play Hare if they are not sure what the other will do. The equilibrium is said to be *risk-dominant* (rather than Pareto superior). In *Firewood*, the convention that "the first possessor of firewood can keep it" spontaneously emerges from repeated interactions between self-interested individuals and creates a *de facto* property right, that may not be fair or equitable but is mutually beneficial. The equilibrium with the largest basin of attraction is likely to emerge as (risk-dominant) conventions – it is the "conventional" outcome. For the stag hunt coordination example see Rousseau, J.-J. (1755) 1988 *Discourse on the origin and foundations of inequality among men*, New York: Norton. For the concept of "risk-dominance" see Harsanyi, J. C., Selten, R., (1988) *A general theory of equilibrium selection in games*, Cambridge, MA: MIT Press.

[18] For contrasting views on the origin of institutions and conventions – "spontaneous" vs. "humanly devised" – see Hayek (1952), Popper (1963) vs. North (1990). Hayek, F. A., (1952) *The counter-revolution of science*, Indianapolis: Liberty Press; Popper, K. R., (1963) *Conjectures and refutations: The growth of scientific knowledge*, New York: Harper; See Colophon, 1965; North, D. C., (1990) *Institutions, institutional change and economic performance*, Cambridge: Cambridge University Press.

broader institutional and cultural fabric. Also, whilst conventions emerge *endogenously*, as the "rules of the game",[19] there is a need for efficient enforcement. Compliance based on external enforcement, public or private, involves weighing the benefits of defection against the penalty imposed once detected; enforcement costs are borne by others.[20] Conversely, compliance with conventions that are internalized is typically self-enforcing and automatic; guilt governs norms which are "rationality-limiting", that is, restrict the domain over which any rational calculus is being applied.[21] Clearly, for any ethic to be evolutionary stable and to efficiently and reliably shape expectations, standards cannot constantly be subjected to situational review or retraced in terms of some implied economic calculus.[22] Acting from internalized principles is more efficient.

Hence, in modeling interaction and learning under uncertainty, rational choice theory transcends the neoclassical limits of short-term self-interest and tackles coordination issues by means of *socializing* institutions. And yet, much of mainstream economics "fails to fully understand that economic actors are driven by more than material short-term self-interest *and need to be* if a market economy is to function efficiently."[23] This may be because governance concerns seem to suggest that "real-life" markets make few demands on people's "elevated motifs" but put pressure on "society-anchored mutually beneficial reasoning" to yield to short-term opportunism. Or it could be because the hype of a market-driven world has come at the expense of advancing economic scholarship on centralized and most-importantly decentralized

---

[19] For a discussion of conventions as "evolutionary stable" means of selecting from alternative Nash equilibria see Sugden (1998).

[20] For a divergent views on the link between conventions as source of law and their legal enforcement see Hart, H. L. A. (1961) *The concept of law*, Oxford: Clarendon Press vs. Fuller, L., (1969) *The morality of law*, 2nd edn. New Haven: Yale University Press. For discussion of conventions and customary law see Parisi, F., (1995) Towards a theory of spontaneous law, *Constitutional Political Economy*, 6, 211–31. Posner, E., (1996) Law, economics, and inefficient norms, *University of Pennsylvania Law Review*, 144, (5) 1697–1744. For a discussion of internalized norms as moral standards see Ullmann-Margalit, E., (1977) *The emergence of norms*, Oxford: Claredon Press.

[21] See Basu, K., (1998) Social norms and the law. In *The New Palgrave Dictionary on Law & Economics*, London: Palgrave Macmillan 476–81.

[22] For a discussion similar to Baier (1995) see Hohmann, K. Kirchner, C., (1995) Ordnungsethik. In Dornreich, P. H. *et al.* (eds.) *Jahrbuch für Neue Politische Ökonomie*, Tübingen: J. C. B. Mohr (Paul Siebeck). Leaning on Luhmann's system theory, the authors use the term "Anreizethik" to denote that "morals in modern society can only be realized in line with incentives – not against them" (p. 196). Given that "situations create incentives" (p. 197), morals may be construed to be merely situational and "market-driven" as opposed to deontologically setting norms of conduct. The implied teleological perspective makes ethics economics-compatible rather than establishing it as a third, independent source of governance. It reflects modern, new institutional economics rather than the concern of classical political economy.

[23] See Wilber, C. K., (1995), p. 61, emphasis in the original.

forms of non-market governance. In fact, current macro-thinking on market-driven life largely comes as either pessimistic cynicism or naïve optimism.

The Marxist and Weberian interpretations of market-driven life are remarkably similar. To the "left," short-term self-interested exchange and productive specialization heighten the division between state and civil society and between public concern and individual interest and thus raise "man's alienation from himself and his fellow men."[24] To the "right," markets drive a powerful process of bureaucratization and rationalization and force man into a fragmented existence. Whereas the Marxist perspective does not consider man capable of linking markets, ethics, and law in jointly constituting civil society, Weber considered him able to somehow preserve his humanity and integrity by applying some form of self-restraint, but did not elaborate this any further. Either way, enduring a market-driven life breeds cynicism.

Conversely, invoking some "society-anchored mutually beneficial reasoning" or Adam Smith's notion of "enlightened self-interest", promises to balance short-term and long-term considerations, individual and societal interests and to fill the gap once markets or explicit rule-based coordination are incomplete. But even if these concepts were operational and broadly understood to be required by reason, it is unlikely that they would inspire all members of society all of the time. Societies tend to be made up of individuals with very different commitments to and interpretations of economic rationality, law abidance, business or social responsibility. Strategies of persuasion may be exploited by some, while strategies of deterrence may undermine the goodwill of others. Once markets and regulation fail, there is a need to either turn to cruder or more intrusive methods of governance *or* to secure "trustworthiness" and benefit from reliable discretion. The latter relies on *socialization* to nurture "the inhabitant of the breast" and inculcate conventions that make self-control in line with overall objectives self-enforcing. The question is how to retain such optimism without being naïve?

3. Rehabilitating moral reasoning

The notion of self-control appeals to Aristotelian virtue as it enables individuals to play a social role rather than to merely achieve individual success. Linked to norms invoking reciprocity or role reversal, from the "brethren in the breast" to "tit-for-tat", it delivers self-enforced and predictable cooperative

---

[24] Marx und Engels Werke, (MEW) Berlin: Dietz Verlag, Vol. 1, p. 252.

outcomes; virtuous behavior spreads as standard of cooperation. Yet, while the principle is clear, reality falls short of this ideal.

US corporate self-regulation programs, for example, induced by the government's recognition of such efforts as mitigating factors in prosecution, do not appear to have led to any measurable improvement in corporate behavior.[25] Instead they have given rise to concerns over the potential worsening of regulatory capture, the likely anti-competitive abuse of endorsement practices, the weakening of the moral force of a less universalistic law, and the growth rather than the reduction of red tape. Similar concerns exist regarding regulatory self-restraints and the delegation of supervision across the broader regulatory community.[26] But, to take incidences of actual or feared abuse of inevitable discretion to justify a retreat from regulatory delegation means accepting the dominance of a base allocation logic over a broader rationale that is essential for efficient economic, commercial and societal cooperation. It also means to discredit non-utilitarian reasoning as a delusion to conceal some deeper pursuit of short-term self-interest. It means to take the market as determining human will.

This is not to invoke some naïve idealism but to challenge those who find in markets every excuse for their action or cynically withdraw in the face of regulatory involvement. Benefits of a market-driven environment and decentralized decision making require necessary short-term instincts to be counterbalanced by long-term rationality. They also call for the rehabilitation of moral reasoning (rather than moralizing) to turn market participants into responsible citizens able and willing to take part in the discourse about the broader agenda of society. Conventions and norms are originated by salient patterns of behavior that endure free riding, attract followers and ultimately set a standards of interaction, from which people derive rights and seek legal enforcement and moral standing. Salience involves accepting risks and taking a lead. It requires individuals able to understand and set society's agenda rather than merely administrating business, economic and political affairs.

---

[25] See Ruhnka, J. C., Boerstler, H., (1998) Government incentives for corporate self-regulation, *Journal of Business Ethics*, 17(3), 309–26; Pitt, H. A., Groskaufmanis, K. A., (1990) Minimizing corporate civil and criminal liability, *Georgetown Law Journal*, 78, 1559–1584. Mathews, M. C., (1987) Codes of ethics: Organizational behavior and misbehavior, *Research in Corporate Social Performance and Policy*, 9, 107–30.

[26] See Schneiberg, M., (1999) Political and institutional conditions for governance by association, *Politics and Society*, 27(1), 67–103. Ayers, I., Braithwaite, J., (1992) *Responsive regulation*, Oxford: Oxford University Press, pp. 123–24. See Stelzer, I. M., (1997) A conservative case for regulation, *Public Interest*, (Summer), pp. 85–97; Weidenbaum, M. (1998) Streamlining the regulatory tangle, *Christian Science Monitor*, May 21, p. 19, Baldwin, R. (1995) *Regulation in question*, London: London School of Economics, chapters 1 and 3.

Index

Printed in the United States
By Bookmasters